# I Am Persuaded . . .

## Daily Meditations for the Year

GW00503535

## Norman L. Harris

Compiled and Edited by Paul L. Harris

It will be obvious to the reader that the Bedford area, where Norman and Jessie grew up, and the history and heritage of John Bunyan, both had a special place in their lives. On their retirement, they became members of Bunyan Meeting and benefitted from the friendship and fellowship within that congregation. Therefore, it seems fitting that any proceeds from the sale of this book will be given to Bunyan Meeting, Bedford, with gratitude to God for the life and witness of that church.

The photograph on the front cover was taken
at Snowshill in the Cotswolds, a place visited over the years
and much loved by Norman and Jessie.

Independently published: TwoWaterloo

In memory

of

Joyce Mary Harris (1932-2013)

# Preface

The following book of meditations for each day of the year was the brainchild of my parents in their retirement to Bedford. Their original homeplace was, of course, Cotton End, a village just outside Bedford, where they both grew up and were nurtured in the Baptist church. After his ordination there and nearly forty years of ministry together in three Baptist churches, namely, Chatteris, Breachwood Green, and Ipswich, Stoke Green – although others had also come under their ministry along the way (such as Witnesham, near Ipswich) – their retirement meant a rather abrupt change of pace and gave them cause for reflection on how they could continue to offer their gifts in ministry. While they each continued to help with leadership of meetings locally, at the Bunyan Meeting church and a few sister causes in the Bedford area (eg. at Elstow and Stevington), they felt that years of accumulated experience in pastoral care and leadership of Sunday worship and midweek devotional meetings, might be somehow expressed in a book of daily reflections for meditation. The title was undoubtedly the choice of my father who was often to be heard preaching with the use of the words of the apostle Paul, 'I am persuaded . . .' at the heart of his message. The titles used for each daily meditation were, generally, his own, as well.

These daily devotional reflections are now being published with the wistful longing that they might have seen the light of day in printed form while my parents were both still alive to see the fruit of their labour published. Sadly, due to circumstance, that never came about, but I have no doubt that they would have been immensely satisfied to see their work made available for others. The typed copies in triplicate (and more!) were cherished by my brothers David and Tim, and I, among many papers my parents left behind in their beloved flat in Waterloo Road, Bedford. My father had actually already given me a complete year set long before he became seriously ill, to keep safe and then to peruse when I had the time. I can only suppose that he hoped that – at some point – they might prove useful to myself and my wife, Karen, together with my family, including my brothers and their families respectively, and arguably, to many more besides. I can only trust that the time has, indeed, come and I sincerely hope this product is a worthy extension of his dream (since the later 1980s) to have these papers collected together, possibly in some published form.

The scripts were lovingly, sometimes perhaps laboriously, written over a period of years in that era after retirement in 1986, and the themes, vocabulary, examples and illustrations used obviously very much reflect his mindset from that pre-personal-computing, pre-internet age. My father's theological training for ministry in the mid-twentieth century (Spurgeon's College, London, 1948-51) is inevitably in the background of the items and thought-forms, though he was quite widely read – liking both biographies and autobiographies – which can be seen from some of the illustrations. My father loved the older translations of the Bible, as well as appreciating some of the newer ones to aid reader understanding, and this is reflected in the quotations, where his beloved Moffatt version is sometimes noted. In view of this, there has since been some light editorial re-working on my part to make the biblical quotations more inclusive where at all possible, and some of the examples have been slightly re-written with editorial licence to reflect the more inclusive language, and less-stereotypical speech forms, acceptable in the early twenty-first century. I trust these have been done modestly in order to keep the overall thrust of these devotional reflections faithful to his original intention. Where a more inclusive modern translation has been substituted for the older one, it has generally – but not always – been taken from the New Revised Standard Version. His original scripts were handed down in typed form – no doubt after being thoroughly checked by my mother. The evidence of my mother's involvement is very clear from her own handwritten 'pages of contents' for each of the months of the year as she assisted in the project with her eye for detail, and her neat, orderly script.

It goes without saying that I am most deeply grateful to Karen who has encouraged this venture and undertaken a vast amount of the production work. She alone has made this publication possible by her meticulous preparation of the original typed scripts in a digital format ready for me to edit, and she has also helped me unfailingly in the final editing to get the complete set of devotions in a manner presentable for self-publishing in this present form. I am thankful to the Lord for the godly parents and my upbringing in a Christian home without which these thoughts would have not come together in this way to bring us cause for reflection on the mercy of the Lord toward us each day. It is the hope of both Karen and myself, that these devotionals will not only be a loving reminder of Norman and Jessie as a couple who served faithfully in ministry together, but also a cause for some encouragement in the spiritual life, together with thanksgiving to God, for all who will read them.

The favourite hymn used often in the church where my parents were members until the end of their lives (and at each of their funerals at Bunyan Meeting in June 2017 and January 2020, respectively) is John Bunyan's hymn 'To Be A Pilgrim'; it is our hope that these humble offerings would perhaps be for each of us, in some small way, an aid to our pilgrimage of faith as we journey on day by day to that 'celestial city'. The choice of the hymns and prayers included is entirely mine, made on the basis of knowing my parents' preferences in cherished hymnody and the prayers of the saints.

The book is dedicated to my father's sister, the late Joyce Mary Harris of Cotton End, who predeceased both my parents, but without whose loving support, companionship, hospitality and prayer my parents would probably never have been as happy and secure as they actually were in retirement, returning to Bedford after decades away. She was to me, and the family, a loving, generous aunt for whom we all give hearty thanks to the Lord whom she served faithfully all her eighty years.

PLH
Eastertide 2021

vi

# Contents

# January

Lead us, heavenly Father, lead us
O'er the world's tempestuous sea;
Guard us, guide us, keep us, feed us,
For we have no help but Thee;
Yet possessing every blessing,
If our God our Father be.

Saviour, breathe forgiveness o'er us;
All our weakness Thou dost know;
Thou didst tread this earth before us,
Thou didst feel its keenest woe;
Son of Mary, lone and weary,
Victor through this world didst go.

Spirit of our God, descending,
Fill our hearts with heavenly joy,
Love with every passion blending,
Pleasure that can never cloy.
Thus provided, pardoned, guided,
Nothing can our peace destroy.

James Edmeston (1791-1867)

Christ be with me, Christ within me,
Christ behind me, Christ before me,
Christ beside me, Christ to win me,
Christ to comfort and restore me.
Christ beneath me, Christ above me,
Christ in quiet, Christ in danger,
Christ in hearts of all that love me,
Christ in mouth of friend and stranger.

St Patrick (5th century)

JANUARY 1st

## THERE ARE PROVISIONS FOR THE JOURNEY

Beginnings are always important! The beginning of a new job, a new school or college, a new friendship, a new commitment or even a New Year, brings a variety of possibilities. On 8th May 1984, James Hatfield (a man who had already experienced major heart surgery) set sail from Penzance on a 'round the world' trip to raise money for charity. A group of relatives, friends, newspaper reporters and a television crew were there to see him off and wish him well. His boat seemed so small for the task ahead! The poignant moment came when he stepped off the harbour wall and descended the ladder to his small boat. There was a moment of pure humour when his small boat reached the harbour mouth and began to head out to the sea. Momentarily, he turned round, shouting, 'Can I come back now?' Yet, he was committed to the challenge ahead.

So often new beginnings are linked to commitment. When Hatfield set sail that day, a host of people were relying on him to make a successful journey, as much depended upon it. Today, we are launching out, as it were, into a New Year and we know that it will bring different days and many different experiences. The Bible truly states: 'You do not know what a day may bring forth' (Proverbs 27:1). However, we do know that God will remain faithful. Tucked away in the Book of Lamentations, amid much woe, there is a helpful passage which gives encouragement for life's journey: 'The steadfast love of the Lord never ceases, his mercies never come to an end; they are new every morning; great is thy faithfulness. "The Lord is my portion", says my soul, "therefore I will hope in him"' (Lamentations 3:22-24). How often this passage is quoted, but the last and most important part is omitted by many speakers. That final clause speaks of our spiritual resources: provisions for the journey, as the reason for our confidence day by day.

James Hatfield had to make fine calculations about supplies: it was vital that there should be adequate provisions for his long journey round the world. As we set out on the journey of this New Year, we can find encouragement from the promises of God's Word, especially this lovely thought, 'The Lord is my portion'. The Lord richly offers us all divine grace, love, mercy, power and blessing: we can draw from them and wholly rely on them. The Old Testament and the New Testament agree on the fact of God's abundant goodness. So the apostle Peter gives believers a very valuable word of wisdom: 'Cast all your anxieties on him, for he cares about you' (1 Peter 5:7). May the God of all grace be known by us this New Year in the calm assurance that, although the journey is a long one, there are provisions for the journey through another whole year as it opens before each and every one of us.

Suggested readings: Psalm 77:11-15 and 1 Peter 5:1-11.

JANUARY 2nd

## VISIBLE THINGS REMIND US OF THE INVISIBLE

In the Old Testament we read how the people of Israel were often in the grip of a numbing fear: a powerful enemy was ready to encircle them or pounce upon them. Their feelings of insecurity were exacerbated by the knowledge that they themselves had been unfaithful to God. They realised they needed God's help but they also knew they actually didn't deserve it! So, on one occasion, they came to the prophet Samuel with this desperate plea: 'Do not cease to cry to the Lord our God for us, that he may save us from the hand of the Philistines' (1 Samuel 7:8). Maybe the Lord would listen to him they reckoned. Indeed, the story did end well for them: the Philistine enemy was overcome and the people of Israel won a mighty victory from the would-be oppressors. Samuel was deeply aware of God's undeserved compassion and we read: 'Then Samuel took a stone and set it up . . . and called its name Ebenezer, for he said, "Hitherto the Lord has helped us"' (1 Samuel 7:12).

How often in human history, people have erected statues, monuments, and buildings to remind them of some outstanding event. Samuel erected a stone to remind the people of unquestionable divine aid. In our world there are thousands of church buildings and each, in its own way, serves to remind the pensive observer of the spiritual dimension to life. Someone has said the every church spire is like a finger pointing upwards to God. Anyone who has seen the magnificent spire of Salisbury Cathedral will understand that poetic description of a church spire as a pointer, in a sense, to the unseen world of the divine presence to support and encourage us all.

Over many centuries Canterbury Cathedral has attracted multitudes of tourists and pilgrims. Very specially, it is loved by international visitors: its history, architecture and beauty have inspired the hearts of many who have come – quite literally – from 'the ends of the earth'. Much has been written and spoken about this special place of prayer and worship. At one great festival, Archbishop Robert Runcie spoke in a television broadcast about the cathedral in these words: 'A visible reminder of an invisible Light'. Surely, to many different generations of people down the centuries, that great edifice of our Christian faith has spoken to their hearts about God: His Grace, His Love, His Power, His Majesty and His Faithfulness.

That simple stone erected by Samuel stood as a monument that reminded the people of the truth he affirmed for them: 'Hitherto the Lord has helped us'. Today, we would do well to remember the significance of many far nobler stones in the walls of churches and cathedrals all around which can still speak the same re-assuring message about the Lord ever near to us, reminding us of 'things invisible'.

Suggested readings: 1 Samuel 7:3-13 and 2 Corinthians 4:13-18.

JANUARY 3rd

## DIVINE LOVE IS BEYOND ALL CALCULATION

In April 1987, a mother was killed in a terrible car accident in Suffolk. It was a tragedy that deprived three children of a mother's love: no one could possibly estimate the pain and loss felt by the husband and the children. In a subsequent court case (many months after the accident), the family was awarded £147,000 in damages for the loss of her life. At the time, it was a large amount, but even a vast sum of money could never be a substitute for her life, or indeed, bring their loved one back. Thinking about the substantial award granted by the High Court Judge, the question inevitably arises, 'How did the judge arrive at this figure?' It must have been an exceedingly difficult task because in our human experience there are things, which are very precious, things truly beyond price!

We think of a good mother's love: all over the world there are men and women who can testify that this special love is beyond the price of any treasure. When children know that their mother loves them – with that deep bond of maternal affection – it is a great blessing. A mother's love is comforting, strengthening, encouraging, and can also be like an anchor amid the storms of growing up in life, even into adult years. In the gospels, we are made aware of the deep love that Mary had for her son, Jesus. It was a very wonderful love and John's gospel tells how, that in the hour of His rejection, suffering and crucifixion, Mary stood keeping vigil near the cross. The simple words used add to the significance of the occasion: 'Now there stood by the cross of Jesus his mother' (John 19:25 AV). Mary's love was unquestionably strong and faithful: it is almost like a window into God's love.

In the Book of Isaiah, the prophet poses an awkward question: 'Can a woman forget her sucking child that she should have no compassion on the son of her womb?' (Isaiah 49:15). The answer is given in plain but moving language: 'Even these may forget, yet I will not forget you' (Isaiah 49:15). God's Word in the Bible declares that divine love is greater than a human mother's love since, even where a mother's love sometimes breaks down, the Lord's love continues unfailingly! This divine love is revealed throughout the sixty-six books of the Bible, in many and varied records where men and women felt God's presence. However, Christians confess that such love was manifest supremely in the life, death and resurrection of Jesus Christ. On the cross, Jesus demonstrated the depths of divine love, the unceasing love of God, which can never be overcome. So when the apostle Paul wrote about that unending love, he urged believers: 'to know the love of Christ which surpasses knowledge' (Ephesians 3:19). That divine love is priceless, quite beyond all calculation or even comprehension!

Suggested readings: John 19:23-27 and 1 John 4:7-12.

## JANUARY 4th

## CHRISTIANS MUST LET THEIR LIGHT SHINE

When Jesus gave the Sermon on the Mount, He challenged people to a high standard of living; so high that some have derided the teaching and even dared to call it ridiculous! However, those wonderful words have been an inspiration to many through the Christian era. What a challenge those words were to the ancient world: there were many evils eroding family life and public life, and Jesus taught a way that confronted such darkness. In this radical teaching the disciples were instructed or, perhaps better, invited, to take their stand in the world: 'Let your light so shine before others, that they may see your good works and give glory to your Father who is in heaven' (Matthew 5:16). It is a fact of history that many accepted the challenge and their light shone out in the darkness, in a benighted world so marred by sin.

We've all known such individuals, even just in ordinary everyday life. East Anglia has produced its share of good Christian characters, people of real faith and commitment. One example of an everyday saint was Ron, a man who worked in a local hospital in the area: he was a person of deep devotion who quietly and humbly lived for Christ. On the day of his retirement, he received numerous cards and presents, but one was very special. A colleague had painted a picture 'just for him': it showed the world, a hand and – in the hand – a little baby. The religious overtones were obvious! On the reverse of the picture were these words:

*Before you came to work here I asked the question who is this Jesus Christ?*
*I have painted this picture in gratitude that I've seen Jesus Christ in you.*

Ron is typical of all those disciples of Jesus who are in a minority position but who let their light shine. There are countless solitary Christians not only at home, but also in offices, canteens, factories, hospitals, schools, as well as other workplaces, who never argue about their faith but just live it out. A light does not have to argue about shining as it just shines on and on! In the early Church there were women and men keeping faith in even the most unusual places. There is a reference at the end of one epistle by the apostle Paul, 'that all the saints greet you, especially those of Caesar's household' (Philippians 4:22). Saints were there in the Roman emperor's own household, which must have been one of the most difficult places to shine for Jesus!

In the same epistle, Paul referred to believers in a striking way: 'Children of God without blemish in the midst of a crooked and perverse generation, among whom you shine as lights in the world' (Philippians 2:15). It is always the right time to resolve anew that, by God's grace, we will let our light shine for Jesus Christ.

Suggested readings: Matthew 5:1-16 and Philippians 2:12-18.

JANUARY 5th

## WE HAVE AN UNDERSTANDING SAVIOUR

The new minister was preaching under some difficulty: he had a very heavy cold. Colds don't matter too much in some professions, but they can play havoc with a preacher's voice. This particular minister had only been in his new pastorate a few weeks so he was anxious to do well. As he preached, he struggled to keep his voice going! Yet, after a few minutes, he lost his place and his mind went blank: the service came to an untimely end and he felt very disheartened. No one likes to flop, especially in the pulpit; it was the preacher's worst nightmare! During the following week, he was visiting one of his older church members who said: 'I think more of you since Sunday! Yes, I like to think my pastor is human, too'. That was a kind thing to say and a wise thing to say, too! If a preacher stands in the pulpit 'six feet above contradiction' as it were, and gives the impression that he or she is superhuman, then pastoral ministry will be far less effective. Ministers of the gospel are very human too, and they can have feelings of joy and sorrow, victory and defeat, happiness and despair. We, and they, alike, all fall short and make mistakes.

John's gospel gives a marvellous picture of the Blessed Saviour: the gospel stresses the uniqueness of Christ in His divinity. Yet, with equal clarity, it also reveals the other side: His humanity. Christians rejoice in this verse: 'And the Word became flesh and dwelt among us, full of grace and truth; we have beheld his glory, glory as of the only Son from the Father' (John 1:14). But they also rejoice in John's detailed account of His human characteristics: the fourth evangelist depicts Jesus as being physically tired, hungry, thirsty, angry and even shedding tears. The cleansing of the temple courts (John 2:13-22) is a passage worth careful thought and study.

It is a good day when any Christian (or unbeliever for that matter) makes a simple resolve to read John's gospel and to think about the One it presents. Readers marvel at the skill of John in revealing the two sides of Christ's nature, as One fully divine but also fully human. We have a Saviour who is approachable: we read how the sad, the lost, the sinful and the outcast found a true friend in Him. One of the secrets of effective ministry is availability and Jesus was always ready to receive people. In one New Testament epistle, there is a wonderful verse which has given comfort and encouragement to generations of believers: 'For we have not a high priest who is unable to sympathize with our weaknesses, but one who in every respect has been tempted as we are, yet without sinning' (Hebrews 4:15). We thank God that we have an understanding Saviour!

Suggested readings: Matthew 8:1-13 and Hebrews 4:14-16.

JANUARY 6th

## OUR GOD IS RICH IN EXPERIENCE

The 'SITUATIONS VACANT' column in any newspaper has always made fascinating reading! It soon reveals that businesses and professions are looking for people of experience; how often we read advertisements there for an experienced chef, experienced legal secretary, experienced social worker, experienced bank clerk and so on. Congregations also put much emphasis upon experience in seeking a new pastor and church members often say: 'We must have an experienced minister'. They mean someone who has had at least two pastorates! We all know that the 'School of Experience' teaches many vital lessons for life. Ralph Emerson put it this way: 'Life is a succession of lessons which must be lived to be understood'.

Today, we ponder the theme of our God being 'rich in experience', by which we mean God as our faithful creator and sustainer. We can rejoice that God is no novice as it were! The psalmist puts it superbly: 'Lord thou hast been our dwelling place in all generations. Before the mountains were brought forth, or ever thou hadst formed the earth and the world, from everlasting to everlasting thou art God' (Psalm 90:1-2). This worshipper believed wholly that the God Whom we approach is always rich in experience, ever seeking to bring us to life and meaning in the deepest sense. Have you possibly ever heard a prayer where God has been instructed by a human tongue? Unfortunately, prayer can degenerate into giving God precise requests, which sometimes sound like orders! We ought to perhaps remind ourselves that, in a reverent way, we can profess that our God has infinite experience; our lives depend upon God's ever new mercies but also, God's unchanging ways.

The opening sentences of the Book of Genesis show how God brought order out of chaos: 'In the beginning God created the heavens and the earth. The earth was without form and void, and darkness was upon the face of the deep; and the Spirit of God was moving over the face of the waters. And God said, "Let there be light; and there was light"' (Genesis 1:1-3). The Old Testament also has many illustrations of people who found themselves in chaotic situations but God – in His own good time – brought order. God has a proven record of being steadfast: He has delivered and can deliver. He has guided and does guide today. He has saved and still saves to the uttermost. On the day of Christ's crucifixion, there was darkness and chaos: it seemed that the power of evil had proven to be victorious. Yet, God, who is rich in experience and plentiful in mercy, brought light out of darkness, order out of chaos and triumph out of defeat! There are days for us all when we may feel helpless and despairing, but we may trust in God!

Suggested readings: Psalm 90:1-16 and Jude 1:24-25.

JANUARY 7th

## REAL CHURCH GROWTH IS THE SPIRIT'S WORK

Sometimes it is a good thing to put detailed instructions away! Some fine people have found exact details very confusing. For example, Hubert von Zeller, a monk and retreat leader, worked as a sculptor and his work was widely recognised around the world. One day he was reading a book about sculpting and discovered how – according to that authority on the subject – he had been doing it incorrectly for all those years! He tried to take the book's precise advice how to grip and angle a chisel but became confused, so the textbook was dispensed with immediately.

We thank God for good Christian books and acknowledge they have been a tremendous help to many. However, especially in this modern age, there has been a tendency towards detailed 'how to' instruction. The books come under numerous titles but the ones on discipleship tend to boil down to such basic topics: 'How to be a successful Christian', 'How to be a successful church', 'How to be a successful minister'. Sometimes these books (by their detailed precision) can bring confusion. We do well to remember our conviction that the Holy Spirit is still the real Teacher!

The opening verses of 2 Thessalonians are a joy to read: 'We must always give thanks to God for you, brothers and sisters, as is right, because your faith is growing abundantly, and the love of every one of you for one another is increasing' (2 Thessalonians 1:3). These friends of the apostle Paul had a growing faith matched by a deepening love; surely, these are the two essentials in any fellowship of believers seeking to serve God's Kingdom in honouring Jesus Christ as Lord, with the aid of God's Spirit.

The key issue is, how can a fellowship really nurture a growing faith and a broadening love for each other? Many Christians would simply answer: 'By the work of the Holy Spirit in the believer's heart'. The Church does need ministers, teachers, leaders, youth workers as well as good books, and other resources. Yet, we must remember that God has given us the Holy Spirit, and a key element of the Spirit's ministry is to encourage growth. While some people today are prone to give precise details on a method for discipleship, the Holy Spirit surely uses many and varied ways, always working within us each as individuals.

Churches are often tempted to judge their work for God by numbers: the numbers on the roll, or people won to faith, or received into membership, or possibly the number of services and activities, or even the amount of money raised. It is good to recall always that there is one part of the Church's life, which is not so easily quantified, namely, the increase of faith and love in individual lives, and so also in the fellowship. Real growth, that both enriches and lasts, is always the Spirit's work.

Suggested readings: Psalm 1:1-6 and 2 Thessalonians 1:1-12.

JANUARY 8th

## TRUE CHRISTIANS KNOW WHERE TO LOOK

Dr. Alexander Whyte was a scholar widely recognised by many of his era to have been greatly used by the Holy Spirit; he was a scholar, preacher, author, lecturer and a humble servant of Jesus Christ. His ministry had a special impact on students and no one could ever estimate how many he influenced for good. Sometimes, as he stood in the pulpit, his honesty was quite astounding: he confessed to profound feelings of unworthiness. Indeed, in his ministry, he did have glorious moments of spiritual joy; but he also knew days of darkness and sadness.

One of his confessions was the following: 'I feel so cold and dead that I might doubt if I had ever come to Him at all; but I go about my work notwithstanding looking in His direction. It is very simple – keep looking'. That reminds us of other words (written many centuries before Alexander Whyte), in the Epistle to the Hebrews: 'Let us run with perseverance the race that is set before us, looking to Jesus the pioneer and perfecter of our faith' (Hebrews 12:1-2). Perseverance is what men and women of faith need. There may be marvellous stretches of the road when life is good and faith is bright, but we all know that there are other, tougher days, too.

Within the Christian Church, there are people who by their attitude make it abundantly clear that – in their opinion – no believer should have a low day! Some Christian literature espouses the same view: the position that believers should always be experiencing sweet faith and glorious hope. However, this clearly flies in the face of indisputable evidence to the contrary. The Old Testament records make it perfectly plain that people of faith do have low days. We think of Sarah, Moses, Elijah, Job, and Jeremiah, to name but a few; the psalmist also had bad days and dark experiences.

Baron Von Hügel had wise words concerning such experiences: he said that, when a traveller encounters a sudden storm on the mountain, he or she stays still and clings hard, for the storm will pass! So when faith is tested, a Christian needs to 'hold fast' knowing that, in God's good time, better days will come again. Dr. Whyte says he always kept 'looking in His direction'. This corresponds with the psalmist's testimony: 'I keep the Lord always before me; because he is at my right hand, I shall not be moved' (Psalm 16:8). As people of God we can look upon life with steady eyes knowing that the normal life of faith consists of many different days and experiences, but the important thing is to remember where to look. As followers of Jesus look steadily in His direction, they receive inspiration, encouragement, strength and blessing; so we are thankful to the Lord for our hope.

Suggested readings: Psalm 16:1-11 and Hebrews 12:1-3.

JANUARY 9th

## CHRISTIANS NEED TO KNOW THE WAY BETTER

There is little doubt that John chapter 14 is one of the best-loved passages of Holy Scripture; its thirty-one verses have been a source of comfort and inspiration to generations of believers. As Jesus reclined at His last meal with the disciples, having washed their feet and taught them about the commandment to love, after some further words of assurance, there is a much-quoted dialogue with one disciple, namely, Thomas. He had remarked to Jesus, 'Lord, we do not know where you are going; how can we know the way?' Jesus' reply was astonishing: 'I am the way, and the truth, and the life; no one comes to the Father, but by me' (John 14:5-6). This wonderful saying 'I am the way . . .' has been a great blessing to multitudes of people. Jesus exuded honest assurance and confidence, graced with humility: before the Father, He both knew the way and, in fact, was the way!

There is a humorous story that highlights the fact that sometimes people are not so confident about us. A Salvation Army officer was walking through a small town in Cambridgeshire. As he strolled along in his uniform, a young lad on a bicycle rode alongside him, obviously 'weighing up' this new resident! The officer asked him 'Can you please tell me the way to the Post Office?' and the boy obliged. The officer (wishing to keep up contact with the lad) continued the conversation 'That's my job to tell people the way, the way to heaven'. He was shaken by the boy's response: 'I can't see how you can show people the way to heaven when you don't even know the way to the Post Office!' The lad was certainly a serious thinker.

It is a sad fact of life that some Christians can occasionally end up appearing to be a bit woolly about their faith: they seem unsure and hesitant, their grasp of Christian truths appears to be, at best, rather hazy. One of the notable things about the apostle Paul was his absolute confidence in the gospel of Jesus Christ. He had a certain sure-footedness about spiritual things. One of his powerful affirmations was in the Epistle to the Romans: 'For I am sure that neither death, nor life, nor angels, nor principalities, nor things present, nor things to come, nor powers, nor height, nor depth, nor anything else in all creation, will be able to separate us from the love of God in Christ Jesus our Lord' (Romans 8:38). Like his gracious Master, he was sure in his own faith; he had an unshakeable confidence in relationship with God.

In the world of today, there is a renewed call for Christians: 'Always be ready to make your defence to anyone who demands from you an accounting for the hope that is in you' (1 Peter 3:15). We thank God today for all those men and women who walk with a great measure of sure-footedness, and who are ready to give an answer concerning their faith.

Suggested readings: John 14:1-12 and 1 Peter 3:8-15.

## JANUARY 10th

## WORSHIP IN GOD'S HOUSE IS IMPORTANT

Every Sunday, around the world, a vast number of people go to a place of worship. Until quite recently, it was claimed in USA that almost forty per cent of the people attended public worship at some point. In Britain, the percentage of the population attending church is now much less, but even so it used to be claimed that more people go to a place of worship on Sunday than to football matches on Saturday! That sounds incredible but is apparently factual! How varied are those places of Christian worship: the chapel in a hamlet or on an estate, the ancient rural church, the suburban or metropolitan town church, the imposing city edifice and the mighty cathedral. The scripture says: 'Now there are varieties of gifts, but the same Spirit; and there are varieties of service, but the same Lord; and there are varieties of working, but it is the same God who inspires them all in every one' (1 Corinthians 12:4-6). The truth remains at the heart of Christian faith: the Word of God is for all, the great hymns are for all, the gifts of the Spirit of God are for all, and the gospel is for all.

There is one beautiful verse in the Psalms, which explores the meaning of worship: 'We have thought on thy steadfast love, O God, in the midst of thy temple' (Psalm 48:9). True worship lifts our thoughts to higher levels: it is the time when we ponder God's love and goodness. The ordinary pattern of worship includes hymns, prayers, readings and some meditation upon the scripture; all these can lift our spirit and renew us. During the week we are literally bombarded by stories of human folly and cruelty rooted in sinfulness, but on the Lord's Day, as believers in the Lord God of all grace, we pause in times of quiet to hear again the good news of Jesus Christ.

In Luke's gospel there is a significant verse about Jesus of Nazareth: 'And he came to Nazareth, where he had been brought up; and he went to the synagogue, as his custom was, on the Sabbath day' (Luke 4:16). That little note conveys so much: 'as his custom was . . .' It was normal for Jesus to attend public worship. So we remind ourselves today that, over many centuries, men and women have found that worship brings real benefits, as it elevates our thoughts, it calms the troubled mind, it inspires the heart; in a sense, the batteries of our inner life are recharged!

When St Augustine wrote about his pre-conversion days, he confessed: 'I lost myself in a multiplicity of things'. How true that can be! In the hectic rush of life, we can think about our work, our family, our home, our pleasures, our concerns and problems, forgetting spiritual things in a way that is self-destructive. There is a real need to slow down and be still; in the quietness of our place of worship, we can offer praise as we ponder the goodness of God.

Suggested readings: Psalm 48:1-9 and 1 Corinthians 12:1-13.

## JANUARY 11th

### PERSEVERANCE WINS MANY VICTORIES

Sometimes we speak of 'breathtaking experiences'. Quite often, we are using rather exaggerated language and other people know it! However, there was a programme shown on television, which was literally breathtaking, so much so that hundreds of people could not watch it through. Catherine Destivelle climbed a sheer African rock face 'free-style': that meant using no ropes or protection of any kind. At one point in the climb, a massive overhang faced her and, quite literally, she had to hang by her fingertips. The slightest error would have meant plunging into an abyss, and certain death for her. It looked an impossible climb but she did it! She climbed to victory by rugged perseverance and sheer courage.

Courage is a wonderful thing: it enables people to press on when the way is exceptionally difficult and hazardous. Some people don't possess it! So we read in John's gospel of a time when the Saviour gave some difficult teaching: 'Many of his disciples, when they heard it, said, "This is a hard saying: who can listen to it?"' (John 6:60). Then a few verses later, we get a dramatic turn of events: 'After this many of his disciples drew back and no longer went about with him' (John 6:66). They failed as they lost their nerve and so they decided to give up. It is fascinating to see how the Blessed Master reacted to all this, as He commented to the Twelve: 'Will you also go away?' (John 6:67). Simon Peter was their spokesman as he replied, 'Lord, to whom shall we go? You have the words of eternal life; and we have believed, and have come to know, that you are the Holy One of God' (John 6:68-69). Peter knew there was no other person, no other way, no substitute for Jesus; they must press on bravely.

When Catherine Destivelle reached the pinnacle of her climb, the African bystanders (who had watched the breathtaking climb with stunned awe) broke out into a truly joyful celebration. They had told Catherine that it was impossible to climb the rock free-style and she had proved them wrong. This reminds us of the inspiring fact that, over many centuries, men and women have pressed on in faith in spite of enormous problems and difficulties. The 'perseverance of the saints' is, indeed, a reality of history. Hebrews chapter 11, is much more than just a potted history of God's people; it is a celebration of faith and faithfulness. The Book of Revelation speaks pictorially of a glorious celebration, as it were, in heaven, where there is rejoicing among those 'who have come out of the great tribulation' (Revelation 7:14). We thank God for all the courageous women and men who have persevered and, by faith, won great victories over all that is against us in life.

Suggested readings: John 6:60-69 and Revelation 7:9-14.

13

JANUARY 12th

## SPIRITUAL BLINDNESS IS A FACT OF LIFE

Two people were standing one day in a busy shopping centre and were engaged in a very animated conversation. They were so taken up with their own concerns that it seemed as if the passersby did not exist! This part of the conversation drifted across loud and clear for all to hear: 'She just cannot see. She says that they do this and that for her, but she just cannot see'. Quite obviously foul play was being suspected, or somehow someone was being conned, but was quite unaware of the menace at hand.

How often people can't – or perhaps won't – see things! This happens within the family circle. For example, a head teacher wrote a short note at the bottom of a child's school report saying that the pupil had a lisp in his speech and ought to have treatment. The parents were shocked, even a little annoyed. They hadn't noticed it at all. Yet, on further reflection, they conceded the point and agreed for their child to go to a speech therapist and have the problem rectified. The parents were grateful and, in later years, looking back on it all, were pleased that the headmaster had taken the trouble to write to them.

We can be blind to defects in ourselves or within the lives of those close to us, and it can be a little sensitive when someone points out the problem. This fact of blindness covers many different areas such as the racist who is blind to the strength and richness of another nationality, the bigot who can never see the good in another person's point of view, or the obscurantist who refuses to consider another theological approach. There is spiritual blindness, too: people who just cannot see any good in the Church or in Christian ways. Sadly, it can even be found within the Church, too, as some fail to acknowledge truth in other traditions.

The New Testament reveals people who were blind to the beauty and wonder of the Son of God. John's gospel often tells of spiritual blindness, and it is clear in one particular verse: 'And there was much muttering about him among the people. While some said 'He is a good man' others said 'No, he is leading the people astray' (John 7:12). It seems incredible to believers but some people actually thought that Jesus Christ was leading people astray! So too, throughout the Christian era, many have simply observed the faith but have been unable to come to see the glory of Jesus Christ, God's Son. Harry Fosdick used to tell the story of how he went with a party of tourists to a famous beauty spot. The lovely scenery was captivating to the tourists, except for one man who, in a strident voice, blurted out: 'Where's this famous view then?' He was, as it were, wholly blind to the beauty manifest before him! One of the lessons that life teaches is that spiritual blindness can be a reality we have to face both in ourselves, and in others.

Suggested readings: John 7:10-18 and Luke 23:18-25.

JANUARY 13th

## THE BIBLE CHALLENGES HYPERACTIVITY

In the normal course of life there is usually a certain amount of waiting. We think of some homely examples: waiting for a bus or train, waiting at the shop checkout, or in the waiting-room at the clinic or surgery, or waiting for something to be delivered or for a job to be completed. Other examples might be more serious such as waiting for exam results to be published, waiting for a major operation in hospital, or for news of a distant relative or friend. Certain daily times of waiting can be quite irritating and, in some cases, tiresome, while in the more serious instances waiting can cause considerable stress and anxiety, as it sorely exercises our patience!

We live in a society, which is hyperactive, with lots of people trying to dash along in the fast lane. A visit to London or another large city confirms an impression that so many people appear to be in a rush heading somewhere: rushing for buses and trains, or rushing to keep appointments or to beat a deadline, or maybe even rushing just to fill leisure hours! All this feverish activity breeds a spirit of impatience and that can be expressed even towards God. So many believers want prayers answered, help divinely granted or guidance given, or healing accomplished with the minimum of delay. Even some of the verses in the Psalms overtly remind God to 'get moving'! We think of two: 'Bestir thyself, and awake for my right, for my cause, my God and my Lord!' (Psalm 35:23) and 'Rouse thyself! Why sleepest thou, O Lord? Awake! Do not cast us off forever' (Psalm 44:23). They remind us of our place before God. The spirit of wanting things 'done yesterday' as it were, conflicts with much of the teaching of Holy Scripture. We think of this wonderful verse which counsels waiting: 'The Lord is good to those who wait for him, to the soul that seeks him. It is good that one should wait quietly for the salvation of the Lord' (Lamentations 3:25-26). How the modern Christian needs to learn the lesson of patiently waiting upon the Lord.

During Dr. Billy Graham's visits to England, many people came to faith or renewed their commitment to Christ. Under the normal process of things, many were connected with churches and some individuals became members of evangelical churches, thus receiving quite a cultural shock! Numerous churches expected their new converts to go from meeting to meeting, to be involved in this and that activity; Sundays were not a day of rest! For a few, this hyperactivity proved to be too much and they grew disheartened, though there were plenty of exceptions to this and, mostly, local churches did a magnificent job in nurturing the new Christians. However, there is a real need for much of the Church of today to be reminded that 'They who wait for the Lord shall renew their strength' (Isaiah 40:31).

Suggested readings: Psalm 37:1-7 and Isaiah 40:27-31.

JANUARY 14th

## WE MUST TRUST GOD'S MERCY

Acute thirst can be a terrible thing! In the Second World War, Russell Braddon was captured by the enemy and made a prisoner of war, and had a terrible experience. At one point, he caught an illness and developed an excessive thirst: this thirst was all demanding and all consuming. It got so bad, apparently, that if any one had offered him a bagful of diamonds or a glass of water, he would have chosen the water! The sensation of thirst is a powerful metaphor. We are reminded in scripture that the human heart can experience a deep spiritual thirst, so strong that nothing else matters at that time. 'My soul thirsts for thee; my flesh faints for thee, as in a dry and weary land where no water is' (Psalm 63:1).

The prophet Daniel knew a deep thirst for God's forgiveness. In the record of his work, we have a deeply moving picture of the prophet concerned about the waywardness of God's people: 'Then I turned my face to the Lord, seeking him by prayer and supplications with fasting and sackcloth and ashes. I prayed to the Lord and made confession' (Daniel 9:3-4). The confession is quite specific: 'We have sinned and done wrong' (v5), 'We have not listened to thy servants the prophets' (v6), 'We have not obeyed the voice of the Lord' (v10), 'We have sinned, we have done wickedly' (v15). Daniel seeks and desires (as with an all-consuming spiritual thirst), on behalf of the people, to have the assurance of God's forgiveness and mercy. Then, he makes a truly remarkable plea: 'We do not present our supplications before thee on the ground of our righteousness, but on the ground of thy great mercy' (Daniel 8:18). Daniel is truly aware of the bankruptcy of the human heart and casts himself, and the people, on the rich mercy of God. The great sixteenth-century reformer of the Church in Geneva, John Calvin, used to put it succinctly: 'Our salvation stands in the mercy of God'.

Luke's gospel contains many references to God's mercy, sometimes in material not found anywhere else in the scriptures: for example, it has a very powerful parable about prayer. Jesus told how two men went up to the temple to pray: one a Pharisee and the other a tax collector. The Pharisee prayed a self-centred prayer telling God what a fine person he was, while the tax collector prayed a God-centred prayer: 'God, be merciful to me a sinner' (Luke 18:13). This parable presents in dramatic form two ideas that have gripped the minds of people though all religious history: some believe in 'Salvation by Works' others believe in 'Salvation by Faith'. Jesus was clearly advocating that we all cast ourselves on the mercy of God.

Suggested readings: Daniel 9:3-19 and Luke 18:9-14.

JANUARY 15th

## PEOPLE SHOULD MOVE FORWARD WITH CHRIST

In our day, it is common for parents to record the stages of development in their children: books printed for this purpose provide spaces to note down weight, height, the first word, the first step, the first sentence, and so much more. One of the joys of parenthood is to see a child develop! In some cases this does not happen and it causes stress and unhappiness. If an otherwise healthy child will not talk, even though he or she is coaxed, encouraged and persuaded, yet still refuses, that child needs a lot of patience and loving attention. We set so much store on progression.

One of the special joys of a Christian fellowship is to see young and old making a sincere commitment to Jesus Christ. However, while some people go on with the Lord and make good progress in the Christian life, sadly, others do not seem to develop and grow in this way. We can perceive from the New Testament epistles that this happened in the early Church: it is an interesting study to seek out how many times people are urged to grow and mature in the faith. The Epistle to the Hebrews says: 'Therefore let us leave the elementary doctrines of Christ and go on to maturity' (Hebrews 6:1). The New English Bible translation of the verse gives the wording a military flavour: 'Let us advance towards maturity'. When an army advances, it is usually by making a costly effort; new ground is won by sheer dogged perseverance. This is often the case with Christian advance, as it is commonly recognised that believers reach Christian maturity through costly discipleship. So we think of the apostle Paul's famous words about his own approach: 'But one thing I do. Forgetting what lies behind and straining forward to what lies ahead, I press on toward the goal for the prize of the upward call of God in Christ Jesus' (Philippians 3:13).

Children normally love to move to a higher class at school! Their progress brings joy and deep satisfaction to their parents. However, some children don't progress quite so well and they have to stay down in the more elementary class. The causes for this vary: it can be laziness, an unhappy home situation, or the lack of ability. Or it may be, occasionally, that they want to conform to a pattern set by others, deliberately holding back, so that they are not too different from their peers. On the spiritual level, there are a considerable number of reasons why some Christians do not worry about spiritual growth; sometimes, it may be that they don't want to be too different from colleagues or workmates in the office or factory. The positive call heard clearly throughout the New Testament is that people should 'Grow in the grace and knowledge of our Lord and Saviour Jesus Christ' (2 Peter 3:18).

Suggested readings: Philippians 3:12-21 and Hebrews 5:11-6:1.

## JANUARY 16th

## SOME PEOPLE HAVE AN INSTRUCTED TONGUE

The Revd. George Bird exercised a remarkable ministry in Bethesda Baptist Church, Ipswich. God used him powerfully as he served within a large congregation; a ministry richly blessed of God. Many people came to faith and confessed Jesus Christ as their Lord and Saviour. There was a wider ministry locally, too, as he encouraged the fainthearted, comforted the sad, encouraged the young and inspired many to serve the Kingdom of God. One of the wonderful things about George Bird was that he always seemed to have just the right words for the right occasion! Whether it was a marriage, a church anniversary, a funeral, an ordination, a conference or a broadcast service, he had the right words to say. So he was in great demand to be the guest preacher at numerous special occasions throughout the British Isles and beyond.

The Bible says: 'A word fitly spoken is like apples of gold in a setting of silver' (Proverbs 25:11). Christian ministers need a great deal of versatility: they need to be 'on their toes' in their talks, addresses, speeches and sermons, and in varied pastoral work, too. Isaiah's own prophecy speaks about the instructed tongue: 'The Sovereign Lord has given me an instructed tongue, to know the word that sustains the weary' (Isaiah 50:4 NIV). We thank God today for all the men and women who have, in their day, given the right words of challenge and inspiration to the Christian Church. Also, we rejoice that in this modern age there are numerous people with an 'instructed tongue' who are ready to speak for their God. There have been many people in Church history who have had limited education, but God has used them mightily to speak right words for the right occasion; one example of that is the American evangelist and preacher, D. L. Moody. While he had limited formal education, he was able to share his faith with many people.

When Jesus went to the synagogue at Nazareth we read: 'And all spoke well of him, and wondered at the gracious words which proceeded out of his mouth; and they said "Is not this Joseph's son?"' (Luke 4:22). Again and again in the gospel records, reference is made to the gracious words of Jesus, one of the best examples being: 'No one ever spoke as this man speaks' (John 7:46). Jesus never failed in His wisdom: He truly had an 'instructed' tongue and always had the right words to say. People with such an 'instructed' tongue stand out 'head and shoulders' above those who simply talk. The gift of wise counsel and true encouragement is to be prized!

Suggested readings: Isaiah 50:4-10 and Proverbs 25:6-13.

JANUARY 17th

## WE ALL NEED SPACES

One of the important things in life is the ability to concentrate. It was said of the famous Scottish preacher, Dr. Alexander Whyte, that he could continue studying in the same room where others were enjoying a tea party. His ability to concentrate was quite extraordinary. Certain people must discipline themselves to concentrate, for example, surgeons, pilots, engineers, gymnasts and jugglers! Jugglers are fascinating: they may have six or more objects flying through the air and must concentrate or some things will drop. It is an art, which can really amaze observers!

At one period in his life Hubert van Zeller was very busy; in fact, he was too busy. He confessed that he felt something like a juggler with so many things going on and he knew that sooner or later something would drop. How easy it is to take on too many tasks! It is also true in Christian work; one can be overwhelmed and concentration can be lost, and then some of the work might be in jeopardy. A full diary can be a source of pride! There is need for wise judgement: life must have a balance between work and leisure, service and recreation, busyness and stillness.

Writing to the Christians in Rome, the apostle Paul included an instruction, which is full of wisdom on this subject: 'I say to everyone among you not to think of yourself more highly than you ought to think, but to think with sober judgement, each according to the measure of faith that God has assigned' (Romans 12:3). Sober judgement: that's what all Christians need in every circumstance. Sadly, some sincere workers take on too much and they cannot cope, or maybe their family life suffers and sometimes even children end up being neglected. We need space to be with friends, family, and also, most important of all, space to be with God in quiet communion. Dr. Alexander Whyte lived an exceptionally busy life but he always made spaces for what was vital, and that included having breaks from work.

So we think of Jesus of Nazareth: the gospels tell of times of prayer, times of fellowship with the disciples, and times when He was alone. So Matthew records: 'And after he had dismissed the crowds, he went up into the hills by himself to pray. When evening came, he was there alone' (Matthew 14:23). The Saviour we acknowledge as Lord, found it absolutely essential to create space in His busy life: He sought space, solitude, silence and quiet communion with His Father regularly. Sometimes, even overheard conversations can be thought provoking! A Christian worker was heard to say 'I'm still juggling with dates'. Juggling? We do well to recall that juggling can have its dangerous moments if one is not very careful! Holy Scripture stresses the need for rest and quiet, as part of our daily walk of faith.

Suggested readings: Psalm 46:1-11 and Matthew 14:22-27.

JANUARY 18th

## OF THE RAINBOW OF GOD'S MERCY AND LOVE

David Watson found much pleasure in telling his friends about an experience which came to him at a crucial turning point in his life. He and his wife Anne were travelling down to Cornwall for a holiday when they saw a beautiful double-rainbow. It seemed almost unreal because the colours were so bright against a dark sky, and at that moment it struck them both as a wonderful assurance of God's blessing and favour. They always remembered it as a very special experience.

In the Book of Genesis, there is the familiar story of a great flood and God's subsequent promise to His servant Noah: 'This is the sign of the covenant which I have made between me and you and every living creature that is with you, for all future generations: I shall set my bow in the cloud, and it shall be a sign of the covenant between me and the earth' (Genesis 9:12-13). To the Hebrew mind, a rainbow was more than one of nature's beautiful sights: it was 'a token for good'. Whenever a rainbow was seen, it was a reminder of God's promise of mercy. So by the eye of faith, many good things can have a far deeper meaning: a sunrise telling of hope, a mountain proclaiming God's greatness, the mighty ocean speaking of the magnitude of divine love, a starry night declaring God's handiwork. Someone has said that God speaks with a thousand different voices: many can testify to that as their own experience. God comes to different people in different ways to make Himself known and heard. The psalmist makes this affirmation: 'The heavens are telling the glory of God and the firmament proclaims his handiwork. Day to day pours forth speech and night to night declares knowledge' (Psalm 19:1-2).

The last book of the Bible, the Book of Revelation, is not the easiest book to read or understand, yet it is wonderful! It tells of a time of crisis and fear, but John's eyes are upon higher things: he has a vision of God's power and authority. There is an exquisite verse, which contains a message for today: 'At once I was in the Spirit, and, lo a throne stood in heaven, with one seated on the throne! And he who sat there appeared like jasper and carnelian, and round the throne was a rainbow' (Revelation 4:2-3). John saw a rainbow round the throne: God's mighty power and supreme authority encircled by grace and mercy. So many of our finest hymns speak of God's greatness and majesty. Yet, this great God of ours is also loving, gracious and merciful for there is a rainbow round the throne. The rainbow mentioned in the first book of the Bible is significant; how much more significant is the one mentioned in the last book of the Bible! It speaks of a hope that extends far beyond this life.

Suggested readings: Psalm 19:1-14 and Revelation 4:1-8.

JANUARY 19th

## PRAYER CAN CARRY PEOPLE

We can all thank God for praying friends as their prayers make a big difference. When we face an important situation such as a new job, a major operation, a family crisis or an especially difficult responsibility it is a positive help to know that Christian friends are upholding us in prayer. In the gospels there is the story of a lame man 'carried by four men' (Mark 2:3) to the feet of Jesus. This lovely story suggests a form of prayer: the prayers of others can carry someone through a difficult situation.

In February 1989, Richard Holloway (Bishop of Edinburgh from 1986 to 2000) had the responsibility of leading the mission to Oxford University, a most important assignment. As he took the long train journey from Edinburgh to Oxford, he had plenty of time for reflection. Previous missions had been conducted by a variety of people of high standing: William Temple, Michael Ramsey, Trevor Huddleston, John V. Taylor, Basil Hume and Robert Runcie. As the train sped along, Richard Holloway knew the burden of the task and felt his own inadequacy. The responsibility of the important mission was now a burden resting upon his shoulders!

There was encouragement ahead. At Oxford, he received a warm welcome and was given a large bundle of letters, all of them assuring him of prayer support. One particular envelope contained a copy of a rota of prayers that would cover every hour of the mission. He felt supported and uplifted; he was, like the man in the gospel story, being carried. The time for the first address was 8:30 pm on the Sunday and there was torrential rain but the University Church, St. Mary's, was packed. For fifty minutes, he spoke on the 'Longing for God': it was a memorable occasion.

The prayers had contributed much on that occasion. Of course, other Church leaders, preachers, evangelists, Christian workers, missionaries have all depended on prayer support. Even the apostle Paul, strong individual that he was, needed the prayers of his friends. We think of Moffatt's fine translation of two verses in Romans: '. . . I beg of you, by the love that the Spirit inspires, rally round me by praying to God for me; pray that I may be delivered from the unbelievers in Judea, and also that my mission to Jerusalem may prove acceptable to the saints' (Romans 15:30-31). The story of the Christian Church abounds with true stories of men and women faced with very difficult situations, who yet gained victory because faithful friends carried them in prayer. It is good to offer our thanks to God for praying friends, and to consider whom we may, in our own way, support through our own prayers.

Suggested readings: Romans 15:25-33 and James 5:13-20.

JANUARY 20th

## THERE ARE RISKS WHICH ARE ACCEPTABLE

The train was slowly moving out of the station: next stop Birmingham. Suddenly, a young woman rushed down the platform, opened a carriage door and struggled to get on board. People looked on helplessly as she fought to board the train. She was in grave danger of falling between the train and the platform and being crushed to death. She actually succeeded in getting on board but only through taking a foolish risk. We know people take unnecessary risks in life: the motorist who overtakes at a blind spot or dangerous bend, the pedestrian who dodges through the traffic, or the cyclist who doesn't have lights, and so on.

We remind ourselves that there are foolish risks and there are acceptable risks, namely, calculated risks. Someone who had many years in counselling work said: 'There is a real sense in which every marriage is a risk'. That is true since we don't really know people until we live with them. Yet, there are other risks in life which we reckon to be acceptable: the investor who puts his money in a pretty sound project, the employer who takes on a young person who's been in trouble with the police, or the test pilot who tries out a new type of plane. There are risks which, on the best human calculation, are acceptable.

In Acts chapter 27 we read how the ship carrying the apostle Paul reached a place called Fair Havens: the wind was strong and 'it was risky to go on with the voyage' (Acts 27:9 NEB). Paul gave definite advice as he thought that to continue the journey would be disastrous. He spoke out against the venture: it was an unacceptable risk. His voice was not heeded, and the ship left port and went to its certain doom. Actually, it is worth reminding ourselves that Paul was a man with steady nerve and on various occasions took risks for the sake of the gospel of Jesus Christ, so he was no coward, but was mindful of the dangers posed to all! In fact, when visiting a certain city to preach, he was stoned and his accusers dragged him out of the city thinking he was dead. Yet, this did not deter him for later he returned! Evidently, Paul was a man of courage and undertook risks in the service of the Kingdom of God.

Earlier in Acts, we read how the church at Jerusalem sent a letter to the church at Antioch and referred to Paul and Barnabas: 'Our beloved Barnabas and Paul, men who have risked their lives for the sake of our Lord Jesus Christ' (Acts 15:26). Since that era, Christian history is studded with the stories of men and women who took risks for the sake of the gospel, in order to be true to Christ. Words in the Book of Proverbs certainly apply to them: 'The righteous are bold as a lion' (Proverbs 28:1). We pray, too, that we might show such courage day by day.

Suggested readings: Acts 15:22-29 and 2 Timothy 2:1-10.

JANUARY 21ˢᵗ

## PEOPLE THIRST FOR PAST HAPPINESS

How often we remember the happiness of life's yesterdays! A loving mother remembers the deep joy experienced in nursing her babies, a man recalls the blissful years of his marriage before the painful separation or divorce, an entrepreneur remembers the pleasant days of keeping an individual shop, but now running a chain of shops is a living burden. So also, perhaps, a person recalls a time of being happily involved in church life and work before other things took priority. Memories of life's yesterdays can be challenging, even painful, as well as satisfying.

So in Psalm 42 we get a loyal worshipper who, for reasons unknown, cannot now go up to Jerusalem to worship. This individual feels deprived: the verses give an illustration of a thirst-crazed deer frantically searching the desert for water: 'As the deer longs for flowing streams, so my soul longs for you, O God. My soul thirsts for God, for the living God' (Psalm 42:1-2). Such worshippers yearn for an experience, which they once possessed, and long for a happiness once enjoyed! The psalmist then includes these poignant words: 'My heart breaks when I remember the past, when I went with the crowds to the house of God and led them as they walked along, a happy crowd singing and shouting praise to God' (Psalm 42:4 GNB). We recall the hymn writer, William Cowper, described this experience of remembering life's yesterdays:

> Where is the blessedness I knew
> When first I saw the Lord?
> Where is the soul-refreshing view
> Of Jesus and His Word?
>
> What peaceful hours I once enjoyed,
> How sweet their memory still!
> But they have left an aching void
> The world can never fill.

One might say that Cowper wrote that hymn with 'the ink of the heart' and with an awareness that, all too often, people long to put the clock back and experience again the joy they once felt. There is good reason, therefore, to recall and to ponder the last verse of this psalm: 'Hope in God; for I shall again praise him, my help and my God' (Psalm 42:11). Those significant words 'I shall again . . .' remind us of the grace and hope that we may know in Jesus Christ.

Suggested readings: Psalm 42:1-11 and John 21:15-19.

## JANUARY 22nd

## SOME WILL ALWAYS WELCOME JESUS

One of the great days of modern history was 21st July 1969. On that day Neil Armstrong, the command pilot of the APOLLO 11 moon mission, became the first human to set foot on the moon. It was a marvellous moment and was watched by millions on television: a thrill of joy swept through the USA and far beyond. When the crew of APOLLO 11 returned to earth they received a rapturous welcome: not only their families but also crowds just wanted to see and listen to these astronauts. One of the most wonderful experiences in life we can each know ourselves is to return to one's home and be given a sincere, loving welcome: it warms the heart like nothing else!

One day Jesus and His disciples boarded a boat on the Sea of Galilee and He then said: 'Let us go across to the other side of the lake' (Luke 8:22). Little did the disciples know what was in store for them! There was a terrible storm and yet Jesus stilled it. Soon after, there was an even greater storm in a poor soul's mental life and yet Jesus calmed it. In the midst of these two miracles of Jesus, the disciples felt a deep sense of awe: 'Who then is this, that he commands even wind and water, and they obey him?' (Luke 8:25). Afterwards, they returned, and Luke gives a moving account of this moment: 'Now when Jesus returned, the crowd welcomed him, for they were all waiting for him' (Luke 8:40). Here is a powerful picture of needy people anxious to receive the Master back to their side of the lake: oppressed people, anxious people, burdened people, confused people and troubled people. A whole host of people – of all circumstances and conditions – welcomed Jesus back!

Through the long centuries, an endless stream of people have sought Jesus' mercy: women and men of every race and culture, people of every class and position, young and old, rich and poor alike have sought His blessing. There is a verse in John's gospel, which has blessed the hearts of generations of people: 'Anyone who comes to me I will never drive away' (John 6:37). These are such comforting and re-assuring words! One modern Bible translation expresses it in unforgettable simple words: 'I will never turn away anyone who comes to me' (John 6:37 GNB). In the gospel story Jesus received an enthusiastic welcome by people who knew He could help them. That's one side of the coin: the other reality is the glorious truth that Jesus Himself gives all people – whoever turns to Him – a loving welcome, too.

Suggested readings: Luke 8:26-40 and John 6:35-40.

## JANUARY 23rd

## TIME IS OPPORTUNITY

It is interesting to see how many verses in Holy Scripture contain the word 'time'. One notable verse is this: 'Trust in him at all times, O people; pour out your heart before him' (Psalm 62:8). For a few moments we might ponder the little phrases people use about time: 'wasting time', 'filling time', 'spending time' and even 'killing time'. The New Testament has a very important verse which really challenges the heart: 'Be careful then how you live, not as unwise people but as wise, making the most of the time, because the days are evil' (Ephesians 5:16). Lots of Christians have accepted that command as vital, and truly taken it to heart in daily life.

There is one important truth which runs like a vein of gold through the Holy Scriptures: time is opportunity. Ideally, everyone should recognise – and use well – life's opportunities! A humorous illustration of this was seen on a very drab day in London as it poured with rain all day. Thousands of people were travelling as usual on the Underground keeping dry but, as they surfaced at their destination, they faced a real problem! At one Holborn Station exit a man stood at a vantage point selling umbrellas, and what a good trade he did, too! He was making excellent use of an opportunity, finding it very profitable in the simplest of ways. The New English Bible nicely translated the verse from Ephesians: 'Use the present opportunity to the full . . .'

We think of various people who – in their work – must always be ready to grasp their opportunities: the barrister takes the chance to press home a legal point, the Army General or Navy Commander takes the opportunity to launch a tactical move, the physician orders more tests or the farmer uses a fine spell of weather to harvest the crops. Faithful Christians have an uncanny knack of knowing when there is a golden opportunity to defend the faith and speak for Jesus Christ. One of the marks of dedication is the unwillingness to waste time! John Wesley is a prime example of a man who just could not bear to fritter time away but was always seeking opportunities to spread the gospel by preaching, writing or simply by conversation. The apostle Paul was a master at grasping openings to serve the Kingdom of God and 'preach Christ'.

There is an ancient proverb, which says, 'There are three things which never return: the spent arrow, the spoken word and the lost opportunity'. We can always remind ourselves that each day we can be presented (probably unexpectedly) with a golden opportunity to witness for Christ in our speech, or to simply show the Lord's love in many practical ways, as the Spirit grants us vision and opportunity.

Suggested readings: Ecclesiastes 3:1-11 and Ephesians 5:7-20.

JANUARY 24th

## GOD CALLS US TO A STEADY FAITH

Even as a child, Susan had one clear ambition as she used to say, 'I want to be a nurse'. She was passionately interested in all things to do with hospitals and nursing. On the day that her mother gave her a present of a child's nursing uniform, she was absolutely delighted. Through all her school years she never wavered from her ambition: the course was set and the day came when she was accepted for training. She looked on that day with the psalmist's attitude: 'This is the day which the Lord has made; let us rejoice and be glad in it' (Psalm 118:24). Susan sailed through her training and became a first-class nurse and, in due time, held a position of much responsibility. So there are some children and young people who have clear objectives for their career and never waver, keeping a steady course in life.

When Joshua became the leader of God's people, he was given a specific instruction: 'Be strong and very courageous, being careful to do according to all the law which Moses my servant commanded you; turn not from it to the right hand or to the left, that you may have good success wherever you go' (Joshua 1:7). In plain language that meant: 'Don't waver but keep to the appointed road'. Actually, the Bible has a lot to say about people having clear objectives and a steady nerve to trust God without wavering. So we read one marvellous verse: 'Let us hold fast the confession of our hope without wavering, for he who promised is faithful' (Hebrews 10:23).

Sailors know that there are days when there are strong crosswinds and the sea is very choppy, so sailing can be both risky and difficult. So it is in life also: there are, as it were, storms and strong crosswinds and we can learn to cope by the mercy and grace of God. Most of the great men and women who have done valiant service for the Kingdom have faced such stormy passages with fortitude and courage, yet have not wavered by reason of God's strength within them. In the New Testament there is a stark verse about doubts: '. . . the one who doubts is like a wave of the sea, driven and tossed by the wind' (James 1:6). Ministers and Christian workers often meet people who have been struck by life's storms, and they have discovered that James' description is strikingly true. People do indeed get blown off course, and it can be both confusing and painful.

The psalmist confesses 'I have trusted in the Lord without wavering' (Psalm 26:1), and many can honestly affirm that! However, numerous people cannot do so, and instead have to testify that the storms and crosswinds have sorely tried them, sometimes unmercifully. We can be thankful that our salvation does not depend on a perfect faith, but on a perfect Saviour who is ever faithful as He promised.

Suggested readings: Psalm 26:1-12 and Hebrews 10:19-25.

JANUARY 25th

## CONVERSION IS A WONDERFUL TRUTH

Many things have been said about the conversion of Saul of Tarsus on the Damascus Road, but one of the most powerful is that of a German theologian who commented that the conversion of Saul 'was like the River Rhine beginning to flow backwards'. The New Testament leaves us in no doubt that the early Christians were astounded by this amazing incident: the persecutor became a preacher, the enemy of the gospel became its foremost champion, and the zealot became a proclaimer of peace and goodwill. Saul became known as the beloved apostle Paul. It was quite incredible, rather like a mighty river flowing in the opposite direction: a remarkable experience indeed! Of course, there are numerous ways in which people come to new faith and commitment: some have a dramatic experience, others a much quieter experience. Some submit to Christ after a long and deep personal struggle, and then, like C.S. Lewis, finally 'give in' to the challenge of the Holy One and come to know that surrender after a protracted experience.

'Conversion' is described in lots of ways: like food after famine, freedom after bondage, light after darkness or life after spiritual death. Conversion is a wonderful truth in the life of faith and untold millions have experienced it as such, although it can be described in different ways. We recall the beautiful testimony of John Wesley: 'In the evening I went very unwillingly to a society in Aldersgate Street, where one was reading Luther's preface to the Epistle to the Romans. About a quarter before nine, while he was describing the change, which God works in the heart through faith in Christ, I felt my heart strangely warmed. I felt I did trust in Christ, Christ alone for salvation; and an assurance was given me that He had taken away my sins, even mine, and saved me from the law of sin and death'. These lovely words have been recited on many occasions, and are viewed by many people as a perfect description of God's work in the human heart.

Sometimes, a person feels alien, cold, or far removed from spiritual things; then, through some humble experience (such as hearing music or watching a play or film or reading a book) she or he feels a warming of the heart, and at that point the Lord Jesus Christ seems so wonderfully near. We can also encounter God's Word through the living word of a preacher or simply the written word on the sacred pages of scripture. We thank God for the very moving conversions we encounter; yet we can also offer thanks for the quieter and humbler conversions, too! Paul's own clear testimony is simply expressed: 'He loved me and gave himself for me' (Galatians 2:20), and that can be the testimony of us each.

Suggested readings: Acts 9:1-25 and Galatians 3:26-29.

JANUARY 26th

## CONCERNING THE DIVINE AVAILABILITY

We can all thank God that there are many helpful people in our world. However, there are perhaps distinctions to be made as to their willingness! There are those who are willing to help if it is convenient, and those who help at any time. In the gospels there is a story told by Jesus of a man who had an unexpected visitor: the real embarrassment was that he had insufficient supplies and it was midnight! However, without a second thought, he went and knocked up his friend. This, incidentally, poses us an interesting question: 'How many friends have you on your midnight list (available and contactable any time of day or night)?' Not everyone has such friends!

In this country there are some lovely villages which often seem to retain a special quality. These communities often seem to have special people living there, and ones to whom other villagers can turn by day or night to receive practical help. These people are the 'salt of the earth' and over the years have earned the respect and trust of the villagers. Of course, there are urban estates and communities in cities, too, where a similar helpfulness may be found from 'available people'.

As we study the four gospel records, we are struck by the humility and kindness of Jesus Christ and His availability. They came to Him from every quarter seeking help: they even invaded His privacy but He proved to be 'a friend at midnight'. In John's gospel, we come across a revealing verse: 'Now there was a man of the Pharisees, named Nicodemus, a ruler of the Jews. This man came to Jesus by night' (John 3:1-2). Jesus was ready to minister even at night! The Scriptures teach, especially through the life and ministry of Jesus Christ, that there is divine humility, which is manifest through divine availability. What a comforting assurance that is as we know our need of God!

There is an unforgettable verse in the Psalms: 'Behold he who keeps Israel will neither slumber nor sleep' (Psalm 121:4). This particular verse is set in a passage, which rejoices in the truth of God's help. We can call upon the Lord by day or night; it is never inconvenient to God! In the story told by Jesus, the man who went to his neighbour at midnight for bread had a shock, as his friend was reluctant to help; yet, his persistence brought results! We can be thankful that, in sharp contrast, our God is never reluctant to receive our prayer for help. Sometimes, when people make an emergency call by dialling 999, they are astounded by the swiftness of the response of the emergency services. If that is true of human agencies, how much more is it true of our God, upon whom we can confidently call anytime, anywhere, and in any condition! We can thank the Lord who is ever close at hand for us all.

Suggested readings: Psalm 121:1-8 and Luke 11:1-13.

JANUARY 27th

## TACKLE THINGS ONE AT A TIME

Sometimes a news item on television has a very special quality and it grips the imagination. One evening a visually impaired man was interviewed and the point of interest centered on the amazing fact that he was keen on mountaineering. A blind mountaineer sounded incredible! The interviewer posed this question: 'As a blind man, how do you manage the boulders?' The blind man paused before giving this significant reply: 'One at a time'. Surely, here is an attitude which is to be emulated, an example of spiritual wisdom worthy of due notice by everyone seeking to live well.

Thank God for the men and women who have been gifted in leading retreats for Christian workers: these have proved to be a blessing and an enrichment to many. Often people who are responsible for a retreat stress the importance of tackling one spiritual problem at a time. Their advice is to 'do one job at a time', 'live one day at a time', 'make spiritual progress one step at a time'. There is so much in the Bible, which reinforces this prudent approach. We recall how, when the Children of Israel were travelling to the Promised Land, they were given manna daily. 'Then the Lord said to Moses, "Behold I will rain bread from heaven for you; and the people shall go out and gather a day's portion everyday"' (Exodus 16:4).

Sometimes, a busy parent or a professional person (even a Christian worker) can see so many tasks that must be done; they feel swamped or completely overwhelmed. This pressure can bring a profound feeling of inadequacy. That is the moment when one needs to stop and ponder: recalling the blind mountaineer, we can see how he tackled the obstacles 'one at a time'. Sometimes, it takes a long time for certain Christians to learn this valuable lesson. At one point in the ministry of Jesus, He was given a specific warning of Herod's hostility. The Master gave a reply which revealed His serenity and faith: 'Nevertheless I must go on my way today and tomorrow and the day following' (Luke 13:33). The Saviour, during His earthly ministry, walked just one day at a time; surely that is a deep spiritual lesson for all Christians to learn.

We might all find it inspiring to listen again to some ancient wisdom found in words of the Lord, through the prophet Isaiah, to God's people facing uncertainty: 'For you shall not go out in haste, and you shall not go in flight, for the Lord will go before you' (Isaiah 52:12). As we face another day with all the unknowns ahead of us, we do well to recall that God is there first; the Lord always stands ready to bless people day by day, if only we would turn in trust and obedience to accept that reality.

Suggested readings: Exodus 16:1-12 and Isaiah 52:7-12.

## JANUARY 28th

## GOD GIVES US TOKENS FOR GOOD

Sometimes in parts of Britain we have a hard and bitter winter which can be especially difficult, and many people just long for the advent of spring. One of the loveliest things is that, in January, the little snowdrops come peeping through; and then, after a short time, the crocuses make their appearance. They are 'tokens for good' in that they herald the fact that spring is round the corner and that better days are ahead. Such signs of hope remind us that the seasons are on the move and the natural world will soon burst forth into new life. It is quite impossible to describe how welcome these small flowers are to so many people because of their simple – but most attractive and reassuring – message that brighter days are ahead.

In Psalm 86, the psalmist prays 'Show me a token for good' (Psalm 86:17). That is a wonderful prayer! When life's circumstances are wintry, or life seems dull and lifeless, God reveals little tokens for good. These tokens can take many different forms: a phone call, a letter, a small gift, an unexpected visitor or a surprise contact can each be uplifting to us. As the snowdrops and crocuses herald a new season ahead, so these small tokens of love can bring us a new dimension to our thinking. We can be lifted up from the humdrum of everyday life.

In the Old Testament story, certain verses show us the deep hostility between Saul and David. In Saul's heart there was a mixture of jealousy and bitterness, envy and hatred; indeed, some of the passages describing Saul's hostility to David make difficult reading. Later in the record, we read this verse: 'And David said, "Is there still any one left of the house of Saul that I may show him kindness for Jonathan's sake?"' (2 Samuel 9:1). This verse stands out for us; that compassionate gesture by David seems to shine forth like a beacon to bring a measure of hope into a rather dark scene.

When we ponder the place called Calvary, it seems a God-forsaken place: the hardness, the cruelty, the mockery and the blasphemy chill the mind. Yet, on the cross, our Saviour uttered unforgettable words: 'Father, forgive them; for they know not what they do' (Luke 23:34). Surely, this saying is like a blossom in the wilderness, like a beam of light in the darkness, indeed a token for good. In His loving purposes, God was going to turn the winter of the crucifixion into the spring of the resurrection; and, because of Calvary, untold millions would find peace and forgiveness. Today, and every day, we can pray: 'Show me a token for good' and we know that God is faithful, and will hear our cry. God is good and gracious; the answer may well be in the next surprise along life's way!

Suggested readings: Psalm 86:1-17 and Luke 23:33-38.

## JANUARY 29th

## TRANSLATIONS ARE IMPORTANT

Politics can have moments of humour! In 1960, Harold Macmillan was making an important speech at the United Nations and was rudely interrupted by Khrushchev, the Russian leader. To the amazement of everybody Khrushchev had taken off one of his shoes and banged the table with it! Macmillan (well known for his keen sense of humour) remarked dryly: 'I'd like that translated, if I may!' How often people speak without saying a word: facial expressions, gestures with the hands, movements of the feet and even bodily postures say much. From the vantage point of the pulpit, a pastor often senses what the congregation might be thinking and saying!

Translations are important: this is true in so many different spheres – political, diplomatic, legal, social and religious areas. One of the most important decisions which J.B. Phillips ever made, was to spend every Tuesday morning translating the scriptures. He had a very busy schedule but he reserved that particular morning each week for this special work. Today, countless people all over the world are grateful for his translations. He certainly opened up the epistles of Paul to the younger generation of Christians, but in fact, all age groups received help from his work. We thank God for modern translations of the scriptures, which give fresh insight into the Word of God to aid understanding; their work is of paramount importance.

In the writings of the apostle Paul there is a verse which speaks of another kind of translation, a translation into life and character: 'You show that you are a letter from Christ, the result of our ministry, written not with ink but with the Spirit of the Living God, not on tablets of stone but on tablets of human hearts' (2 Corinthians 3:3 NIV). What a wonderful thing it is when the gospel of Jesus Christ is translated so beautifully into a consecrated life dedicated to Him.

The Holy Bible is a bestseller and millions of copies are purchased or given as presents each year. However, in spite of this good news, we remind ourselves that some people never read the scriptures. It is therefore important to remember that the only translation these people read is the life of a believer they know; this fact places an enormous responsibility on our Christian witness, as we hear again the apostle Paul's words: 'You show that you are a letter from Christ'. There is a clarion call for Christian people to translate truth into life and so witness to others. One young Christian wrote to another: 'You make it easier for me to believe in God'. That is true service, which results in vital witnessing to others, all to the glory of God.

Suggested readings: 2 Corinthians 2:12-3:6 and 1 Timothy 2:1-8.

## JANUARY 30th

## GOD MOVES IN A MYSTERIOUS WAY

One of the most popular quiz programmes on British Television in recent decades has been MASTERMIND. It is a severe test of intellectual ability and it is fascinating to watch the contestants. It is quite absorbing to watch people closely questioned on their chosen subject, such as, 'The works of Shakespeare', 'The history of Ireland', 'The music of J.S. Bach, or 'The French Revolution'. Lots of viewers feel their own ignorance as these brilliant men and women answer the most remote and awkward questions! It is very entertaining to see their general and specialist knowledge.

What of God? In the Epistle to the Romans we have a magnificent verse: 'O the depth of the riches and wisdom and knowledge of God! How unsearchable are his judgments and how inscrutable his ways' (Romans 11:33). Dr. J. Moffatt translates the last part of that verse as 'How mysterious his methods'. We are reminded of William Cowper's famous hymn:

> God moves in a mysterious way,
> His wonders to perform;
> He plants His footsteps in the sea
> And rides upon the storm.

In times of emergency (say, wartime) our national leaders sometimes make strange decisions, which seem to be rather mysterious ones. So often these very important decisions are made because they possess a far greater knowledge of the total situation. Afterwards, official papers and the diaries of these leaders are often published, and the public then begins to understand what was actually going on behind the scenes! Today, we recall that our God has a wealth of wisdom and knowledge. The Lord God sees the total situation: God surely sees the end from the beginning!

Such is the story of the cross of Jesus Christ. In the ancient world the cross was a sign of deepest shame; Jesus died in such a humiliating way on a cross. He suffered pain and rejection, mockery and cruelty, and He had a crown of thorns put upon His head. Yet, His cross is now a place of glory: the place where we may find forgiveness, restoration, new life and peace with God. How mysterious are His ways! The human observer perceived only crucifixion; but God saw glorious resurrection. When we find life very puzzling or perhaps sometimes even feel that God has failed us, we may remember our faith that God can be trusted. For God knows the whole situation and can, by His power, turn darkness into light and shame into glory. God has done this in the past and still does so today.

Suggested readings: Romans 11:26-36 and 1 Peter 2:11-25.

JANUARY 31st

## CONCERNING THE STIRRING QUALITY OF CHRIST'S MINISTRY

When we ponder the last few days of the ministry of Jesus before He was put on the cross, we are struck by the unfairness, indeed the blatant injustice. One accusation was this claim: 'We found this man perverting our nation' (Luke 23:2). Perverting the nation was the allegation: they accused Jesus of misleading and corrupting the people! The hardness, blindness, cruelty of the religious leaders who acted as Christ's accusers is staggering. However, sometimes those hostile to Jesus unwittingly spoke a true word, indeed, a far deeper truth than they realised. An example of this is found in Luke's gospel, in the complaint about Jesus: 'He stirs up the people all over Judea by his teaching' (Luke 23:5 NIV). Of course, it is true that the Saviour stirred the minds and the hearts of people, but as a good act, in seeking to draw them to repentance.

In the Epistle to the Hebrews, we have a challenging verse: 'The word of God is living and active, sharper than any two-edged sword' (Hebrews 4:12). It is profoundly true that the words of Jesus Christ had – and still have – a stirring quality. So often His gracious words cut through the complacency of people, and today His words can still move individuals to inner change and to positive action. We acknowledge that a person may attend worship, or hear the gospel in another way, and be disturbed by the message such that he or she hears anew Christ's gracious yet persistent call to follow.

There is another side of the coin! One person used to attend church each Sunday evening until one week, an old preacher spoke on the text: 'For what shall it profit a man, if he gain the whole world, and lose his own soul?' (Mark 9:36 AV). This man listened intently to the sermon, but never came to church again. The challenge had hit home hard and was not well received. Truth can really hurt as it presents a stark challenge: it can surely stir the heart and mind.

In John's gospel we get a vivid picture of how Jesus stirred people: 'And there was much muttering about him among the people. While some said, "He is a good man", others said "No, he is leading the people astray"' (John 7:12). We see how some were strongly opposed to Him but others were equally supportive of Him. In the Christian fellowship we talk of stirring hymns, passionate sermons, and challenging testimonies. It is a fact that the truth of the gospel is both challenging and motivating: some are thus stirred to decision, or to Christian service, or to renewed commitment. The message of Jesus Christ continues to stir the hearts and minds of people!

Suggested readings: Luke 23:1-25 and John 7:10-18.

# February

Come down, O Love divine,
Seek Thou this soul of mine,
And visit it with Thine own ardour glowing;
O Comforter, draw near,
Within my heart appear,
And kindle it, Thy holy flame bestowing.

O let it freely burn,
Till earthly passions turn
To dust and ashes, in its heat consuming;
And let Thy glorious light
Shine ever on my sight,
And clothe me round, the while my path illuming.

Let holy Charity
Mine outward vesture be,
And lowliness become mine inner clothing;
True lowliness of heart,
 Which takes the humbler part,
And o'er its own shortcomings, weeps with loathing.

And so the yearning strong,
With which the soul will long,
Shall far outpass the power of human telling;
For none can guess its grace,
Till  He become the place
Wherein the Holy Spirit makes His dwelling.

Bianco da Siena (c.1350-1434)

Make us to remember, O God, that every day is thy gift,
and ought to be used according to thy command;
through Jesus Christ our Lord.

Samuel Johnson (1709-84)

## FEBRUARY 1<sup>st</sup>

## THERE IS A VAST MINISTRY OF GOOD

He sat on the edge of his bed in a hospital ward, a picture of hopelessness. It just seemed that years of sorrow had been heaped on his back, and he was, as it were, a study in despair. To the observer, the question arose: what circumstances had so crushed his spirit such that this man became so sad and despairing? It was obvious to all that he had reached 'the end of his tether'. Then, in came the nurses who, with great care, washed him, fed him, dressed him and coaxed him to say a few words. With much patience, they showed this man true human compassion. It was a picture of love at work. No doubt, some of those nurses had little time for organised Christianity and rarely, if ever, went to church. Yet, that is the marvel of God's grace; God can use many instruments and a variety of people whether or not they are Christians or, indeed, believers of any faith tradition. We remember that our God, in His sovereignty, can use all people!

Every single day of the year the media – radio, television, the press and so on – splash news of 'man's inhumanity to man'. Yet, there is another picture, too. Day by day in hospital wards and other places of caring, men and women display the dignity of human nature: they show love, tenderness and compassion. No one can calculate the multitude of works accomplished by the Lord who uses ministers, missionaries, Christian workers and a host of dedicated individuals to accomplish His purposes. Today, we remind ourselves that God's Spirit powerfully uses others too, including agnostics! How difficult it always is to estimate the scope of the Lord's ministry, as one verse in John's gospel hints tantalisingly: 'But there are also many other things which Jesus did; were every one of them to be written, I suppose that the world itself could not contain the books that would be written' (John 21:25). The Master graciously ministered through lots of very different people, in so many varied ways and places, and still does!

The New Testament has a lot to say about simply doing good. One wonderful verse from Romans puts it thus: 'But glory and honour and peace for every one who does good, the Jew first and also the Greek. For God shows no partiality' (Romans 2:10-11). We thank God that, in this troubled world, there are countless people being used by God; while some are conscious of being used, many are not. The good news is that daily there is a vast outpouring of good in our world: we rejoice in the rich ministries of love, kindness, care and compassion that continue day by day in countless places and situations.

Suggested readings: Romans 2:1-10 and I Thessalonians 5:12-22.

FEBRUARY 2nd

## LOVE BUILDS UP CHURCHES

God is to be praised for the variety of gifts and talents found within the Christian Church! There are gifts of preaching, administration, healing, teaching, among those listed by the apostle Paul, while we might add to those gifts of artistry and music, as well as so many more. So Paul writes: 'Having gifts that differ according to the grace given us, let us use them' (Romans 12:6). While that truth can be overlooked, if every Christian worldwide obeyed that advice, there would be a dramatic increase in the work done for the Kingdom of God! Many are shy or bashful, some seemingly even disobedient or lazy, while others might be frustrated in their service, but many gifts are not used, and rich resources are left untapped. Some people even enter into dissent with God about the way they are talented, wishing they possessed a different gift, one that they think they would prefer themselves.

Paul had a wide experience of church life, and he wrote these words to the fellowship at Corinth: 'Since you are eager to have spiritual gifts, try to excel in gifts that build up the church' (1 Corinthians 14:12 NIV). Anyone familiar with Paul's letters to the Corinthian church is acutely aware that he wanted the Christians to show greater love. Indeed, he urges them to make authentic, enduring love their aim (1 Corinthians 14:1). Genuine Christian love both strengthens and builds up local churches. It is vitally important as it enriches and fortifies congregational life.

In the modern world there is so much competitiveness: much of this can be healthy in commerce and, of course, in sporting endeavours. Many people enjoy entering competitions in the media for fun and social well being, and some appear to be born with a very competitive nature. However, there can be a darker side to the competitive spirit where it impairs relationships. Sometimes the spirit of jealousy is evident, too. The scriptures indicate that the best competition is gently provoking one another to excel in love, which always builds up true fellowship. Love is at the heart of all faithful Christian living. It has been commented that Dr. Billy Graham was a fine evangelist but, actually, the best expression of evangelism is not grand eloquence or spectacular visual presentation but our love reflecting God's love!

Genuine love is satisfied not to be trumpeted, or even recognised by others, when bringing help or offering encouragement. Love builds churches: anyone can build the material structure of a sanctuary, but it takes real Christian love to build fellowship. It is recorded that Jesus said: 'I will build my church' (Matthew 16:18). However, love is always the building factor: 'By this everyone will know that you are my disciples, if you have love for one another' (John 13:35). It is on the basis of love, which is focused on Him, that we live.

Suggested readings: John 13:31-35 and 1 Corinthians 13:8-14:1.

FEBRUARY 3rd

## WORDS CAN HAVE HEALING POWER

The Bible has a tremendous amount to say about human speech: words can be a power for good or a force for evil. In the Epistle of James, this comment is made about the human tongue: 'With it we bless the Lord and Father, and with it we curse those who are made in the likeness of God. From the same mouth come blessing and cursing' (James 3:9-10). From our own experience, we know how friends can both hurt us and help us: one day we can rejoice in their encouragement and another day we might feel dispirited by their criticism.

Modern Bible translations now abound, but before they became widely available many Christians were helped and inspired by versions of the scriptures such as Moffatt's translation in the early twentieth century. It is a wonderful experience to read his version of the Book of Proverbs. We find one such thought-provoking translation of an intriguing verse: 'A reckless tongue wounds like a sword, but there is healing power in thoughtful words' (Proverbs 12:18 Moffatt). It is worth thinking about how easy it is to be deeply wounded and hurt by malicious comments. Yet, on the positive side, surely we have all been helped and encouraged by thoughtful words. It is true that there is healing power in good, well-judged words, whether spoken or, indeed, written. We can all be thankful for encouraging words, or comforting words, which can bring a measure of healing in difficult situations. At the same time we can rejoice in the inspiration known through visionaries, hymn composers, songwriters, dramatists and poets whose words somehow truly strike a chord deep within us.

In some cases, it might be an understanding and diligent, well-trusted physician who offers the right words in a context of physical, mental or emotional trouble. He or she uses professional expertise to diagnose a problem and prescribe treatment, or maybe refer the patient to clinics or consultants. Often a key element in the work is the manner used: the gift of communication can mean that troubled people find help, sometimes just through healing words. The ministry of healing through therapeutic interaction (including healing words) is not confined to professionals; there are many very ordinary folk in this ministry, too. Some people have a natural way of employing helpful words to encourage others on the journey of life, and ultimately bring glory to God! As we think about the ministry of Jesus Christ, we see how often He spoke words that comforted and encouraged needy people. Jesus once said: 'Come to me, all who labour and are heavy-laden and I will give you rest' (Matthew 11:28). Those words have brought comfort down the ages. In our own small way, we too, can each use words in our daily lives to help someone needing encouragement!

Suggested readings: Proverbs 12:10-12 and Matthew 9:1-8.

FEBRUARY 4th

## THE LORD LIVES

In 1984, there was a great tragedy in India: something went wrong with a very large chemical plant and a massive cloud of poisonous gas escaped. The death toll was in excess of 2000 and many were seriously injured. It was a tragedy, which shook people around the globe. Without belittling the horror of that disaster, in a sense, it could also be seen as an analogy of our broken world. In fact, one might say that there is another poisonous cloud, which does incalculable damage in the lives of people, namely, the cloud of unbelief. Unbelief can be destructive to life and well-being, with the result that there is no personal relationship with God, no lasting hope, and no spiritual anchorage amid the storms of life. Any sense of the divine as a reality for us is excluded, but the Bible includes a stark warning to those who dismiss faith in this way: 'The fool says in his heart "There is no God"' (Psalm 14:1).

In another psalm there is a glorious affirmation of faith: 'The Lord lives' (Psalm 18:46). Life can be difficult. Tragedy strikes, sorrows can be burdensome, the way ahead may seem daunting and the forces against us appear very strong, but the affirmation of the Bible is that the Lord lives. Inevitably, people change, communities and nations change, and our circumstances change, but God remains the faithful, unchanging One, indeed, the eternal Lord at the heart of all life.

When visitors go to Italy, many plan to see the leaning tower of Pisa as a great tourist attraction. Actually, it stands – perhaps awkwardly – as a dramatic reminder that sound foundations are important. If solid foundations are ignored or neglected, a building will not stand safe and secure. An architect, in designing any tall building, ensures that foundations are especially deep and strong. Christians believe that their faith stands on the solid foundation that 'The Lord lives'.

There is another challenging verse in the New Testament: 'And without faith it is impossible to please him. For whoever would draw near to God must believe that he exists and that he rewards those who seek him' (Hebrews 11:6). Does God exist? Prophets, teachers, psalmists, together with the evangelists and apostles, and – since biblical times – countless people of faith would affirm, 'Yes'! It is possible to testify that God has not left Himself without a witness: the splendour of creation, the beauty of nature, the marvel of human life in community and the wonder of the inner life of the spirit in tune with the divine Spirit, may be interpreted as bearing witness to God's existence. Best of all, God has been revealed in the ministry of our Lord Jesus Christ. This phrase, 'The Lord lives', underlies all that makes for faith, hope and love, and it surely gives us courage to face each new day, whatever is ahead.

Suggested readings: Psalm 18:1-6 and Psalm 18:43-50.

FEBRUARY 5th

## WE MUST CONTINUE IN PRAYER AND NOT LOSE HEART

One of the best-known and most remarkable conversions in the story of the Christian church is that of St Augustine of Hippo. A man in the grip of worldly ways enjoying the pleasures of the flesh and wandering far from Christian standards and ideals, amazingly came to profess faith in Christ! What became clear was the fact that behind this wayward son was a strong mother, Monica, who continued in prayer for him. One can only just imagine how she felt when reports percolated through about her son's waywardness, and she wondered why her prayer for Augustine was not answered? She kept on praying earnestly, and eventually after much persistence in prayer, the change in his life came about. No one could ever calculate all that God did through St Augustine: his life, faith and writings have left an inestimable impact on history.

In the New Testament, there is a parable of Jesus about persistence in prayer: 'He spoke to them in a parable to show that they should keep on praying and never lose heart' (Luke 18:1). The critical issue was never to lose heart: Jesus spoke of an oppressed woman who was continually seeking vindication of her cause, but it was denied her. She was a helpless widow facing the hardness of a judge who didn't care at all, and her cause seemed lost from the outset. Yet she didn't lose heart, and with her bold persistence she kept seeking justice and her importunity won through in final victory over her adversary. The judge said 'Though I have no fear God and no respect for anyone, yet because this widow keeps bothering me, I will grant her justice, so she that she may not wear me out by continually coming' (Luke 18:4-5). The lesson for us is how much more believers ought to persevere in prayer before their heavenly Father Who, of course, stands in sharp contrast to a hard-hearted, unjust judge reluctant to listen to a vulnerable woman's persistent plea!

Men and women of every age have continued in prayer, including many who have persisted in prayer when they were facing enormous difficulties and setbacks. They kept on praying when it appeared that an answer was not forthcoming. They did not lose heart, but truly believed that God would heed their faithful prayers. We think of William and Catherine Booth, founders of the Salvation Army, who had to face huge problems in their work for the Kingdom. In spite of determined opposition, they continued to pray and work. They never lost heart when their difficulties seemed insurmountable. Today, the Salvation Army is an honoured and respected institution worldwide, the fruit of many faithful prayers. So we can find inspiration that all Christians, whatever their background or situation, have a vocation day by day to 'keep on praying and never lose heart'.

Suggested readings: Luke 18:1-8 and Thessalonians 5:12-24.

41

FEBRUARY 6th

## DISTRACTIONS ARE A SOLID REALITY

It was a special service, and the church was packed with young people and their parents. As the minister was giving the address, a beautiful butterfly appeared and buzzed him not just once, but many times! Doubtless, few present remembered the message that morning; the butterfly had claimed most of the attention. How little it takes to distract our attention and it plays havoc in so many areas of life. A motorist who had crashed into another car causing extensive damage, once made it his defence that, since a bee had distracted his attention, the bee was to be blamed for the accident!

In Luke's gospel we have the well known story of Jesus going to the home of Mary and Martha, and it contains this revealing passage: 'Mary sat at the Lord's feet and listened to his teaching. However, Martha was distracted with much serving; and she went to him and said, "Lord, do you not care that my sister has left me to serve alone?"'(Luke 10:39-40) This story has been used countless times in devotional talks, weighing up the virtues of each sister! Yet, the fact remains that, according to the Master, Martha was distracted and this is true insight into the situation of so many over the Christian era; maybe we can also sometimes see that in ourselves today!

The apostle Paul often stressed in his letters to the churches that priority should be given to the work of the Kingdom. He even expressed the view in one letter, echoed in some traditions down the centuries, that there is an advantage in remaining single! He put it this way: 'I have no wish to keep you on a tight rein. I am thinking simply of your own good, of what is seemly, and of your freedom to wait upon the Lord without distraction' (1 Corinthians 7:35 NEB). While he was undoubtedly referring to a specific situation, it may be that there is a time when – in some missionary situations or other areas of life – celibacy might be one solution to help give undivided attention to the work. However, married couples might also point out the advantages of being a Christian team in God's service. In so many instances, valiant service has been rendered by a couple together, and so it is a matter of individual calling.

The Evil One, as enemy of souls, could be regarded as the master of the art of distraction. One saintly figure in later Church history, Andrew Bonar, wrote of his determination to fence off time for prayer and study, but he acknowledged there was always a conflict of interests. He claimed that he could always find something else very pressing at the time which needed doing. It is an issue, which can mar even the most disciplined soul: we can but pray for divine aid to overcome such distraction!

Suggested readings: Luke 10:38-42 and Psalm 119:25-32.

FEBRUARY 7th

## PRAYER IS A HOMING INSTINCT

One does not have to be an ornithologist to be interested in the homing instinct of birds: it is a marvel, which surely fascinates anyone who is interested in nature. Various explanations have been given, but there is still a considerable amount of mystery about it. A simple experiment was made with seagulls living in Wales some time ago: they were taken to South America and, within a matter of days, they were back 'home' in Wales, a wonderful achievement. It raises the curious question: how do birds have both the stamina and ability to cross the sea and land to find their way back home? One thing is sure: the homing instinct is amazingly powerful and mysterious.

Prayer can be likened to the homing instinct. Many people pray: people of all backgrounds, cultures, beliefs and traditions, including those who do not even go to church as much as others who do so attend. How often people – with or without religious inclination – faced with a complex situation, a problem, a sad loss, a great burden or an important decision, feel the need to pray. It is as if by instinct people turn to God in prayer. In Psalm 107, reference is made to a ship caught in a storm as an illustration of such a turning to God: 'They reeled and staggered like drunken men, and were at their wit's end. Then they cried to the Lord in their trouble, and he delivered them from their distress; he made the storm be still, and the waves of the sea were hushed' (Psalm 107:27-29).

James Boswell was notable for his record of Dr. Samuel Johnson's wise sayings. On one occasion Johnson was asked 'What is the strongest argument for prayer?' His answer was disarmingly simple: 'There is no argument for prayer'. There is a deep sense in which the urge to pray is like the homing instinct: under a variety of circumstances, people pray quite naturally, perhaps almost as naturally as eating and breathing, even without instruction. Malcolm Muggeridge once testified that, when he was a journalist (long before he was received into church membership), he used to cry to God in prayer. He would pray secretly such prayers as 'Help me', 'Guide me' or 'Use me'. Evidently others also, who normally appear to be very little concerned with the inner life, sometimes pray like that on certain occasions.

Of course, there are higher levels of prayer and, when a person has made a sincere commitment of faith, it is important to foster growth in prayer. Short so-called 'arrow prayers' have their place, but God's Spirit surely prompts people to have a richer and deeper experience of prayer. It might begin rather like a simple homing instinct but, in real faith, prayer can truly deepen to something far richer!

Suggested readings: Psalm 107:23-32 and 1 Thessalonians 5:12-25.

FEBRUARY 8th

## LIFE HAS ITS AWESOME FINALITIES

How often a very homely scene can elicit an eternal truth, and we get a glimpse of the spiritual in the midst of the ordinary. A true story is told of an elderly lady who was being settled into a hospital ward after an operation. She asked for several things, and one of her requests was for a little stool to rest her leg. The kind nurse helping her quietly said: 'No, my dear, you will not need that now, your leg is not there anymore'. It was just a familiar request the patient made out of habit: actually she had faced leg amputation in another hospital, and was now entering on a period of convalescence, but was still coming to terms with her loss of the limb. There is a terrible finality about an amputation: a leg may have been painful for years, but people find it very difficult to accept that such drastic action should be taken. So also in life, there are other respects in which there can be an awesome finality about things: then, as the old expression put it, 'the Rubicon is crossed', and a momentous change seems to be realized, and life takes on a different dimension!

John the Baptist, who prepared the way for the Messiah, was a brave prophet of God. He conveyed a stark message of repentance: it must have taken extraordinary courage to challenge even the political and religious leaders to repent. We think of him as an austere, rugged and bold preacher, and the gospel narratives indicate that his ministry brought about sweeping renewal. However, the most courageous thing he did was to challenge Herod Antipas, the tetrarch, about his illicit relationship with a woman: 'It is not lawful for you to have her' (Matthew 14:4). His condemnation proved costly, and from the moment his words were uttered, life was never the same again: John's life was immediately under threat. The woman involved, Herodias, yearned for revenge and when the moment came, she took the opportunity to silence him, and John lost his life for his righteous stand as God's prophet.

In one sense, other moments may seem rather final: the moment of making a costly decision, the loss of a friendship, the death of one's partner, the loss of reputation by some foolish deed, or the loss of faith through a crisis of life. The crucifixion scene narrated in Matthew's gospel, presents the cry of Jesus in a rather stark and final way: 'My God, my God, why have you forsaken me?' (Matthew 27:40). No theologian, Bible scholar or devout Christian has ever plumbed the depth of those terrible words of anguish: it seems that the Saviour drank to the very bottom of the cup of suffering. Thus we can testify that, in bearing our sin as Saviour, Jesus knew a depth of dereliction for our sakes, so we can affirm that we know we shall never face the finality of being forsaken. God's work on the cross in Christ is final: so here is our blessed assurance and our glorious hope!

Suggested readings: Matthew 14:1-12 and Matthew 27:45-50.

FEBRUARY 9th

## JESUS CHRIST OPENS EARS THAT DON'T HEAR

One of the great blessings of life is a good sense of hearing. We are surely grateful for lovely sounds: church bells ringing in the distance, the song of birds, the laughter of little children, the ticking of a grandfather clock, the sound of familiar footsteps, a gentle breeze rustling leaves, the crashing of waves or a babbling brook. It seems that sometimes we show a lot of sympathy for the blind but much less for the deaf. How often people become impatient – even cross – with the hearing impaired.

People occasionally can recover the ability to hear. A story is told of a woman who had faced hearing loss for seventeen years. It had been a sore trial for her. However, by a new therapy, her hearing was restored! She said: 'It was like entering a room that I had not visited for a long time'. Memories were revived to her great delight. In a sense, that could be seen as a kind of parable of the spiritual life. We think of someone who goes regularly to church and loves it: the singing of the hymns, the fellowship with others, the genuine sharing, and the zealous service for the Kingdom bring joy. Then things go wrong: a new interest or pastime takes over, and other activities militate against church attendance. Gradually this person becomes, as it were, spiritually deaf and fails to respond to God's gracious call. Yet, thankfully, God does not let someone go away so easily, and occasionally, the person may be drawn back afresh, through the loving support and prayers of others.

Luke chapter 15 includes the lovely parable of the diligent shepherd who is willing to 'go after the one which is lost until he finds it' (Luke 15:4). So, likewise, we know that spiritually, when a straying soul is found, the wanderer's senses are renewed, a person's eyes are opened and hearing is restored! Surely, it is like entering a long-neglected room and memories are revived! The hymn writer puts it beautifully:

> Down in the human heart, crushed by the tempter,
> Feelings lie buried that grace can restore;
> Touched by a loving hand, wakened by kindness,
> Cords that were broken will vibrate once more.

There are plenty of people who can testify that Jesus Christ has restored them to newness of life, a wholly new life in God filled with joy and peace. Still today, in the realm of the spirit, Jesus Christ can open deaf ears as well as blind eyes of men and women seemingly shut off from faith, to bring fullness of life in union with God!

Suggested readings: Mark 7:31-37 and Luke 15:1-7.

FEBRUARY 10th

## ABOUT TURNS ARE OFTEN NECESSARY

Each year the Baptist Missionary Society normally holds a special valedictory service for men and women who are sent abroad on their work for God. It is always a crowded service and delegates from churches come from long distances to be there. The singing is warm and hearty; the addresses are packed with interest and challenge. However, the most moving part is when the missionaries who are then returning to the field, or new missionaries going out for the first time, give a few brief words concerning their commitment. Often they quote a verse of scripture, and they speak sincerely of a real and tangible experience with God. They have sensed God's call, and many have had to make an important 'U turn' to be obedient to it: often their life-style has undergone a significant revolution, and it has involved cost to their family, too!

One of the passages in Acts is known popularly as 'the Macedonian call', and it is a very well used passage in missionary circles. It tells how the apostle Paul and his companions were guided not to fulfil their own plans. In fact, the record shows how they were forbidden to do so: 'They attempted to go into Bithynia but the Spirit of Jesus did not allow them; so, passing by Mysia, they went down to Troas' (Acts 16:7). That same night, Paul had a vision of a man of Macedonia standing with a plea: 'Come over to Macedonia and help us' (Acts 16:9). They duly obeyed that call and, since Luke penned his account, that story has challenged many people to venture in Christian service. Paul made an important 'about turn' under a sense of obedience to God. All through Christian history, there have been people who have been willing to abandon their own plans and grand ambitions, to obey a call from God, and to be self-denying for the furtherance of the work of Christ.

The Bible has many stories of people who, under the influence of God's Spirit, changed their plans. Generations of believers have done the same: David Sheppard, a brilliant cricketer, who played for England, left that successful post to become an Anglican priest. Also, James Irwin (one of the few who went to the moon) left his career as an astronaut to do Christian service. Those telling words, 'Come over and help us', have challenged many and brought change in numerous lives. God's Spirit has inspired people in other directions, too. Today, there is a noble army of people who work earnestly to improve the lot of the physically and mentally challenged. Many others reach out to those who are on the margins of society, the oppressed, the deprived, the refugee, as well as prisoners, addicts and the 'down-and-out', simply because they have willingly left their own plans to obey God's will.

Suggested readings: Acts 16:6-15 and Philippians 1:3-11.

FEBRUARY 11th

## JESUS CHRIST COMES TO SMALL FELLOWSHIPS

One of the great joys of the Christian life is to worship in a large church in fellowship with hundreds of other Christians. It is a thrilling and enlivening experience, which moves the heart and inspires the mind. Such times of worship are precious. However, it is also true that some people find it equally enthralling to worship in a much smaller fellowship; those times can be very special too, as God has been found to be so near and His blessing so real, even among the faithful few.

A Christian family on holiday spent a Sunday afternoon exploring in the Cotswolds and visited a very tiny church tucked away in the depths of the lovely countryside. Unbeknown to them, they had arrived just before Evensong and they were invited to stay! The congregation was small (the family actually doubled the congregation), but the worship was warm and sincere. Here was a small group of people in the heart of the countryside praising and serving God. The visitors that day testified later that it was a lovely experience: God's presence was so clearly felt there.

This reminds us of the promise given by Jesus Christ: 'For where two or three are gathered in my name, there am I in the midst of them' (Matthew 18:20). This promise has been proved true by many small groups of believers all around the world. A tiny congregation in a village church, a small group of believers on board ship, a few friends at a Christian guesthouse, a chaplain on a hospital ward; all testify to experiencing God's presence in a vital way. The Christian author, H.A. Williams, testified to that sense of divine presence he had known at a simple service held on the shores of the Lake of Galilee, in the presence of a few close friends: it was a rare and wonderful experience, and one he never forgot.

In the modern world, there is a great stress on numbers and big is equated with beautiful and best. Of course, numbers are important and it is a splendid thing to see a church fellowship prosper. Yet, we recognise that numbers are not everything! Throughout Scripture, we are told that our God can use many or, indeed, just a few. We recall that on the first Easter, two sad people were walking on the Emmaus Road: the events of the previous few days were very much on their minds. They were in a deep conversation: 'Jesus himself drew near and went with them' (Luke 24:15). In the story, these two were transformed and enriched in fellowship with Him once they realised the reality of His risen presence; this was not just an isolated event! Disciples of the risen Lord bear witness to how He still draws near, even to the twos and threes, to bless them with His presence. So we thank God for the smaller fellowships where people experience God's love, grace and forgiveness. Great Christian service is undertaken on quite a scale in large churches, but it is true that God's Spirit is powerfully at work in and through small fellowships, too.

Suggested readings: Matthew 18:10-20 and Luke 24:13-31.

FEBRUARY 12th

## PEOPLE DO FORGET ESSENTIALS

They arrived at the airport with a great sense of excitement; this was their holiday of a lifetime. 'Australia, here we come', they happily exclaimed. Then came the awkward question: 'You did pick up the passports from the telephone table?' The silence was unbearable, before the embarrassed 'No' was painfully uttered. They had forgotten the essentials and felt devastated beyond words: one error had plunged them from the heights of happiness to a misery beyond description. They obviously missed the plane and the whole trip was thrown into confusion.

In every area of life there are moments when people forget the essentials: the motorist who runs out of petrol on the motorway, the busy parent who forgets to turn on the oven, the business executive who misses an important appointment or the barrister who leaves the briefcase on the train, to name but a few mishaps. In the Book of Jeremiah there is a fascinating passage: 'Does a young woman forget her jewellery, or a bride her wedding-dress? But my people have forgotten me for more days than can be counted' (Jeremiah 2:32 GNB). To his first hearers, as also to us, this sounds incredible: a bride forgetting her wedding-dress. Yet, it is in this way, the prophet laments, that the people of God had astonishingly forgotten their Saviour.

The Old Testament records instances of human forgetfulness and ingratitude. Two verses from Psalm 106 speak volumes: 'Our ancestors, when they were in Egypt, did not consider your wonderful works; they did not remember the abundance of your steadfast love' (Psalm 106:7). Later there is a similar indictment: 'They forgot God, their Saviour, who had done great things in Egypt' (Psalm 106:21).

A couple forget their passports! A holy people forget their God! Every minister of the Gospel can testify that he or she has known people who have enjoyed numerous blessings from the Lord's hands, and then completely forgotten God. What unbelievable omissions! Yet, we have to face the fact that forgetting God is at the core of human frailty and sin.

In our age, the great pictures once painted by John Constable carry a massive price tag. We may ponder how he became such a wonderful artist. In real terms his gift was the ability to select the significant: he had the sensitivity to know what was important, essential and effective. So he looked at an English country scene with discerning eyes. Seeing what is truly essential and significant above all else, is actually the secret of successful living. It's vital to glimpse and to acknowledge what is fundamentally important, and then not to forget it.

Suggested readings: Jeremiah 2:26-32 and Isaiah 51:11-16.

FEBRUARY 13th

## THERE IS ROOM FOR IMPROVEMENT

In Mark's gospel there is a deeply moving story about the defeat of the disciples. A man brought to them his young son suffering from epilepsy, but they could not cure him, and the situation seemed hopeless. Then, they brought the child to Jesus and, right in front of Him, the child had another terrible convulsion. The words of the desperate father stir the heart: 'If you can do anything, have pity on us and help us' (Mark 9:22). What is notable is the small but significant word 'if'. Then later, in his dialogue with Jesus, came the man's confession of faith: 'I believe, help thou my unbelief' (Mark 9:24). We notice the complete honesty of the father; he did not pretend to have fullness of faith, but he came to Jesus with what faith he had.

During his ministry at the Metropolitan Tabernacle, London, C.H. Spurgeon used to refer to man's 'little faith' placed in a great Saviour. The line that carries electricity may seem thin, but it provides power. The artery, which carries blood to the heart, is small compared to its vital importance. In the same way, the prayer, 'I believe, help my unbelief', is a brief one, but it remains as a truly marvellous prayer, wholly acceptable to God.

When a plane flies over certain areas in Australia it provides a panoramic view of the dual landscape: there are parts richly cultivated and parts which (for a whole variety of reasons) stubbornly resist cultivation. The uncultivated parts look like ugly blemishes on an otherwise lovely vista! Similarly, if we take an 'aerial view' of a Christian life, it reveals places where faith has conquered but also places where doubt still lurks, a mixture of belief and unbelief. There are some Christians who claim that they have no doubts, no lack of faith, no 'fainting of spirit', but surely they are the exceptions which prove the rule! This little prayer 'I believe, help my unbelief', so stark in its brevity and honesty, truly rings a bell for the majority of believers.

There is an old saying that 'The largest room in the world is the room for improvement'. How true that is in the realm of the spiritual life: countless Christians feel the yearning for growth in love, faith, obedience and hope. Indeed, the New Testament epistles of Peter speak of the need to grow in faith. One verse in particular expresses the apostle's profound wish: 'But grow in grace and knowledge of our Lord and Saviour Jesus Christ' (2 Peter 3:18). Sometimes, of course, we may feel that our faith is weak and there is no possibility of spiritual growth or improvement in our devotion. In those moments, we may turn to Jesus with the simple prayer: 'I believe, help my unbelief' knowing that even if our faith is small, God hears our prayers and longs to bless and transform us.

Suggested readings: Mark 9:14-29 and 2 Peter 3:14-18.

FEBRUARY 14th

## THERE IS A POWER OF EVIL

One of the big concerns in the modern world is the way in which forests are being destroyed. Acres and acres of trees are being felled: the great land of Brazil is losing stretches of forest at an alarming rate, and it happens elsewhere, too. Scientists are concerned that there are changes in the climate patterns; also that natural habitats for birds and animals are being destroyed. A news item a while ago gave a vivid, even stark, demonstration of the problem. Viewers were shown a fine mahogany tree which had taken over one hundred years to grow to its majestic size. A worker came along with a chain saw and, in precisely one hundred seconds felled the tree. The tree took one hundred years to grow, and just one hundred seconds to fell. In one sense, that seemingly innocent act of tree-felling could be likened to the power of evil.

A person who has taken a whole lifetime to develop his character, known and respected by peers for his devotion and integrity, comes to a sad demise. He held a position of great authority and influence, and many had sought his wise counsel. Then, he made a very foolish mistake – a lapse into immorality – and his character and reputation were seriously damaged. The story of the Israelite King David, is a powerful illustration of what evil can do: he committed adultery and, in the time that followed this failing, the Bible story records that he stumbled from one sin to another. The account of David's fall may be described as being like the fall of a mighty tree, because he sinned against the Lord. Since the very beginning, men and women have faced the awful power of evil, and the havoc it can wreak upon lives and individual homes, as well as upon families and communities.

Evil is a reality and the media daily reminds us of human failings: there are always stories of violence, abuse, unfaithfulness, treachery, cruelty and neglect. There are large cities which are notorious for high levels of serious crime daily; even smaller places often also tell a sorry tale. Some time ago, a beautiful parish church in a lovely English village was marvellously and carefully restored. Inside the church a notice reads: 'This Lady Chapel is offered as a quiet place for private prayer'. Then the visitor observes another notice (not far from the first one): 'Please do not touch the ornaments. Burglar alarm is fitted'. There, in the most serene surroundings, stands a place of prayer, with the sense that evil is not far away. Sadly, vandalism and theft from parish churches has reached such levels that many churches cannot be safely left unlocked: an acknowledgement that we still reckon with evil in the world.

As the Bible testifies, everyone has sinned and, in a sense, 'fallen to evil'. Yet, there is always forgiveness for all who truly repent. In recalling the power of evil, we can also rejoice in the grace of God which still brings hope and healing today.

Suggested readings: Luke 22:54-62 and 1 Corinthians 10:11-13.

FEBRUARY 15th

## THERE'S A NEED TO MEDITATE

Someone seeking a house-companion placed an advert in a newspaper, and the last few words arrested the reader's attention: 'Impeccable references essential'. We remind ourselves today that our gracious God is faithful and true, and there are many impeccable references in scripture testifying as much. The psalmist speaks for a vast multitude of believers when he says: 'For the Lord is good; his steadfast love endures for ever, and his faithfulness to all generations' (Psalm 100:5). In the modern era of feverish busyness and activity, it is a good thing to fence off time to ponder and meditate upon God's loving and merciful character. It is very easy for life to become filled with so many things that we can overlook the Eternal One at the heart of all creation, and forget to take time to be still and to know God at hand.

The New English Bible has a fine translation of a verse from Psalm 107: 'Let the wise . . . lay these things to heart, and ponder the record of the Lord's enduring love' (Psalm 107:43 NEB). What a marvellous phrase: 'ponder the record'. It is a wise plan for the Christian to give time each day to ponder the record of God's love and goodness contained in the Bible. Of course, the record extends outside the scriptures too: the biographies of God's faithful servants can stimulate (in the words of the hymn writer) 'new thoughts of God, new hopes of heaven'. We should remind ourselves continually that waiting time is not wasted time: one can ponder God's grace as one stands waiting in a queue in a shop or at a bank or post office, or out on the street, or at a station, and many people do exactly that.

One of the loveliest thoughts given by Catherine Marshall about God is this one: 'He can make all the difference in every human situation'. Those ten words are gloriously true and wonderfully comforting! We might consider our own situation today, or that of someone we know well. If it is a matter of facing illness, weakness, bereavement, disappointment, trouble, or some other knotty problem, we can 'ponder the record' and consciously remind ourselves of what God has done, and what He has promised to do for His children. Countless ones testify that God does make all the difference: sometimes God removes the burden and sometimes He just strengthens our back to bear the load.

The lovely words from Isaiah are refreshing, like gentle rain after prolonged drought: 'Those of steadfast mind you keep in peace – in peace because they trust in you. Trust in the Lord for ever: for in the Lord God you have an everlasting rock' (Isaiah 26:3-4). This solid truth has been proved and tested by generations of believers. Each day we surely ought to reflect on this wonderful assurance by making time to ponder the record of God's marvellous, enduring faithfulness.

Suggested readings: Psalm 100:1-5 and Isaiah 26:1-8.

FEBRUARY 16<sup>th</sup>

## JESUS CHRIST LOVED CHILDREN

It is wonderful to hear the voices of children praising God! There is a verse in Psalm 8 that says: 'From the lips of children and infants you have ordained praise' (Psalm 8:2). Indeed, there is a special quality to the songs when children sing: 'Tell me the stories of Jesus', 'All things bright and beautiful' or 'Away in a manger'. Of course, sometimes their questions and responses about God and faith bring penetrating insights or make us pause for thought.

On one occasion, Bishop Malcolm Menin went along to a Church primary school in Leeds to talk about the life of a bishop. He showed the children his staff and his mitre and they were fascinated. Right at the end, the teacher asked whether the children had any questions. A small voice from the back row said 'Miss, he's got black leather elbow-pads on his jumper just like me!' The boy had listened to the talk and watched the bishop show his symbols of office, but the important thing for him was the point of identification, namely, black leather elbow-pads. All bishops are, after all, just ordinary people in a special role.

Matthew's gospel leaves us in no doubt that Jesus had time for children. We read in the gospel that on one occasion Jesus said this prayer: 'I thank thee Father, Lord of heaven and earth, that thou hast hidden these things from the wise and understanding and revealed them to babes; yea, Father, for such was thy gracious will' (Matthew 11:25 AV). The gospel writer also says: 'Then little children were brought to Jesus for him to place his hands on them and pray for them. But the disciples rebuked those who brought them. Jesus said "Let the little children come to me, and do not hinder them, for the kingdom of heaven belongs to such as these"' (Matthew 19:13-14). As we reflect on these readings, we can imagine (without any difficulty whatsoever) that children saw in Jesus a friend. Though unique as God's Son, He came among us and belonged to the human race sharing our lot as one of us; at so many points and in many ways, He identified Himself with ordinary people.

It is right that Christians should stress the divinity of the Lord Jesus Christ as it is fundamental! Yet, equally, Christians should acknowledge His humanity, too. He is One who readily identified Himself with the human race and people can say, very reverently: 'He is one of us'. The Saviour of the world knew weariness, hunger, thirst, disappointment, pain and grief and He understands us. As He loved children, so His love extends to us all. In the words of the much-loved Christmas carol: 'He is our life's true pattern, tears and smiles like us He knew'. We thank the Lord that God's children of all ages know the Saviour's love!

Suggested readings: Matthew 11:25-30 and Matthew 19:13-15.

FEBRUARY 17th

## PRAYER CAN OPEN AWKWARD DOORS

A vicar writing in his parish magazine gave a report concerning the House Groups held for Bible Study. He was pleased to report that the series of studies was progressing well, with the studies proving both helpful and rewarding. He mentioned (as a humorous aside) that one of the homes used for the House Group had an awkward door! How often this problem arises in a home, and the amazing thing is that people just 'put up with it'. They regularly say to visitors: 'Oh, sorry, this door is a bit awkward'. That scene can provoke an interesting meditation on life.

One of the facts of life is that, some people who hold positions of trust and authority, are just like an awkward door: it can be difficult to get past them for various reasons. These people range from controllers or inspectors to enforcement officers: people from many different walks of life including people with positions in church life can seem to be a little like awkward doors! They don't respond easily and readily, and maybe sometimes they need a gentle but firm push to shift them. In all sorts of scenarios it can be hard to overcome bureaucracy: missionaries and aid workers have stories about the awkwardness of getting visas through, as needed, at the right time!

Luke records at the opening of Acts chapter 12: 'Herod the king laid violent hands upon some who belonged to the church'. He notes how Peter was arrested and put in prison, with very tight security. Escape seemed impossible! According to the account, one unforgettable night, Peter had a marvellous experience of deliverance, and the only thing barring his way to freedom was a strong iron gate, a very tough 'awkward door'. The account of the angel delivering Peter continued astonishingly: 'They came to the iron gate leading into the city. It opened to them of its own accord and they went out' (Acts 12:10). We might well ask how this awkward door could yield and open. We need to refer to an earlier part of the narrative: 'So Peter was kept in prison; but earnest prayer for him was made to God by the church' (Acts 12:5). There is little doubt that Luke intends his readers to make the vital link between the believing prayer of God's people and Peter's amazing deliverance. Prayer is the key to many doors! Faithful intercession is offered and it can be our experience that doors are unlocked, ways seem to open up and new vistas can begin to appear ahead of us.

The ordinary house door that is proving difficult to open can usually be fixed quite easily; an experienced carpenter can do the job in minutes. There are other doors, 'awkward doors', which can indeed be opened by believing prayer.

Suggested readings: Psalm 24:1-10 and Acts 12:1-17.

FEBRUARY 18th

## OUR GOD USES GOOD BOOKS

How can one place a value on a good book? Patrick Moore tells how that when he was a boy someone gave him a book about the stars; he was absolutely fascinated and it sparked off a lifetime's interest in astronomy. His popular series on television 'The sky at night' has given pleasure to millions of viewers and provoked much interest in the stars. One small book set Patrick Moore on his life's work. In essence, not only can a book inform, entertain or inspire us, it can shape us or even be life-changing!

In Psalm 102, there is a beautiful verse about the value of a written record: 'Let this be recorded for a generation to come, so that people yet unborn may praise the Lord' (Psalm 102:18). Thank God for all the faithful men and women who have written down their spiritual thoughts and experiences so that others could benefit. We can think of wonderful volumes such John Wesley's *Journal*, John Bunyan's *Pilgrim's Progress*, William Temple's *Readings in St John*, William Sangster's *The Pure in Heart* or Amy Carmichael's *The Edges of His Ways*, among many others known to us. How often one good book can spark off a renewed interest in the Holy Scripture or the spiritual life: this has happened time after time.

We can purchase a substantial book (or, indeed, a modern translation of the Bible) for the price of a meal in a restaurant, and that one book can give us spiritual food for a lifetime! Christians all thank God for the Bible, but surely also for inspiring good books, too. We know how lives have been changed as faith has been fostered, encouragement has been given and comfort has been granted, sometimes simply through the reading of a book, even a book written a long time before the reader was born! The Methodist Church can never forget that John Wesley had his heart-warming experience because he heard someone else reading one of Martin Luther's books; it was even just the preface of that important book!

Bedford is rightly proud of the fact that one of its most unlikely citizens, John Bunyan, brought it honour and fame by his seventeenth-century work. Today, Christians the world over, testify how the Holy Spirit enabled Bunyan to use his pen, even in Bedford gaol, to the glory of God. It is interesting to see how Luke explains why he wrote his gospel: 'I myself have carefully investigated everything from the beginning, it seemed good also to write an orderly account for you' (Luke 1:3 NIV). That marvellous Gospel written by Luke, as well as his second volume – the Acts of the Apostles – has been used of God to bring about so much for the Kingdom, and, of course, other scripture books have been equally inspired and inspiring!

Suggested readings: Psalm 102:12-22 and Luke 1:1-4.

FEBRUARY 19th

## CONCERNING THE BLESSINGS OF THE DIVINE OCTAVE

One of the marvels of life is the octave – the eight basic notes of music. It is simply impossible to estimate the rich variety of music which has flowed from these eight sounds: it is one of the wonders of the world! When we think of the great classical composers such as Bach, Mozart, Beethoven, Handel (to name but a few of the much-loved classical composers of the past), using these basic notes to write their famous compositions, it is a thrill to perceive and appreciate the 'miracle of the octave'. It is just incredible to think that, for centuries yet still to come, there will still be men and women producing more lovely compositions from the octave.

There is a verse which could be called the 'Divine Octave': an eight-word promise found in the Epistle to the Hebrews. The epistle includes this divine promise: 'I will never leave you or forsake you'. (Hebrews 13:5). Those eight words in the translation (the Divine Octave), have brought untold blessings into countless lives. This promise has given inspiration, comfort, encouragement, strength and blessing to individuals, families, and entire congregations. Like the octave in music, its power to be fruitful in the spiritual life is undiminished by time: God never fails us!

One of the sad facts of life is that people fail us. Joseph was persecuted by his own brothers, David was betrayed by his own son, the disciples who followed Jesus forsook him, the apostle Paul faced criticism and was deserted by Demas, and John wrote of setbacks in the churches. One of the most painful disclosures of broken fellowship is in Psalm 55: 'It is not an enemy who taunts me – then I could bear it; it is not an adversary who deals insolently with me, then I could hide from him. But it is you, my equal, my companion, my familiar friend. We used to hold sweet converse together; within God's house we walked in fellowship' (Psalm 55:12-14).

Today we rejoice in the glorious fact that God's promise of never failing us stands as the melodious 'Divine Octave': countless people, have delighted in its spiritual music, as it were. It is a promise that stands sure and remains in every circumstance, every day of the year. As we look into the future, we are aware of the words of scripture: 'Do not boast about tomorrow for you do not know what a day may bring forth' (Proverbs 27:1). Experience impresses upon us the truth that life is full of uncertainties, but there is the Lord's affirmation: 'I will never leave you or forsake you'. This promise is like a solid foundation, and we can build our life upon it with confidence; so in every generation there have been men and women who have trusted God's utter faithfulness, and their lives have been wonderfully enriched. We can still prove that glorious affirmation to be true in our own experience today.

Suggested readings: Psalm 55:12-14 and Hebrews 13:1-16.

FEBRUARY 20th

## BELIEVERS SHOULD BE A PEOPLE NEAR TO GOD

In the New Testament we are told of an exciting time of blessing at Antioch. The scripture says 'And the hand of the Lord was with them: and a great number believed, and turned to the Lord' (Acts 11:21). The church at Jerusalem heard of this and sent Barnabas to investigate; what he saw thrilled his heart! Then we read this sentence rendered so eloquently in the Living Bible: 'Then he arrived and saw the wonderful things God was doing, he was filled with excitement and joy, and encouraged the believers to stay close to the Lord, whatever the cost' (Acts 11:23). In the Bible there are many descriptions of the people of God as God's flock, His children, His jewels, His servants or His portion. The Psalmist surely gives one of the loveliest of them all: 'A people near unto Him' (Psalm 148:14).

There is no substitute for living near the Lord! A church can be wonderfully organised, it can rejoice in an abundance of talented workers, it can have ample financial resources, but one other thing is necessary: to be 'a people near unto the Lord'. Christian history reveals with great certainty that the people who lived near to God have brought rich blessing to the Church and to the world. In fact, both the Old and New Testaments teach that there is no substitute for close fellowship with God. It is interesting to note that, when Jesus called the twelve disciples, Mark's gospel gives this significant verse: 'And he appointed twelve to be with him' (Mark 3:14). The primary requisite was simply to be with Him.

In his gospel, Luke tells us that when Jesus was arrested and taken to the house of the high priest 'Peter followed at a distance' (Luke 22:54). How do we measure that distance? Is it a distance of yards or a spiritual distance? We know that it was both: Peter followed at a distance, and then within a short time denied his discipleship. When it comes to faith, it is always dangerous to follow at a distance. Individuals, married couples, families, church fellowships are challenged to be 'people of God', and the effective way to obey this is to have close fellowship with the Lord.

A minister was called to a large church but was dismayed that the bulk of the people sat at the rear section. A complaint was voiced at a subsequent church meeting that some couldn't hear the new minister. His reply came quietly, but firmly: 'If you sit at a distance you won't hear'. That's clearly also a significant spiritual truth; so James in his epistle exhorts the believers: 'Draw near to God and He will draw near to you' (James 4:8). Drawing near to God is the Lord's will, and it always helps the hearing problem, too!

Suggested readings: Mark 3:7-14 and Luke 22:54-62.

FEBRUARY 21st

## GOD'S GRACE GIVES NEW BEGINNINGS

The broadcasting of the Daily Service on BBC Radio 4 (LW) down recent decades has been a blessing to so many. The fact that this broadcast of a morning act of Christian worship has been a feature for well over six decades gives some indication of its value. Lots of people have testified to what this short religious broadcast has meant to them. It has obviously been a great help to the sick, the troubled, the bereaved, those shut in and lonely, as well as countless others. One woman tells how she was in her study at Felixstowe facing a crisis in both her personal life and her professional life. She listened to the Daily Service when the prayers that particular morning were concerning the grace of God. It started a train of thought and she went back to the Prayer Book to study the word 'grace'. Before the day closed, she had entered into a new experience: it was a turning point which eventually brought her into Christian ministry to serve Jesus Christ and His Kingdom. The service had been used of God to do a mighty work within her mind and heart!

God's grace is wonderfully rich toward us. The Holy Scriptures tell of divine grace to forgive, to sustain, to restore, to comfort and to strengthen, beautifully summed up in one verse: 'grace to help in time of need' (Hebrews 4:16). In a marvellous way, grace is like the famous Niagara Falls, ever-flowing season by season, day by day, hour by hour: awesome, abundant and magnificent! However, there is one essential difference. At least once in recent years, those cascades actually froze solid in the intense cold, and the waters actually stopped flowing: to observers it seemed incredible! Today, we rejoice that God's grace never stops: it flows constantly and we can utterly depend upon it. Even when there is a deadly spiritual coldness in the atmosphere and it seems that evil is triumphant, the wonderful grace of God keeps flowing.

Whatever we might face, whether a particular crisis, or simply feeling quite overwhelmed or having in our heart a sense of foreboding, there is unfailing grace to help in that time of need. It is always good to pause and remember God's rich grace, especially as described in this lovely verse in the New Testament: 'And God is able to make all grace abound to you, so that in all things at all times, having all that you need, you will abound in every good work' (2 Corinthians 9:8 NIV). If we truly let that verse sink into our mind and heart, and allow that key little word 'all' to exercise its own powerful work of encouragement and transformation, we can know the blessed assurance of our faith. At the heart of our faith is the knowledge that God's grace is available to us each and every one, here and now.

Suggested readings: 2 Corinthians 9:1-11 and Ephesians 2:4-10.

## FEBRUARY 22nd

## THERE ARE FORCES WHICH HINDER

All Christian believers who seek to serve are conscious that they have a 'Helper'! To them, the powerful ministry of the Holy Spirit, the divine 'Advocate' (or 'Helper'), is both obvious and essential. They are convinced that they have an ally, while they also understand that there are forces working against the Kingdom. So often, Christian work is hindered – sometimes wrecked – by such unleashed, unseen, enemy forces. It is recorded in Matthew's gospel that Jesus told the parable of a man who sowed good seed in his field but, while he slept, an enemy came and sowed weeds. As a result, the wheat and the weeds grew together. In conversation with his servants, who were questioning why there were weeds, the farmer said, 'An enemy has done this' (Matthew 13:28). The obvious conclusion was stark: an enemy has done this!

How true that is to life as we all experience it. One apostle was quite clear: 'We wanted to come to you – I, Paul, again and again – but Satan hindered us' (1 Thessalonians 2:18). Paul recognised a persistent 'hinderer' at work. On 21st October 1966, the world was shocked to hear the news of a great tragedy in Wales which resulted in much loss of life; that fateful day a huge slag-heap became unstable and shifted, sliding down on houses and a school, with many people – including lots of children – tragically killed. Within hours, this remote village in Wales became a household word in numerous countries. In record time another mountain moved, as it were, a mountain of goodwill, generosity and love. People from all quarters were eager to help and offered their services. Then, sadly, around this wonderful act of kind-heartedness, arose much bickering, jealousy, quarrels, and strife. The money intended for good purposes became the focal point for animosity and division. The wise ancient word of the apostle Paul seems to be very relevant here: '. . . but Satan hindered us'.

It is one of the sure facts of life that often things go sour. Individuals, couples, families, churches and nations have experienced this hindering menace. There are forces which are very powerful and disruptive: many believers can testify of plans upset, of good intentions twisted and of hostility experienced. The story is told of a certain church experiencing much blessing with new people coming to join the fellowship, and the influx of people meant new arrangements had to be made about the seating for the Holy Communion service. At this point, when people should have been rejoicing and praising God, church officials quarreled bitterly over seating arrangements! Sad, but true, and the minister recalled the words of Paul: '. . . but Satan hindered us'. Some argue against belief in the Evil One; however, the words of C.S. Lewis are pertinent. He wrote: 'The devil's cleverest trick is to make people believe he does not exist!' We rejoice that Jesus promised us the Helper (John 14:16).

Suggested readings: Matthew 13:24-30 and I Thessalonians 2:13-20.

FEBRUARY 23rd

## THERE IS VALUE IN THE OLD PATHS

In our contemporary era, there is a great passion for new things! Many people are interested in new tools, new attitudes, new religions, new philosophies, new methods and standards. In the home, we are all grateful for the new labour-saving gadgets because the better devices, machines, processors and cleaners have made life in the kitchen, utility room and elsewhere so much easier. However, it's very clear that not all new things are necessarily good. Some of the new attitudes and standards leave much to be desired. At one point, Jeremiah the prophet looked at his world and saw the disobedience and the selfishness, and the refusal to listen to God's Word. He boldly proclaimed a direct command of God: 'Stand at the crossroads and look; ask for the ancient paths, ask where the good way is, and walk in it, and you will find rest for your souls' (Jeremiah 6:16 NIV).

In this modern age, many feel that our own country is likewise at a crossroads: there is violence, vandalism, abuse, injustice and unrighteousness in many respects. At times, it seems that cherished old paths have been forsaken and many believe that God's clear message has been spurned. Christians rightly feel they make a strong case in advocating that the ancient paths of obedience and unselfishness are the good paths. The path of those who follow Christ is surely one of selfless service as we 'bear one another's burdens' (Galatians 6:2). Of course, at times Christians can become closed in upon themselves and seemingly unable to consider others. A.J.P. Taylor tells how that in Lancashire there is a church without windows! No windows whatsoever! This picture might represent the attitude of some individuals and churches! However, there are those who, when they stand at a crossroads in life, are determined to choose the way of self-giving service.

The story is told of a time when Albert Schweitzer stood at the crossroads of life: he was a man of many talents and could have made a fortune for himself. However, he chose the ancient path of unselfish service. As a result of that decision, through his medical skills exercised in his hospital at Lambaréné, he brought health and healing to multitudes of African people. Sometimes it can be like that for us: we arrive at a turning point in life and we have to make an important decision. Perhaps there are a variety of choices. In such moments of decision, the profound words uttered by Jeremiah – about probing how the old, well-trodden paths appear in respect of our own situation – can be very helpful, indeed enlightening. For those who follow Christ, the new way He has opened up is, in fact, true to the old path and we also know the guidance of the Spirit to help us make the right choice.

Suggested readings: Jeremiah 6:16 and Galatians 6:2-10.

FEBRUARY 24th

## CHRISTIANS HAVE A GREAT INHERITANCE

When Christina Onassis died on 19th November 1988, the press sought to assess her life. This wealthy woman died at thirty-seven years of age: she was married four times and divorced four times. The newspapers agreed on one thing: she sought lasting happiness but it seemed to elude her. Apart from short periods of contentment, she lived a life dogged by tragedy, disappointments and unhappiness. She was fantastically wealthy, but desperately unhappy. However, there was one lovely ray of sunshine in her life, namely, her baby daughter Athena: this little child brought more joy than all her wealth. On the death of Christina, this child was set to inherit a vast fortune, said to be five billion pounds! The question arose: does a child understand about such an inheritance? Evidently, she wouldn't have the least idea of its magnitude and potential.

Of course, an inheritance is not simply calculated in terms of financial gain. There are numerous passages of scripture that speak about the glorious inheritance of the people of faith. In the Book of Joshua we find an important passage which tells of the division of land between the various tribes of Israel, and it concludes with this wonderful verse: 'But to the tribe of Levi Moses gave no inheritance; the Lord God of Israel is their inheritance' (Joshua 13:33). Similarly, we might recall three other thought-provoking verses on this subject. First, 'The Lord is the portion of my inheritance' (Psalm 16:5), and secondly, 'Blessed be the God . . . who has blessed us in Christ with every spiritual blessing' (Ephesians 3:1). A third verse is rich indeed in the description it spells out: 'By his great mercy we have been born new to a living hope through the resurrection of Jesus Christ from the dead, and to an inheritance which is imperishable, undefiled, and unfading, kept in heaven for you' (1 Peter 1:3-4). Every Christian is truly, as it were, a spiritual millionaire!

Pondering the blessings believers know now, one could list God's free forgiveness, and amazing grace, as well as God's sure help and unfailing presence. There is so much more promised here, and in the life of the world to come, too; blessings beyond description. Like the little child, Athena, we have no idea of the magnitude of our inheritance. Just as no one person could describe what a five billion dollar fortune is, so no Christian (however mature) can fully comprehend the blessings we have 'in Christ'. The poet said, 'The best is yet to be', and that is literally true for those who know the love God has for them, though there may be very difficult times to face along the way. So today, Christians can rejoice in their inheritance, praising God both for blessings received, and blessings yet to come.

Suggested readings: Joshua 13:32-33 and 1 Peter 1:1-9.

FEBRUARY 25th

## SOME PLACES ARE VERY SPECIAL

During his ministry as priest, author and broadcaster, Kenneth Leech has given people of all backgrounds and beliefs much food for thought. One such reflection reads: 'For many people a relationship with a place is of as great importance and value as that with a person'. There are places which are very special. Over many centuries the Jewish people have been attracted to Jerusalem with a deep-seated affiliation to the place. For them it is a very special city, cited in scores of places in the Bible, and often referred to as Zion. The Old Testament reveals the joy people felt as they entered the Holy City: 'I was glad when they said to me "Let us go to the house of the Lord!"'(Psalm 122:1). Their joy at the opportunity to go to worship in Jerusalem was real, palpable and vibrant.

We all have special places, such as a family home, a particular church, a holiday resort, an area of lovely countryside, a hill, river, lake or beach. Bishop Mervyn Stockwood had a great love for the Chanctonbury Ring (the famous circle of trees standing on a hill in southern England), and it was a place of memories for him. He had been there at crucial moments in his ministry and he felt drawn there to meditate and to pray concerning important decisions. A Christian nurse visiting the Holy Land found that the Sea of Galilee had a unique quality about it: she had visited the famous landmarks and sites, but found there were things which really jarred. At Bethlehem, her purse was stolen, and some other places smacked of commercialism. However, the Sea of Galilee stimulated memories of her Saviour's own dealings with needy women and men; for her, Galilee was a very special place for reflection.

In 1988, a report was given about the number of visitors to well-loved places of worship in England: Westminster Abbey attracted three million people each year, St Paul's Cathedral two million, while York Minster and Canterbury Cathedral each had two million visitors. These are four very grand places of worship but, for many ordinary Christians, just a humble place of worship – hallowed by many beautiful memories – is their favourite place to meet with God. Sometimes, at a given spot, people have had a vital experience of God and that leaves an indelible memory.

There is a significant brief record in Luke's gospel: 'And Jesus came out, and went as was his custom, to the Mount of Olives; and the disciples followed him' (Luke 22:39). We note those words 'as was his custom'; even Jesus Christ loved certain times and places for prayer, and returned again and again to them. Today, we can thank God for special places hallowed for us by precious memories.

Suggested readings: Psalm 122:1-9 and Luke 22:39-46.

FEBRUARY 26th

## THE LORD DOES UNDERSTAND

'You just don't understand!' These words rang out so loudly that even the neighbours could hear. This was no ordinary flash-in-the-pan quarrel, but something that had been brewing for many months. It was a quarrel erupting like a volcano, as it were, and the words 'You just don't understand' were spoken with vehemence, an experience many of us have probably faced in some way or another. Too often, perhaps, they are quite true words. The plain fact is that there are times when, with the best will in the world, our nearest friends or relatives do not really understand us, and our human perception of another can prove deficient.

In the Psalter there is a verse on this theme which highlights God's understanding, contrasted with ours: 'Great is our Lord, and abundant in power; his understanding is beyond measure' (Psalm 147:5). The New International Version of the Bible puts it plainly: 'His understanding has no limit'. How wonderful is that assurance; how precious and comforting it is to us in our weakness. There are moments when others cannot fully understand our feelings: the crushed feelings after the death of a loved one, the confused feelings after a great disappointment, the bewildered feelings after major surgery, the distressed feelings when doubts threaten to overwhelm and the frustrated feelings when cherished plans are thwarted. However, we know God truly understands us and upholds us, whatever our feelings.

When Jesus hung upon the cross, He had to endure 'the contradiction of sinners', so one New Testament witness testified. He faced cruelty, injustice, mockery and evil taunts. One part of the narrative states: 'So also the chief priests mocked him to one another with the scribes, saying, "He saved others; he cannot save himself"'. In this taunting, they revealed their lack of perception and comprehension: Jesus was not understood. They failed to understand His ministry and His message. The Bible affirms that the One who was so cruelly misunderstood knows how we feel. The writer of the Epistle to the Hebrews puts it in unforgettable words: 'For we have not a high priest who is unable to sympathize with our weaknesses, but one who in every respect has been tempted as we are yet without sinning. Let us then with confidence draw near to the throne of grace, that we may receive mercy and find grace to help in time of need' (Hebrews 4:15-16).

One of the most painful things to endure is misunderstanding; how easy it is for others to misinterpret our motives and aims! As we begin each new day, it's easy to feel frustrated – even irritated – because so few, if any, understand our present situation and the problems we face. We can take comfort in recalling that the Lord fully understands.

Suggested readings: Psalm 147:1-11 and Mark 15:21-32.

FEBRUARY 27th

## GOD USES UNLIKELY EVENTS

Visitors who go to the Greek island of Santorini learn of the very powerful volcanic eruption which took place many centuries ago. This eruption was so enormous that it totally altered the shape of the island; the devastating shock waves from this massive disturbance were felt many miles away. It was no doubt a hugely destructive and terrifying episode to the civilisation of that era in millennia past. That event can remind us today of the course of life; sometimes a particular event brings a similar shock to a community or nation as a disaster or tragedy is faced. It was rather like that for the early Church when a key leader, Stephen, was killed. Indeed, the shock waves were felt in a variety of ways, and it proved to be a significant turning point in Church history, too.

Luke records how on the day that Stephen was stoned to death for his faithful ministry, a wave of persecution began: 'And on that day a great persecution arose against the church in Jerusalem; and they were all scattered throughout the region of Judea and Samaria, except the apostles' (Acts 8:1). All but just a few were widely dispersed as the Christian fellowship was violently disturbed, and many fled for their safety. At first glance, this looks all bad: it was a testing and frightening time for the early believers. Some may have asked themselves, 'Where is God?'

Now, looking back, we can see how God used this experience: even the terrible experience of being fearfully scattered was woven into God's ultimate purpose. One verse puts it simply: 'Now those who were scattered went about preaching the word' (Acts 8:4). The Christians were rather like seed scattered, with growth occurring wherever it took root! Wherever they went for safety, they spoke the good news of Jesus Christ. Nature relies, in part, on the wind to scatter seed so it can be spread, then to germinate and grow. Here, in the story, as it were, the strong wind of persecution drove the believers into new areas and so the faith was widely spread. One Bible expositor liked to put it this way: 'Here we get the Devil's greatest mistake! The Christians were persecuted and scattered but the gospel spread'.

Stephen's martyrdom may serve as a reminder of the ongoing work of God, through even the darkest of events, to bring hope. Sometimes it looks as if God's purposes are being thwarted and that evil is rampant, seemingly giving us little ground for hope, but even so God can work powerfully for good. In the story of Jesus, the day of crucifixion and shame led, by God's mysterious and mighty power, to the day of resurrection and glory. As one Australian pastor used to say to his people: 'Give God time . . . give God time'.

Suggested readings: Acts 7:54-8:8 and Ephesians 1:7-14.

FEBRUARY 28th

## THAT BALANCE IS ESSENTIAL

It sometimes pays to stop and consider carefully all the things that scripture tells us to avoid. With clarity it tells us to avoid quarrelling, envy, selfishness, slander, dishonesty, idolatry and, indeed, all manner of evil. In one contemporary translation of the Bible, we read this verse: 'The man who fears God will avoid all extremes' (Ecclesiastes 7:18 NIV). It is a provocative, but sobering thought for anyone of any age or background. One older interpreter of the scriptures, put it this way: "If I were allowed to put one extra verse in the Bible it would be "Blessed is the man who is balanced"". That's quite a thought: namely, the 'balanced person' is one who is blessed by God. If one looks carefully, it would appear that this is implied in so many Bible passages, with respect to both our worship and our daily life and work.

We all know that the extremist can do so much harm to people or damage to the environment. Here is an actual illustration: in a quiet close hidden in the depths of the English countryside with about fifteen bungalows around, there lived a devout Christian. He was a sincere, earnest, hardworking person but one with a tendency to go to extremes! One quiet Sunday afternoon, when his neighbours were enjoying peace and relaxation, he fixed a loudspeaker to the side of his bungalow and broadcast a Christian message loud and clear. As he did this, the man sincerely thought he was doing a good Christian service in bold witness, but he lacked balance!

The Church of Jesus Christ needs people with zeal and energy, and leaders with powers of persuasion and encouragement. However, it is vital to remember that Christian history teaches us that religious fanaticism does untold damage to communities, and to fellowships. Ministers occasionally encounter such people from time to time and they can be a real 'thorn in the flesh'. God's Word says, both explicitly and implicitly, that we need a sense of balance and the apostle Paul expresses it in these words: 'Let your moderation be known unto all' (Philippians 4: 5).

One figure who embodied the balanced life was Dr. J. H. Jowett: he held pastorates at Carr's Lane, Birmingham, Fifth Avenue Presbyterian Church, New York, and Westminster Chapel, London. He had no time for extremism: indeed, his life was an example of poise and balance. However, at the same time, he wrote an influential book entitled *The Passion for Souls*; he demonstrated that a person can be earnest, sincere and passionate without being extreme. Such true composure and balance we find in the perfect life of the Saviour: He had a passionate desire to do His Father's will, but He always remained balanced and serene.

Suggested readings: Philippians 4:1-7 and I Timothy 4:6-16

# March

Angel voices ever singing
Round Thy throne of light,
Angel harps, forever ringing,
Rest not day nor night;
Thousands only live to bless Thee
And confess Thee, Lord of might.

Yea, we know that Thou rejoicest
O'er each work of Thine;
Thou didst ears and hands and voices
For Thy praise design;
Craftsman's art and music's measure
For Thy pleasure all combine.

Thou, who art beyond the farthest
Mortal eye can scan,
Can it be that Thou regardest
Songs of sinful man?
Can we know that Thou art near us
And wilt hear us? Yea, we can.

In Thy house, great God, we offer
Of Thine own to Thee;
And for Thine acceptance proffer,
All unworthily,
Hearts and minds and hands and voices
In our choicest psalmody.

Honour, glory, might, and merit,
Thine shall ever be:
Father, Son, and Holy Spirit,
Blessèd Trinity:
Of the best that Thou hast given,
Earth and Heaven render Thee.

Francis Pott (1832-1909)

O Gracious and holy Father,
Give us wisdom to perceive thee,
intelligence to understand thee,
diligence to seek thee,
patience to wait for thee,
eyes to behold thee,
a heart to meditate upon thee,
and a life to proclaim thee;
through the power of the Spirit of Jesus Christ our Lord.

St Benedict (480-543)

MARCH 1st

## THAT GOD HAS A SECRET ARMY OF WORKERS

Even a casual reading of the first few chapters of the First Book of Kings gives an impression of the magnificence of the temple that King Solomon had built at Jerusalem. It must have been a marvellous experience to enter it: the size, beauty and craftsmanship, meant that its glory was awe-inspiring. We read: 'And when the priests came out of the holy place, a cloud filled the house of the Lord, so that the priests could not stand to minister because of the cloud; for the glory of the Lord filled the house of the Lord' (1 Kings 8:10-11). At its consecration, Solomon stood and prayed before the altar of the Lord and so dedicated this wonderful house of prayer for the worship of the God of Israel.

In the account of the building of the temple, we read how the workmen used wood, brass, silver and gold, but there is one small detail which attracts special attention: 'And upon the tops of the pillars was lily-work. Thus the work of the pillars was finished' (1 Kings 7:22). It might be asked how many people saw this particular piece of work and fully appreciated it. This little detail actually speaks volumes! In church circles, when a vote of thanks is given, mention is often made of 'all who worked behind the scenes'. In the Christian Church, there is a vast host of people – God's secret army, one could say – who quietly do valuable work for the Kingdom of God.

A small village church needed a caretaker and the job was duly advertised; though there seemed little hope that anyone would take on this work, yet one woman kindly offered her services. The church fellowship was more than a little surprised as no one had anticipated that the person would offer to do it. Humbly and quietly she gave the reason: 'I will do it for Him'. That she did, and she proved to be hardworking and faithful. So in every Christian fellowship, there are good people who do the humbler – often inconspicuous – tasks 'for Him'. This story of genuine, humble, background service has been repeated countless times in Christian history.

Charles H. Spurgeon stood in his London pulpit and preached to five thousand people at each Sunday service: people came from near and far to hear him expound the glorious gospel of God's grace. But how few knew then the name of the humble minister who, as it were, 'primed Spurgeon's pump', giving him sermon ideas and outlines! Like the craftsmen who did the lily-work on top of the pillars of the ancient temple, there is a secret army of women and men who quietly, but very effectively, do valuable work faithfully 'behind the scenes', so often unnoticed. We may never know their names but surely God does, and we trust God honours all who so quietly serve!

Suggested readings: 1 Kings 1:13-22 and 1 Kings 17:8-16.

MARCH 2nd

## CHRISTIANS SHOULD BOAST OF THE LORD

Have you ever been embarrassed by someone's conversation on a train? A crowded train was speeding through the beautiful Yorkshire countryside, and a man who'd recently returned home from Australia was holding forth, loudly boasting! He had journeyed to Australia as a young man and 'struck it rich'; as passengers learned, he now owned five luxury cars, and had a large, prosperous farm, and so it went on. More than one person in that carriage felt uncomfortable, and even a bit embarrassed for him, as he was making such a fool of himself in front of a captive audience!

Actually, it is surprising how many people – young and old – enjoy boasting. People boast about their house, car, or garden or some other prized possession! Some boast of their accomplishments or their academic achievements, or maybe those of their offspring! Buses, trains, trams and planes are the good stomping grounds of the boastful. It is helpful to turn to Holy Scripture on this subject: 'Thus says the Lord "Do not let the wise boast in their wisdom, do not let the mighty boast in their might, do not let the wealthy boast in their wealth; but let those who boast, boast in this, that they understand and know me, that I am the Lord; I act with steadfast love, justice, and righteousness in the earth; for in these things I delight", says the Lord' (Jeremiah 9:23-24).

It could be argued that, right at the heart of divine grace, there is the reality that those who pursue 'salvation by works' foster only boasting. However, those who delight in the biblical truth of 'salvation by grace through faith' turn from any such boasting. The apostle Paul is quite unequivocal: 'For by grace you have been saved through faith; and this is not your own doing, it is the gift of God – not the result of works, so that no one may boast' (Ephesians 2:8-9). Once we accept the truth that our salvation is because of the abundant and free grace of God, there is no room for boasting. We can surely affirm that eternal life is not merited or earned by any achievements of ours, but is the free gift of God to all who will receive it!

There is, of course, a place for rightful boasting. The psalmist wrote: 'My soul makes its boast in the Lord' (Psalm 34:2). This boasting is about God's goodness, God's provision and God's compassion. In the New Testament, Paul cautioned the Corinthian Christians against rivalry or disparagement of others in the fellowship: 'Let the one who boasts, boast in the Lord' (1 Corinthians 1:31). When our eyes are truly opened to the Lord, we are able to focus wholly on God's glory and not be taken up with ourselves! Thus we have the basis for sound living day by day in relationship with God, serving the Lord with gladness, as we have opportunity, to His glory.

Suggested readings: Psalm 34:1-18 and 1 Corinthians 1:26-3.

MARCH 3rd

## THE TIDE DOES TURN SPIRITUALLY

Papworth Hospital in Cambridgeshire has a reputation for being a place of miracles: it is a place where numerous people with severe heart conditions have received new health. One man who had a heart operation there said afterwards: 'It was like being born again!' Some people arrive at Papworth almost too ill to walk and, after major surgery, they can, quite often, some months later, run, cycle, swim and do other things such as house-work and gardening. The return to renewed health is truly wonderful.

In the psalms there is a verse which was powerfully translated (albeit in the older language of the original New English Bible) in this way: 'When the Lord turned the tide of Zion's fortune, we were like men who had found new health' (Psalm 126:1 NEB). There was a point when the Holy City of Jerusalem suffered a crushing defeat and 'hope burned low': it seemed as if God had forsaken the city and there was distress, confusion and deep sorrow among the people. However, the day came when 'the tide turned' and the city was visibly under the blessing of God. It was like a new era: it could only be described as like recovering from illness to new health.

So in the experience of men and women there are times when the tide ebbs, but there are also times when the tide flows, and we can, indeed, thank God. We know that individuals, couples, families, communities and church fellowships each in their own way experience such changes. When the tide is out it may feel like an illness besetting us. Yet, when the tide turns and flows in its fullness, it is like renewed health. One practical illustration of this truth would be the experience of a young couple who decided (for a whole variety of reasons) to move to a completely new area: this move involved a new house, a new job and a new church. Initially, it was far from a success! Looking back, the wife testified afterwards 'we had two whole years without laughter'. Those few words are very descriptive of a 'low tide' in family life: life without laughter and devoid of shared joy. Yet, when the people of God experienced the turning of the tide, and they came to know anew God's rich blessing, there was a renewal of laughter because of the experience of holy joy.

The next verses of the psalmist put it perfectly 'Then our mouth was filled with laughter and our tongue with shouts of joy; then they said among the nations, "The Lord has done great things for them". The Lord has done great things for us; we are glad' (Psalm 126:2-3). We surely owe thanksgiving to God for those days when we know, in the depths of our being, that better things have arrived; like renewed health and regained strength, such days bring refreshing joy and delightful laughter.

Suggested readings: Psalm 126:1-6 and John 20:26-31.

MARCH 4th

## WE SHOULD ENJOY LIFE

Some of our best-loved hymns remind us that God has freely given us so much, and all these things are a cause for praise. A reading of Psalm 148 (with its recurring phrase 'Praise the Lord') gives us some idea of the things God has given to us on this planet. The people are urged to extol God and join with all creation in giving thanks to God. Elsewhere, the psalmist reminds us to give thanks for hills and valleys, fields and trees, streams and rivers, sun and moon, flowers and birds, indeed the whole natural world in the created order. Along the Embankment by the Great Ouse at Bedford, there are a number of seats provided so that people can sit and enjoy the beautiful riverside. Some of the seats have a special dedication plate to a loved one, and there is one dedicated to a lady 'who enjoyed all God's gifts like rivers, trees and flowers'. One imagines that she spent many happy times near the river admiring the lovely gardens and the peaceful scenery, thus thoroughly enjoying life!

There is a verse in the New Testament which speaks of 'God who richly provides us with everything for our enjoyment' (1 Timothy 6:17). There are those who refer to the New Testament as 'The Book of Joy', meaning that joy not just in the things of the Spirit, but also in the world God has given. Today, many people are becoming more aware of the rich beauty of this world and actively campaign against spoiling, exploiting or polluting it. This marvellous planet Earth is given to us all by God to share and to enjoy. Life's greatest things, in the whole world about us, are free for us to delight in day by day, even as we long for others to know that joy in abundant living, too!

Sometimes, men and women can be pessimistic and look out on things with unseeing eyes, not noticing the beauty that is all around them in the world and in people's lives. In Mark's gospel we find a verse where Jesus Christ rebuked the disciples: 'Do you not yet perceive and understand? Are your hearts hardened? Having eyes do you not see, and having ears do you not hear? And do you not remember?' (Mark 8:17-18). How unobservant we can be! It is surely fitting and right always to remember the good things we can enjoy, giving praise to God. So we can be grateful for family, friends and companions, and those in shared fellowship, as well as the beautiful natural world about us. God has given us all these lovely things for our enjoyment, and that includes preserving the Earth for future generations. Thanksgiving to God is surely always timely!

Suggested readings: Psalm 148:1-14 and 1 Timothy 6:17-21.

MARCH 5th

## GOD CAN USE LIFE'S INTERRUPTIONS

How often one of life's interruptions can prove to be a blessing in disguise! Interruptions can take so many different forms: a phone call, a surprise visitor, an unexpected letter, a change of plan, a stay in hospital, an accident or injury, even a radical change in the weather. At the time, these interruptions can spoil the smooth running of one's life so they can be very frustrating, and even annoying! However, sometimes, we can look back and discern a blessing which was far from evident at the actual time of the interruption. Occasionally, we perceive, looking back later, that the gracious 'divine hand' has been mysteriously, but marvellously, at work in the midst of our lives.

When F.W. Boreham was a lad of fifteen, he had two great loves: hiking and sport. He was fortunate to get a job on the railway where he could be out in God's fresh air. All was set fair for a life he loved, and he was both healthy and happy. Then, one unforgettable day, through absentmindedness, he was involved in a shocking accident, and his right foot was severed. For five long and weary months he stayed in hospital, and his whole future had a big question mark hanging over it; his life had been seriously interrupted. When his strength began to return, he made a decision to use his time profitably by studying shorthand: he became very proficient and, when he eventually left hospital, attended services on Sunday to put his new skills to good use! He made exact records of the sermons he heard preached. During this time, he felt the call to the Christian ministry and was accepted for training at Spurgeon's College, London.

Life had taken an unexpected turn, and it proved to be beneficial! Apart from preaching and lecturing, Boreham came to use his skills in the cause of the Kingdom of God, writing over fifty books! They were so well written that they won the attention of many in various denominations in places all round the world. Yet, it all began with an unforeseen event which led to that long spell in hospital, and the drastic change which came about by it.

In the Book of Isaiah we read these lovely words 'I will give you the treasures of darkness' (Isaiah 45:3). It is a puzzling word, and yet many have discovered that experience for themselves. In the Psalms, there is another verse akin to this sense of God's leading, even in unforeseen ways: 'It is the Lord who directs a person's steps' (Psalm 37:23). C.H. Spurgeon, the famous preacher used to deliberately 'misquote' the old translation of this verse: 'The stops of a good man are ordered by the Lord'. Interruptions can bring transformation for good, and as such are used by God.

Suggested readings: Psalm 37:11-23 and Romans 15:4-13.

MARCH 6th

## MEMORY NEEDS TRAINING

In a rather strange way, memory is like a magnet and it attracts certain things to it, pleasant or otherwise. Like the draw of a magnet, the memory of some people tends to attract the recollection of all the unpleasant and bad things which have happened. If you converse with such people, they give a long catalogue of their disappointments, illnesses and grievances! Other people, with sunny personalities, are just the opposite. They cheerfully recall all the good things of life and seem to put to one side the more unpleasant happenings. Indeed, one's memory can be very selective and, as a result, it sometimes takes concerted effort to train it to be more impartial and balanced!

A.L. Rouse (the historian and writer) tells how he was reared in a home where there were no books at all. However, his auntie had a history book and, whenever he visited her, he enjoyed reading it. Over the ensuing years, he developed an appreciation for many things such as music, poetry, and politics; however, his love for Tudor history remained dominant and he spent many hours focusing on it. One might say that he endeavoured to train his memory to recall various details of history.

For Christians, amid the different interests we have, there is a dominant call to read and study God's Word in the Holy Scriptures. Indeed, the study of scripture is a fundamental means for training our minds and hearts. In such study, we discover that again and again, the Bible challenges men and women to remember God's love and mercy. The psalmist puts it beautifully: 'They shall abundantly utter the memory of thy great goodness and sing of thy righteousness' (Psalm 145:7 AV). When we come to think about the life of faith, we soon realise that God's people always have something to celebrate: God's provision, guidance, and deliverance. However, at the root of our faith is the confession of God's faithfulness and, of course, there is the blessed assurance which comes through God's gift to us all in sending Jesus Christ to be the Saviour of the world. One version fittingly translates the above verse as follows: 'They will celebrate your abundant goodness' (Psalm 145:7 NIV).

In the regular life of the Church year there are special celebrations: we think of Christmas, Easter, Whitsun, and Harvest Thanksgiving. Yet, in reality, every Sunday is a celebration. Dr. R.W. Dale (one time minister of Carr's Lane Church, Birmingham) used to include an Easter hymn in every Sunday's worship! There is a challenging verse in Deuteronomy which we might ponder: 'And you shall remember all the way which the Lord your God led you' (Deuteronomy 8:2). We might note that it says: 'all the way'! How important it is, before the Lord, ever to ponder 'the memory of thy great goodness'. Setting our mind on scripture, we can be sure that the Lord will keep our memories focused on God's goodness all the way.

Suggested readings: Deuteronomy 3:1-14 and Psalm 145:1-7.

MARCH 7th

## BURDENS CAN BE GIVEN TO GOD

In July 1988, the U.S. warship USS VINCENNES came under fire from gunboats in the Persian Gulf. Just at this distressing time, the radar system showed an aircraft approaching, and it looked like an air attack was imminent. The captain of the ship, thinking it was a fighter plane, ordered missiles to be fired and the plane was blasted out of the sky. The plane was, in fact, a civilian Iranian Airbus and there was a terrible loss of life; two hundred and ninety people were killed including sixty-six children. It was a tragic mistake and Captain Will Rogers who gave the order to fire has spoken of his deep distress and guilt. As he put it: 'I alone am fully responsible. This is a burden I shall carry for the rest of my life'. One thing is certain, millions of people all over the world felt deep grief for the loss of life, but also much sympathy for the captain, who must forever live with his mistake. The tragic error of judgement led to a crushing and terrible burden.

We all know that on life's pilgrimage there are burdens to be carried. Some of them come by choice, others we just have to bear: the burden of responsibility in office, the burden of leadership and decision-making, the burden of our mistakes or those of others, and even the unrelieved burden of sin and guilt. This latter is a particularly hard one to bear; it is much more widespread than perhaps most people imagine. So many can echo David's prayer, 'For I know my transgressions, and my sin is ever before me. Against thee, thee only, have I sinned and done that which is evil in thy sight' (Psalm 51:3-4 AV). There are other forms of guilt, too, beyond simply personal culpability; for example, persons involved in a serious road accident (which was not their fault) where someone was killed or seriously injured. There can be awful feelings of guilt. There are scores of human situations where guilt is a terrible reality and is felt as a very heavy burden.

The question therefore arises: 'What can be done?' Such a guilt-stricken person can be realistic and say that certain situations cannot be unscrambled; the person may be self-condemning, and in subtle ways resort to self-punishment or the person may humbly turn to God, seeking forgiveness and peace. With God, forgiveness is indeed a reality and it can bring a deep healing within. It is said there are three kinds of burdens: those we carry alone, those we share with others, and those we cast upon God. A verse in the First Epistle of Peter puts it succinctly: 'Cast all your anxiety upon him, for he cares for you' (1 Peter 5:7). Multitudes of people have discovered in their own experience, that God is willing and able to forgive. For Christians, the place called Calvary is experienced by so many as a place to find such glad release from the burden of guilt and to discover healing deep within!

Suggested readings: Galatians 6:1-10 and 1 Peter 5:6-11.

MARCH 8th

## GOD KEEPS HIS PROMISES

Lots of motorists put small stickers on or in their cars, and it is quite a modern craze. Frankly, many are very humorous, others are quite vulgar, and some just plainly ridiculous! A number of Christians have taken the opportunity to use this modern trend for Christian purposes, so we get vehicles bearing wise sayings or biblical texts. One such car had a neat little sign simply declaring the faith: 'GOD KEEPS HIS PROMISES'. It was printed with a rainbow in the background; just four words but what a world of inspiration and comfort they contain for those who believe!

We live in a world of broken promises: business promises, marriage promises, political promises and everyday life promises are broken. It is part of life and something we all have to face when appointments are not honoured, a taxi arrives later than we booked, a repair is not done on the day promised, or a special home delivery comes days later than we expected. Yet, we can thank the Lord with confidence in His faithfulness, for God always keeps His promises forever.

In the Old Testament, we have the deeply moving story of the dedication of the temple at Jerusalem. In that story, recorded for posterity, is the beautiful prayer offered by Solomon and the blessing after the prayer: 'Blessed be the Lord who has given rest to his people Israel according to all that he promised; not one word has failed of all his good promise, which he spoke through his servant Moses. The Lord our God be with us, as he was with our ancestors; may he not leave us or abandon us' (1 Kings 8:56-57). The central part of that passage commands our attention: 'Not one word has failed of all his good promise'. What a marvellous testimony to the Lord.

In the Authorised Version of the Bible, we read these lovely words: 'Hereby are given unto us exceeding great and precious promises' (2 Peter 1:4). As so many Christians can testify, that is gloriously true! We can recall two other promises: 'God is our refuge and strength, a very present help in trouble' (Psalm 46:1), and 'My grace is sufficient for you, for my power is made perfect in weakness' (2 Corinthians 12:9). It is most interesting to note how the New English Bible translates the apostle Peter's testimony about God's promises 'He has given us his promises, great beyond all price'. We have to ask ourselves: where is the person who could possibly calculate the value of one of God's gracious promises? Of course, they are quite beyond human measurement! One thing we do know is that they are all very precious: they have helped, inspired, enriched and comforted generations of believers. A wise believer takes time to ponder these promises and let them truly sink in so as to inform and shape his or her life; on God's promises every person's life can be built with confidence and hope placed firmly in the Lord.

Suggested readings: 1 Kings 8:54-61 and 2 Peter 1:1-8.

MARCH 9th

## GOD HEALS OUR BACKSLIDING

Sleeplessness is a sore trial! Every night of the year, for a whole variety of reasons, some people cannot rest or sleep. Besides the medical reasons there are of course many others, one being worry and emotional upset, such as through facing infidelity; the pain of a partner's betrayal and unfaithfulness is one of the worst inner pains to handle as it strikes at the heart. Most ministers and counsellors have spent time helping and comforting people who have endured this terrible experience.

A young couple were going through a difficult patch in their marriage. The husband was restless and sleepless; outwardly, there seemed no obvious reason for his restlessness, but he knew: he was being unfaithful. He carefully covered the tracks of his infidelity but the whole matter weighed on his mind. He thought he would go insane. He decided – slowly and painfully – that his wife must be told and confession made. On the unforgettable evening that she was told, her response was swift and moving: 'Your body belongs to me'. In those five words, wittingly or unwittingly, she illustrated a key aspect of the Christian concept of marriage. A true marriage literally involves the giving of oneself wholly in covenantal trust to another.

Jeremiah chapter 3 is not the easiest one for a daily reading! It speaks of the unfaithfulness of God's people in terms of infidelity, as spiritual adultery: 'Surely, as a faithless wife leaves her husband, so have you been faithless to me, O House of Israel, says the Lord' (Jeremiah 3:20). God had every reason to be aggrieved because the people had returned unfaithfulness for His faithfulness; yet, in this chapter, there is revealed the mercy of God as well as His wonderful tenderness: 'Unfaithful people, come back; you belong to me' (Jeremiah 3:14 GNB). We can see, in essence, that very same claim of 'ownership', in those marvellous words: 'You belong to me'.

It is a joy to record that the young couple experienced a healed relationship; it took much time and patience, but love won through. In fact, that relationship became enriched by a deeper and more understanding love. There are lots of people who have both grieved the Lord and failed Him, but have come back. Their own experience of divine mercy and love has enabled them to be wise counsellors to others: it is true that a particular experience can be painful, even traumatic, but it can teach life's deepest lessons. So we listen again to God speaking through His prophet: 'Return, thou backsliding Israel, saith the Lord, and I will not cause my anger to fall upon you: for I am merciful, saith the Lord, and I will not keep anger for ever'. We have cause for vibrant, unbounded thanksgiving, because our God is merciful and gladly welcomes back all those who will return, offering to all who are open to it a new beginning.

Suggested readings: Jeremiah 3:6-18 and John 21:14-19.

MARCH 10th

## CHRISTIANS MUST GET THINGS IN PERSPECTIVE

George was very proud of his new car! As he looked at it standing outside his home, he reflected that all the overtime hours at work that he had done in recent months had paid off handsomely. It was with much pleasure and pride that he drove round his neighbourhood hoping that his friends would spot him. He had been driving the car three weeks when the accident happened: a car came straight out of a side road and smashed the front wing of his new car. George was livid! In the days that followed, he droned on about his bad luck. Friends began to avoid him; they grew bored with hearing his complaints. Then one evening, a good friend gently took him by the shoulder: 'Listen George! Listen to me and get this thing in perspective. You haven't got a bad injury, or lost a limb, or been killed. You've just got damage to your car'. George was shocked, but he did listen and realised that he had lost his sense of perspective. He had made a minor road accident sound like a disaster and in doing that had, so to speak, made 'a mountain out of a molehill'!

Jesus Christ challenged the scribes and Pharisees of His day: He could see so clearly that they sometimes got things out of perspective. He challenged them with these words: 'For you tithe mint and dill and cummin, and have neglected the weightier matters of the law, justice and mercy and faith; these you ought to have done without neglecting the others' (Matthew 23:23). Then in a withering comment (a saying which is quoted in a wide variety of circumstances in modern life), Jesus said: 'You blind guides, straining out a gnat and swallowing a camel . . .' (Matthew 23:24). How important it is to get things in perspective in spiritual matters, too. As Christians, we need both balance and perspective in our faith and practice day by day.

We are reminded by our own experience that it is easy to get things out of perspective. One might recall the man who quipped: 'I can cope with a major operation but not with toothache!' There are people who seem to cope quite well when there is a real crisis, but go to pieces when there is a minor misfortune. An elderly Christian, who had served God's Church for over fifty years, had a simple tactic when dealing with a whining believer, he would look at them and say: 'Remember someone in hospital will be having their leg amputated today!' The shock of this stark rebuke brought a number of people to their senses. It certainly points out the need for keeping things in a right perspective before the Lord in all His glory and grace.

Suggested reading: Psalm 37:1-11 and Matthew 23:23-28.

MARCH 11th

## THERE IS A DIVINE LADDER

One of the saddest things in life is to see hatred between two brothers. In Genesis, we read how Esau hated Jacob, and their mother strongly advised Jacob to make his escape, until the situation improved. So Jacob came to Haran and his heart was really troubled. Three things troubled him: (1) he had aroused his brother's strong anger, (2) he was alone in a desert place, and (3) he was away from his family circle. However, he tried to find rest and that night he had a remarkable dream: 'And he dreamed that there was a ladder set up on the earth, and the top of it reached to heaven; and behold, the angels of God were ascending and descending on it; And behold, the Lord stood above it and said, I am the Lord, the God of Abraham your father and the God of Isaac' (Genesis 28:12-13).

Yet that was not all! God gave Jacob a marvellous promise which included these encouraging words: 'Behold I am with you and will keep you wherever you go, and will bring you back to this land' (Genesis 28:15). Then Jacob woke up! There are many different dreams: some we forget very quickly, others remain with us for a few days, and still others we can never forget. Jacob could never forget the dream about the ladder which stretched from earth to heaven. We can think of its profound significance as a pointer to our faith in God, even today: (1) there is a link between earth and heaven, (2) God has spiritual agents who do His bidding, whether seen as angels or other special messengers, (3) there is divine mercy toward the imperfect person, and (4) God comes at unexpected times and places.

According to the fourth gospel, Jesus Christ gave some wonderful truths about Himself in the 'I am' sayings. He said 'I am the door', 'I am the bread of life', 'I am the good shepherd' and so on. In fact, Jesus could have said 'I am the ladder' because the ladder seen in Jacob's dream is, in a real sense, perfectly fulfilled in the ministry of Jesus. He is that vital link between earth and heaven and, from His divine life, mercy and grace flow in abundance. Alluding to that experience of Jacob, Jesus said to Nathaniel (but with an actual phrasing clearly directing the reference beyond simply Nathaniel alone, to include all who will accept the Word): 'Truly, truly, I say to you, you will see heaven opened, and the angels of God ascending and descending upon the Son of Man' (John 1:51). Surely this is a reminder to us all that, in Jesus, we see the One who was in Himself, as it were, that divine ladder, the gracious link between earth and heaven. In Him is true hope and complete forgiveness to heal and to renew us. Thus, with true assurance, the hymn writer puts it plainly: 'So seems my Saviour's cross to me, a ladder up to heaven'.

Suggested readings: Genesis 28:10-22 and John 1:47-51.

MARCH 12th

## GOD USES ONE PERSON

The Bible contains the thrilling story of Joshua, who took over the leadership of God's people after the death of Moses. He led them over Jordan into the Promised Land and, according to scripture, he had a rich variety of experiences which helped him understand more about God's ways and purpose. In Joshua chapter 23, we have a delightful picture of Joshua calling together the leaders and the people to give them his last words of counsel. Here was a man deeply experienced in the ups and downs of life, and his central message was 'Cleave to the Lord your God as you have done to this day' (Joshua 23:8). He also told them: 'One man of you shall chase a thousand' (Joshua 23:10 AV). He was underlining, of course, the importance of just one person in the Lord's sight: God uses individual men and women in His plans for His people.

We all know the significance of just the one in ordinary living: a person can win a cricket match by scoring two hundred runs; a footballer at the Cup Final at Wembley Stadium can score goals and win the match for his team. However, this truth has much deeper dimensions, too: one devout believer can achieve so much for God and His Kingdom. We think of Abraham, Moses, Deborah, Elijah, Mary, Peter, Paul, and in later times, Martin Luther, John Wesley, Mary Slessor, Amy Carmichael to name but a few! Each made a very powerful and significant contribution by his or her own individual efforts (though, actually, there were no doubt always others in the background). However, they would all hasten to say that they were called of God to undertake what they accomplished. We might say, that each one of these was, individually and uniquely, used by the Holy Spirit of God in the service of the Kingdom. God can use individuals who are open to Him, as well as whole communities of faith.

At the age of fourteen, Dr. Stanley Browne gave his life to Jesus Christ. What a thrilling story flows from that decisive step! As a surgeon he performed thousands of operations, as a missionary he taught many people, as a writer he instructed the medical world (especially on the subject of leprosy), and as a dedicated Christian he was a channel of blessing to a multitude of people. If ever we wanted an illustration of Joshua's words, 'One man of you shall chase a thousand', it is seen in the life and witness of this outstanding physician; he exercised an amazing gifting by God. God delights to use individuals in His work, and that includes each of us, too!

Suggested readings: Joshua 23:1-11 and Psalm 143:5-8.

MARCH 13th

## A SENSE OF WONDER IS ESSENTIAL

All down the centuries, the Book of Psalms has been a vital source of comfort and inspiration to women and men, especially those who have been treading, as it were, the uphill path. It has an inexhaustible supply of wisdom and spiritual insight such that, whatever our mood or our circumstance, there seems to be a helpful passage in the Psalms to sustain and encourage us. We do well to remember the rich notes of thanksgiving found in this truly remarkable section of the scriptures. So many verses express praise, and one verse in particular seems to sum up all these tones: 'Great is the Lord, and greatly to be praised, and his greatness is unsearchable' (Psalm 145:3).

One of the best things about the Book of Psalms is its delight in the world of nature: 'Thou visitest the earth and waterest it, thou greatly enrichest it; the river of God is full of water; thou providest the grain . . .' (Psalm 65:9). God has enriched this lovely planet: there are scores of verses which underline the goodness of God expressed in sea and sky, mountains and hills, trees and flowers, fields and valleys, vineyards and cornfields, rivers and streams. Of course, the whole world of living things points to our great Creator. So the psalmist cries out in praise 'The Lord has done great things for us, and we are filled with joy' (Psalm 126:3 NIV). What a wonderful thing it is to have our eyes wide open and to revel in the beauty and splendour of nature on this fair planet we call Earth.

In his later years, Hugh Maycock (Principal of Pusey House, Oxford, 1952-70), took a continuous delight in natural beauty. He would frequently get up early and drive to Herne Bay in Kent, to watch the sunrise. He could often be heard saying: 'It's amazing . . . it's amazing!' Lots of people have a deep sense of wonder; their minds and hearts are always ready to appreciate the marvels of the natural world. However, it is also true, that some people don't seem to have any sense of wonder; they never seem to look around or up to the heavens. To miss out in this way, is loss indeed, and it shows! Without the sense of awe, ingratitude can prevail.

The first chapter of Genesis gives us the ancient creation story and the whole of the chapter is punctuated with the refrain ' . . . and God saw that it was good'. Then, right at the end of that marvellous chapter, we read: 'And God saw everything that he had made and behold it was very good' (Genesis 1:31) So the psalmist exclaims: 'From the rising of the sun to its setting the name of the Lord is to be praised' (Psalm 113:3). Indeed, wonder is a crucial part of true spirituality.

Suggested readings: Psalm 65:1-13 and Luke 12:22-31.

MARCH 14th

## THE HUMAN HEART IS VERY COMPLEX

A Christian woman was deeply respected by her friends for the magnificent way she nursed her husband during his terminal illness. Indeed, she well deserved to be a priority in the allocation of bravery awards! In a thousand and one ways, she sought to care for her husband in the time of his weakness and illness. One day, when she was talking to a friend she made a telling comment: 'I've been three people: the person seen by outsiders, the person seen by my husband and the person seen by myself in the wakeful hours of the early morning'. There are, of course, lots of people who can identify with her frank admission!

One university don, speaking about the heart, once made an intriguing remark: 'My heart is like a zoo!' That is a perceptive description of the human condition, for one could argue that, in the human heart, there is – in a sense – a tiger, an ostrich, a fox, a monkey, a snake, a gazelle and much more! How often we realise (sometimes with a great shock) that we are, as it were, many things; we are complex personalities and the very language we use underlines the fact that we have many selves. For example, we speak about our inner self, our better self, our higher self; also, in honest self-appraisal before God, we all know from painful experience that there is a lower self.

In Jesus' parable of the prodigal son, we read how a man took his inheritance, went to a far country, squandered his money and so found himself there in serious difficulties. Then we read these thought-provoking words: 'But when he came to himself he said, 'How many of my father's hired servants have bread enough and to spare, but I perish here with hunger! I will arise and go to my father' (Luke 15:17-18). In the story, the son decided he would then confess: 'Father, I have sinned against heaven and before you. I am no longer worthy to be called your son' (v18). The turning point was when he came to himself. The prodigal son found his wiser self, his better self, his higher self. How often in life, men and women have second thoughts and, in a moment of truth, they come to their senses, and see a much wiser course of action. Recognising this dimension in ourselves is very important.

Sadly, in this modern age, a vast number of marriages end in divorce, causing distress to the families and friends, especially any children of the marriage. Regrettably, so often couples get caught up 'in the machinery' of divorce when it might have been avoided. In fact, it is possible that many relationships could be saved if the 'dove' took over from the 'tiger' in us! The tiger tears things apart, but the dove is the symbol of peace: the latter is the way to reconciliation. The Lord longs for people to be in true communion with each other, in openness above all, to God.

Suggested readings: Psalm 23:1-6 and Luke 15:17-24.

MARCH 15th

## OUR GREAT GOD GIVES INNER RESOURCES

Mid-March brings the onset of spring, and thoughts turn to new growth with the blossom and leaves sprouting forth. One of the most beautiful sights in the English countryside is an oak tree in full leaf! It is fascinating to look at a magnificent oak and realise that it has weathered many storms and stood for several centuries. The English oak has played a very important role in architecture: cathedrals, churches, state buildings, country houses, and many other residences have relied on its strength and durability. Also, the Navy has had close links with the oak and, at one stage in British history, the oak tree played a vital role in the building of fine, sturdy ships.

How interesting to recall that the oak is a secret battlefield, in a sense, as it is the scene of much conflict. The massive oak has to withstand onslaughts from fungi, insects, birds, and animals. Also, there is the constant battle against heat, damp, frost, high winds and other extreme weather conditions. There are seasons when the oak tree has a very hard time and, long before the autumn months, it loses most of its leaves. Yet, this tree battles on, putting up a mighty fight and, summoning deep resources, can even produce a second flush of leaves! It can survive difficulties, and its endurance through the ages reflects the fact that it is resilient and resourceful.

Like the oak tree, many people have to weather times of extreme difficulty; they, like Job in the Old Testament, have a whole series of problems. The wonderful thing is that many of these people find deep resources, and so come to a wholly new beginning; this is profoundly true of people with sincere faith in God. The psalmist speaks for many such believers: 'I was pushed hard, so that I was falling, but the Lord helped me' (Psalm 118:13). How important is that word 'but' in that affirmation of faith. It indicates God's sure help, and loving support, in coming to our aid.

In the Christian life, there are numerous faithful people who have soul-searing experiences and touch the depths of despair, but they win through by divine grace. Relying on God's help and the deep inner resources within our personality, we may both survive and start anew. There is an important word of both encouragement and exhortation in this prayer to the Lord: '. . . he may grant that you may be strengthened in your inner being with power through his Spirit, and that Christ may dwell in your hearts through faith' (Ephesians 3:16-17). The apostle Paul's courage was unrelenting: 'So we do not lose heart. Though our outward nature is wasting away, our inner nature is being renewed every day' (2 Corinthians 4:16). That kind of faith and courage can be ours, if we are open to God to keep on leading, guarding and guiding us through all the ups and downs of life.

Suggested readings: Psalm 118:5-14 and 2 Corinthians 4:13-18.

MARCH 16th

## GOODNESS IS A WISE INVESTMENT

One of the dominant questions in our modern society is, 'How can I make a good profit?' If you travel on an early morning train into London loaded with commuters you will quickly notice how many of them are avidly reading *The Financial Times*! Lots of ordinary people who make no claim to 'stockbroker skills' are most interested in good investments, too. Of course, there is nothing wrong with a wise, ethical and sound investment; it can be a prudent provision for our family or, indeed, various charitable causes or our church, at the right time.

There are other investments too: we can invest time, skills, talent or we can invest our life. On numerous occasions, Dr. Billy Graham testified that the Book of Proverbs was always of importance to him in his spiritual life. We recall one of its wise sayings: 'Good yields a lasting profit' (Proverbs 11:18 Moffatt). A good life is surely profitable!! One of the most admirable characters in the New Testament is Barnabas. So often, he seems to be expressing generosity of one kind or another: kind friendship, generous giving, genuine forgiveness and self-denying service for the Kingdom of God. We are reminded of the beautiful words of Jesus: 'The good man out of his good treasure brings forth good' (Matthew 12:35). So Barnabas enriched the lives of people by his sheer generosity of spirit and the rich goodness of his heart. Actually, overall, the Bible is very sparing in the number of people it calls good; but it's worth pondering what Luke eloquently says in his record commending Barnabas: 'For he was a good man, full of the Holy Spirit and of faith' (Acts 11:24).

The name of Percy Wilson is lovingly remembered by Christians in the Suffolk area. He was a truly remarkable character; Percy served as church secretary of a village chapel for over fifty years. He was witty, wise, loving and devout; and, to those who knew him, just plain good. Like his Lord, who 'went about doing good', so Percy was a person, who with deep devotion, served Jesus Christ with dedication and faithfulness. In life, he received no medals or special honours. He was simply a humble and sincere Christian to the end. Yet, in a deeper sense he was honoured: people in that area (believers and unbelievers alike) readily recognised that he was a man of sterling character. He was a living demonstration of a life invested in goodness. In that lovely sense, he undoubtedly represented in himself, as it were, that whole host of faithful men and women who will surely, at the last, hear the gracious words of the Master, 'Well done, good and faithful servant' (Matthew 25:23).

Suggested readings: Matthew 12:33-37 and Acts 11:19-26.

MARCH 17th

## JESUS CHRIST OUTLIVES HIS CRITICS

How frustrating it is to go into the beautiful English countryside and wend your way to an old parish church and find its door firmly locked! However, regrettably, this is a sign of the times. There has been a great increase in vandalism against churches: numerous country churches have been desecrated, and have even been robbed of their ancient treasures. Thieves have scandalously stolen silver candlesticks, precious communion plates, and money. They have even taken crosses off the altar! To the average citizen this behaviour is quite shocking and thoroughly reprehensible. One act of vandalism which shocked the town of Ipswich, some years ago, concerned the Church of St. Lawrence: a vandal painted on its door 'JESUS WAS A LIAR'. A photograph of the vandalized door was published in the local newspaper and Christians felt a stabbing pain, for it was a terrible deed. Thinking of this act of vandalism now serves as a reminder that people have put the Blessed Master into various categories: Jesus was deluded, or He was a deceiver or even a liar, or indeed, He was, as He Himself claimed – and as countless souls in Christian history have professed – One imparting the truth.

In various places, John's gospel highlights how people argued about Jesus Christ, and one small verse sums it up concisely: 'So there was a division among the people over him' (John 7:43). It is evident that people have always tried to categorise Him. Yet, when we listen to the words of Jesus in John's gospel, we find a different message: 'I am the way, and the truth, and the life; no one comes to the Father but by me' (John 14:6). That plain statement is either true or false. We rejoice that in every age of the Christian era, faithful people from all nations upon earth have simply believed that Jesus is 'the Truth', and so have solidly committed their lives to His teaching.

The blatant statement, 'Jesus was a liar', shocked people as these words painted on the door of an ancient church seemed so blasphemous. Believers and unbelievers alike, in Ipswich, were upset. Of course, it could be suggested that many people who were so shocked to see the press photograph might have been conveying the same thing by their lifestyle! The words of John's first epistle are stark and challenging: 'Those who do not believe in God have made him a liar, by not believing in the testimony that God has given concerning his Son' (1 John 5:10). What challenging words; we do indeed, by our daily lives, make a very plain statement as to our view of truth, and our estimate of Christ in His place as the Saviour of all!

Suggested readings: John 7:40-52 and 1 John 5:6-12.

MARCH 18th

## RIGHT CALCULATIONS ARE ESSENTIAL

Life can indeed be stranger than fiction! A man purchased a brand new car: he arrived home with his 'pride and joy', but then received a nasty shock, as the garage was too small for it! To be exact, he could actually just get the car into the garage, but then he couldn't open the door to get out! We hear a story like that and we are, perhaps, tempted to mutter under our breath: 'How foolish'! A simple measuring of the car and the garage would have saved him a lot of trouble. In life, men and women do not always measure up a situation, and so get into difficulties! In the teaching of Jesus Christ, there is clear advice about making right calculations.

In Luke's gospel we find these words of Jesus: 'For which of you, desiring to build a tower does not first sit down and count the cost, whether he has enough to complete it?' (Luke 14:28). In East Anglia, there is a church where the bells are kept in a cage on the ground! The story is told that there were insufficient church funds to complete the tower and so, the bells were sited on the ground. These caged bells are now a tourist attraction, and they remind people that it is important to count the cost before beginning a project. We do well to listen to the Master's comment about the necessity to calculate the cost of tower-building: 'Otherwise, when he has laid a foundation, and is not able to finish, all who see it begin to ridicule him, saying, "This fellow began to build, and was not able to finish"' (Luke 14: 29-30).

It is true that numerous people do not weigh up the situation by doing the necessary calculations or thinking, as Jesus said, to 'count the cost'. During various Billy Graham missions in this country thousands of people made a sincere commitment to Jesus Christ. This gave much joy and encouragement to Christian leaders and workers. However, it is also evident that many who made a response did not 'go on with Christ'; perhaps they had not counted the cost of discipleship. We find a very revealing verse in John's gospel on this subject: 'From that time many of his disciples went back, and walked no more with him' (John 6:66 AV). John says 'from that time', namely, the time when Jesus' teaching seemed too demanding, some found His teaching too difficult to accept, and so they left Him.

There are many decisions to be made in life. Some are related to work, business, family, relationships, or the important decision of committing ourselves to follow Jesus Christ. Whatever our situation, it's always right to consider before the Lord these issues: have the right calculations been made and has the cost been truly counted? Even if we are hesitant and unsure, the heavenly Father will unfailingly help us. As the words of Scripture remind us: there is always 'grace to help in time of need' (Hebrews 4:16).

Suggested readings: Luke 14:25-33 and Hebrews 4:14-16.

MARCH 19th

## THE LORD IS THE DIVINE VISITOR

The New Testament gives ample evidence that Jesus of Nazareth wrought numerous wonderful miracles. One extraordinary miracle which has attracted much attention – though short on detail – is found in Luke chapter 7: Jesus was near the city gate when He met a group of mourners. There was palpable, deep sadness because the only son of a widow had died; a young life cut off in its prime. The record states that Jesus looked upon the widow with compassion, and Luke tells how He miraculously restored the young man to life. It was a marvellous moment and in the sequel we read this account: 'Fear seized them all; and they glorified God saying, "A great prophet has arisen among us!" and "God has visited his people"' (Luke 7:16).

This particular miracle poses many difficult questions, especially for those who have lost a child in tragic circumstances. Yet, while acknowledging these questions, we may also profitably dwell on the great affirmation 'God has visited his people'. For untold numbers, God seems remote, as though a million miles away, but the uncompromising affirmation, in both the Old and New Testaments, is that God does come near to His people. The great Christian festivals of Christmas, Easter and Whitsun, all give this united testimony that God has 'drawn near' to us as those who inhabit this planet Earth. At the season of Harvest, also, there is a reminder that God reaches out to us in other ways, too. Speaking of God's care, the psalmist wrote: 'Thou visitest the earth and waterest it' (Psalm 65:9 AV).

When the astronaut James Irwin came to Britain to address large audiences about his experience on the moon, people were thrilled. It was remarkable to see a man who had done the seemingly impossible thing: he had, indeed, walked on the surface of the moon! At one point, he reminded his audiences that the great thing is, not that men have walked on the moon, but that God's Son once walked on planet Earth; he stressed that we have had a divine visitor. This simple truth (so vividly and graphically explained) made lots of people think again: 'God has visited his people'.

It is inspiring to note that God has 'visited' in many different ways: to Moses at the 'burning bush', to Jeremiah in the potter's house, as well as to Miriam and Hannah, and uniquely to Mary, who bore the Saviour of the world. God visited our world supremely in the person and work of Jesus Christ, and so Paul wrote these awesome words: 'God was in Christ reconciling the world to himself' (2 Corinthians 5:19). Bible scholars think of the total ministry of Jesus Christ in this affirmation: He came, He still comes, and He will come. Even this day, whatever we face and however we feel, God can in His own mysterious way visit us, drawing especially near to offer comfort, encouragement and blessing.

Suggested readings: Psalm 115:9-13 and Luke 7:11-23.

MARCH 20th

## ANGER OFTEN PRODUCES A VICIOUS CIRCLE

Janet and Simon had a nasty quarrel, the first of their married life. They had agreed to meet outside the town shop at 3.00pm, but Simon turned up twenty minutes late! When they arrived home the atmosphere was tense. Janet absolutely exploded: 'Why did you keep me waiting? I'm absolutely frozen to the bone!' Her fury poured forth like molten lava; her seething anger was palpable. Suspecting that Janet's rage would last a long time, Simon got up and rushed out of the front door and slammed it violently; the loud slam revealed his anger and resentment! However, a couple of hours later it all ended happily, and was then resolved sweetly.

People do express anger and annoyance in a wide variety of ways: people kick machines that won't work, slam things down, or even throw items. There is the story from the Bible, when Moses had a dilemma as there was no water for the people to drink in the wilderness. They were angry: 'Why have you made us come up out of Egypt, to bring us to this evil place? It is no place for grain, or figs or vines, or pomegranates; and there is no water to drink' (Numbers 20:5). Moses and Aaron retreated from this fury and sought the Lord's presence. They duly received specific instructions: 'Take the rod and assemble the congregation, and tell the rock before their eyes to yield its water' (Numbers 20:8). So Moses and Aaron assembled the people and Moses rebuked them: 'Hear now, you rebels; shall we bring forth water for you out of this rock?' It must have been a picture to see Moses' face. We read: 'Moses lifted up his hand and struck the rock with his rod twice; and water came forth' (Numbers 20:11). We can imagine Moses' face when he struck the rock; his anger, his frustration and his bitterness were given release in those two blows. God had actually said 'Take the rod and speak', but Moses did his own thing; he took the rod and hit the rock hard, twice. His bitterness of spirit did not go unnoticed.

There is a comment on this story in the Psalms: 'They angered him at the waters of Meribah and it went ill with Moses on their account; for they made his spirit bitter, and he spoke words that were rash' (Psalm 106:32-33). So we see the circle of bitterness: the people were angry and bitter with Moses, and he reacted in anger and bitterness towards them, and failed to obey God's specific instructions. An old biblical commentator, Matthew Henry, aptly commented on this incident in the life of Moses: 'The best of men have their failings'. So we may well ask ourselves how we handle conflict and whether we provoke anger or bitterness by our lives. The challenge always to Christians is to seek to break the circle of bitterness wherever we find it and, with God's help, to respond in love.

Suggested readings: Numbers 20:1-13 and Psalm 106:32-33.

MARCH 21st

## GOD HELPS PEOPLE

There is one experience of deliverance which is mentioned many times in the Old Testament: the Psalmist puts it in a nutshell, 'He turned the sea into dry land; they passed through the river on foot. There we rejoiced in him' (Psalm 66:6). God helped in the hour of need and the people knew this was God's work. In this striking verse from the Psalter, we note the last five words: 'There we rejoiced in him'. There is profound significance in that first word: it directly points both to a particular moment in time and to a particular place!

In our day and age, men and women in all parts of the world, living in a vast variety of circumstances, can gladly testify they have also experienced God's help. Many can also still point to a particular place and testify: 'There I was guided' or 'There I was delivered'. The same could be said of being strengthened or, indeed, protected. So, in the experience of all believers, there are memories of times and places where God, in His infinite mercy and goodness, blessed them through helping them. If we turn our minds to the Holy Scripture, we can recall the men and women there who witness to the truth that God came to them. Moses paused close to a burning bush, Joshua waited by the River Jordan, Elijah hid in a cave, Daniel languished in a den of lions, Hannah prostrated herself at the sanctuary, Jeremiah stood in the potter's house, while numerous other characters, such as Ruth, could say that God was their helper at a particular moment in their lives.

An elderly Christian was in hospital after an accident; he had been crossing the road and a car knocked him over causing serious injury. When his minister visited him, he comforted the injured man by reading Psalm 121: the first two verses are so beautiful: 'I lift up my eyes to the hills. From whence does my help come? My help comes from the Lord, who made heaven and earth' (Psalm 121:1-2). As the words of the second verse were read, the semi-conscious man opened his eyes and spoke: 'That was true fifty years ago and it's still true today'. There, in the extremity of his dire physical condition, he was acutely aware of God's help. When the man recovered, he was able to testify from the heart that it was there the Lord helped him, kept him and blessed him.

Our God does, indeed, come to our aid and believers can often point to specific times and occasions where they were supremely aware of His blessing. We can rejoice as we remember, God does help us in our place of need and, through that, we may come to experience spiritually, new beginnings and fresh awakenings, too. For that confidence we know in the Lord as our eternal maker and our true keeper, we can offer hearty thanks to God.

Suggested readings: Psalm 121:1-8 and Joshua 3:7-17.

MARCH 22nd

## OUR LONELINESS IS EASED BY THE LORD

There are lots of ways in which people can show courage: there is the courage of the firefighter (and others of the rescue services), the disaster-zone medic, the soldier, sailor or airman in the armed forces, the mountaineer or the astronaut, not to mention others who also risk their lives, including prophetic figures and reformers. Baron Von Hügel used to talk about 'heroic virtue': the courage to be good. In fact, many of the world's good people of all faiths, or none, have walked a lonely path in the pursuit of what is good. These include the Old Testament prophets, as well as John the Baptist and, of course, Jesus of Nazareth. Yet, it is, admittedly, never the easy way to live! How often men and women committed to the Kingdom of God, plough a lonely furrow, as it were, and in the Bible, there are examples of individuals called to serve in this way. Moses was summoned to receive the Ten Commandments: 'Be ready in the morning, and come up in the morning, to Mount Sinai and present yourself there to me, on the top of the mountain. No one shall come up with you . . .' (Exodus 34:2-3). The loneliness of leadership is something which many servants of God are summoned to face and it can be tough indeed.

In the gospels, we have the fascinating story of the feeding of the crowd numbering five thousand near Galilee. It is a dramatic, mysterious and thought-provoking story, and the sequel is also significant: 'He made the disciples get into the boat and go before him to the other side, while he dismissed the crowds. And after he had dismissed the crowds, he went up into the hills by himself to pray. When evening came, he was there alone' (Matthew 14:22-23). The Blessed Master needed solitude just as much as the crowd had needed food. He needed rest and quietness; indeed, He needed a space alone and apart for reflection, and prayer to the Father.

In a profound sense, Jesus was always alone; He bore the loneliness of responsibility, the loneliness of dedication and the loneliness of sacrifice, which was supremely the loneliness of the Saviour. John the Baptist pointed to Him and said: 'Behold, the Lamb of God, who takes away the sin of the world' (John 1:29). Although the place called Calvary bore three crosses that first Good Friday, His cross was actually a solitary place for Him. Even with the few courageous women and men who dared to stand in close proximity, He was alone as the Saviour, enduring the moment of deepest self-giving and sacrifice for our sake.

We may sometimes feel alone, but we are not actually ever wholly alone. The Lord is unfailingly present and so we will never have to face life's challenges on our own. We can trust because the Lord Jesus Christ gave the disciples a marvellous promise: 'Lo, I am with you always to the close of the age' (Matthew 28:20).

Suggested readings: Matthew 14:22-33 and Matthew 28:19-20.

## MARCH 23rd

## THERE'S A REAL NEED FOR WATCHFULNESS

In our world, there are numerous people who spend much time in restoration work: restoring furniture, buildings, paintings, antiques, manuscripts and historical artefacts. The story is told of a group of men who took an old Blenheim plane and very patiently, with great skill, restored it. It took them twelve years and cost the huge sum of £100,000; then, in 1987, it passed the Civil Aviation's stringent air-worthiness safety test. Later, on 21st June 1987, it took part in a private display and disappointingly crashed. It took twelve years to restore, but only a few seconds to undo all the patient work as the crash caused awful damage. In this we see a parable of life as we so often know it.

A man had a serious drink problem and slid into a severe condition of helpless alcoholism, sinking down to an abysmal depth. Good days were a thing of the past; he caused much misery to his wife and family. One unforgettable day, he came face to face with his condition, and stopped drinking completely. For eight long years, in spite of all the fierce inner struggles, he kept on an even keel and won victory after victory over his addiction. His family was overjoyed, as it seemed like a miracle! Then, one Christmas season, some friends encouraged him to drink, and unfortunately, he did so, and all the patient work of restoration was devastatingly ruined in one night. Eight years of valiant struggling were destroyed in hours and, sadly, he never recovered from that terrible mistake.

The tenth chapter of Paul's first Epistle to the Christians in Corinth is not easy reading! However, it contains a verse that stands out in its simplicity and realism: 'So if you think you are standing, watch out that you do not fall '(1 Corinthians 10:12). A person can spend a whole life in serving Jesus Christ but, in just a few moments of foolishness, lose his or her reputation, credibility and character. Does not the Bible tell us that Judas was with Jesus of Nazareth for three years, but one terrible night, he betrayed Him for thirty pieces of silver? It seems utterly unbelievable but it certainly happened. Peter, in a very vivid passage in his first Epistle, speaks of such apostasy: 'The devil prowls around like a roaring lion, seeking someone to devour, resist him firm in your faith' (1 Peter 5:8-9). We might note that lions are pretty cunning and ruthless, never announcing their arrival, and they move with frightening speed. In the same way, we could envisage, as it were, the 'enemy of souls': cunning, swift and intent on wreaking devastating harm. We recall that Jesus, in the Garden of Gethsemane, said to His disciples: 'Watch and pray' (Matthew 26:41). Over the Christian era, multitudes of Christian people have taken it as their motto: 'watch and pray'.

Suggested readings: 1 Corinthians 10:6-13 and 1 Peter 5:6-14.

MARCH 24th

## 'WITS' END CORNER' CAN BE A PLACE OF REAL FAITH

Many people's atheism is just skin deep! Just below the surface, untold millions have some kind of belief in God; they have a veneer of worldliness, but underneath, there is an awareness of a spiritual dimension. That belief in God might be rather hazy, but in a strange way, it is real. There are plenty of illustrations of people who, when caught in a difficult situation, appeal to God for help and deliverance, even though it might be a last resort. For example, Mike Tomkies professed to be an agnostic and had little time for orthodox belief. One unforgettable day, when he was in a small boat off an island in British Columbia, he was surrounded by a number of killer whales. He was in grave danger, and he found himself crying out to God for help.

In Psalm 107, we have a dramatic description of a storm at sea and it tells of the reaction of the terrified sailors: 'In their peril their courage melted away. They reeled and staggered like drunken men; they were at their wits' end, then they cried out to the Lord in their trouble, and he brought them out of their distress' (Psalm 107:26-28 NIV). We note the significant word 'then'. How often when people get to 'wits' end corner', they discover that, under the veneer of unbelief, there is some residual level of belief in God! Of course, their belief may be faulty, fear-linked or manipulative and theologically inaccurate, but it is there to a degree. A sobering thought is that if we were to suppose God only listened to those people who were theologically literate, few if any prayers would be heard! The good news of our faith is that God will, indeed, hear the real prayer within any 'cry for help'.

Countless books and pamphlets have been written on the subject of prayer: some of these publications are very helpful, others are rather confusing, misleading or even frightening! Some volumes on prayer are so dense and so complex that one needs to be a trained theologian in order to understand them. Surely, we might ask, there are words of help and comfort for ordinary people in the everyday world? Thankfully, some verses in the scriptures are quite plain to us all! There is a marvellous verse in Psalm 138 which has been a blessing to generations of people: 'On the day I called, thou didst answer me, my strength of soul thou didst increase' (Psalm 138:3). As those who have been created by God and formed in His image, we are drawn to pray in the hour of crisis or danger, and that is, as it were, a baseline. Yet, there is much more to prayer than the desperate 'plea for help'; the gospel affirms that God is our heavenly Father, and we can draw near to Him in supplication and gratitude for granting us blessings beyond number at all times! Nevertheless, it is true that 'wits' end corner' can turn out to be a place for the kindling, or indeed, the renewing, of a truly whole-hearted and informed faith. If we are open to the Lord, even in difficult times, God can draw us closer to Himself.

Suggested readings: Psalm 107:21-43 and Matthew 14:22-33.

MARCH 25th

## WE SHOULD NOT SEE EVERYTHING

At one British Baptist theological college (Spurgeon's College, London) this piece of advice used to be given to those who were training for ministry: 'A Christian minister needs one blind eye and one deaf ear'. This is perhaps a strange, but very true, reflection. What a happier world it would be if men and women did have one 'unseeing' eye, as it were; it is also true that lots of marriages might possibly be better and more contented if each partner had one ear not 'hearing' quite so well! The story is told of a man who looked after the home while his wife was in hospital facing major surgery. He had a busy time cooking, cleaning, doing all the housework, and looking after the children, as well as regularly visiting his wife in hospital some distance away. On the day his wife came home from hospital, she walked into the lounge and said in a reproachful voice: 'Look at the dust on the television!' If only she had been wise enough to have had one 'unseeing' eye.

In the old King James Version of the Bible, we come across a unique verse, curiously telling of the time 'God winked', and it is worth studying closely. 'And the times of this ignorance God winked at; but now commandeth all men everywhere to repent' (Acts 17:30 AV). Most modern versions replace the word 'wink' by the word 'overlook', so the Good News Bible puts it, 'God has overlooked the time when people did not know him'. What abundant mercy is evident in that verse as we are reminded of Psalm 103. Two verses stand out in particular: 'The Lord is merciful and gracious, slow to anger and abounding in steadfast love' (Psalm 103:8), and this verse: 'He does not deal with us according to our sins, nor requite us according to our iniquities' (Psalm 103:10). The New English Bible puts it: 'He has not treated us as our sins deserve'. We can all thank God for that assurance of faith.

There are many board games that people play at home such as chess, draughts, Scrabble, Monopoly, and so on, but it is worth remembering how easy it is to play relational games, acting out – sometimes very inappropriately – the roles of the child, the parent, the clown, the victim, and so on. One very harmful game is that of constant fault-finding! Some individuals, with both eyes and ears, all too readily find fault with others and it wreaks untold damage. While at times, it may be appropriate to gently point out some error (even as we acknowledge our own faults), perhaps rather more often, we should practise overlooking a person's faults, on the grounds of compassion. The apostle Paul wrote: 'My friends, if anyone is detected in a transgression, you who have received the Spirit should restore such a one in a spirit of gentleness. Take care that you yourselves are not tempted' (Galatians 6:1). Timely words for us all!

Suggested readings: Acts 17:22-31 and Galatians 6:1-5.

MARCH 26th

## CHRISTIANS NEED FISHERMEN'S VIRTUES

How dependant we are upon each other! One of the ways of proving this is to consider all the places which supply us with food and goods: north and south America, Africa, Asia and Australasia, indeed all parts of the globe! One of the groups of people we depend upon is the fishermen: the all-weather people who, in the words of the psalmist, 'go down to the sea in ships, that do business in great waters' (Psalm 107:23 AV). These brave souls supply us all year round with a variety of fish and other seafood to eat: the sad fact is that so often we forget their courage and fortitude in providing such essential and delightful food.

It is fascinating to recall that, when Jesus began His ministry, He called some fishermen to be His disciples. Mark tells the simple story of how Jesus came to the Sea of Galilee and called Simon and Andrew, James and John: 'And Jesus said to them "Follow me and I will make you fish for people"' (Mark 1:17). It is evident that Jesus saw in the fishermen special potential and particular qualities that would help them to be good servants in the service of the Kingdom of God. We can observe two obvious qualities in good fishermen: courage and patience. Sometimes, when the weather forecaster warns of gales offshore, it is a timely reminder of the brave people who fish in the deep waters facing the rigours and dangers of the stormy seas. We recall the fact that the Sea of Galilee was quite notorious for its sudden storms, so even there the fishermen needed much courage. Galilee on a lovely calm and sunny day looks absolutely beautiful, and most people who visit the Holy Land are captivated by its charm, but the lake does have another face, as recorded in other gospel stories of the storms.

Besides courage, fishermen need patience, too. The business of catching fish at sea can have a very irregular pattern about it; some days the catch is large and some days negligible. Even the anglers who sit on the banks of a river in Britain need the quality of patience, as there may be little result after long hours of endeavour. So too, a day or a night of fishing on the Sea of Galilee could be fruitless, until even the last few minutes, a task requiring utmost patience. Similarly, in the service of Christ's Kingdom, a Christian worker needs these two fine qualities: courage and patience. We live in a world which demands quick returns, but in the service of Jesus Christ, we need both the courage and the patience to continue on, even when the returns seem slow or small. To be frank, true Christian service and, indeed, day to day living of the true Christian life, is not for those who easily grow faint-hearted or impatient!

Suggested readings: Mark 1:14-20 and Psalm 107:21-31.

MARCH 27th

## GOD NEEDS FAITHFUL ROAD-MAKERS

One of the busiest and most important motorways in England is the M25, the orbital road which encompasses London. The building of this road was a costly, protracted and massive undertaking. Those involved in its construction needed detailed plans, machinery, tools, materials and a whole variety of skills. Road-makers are important and they often have to work unsocial hours for the good of others. Now, every day of the year, the M25 takes a huge volume of traffic carrying both people and freight, and so we are all indebted (whether we acknowledge it or not) to the diligent road-makers who made this vital route possible and accessible for the nation.

In a spiritual sense, there are true road-makers too. As we look at the ancient story of God's people, we see many road-makers: Abraham and Sarah, Moses, Joshua, Deborah, Esther, Nehemiah and Ezra to name just a few. Also, in Isaiah, chapter 40, we read of road-building: 'In the wilderness prepare the way of the Lord, make straight in the desert a highway for our God. Every valley shall be lifted up, and every mountain and hill be made low; the uneven ground shall become level, and the rough places a plain' (Isaiah 40:3-4). Many people relate this passage of scripture to John the Baptist, who came to 'prepare the way' for the Messiah. Indeed, Matthew's gospel tells of John the Baptist's preaching and his ardent work of calling the people to repentance, and then continues with these words: 'For this is he who was spoken of by the prophet Isaiah when he said, "The voice of one crying in the wilderness: Prepare the way of the Lord, make his paths straight"' (Matthew 3:3).

Today, there are other road-makers for God who faithfully, and often inconspicuously, 'prepare the way': pastors and evangelists, Bible class or Sunday-school teachers, tutors in Christian training colleges or leaders at retreat centres, authors, translators and publishers, together with a whole host of others, including those who do menial tasks for the Kingdom. We might recall the pioneering work of missionaries overseas in how they prepare the way; often it is very hard service with few visible results. We may rejoice in the vast number of believers who, by practical acts of kindness and Christian service, make it easier for others to come to personal faith in Christ. Who could ever measure the major contributions of Helen Keller, C.S. Lewis, Billy Graham, Cliff Richard or Mother Teresa, and the list goes on and on. We thank God that so many of the Kingdom's road-makers have been people who have served the Lord, and so made a noticeable difference in the life of the world! God still needs faithful road-makers today.

Suggested readings: Isaiah 40:1-8 and John 5:32-36.

MARCH 28th

## GOD'S METHODS ARE NUMEROUS

One of the classic national radio programmes which has brought enormous pleasure to millions of listeners in Britain is *Desert Island Discs*. The records selected by the privileged guest are quite revealing, but even more fascinating is the conversation between records. The guest is often very relaxed and in the off-guard moments sometimes tells interesting secrets. When Dr. Robert Runcie, the Archbishop of Canterbury, was interviewed by Sue Lawley, he told how his interest in the church began in a different way than expected. Dr. Runcie confessed that as a lad he was interested in a twelve-year-old girl named Betty. When he discovered that she was going to confirmation classes, he thought it a splendid idea to go along, too. That was how his interest in the church began! He said: 'She was the unknown agent of my being led into the way of religious orthodoxy'. This particular girl did not subsequently figure in his life at all, but she unwittingly introduced him to the faith. So we get the thought-provoking verse written by the apostle Paul to the Christians in Rome: 'What a fathomless wealth lies in the wisdom and knowledge of God! How inscrutable his judgement! How mysterious his methods' (Romans 11:33 Moffatt).

It is said that God speaks with a thousand different voices; yet it is also true that God uses a thousand different methods to draw people to the faith. Imagine a book in a public library with this title: 'How I was introduced to the Christian Faith'. What testimonies it would surely contain, and in fact there would have to be a whole series of books because God's methods are both mysterious and numerous! Some come by direct routes: a Christian home, an evangelistic meeting, regular attendance at public worship. For others, there are more indirect ways: a chance conversation, a book or musical recording given as a present, a poster at a bus or railway station, a letter or card in the post, a tract given by an unknown Christian, and countless other ways. There is no limit to the working of God's Spirit.

In the New Testament we're told how Philip received a message: 'Rise and go toward the south to the road that goes down from Jerusalem to Gaza' (Acts 8:26). He obeyed the call and seemingly 'by chance' he met a person in spiritual need, an Ethiopian royal official who was puzzling over a passage in Isaiah, whom Philip duly instructed in the faith: 'Then Philip opened his mouth, and beginning with this scripture he told him the good news of Jesus' (Acts 8:35). This then led to a commitment to Christ. We ask ourselves: was this a chance meeting or one brought about by the unseen hand of the Lord? In our day, too, God still uses such 'chance meetings', as well as innumerable other mysterious means beyond our knowing, to accomplish His purposes and draw people into the life of the Kingdom.

Suggested readings: Acts 8:26-38 and Romans 11:33-36.

MARCH 29th

## THE MAKER HAS GIVEN INSTRUCTIONS

A visit to any well-known toy shop gives some indication of the wide variety of toys, games and puzzles available for boys and girls, quite apart from the new modern electronic games. Some of the toys are brand new ideas but the amazing thing is, that some of the older ideas are still popular, for example, assembly products and building kits. It is possible to purchase such a kit so that a child – or maybe an adult – can build a car, plane, ship, tank, train or other vehicle. Of course, in using one of these packs to make the desired item, it is essential to obey the basic rule: 'Follow the instructions'. It is a shame that many of these items to be built remain half-finished because the one assembling it decided to 'go it alone' and not follow the instructions!

Some time ago, there was a poster available for use in churches which showed a large globe of the world and attached to it was a small ticket saying, 'Follow the Maker's instructions'. We can pause to reflect on how very true that is, and what a different world it would be if this principle were kept. Within the Holy Scriptures, the heavenly Father has given us the ground rules for living on this planet Earth: these basic rules show how people of different races and ethnic groups, cultures and backgrounds can live together in peace, justice and harmony. The plain fact is that so many people do not adhere to 'the Maker's instructions' and the end result is chaos.

We think of the Ten Commandments: what a transformation would come over the world if people adopted these ground rules as a basis for daily living. In the gospels we read how a lawyer came to Jesus to ask a question: 'Teacher, which is the greatest commandment in the law?' (Matthew 22:36). He had a direct answer from Jesus: 'You shall love the Lord your God with all your heart, and with all your soul, and with all your mind. This is the great and first commandment. And a second is like it, you shall love your neighbour as yourself. On these two commandments depend all the law and the prophets' (Matthew 22:37-40). That was a most profound answer to the lawyer's question! The Saviour's authority and wisdom, as well as His own spiritual devotion to His Father, are plainly revealed in this remarkable teaching.

In our age, we can put it very simply: the ground rules for this planet are 'Love God, love others'. These two commands, and all they represent, are found often in the Bible. Sadly, many lives have been spoilt because these words have been neglected or ignored. It may be foolish of a child to try to assemble a model kit unless the instructions are followed; it is certainly foolhardy of a person of any age to live without reference to the teachings of Jesus Christ, our Teacher and Master. It is easy to see how others fall short in this respect; the challenge, of course, is to look at ourselves and to acknowledge fully what these rules mean for our own lives.

Suggested readings: Exodus 20:1-17 and Matthew 22:34-40.

MARCH 30th

## HIS PRESENCE IS A REALITY

As we all know, saying farewell can be a very painful experience! A missionary going to a distant land to be, say, a pastor, teacher or nurse there, is going to be away a number of years. Parents go to the station or airport to say goodbye, and this proves to be a deeply moving and tearful experience. Every day at stations, seaports and airports people are seen bidding their farewells. It is an experience no one can get used to as it hurts. In the last chapter of Matthew, we read about the Master parting from His disciples. His earthly ministry is over; He had taught much and done many wonderful things, He had experienced fellowship with those who followed, He had suffered the pains of betrayal and rejection, and then endured crucifixion. Raised from the dead, He meets His own, and after the encounter on the mountain in Galilee (described by the first evangelist) comes the farewell. At this significant moment, the risen Lord Jesus gives the disciples a marvellous promise to comfort and sustain them: 'Lo, I am with you always, to the close of the age' (Matthew 28:20).

We have to admit we live in an age of broken promises: it is a sad fact of life but in business, in politics, in professional life, in marriage and in the home, promises are frequently broken. Yet, the promises of Jesus Christ are sure and steadfast. The special pledge given by the Saviour at the close of His earthly ministry has been a source of comfort and inspiration to Christians down the centuries. It affirms that He is with us in our joys and sorrows, our victories and defeats, whether at home or far away, and however we may feel. He is with us always. Truly a daily experience! We admire the courage and fortitude of Christians who continue serving in 'impossible situations', wholeheartedly relying on this faithful promise of the Master. Testimonies abound telling of people who have experienced His presence in their hour of need. By this marvellous promise, life is enriched, problems are tackled, dull days are enlivened and battles are won.

It is natural to link this promise with a verse in the Epistles: 'Jesus Christ is the same yesterday and today and for ever' (Hebrews 13:8). The total ministry of Jesus Christ can never be wholly delineated, as it is beyond all our human description and classification, but the glorious promise stands. He is unchanging and stands with us in every circumstance of life. Therefore, we can wholly and assuredly rejoice in the Lord's presence today and everyday.

Suggested readings: Psalm 130:1-8 and Matthew 28:16-20.

MARCH 31st

## POSSESSIONS ARE NOT THE MEASURE OF LIFE

On 20th January 1989, George W. Bush was duly installed as the 41st President of the USA. Tens of thousands gathered that day in the Washington Mall to witness the inauguration; but literally untold multitudes throughout the world, watched the ceremony on television. It was a magnificent occasion! In his inaugural address, George Bush spoke on a number of relevant subjects: the deprived in society, the drug problem and crime on the streets, the budget deficit and the international situation, including relationships with other nations. He gave this vision: 'It is to make kinder the face of the nation and gentler the face of the world'.

On this important occasion, it was Dr. Billy Graham's responsibility to lead the prayers of the nation: he did so with reverence and understanding. This gesture of inviting a well-known and respected Christian figure to share in the ceremony brought deep pleasure to Christians, as it seemed to reflect a profound recognition of the place of spiritual values. Yet, there was another thing which caused Christian hearts to beat faster, for the new president said in his address: 'My friends, we are not the sum of our possessions. They are not the measure of our lives'. The message was clear: life is more than our accumulation of possessions and attainment of various achievements.

Of course, that truth is central to Christian teaching. In Luke's gospel, we're told the story of a man who approached Jesus about an inheritance issue. He must have been surprised by the answer he was given: 'Take care and be on your guard against all kinds of greed, for one's life does not consist in the abundance of possessions' (Luke 12:15). The Good News Bible gives a little sharper edge to the reply which Jesus made: 'A person's true life is not made up of the things he owns, no matter how rich he may be'. Sometimes, it seems that materialism has a grip on people: a quest for what is bigger and better, whether it is the house, the car, the bank balance or whatever! The truth is that some of the wealthiest people are truly poor inwardly, as Harry Fosdick, the famous preacher, claimed in a telling phrase in one of his hymns: we can be 'rich in things and poor in soul'. Conversely, there are lots of materially poor people who are rich in so many other ways. Possessions have a rightful place, but they certainly are not the measure of our lives. Indeed, true life is found in relationship with God and others, and not in the things we may own.

Suggested readings: Psalm 49:5-12 and Luke 12:13-21.

# April

Thine be the glory,
Risen, conquering Son,
Endless is the victory
Thou o'er death hast won;
Angels in bright raiment
Rolled the stone away,
Kept the folded grave-clothes
Where Thy body lay.

No more we doubt Thee,
Glorious Prince of life;
Life is naught without Thee:
Aid us in our strife;
Make us more than conquerors
Through Thy deathless love;
Bring us safe through Jordan
To Thy home above:

Lo, Jesus meets us,
Risen from the tomb;
Lovingly He greets us,
Scatters fear and gloom;
Let the Church with gladness
Hymns of triumph sing,
For her Lord now liveth,
Death hath lost its sting.

Refrain:

*Thine be the glory,*
*Risen, conquering Son;*
*Endless is the victory*
*Thou o'er death hast won!*

Edmund Budry (1854-1932)
tr. R. Birch Hoyle (1875-1939)

Thanks be to thee, my Lord Jesus Christ,
For all the benefits thou hast won for me,
For all the pains and insults thou hast borne for me.
O most merciful Redeemer, Friend, and Brother,
May I know thee more clearly,
Love thee more dearly,
And follow thee more nearly:
For ever and ever.

St Richard of Chichester (c.1197-1253)

APRIL 1st

## GOD USES THE WORD OF REBUKE

Some New Testament scholars believe that 2 Timothy chapter 4 is the last passage which Paul wrote, so it commands special interest and study. It is often read at an ordination service as verse two is a favourite text for the ordination sermon: 'Preach the word, be urgent in season and out of season, convince, rebuke, and exhort, be unfailing in patience and in teaching' (2 Timothy 4:2). As well as being told to encourage, it is suggested that while it may be difficult to do, a minister must also be ready to offer the 'Ministry of Rebuke'. While this is not an easy task, exercised gently and wisely, it can be much used by God; it can be like a new door opening, as the rebuked person enters into another room of experience, and so is richly blessed.

When Norman V. Peale was a young man, he had opportunity to preach in a local church. He wrote a sermon on the Atonement; it was a complicated exposition! Before preaching it, he read it to his father and invited comment; there was a fair chance he would receive a few compliments. Much to Norman's surprise, his father gave a short and terse reply: 'Burn it'. That was a most painful rebuke, but he learnt a valuable lesson, that the way to the human heart is through simplicity not through long and complex theological argument. A sincere rebuke can be life-giving: 'The ear that heeds wholesome admonition will lodge among the wise' (Proverbs 15:31).

The apostle Peter was an imperfect man and sometimes he made quite serious mistakes. The scriptures tell how in one delicate situation Peter, motivated by fear, did an unwise thing and Paul rebuked him! One short verse in Paul's epistle records the problem: 'When Peter came to Antioch, I opposed him to his face, because he was in the wrong' (Galatians 2:11 NIV). The insight that this gives into the character of Paul is revealing: he was quite willing to rebuke a 'pillar of the Church' for the sake of the gospel! Truth was so important to Paul in defending the integrity of the gospel, that he was ready to risk a friendship.

Late one evening, a good Christian woman rang her pastor with a request: 'Will you agree to an all-night prayer meeting at our church?' The pastor realised that she very rarely came to the regular church prayer meeting held mid-week, so he replied: 'We meet for prayer one evening every week, so why not start there?' She accepted this as a gentle rebuke and began to attend regularly, showing that people can profit from such an admonition. So we have this verse in Proverbs: 'The wise, when rebuked, will love you' (Proverbs 9:8). Sometimes a word of rebuke is necessary, though it is not easy. If we ponder the gracious ministry of Jesus we see how He did this so well, with great compassion and yet with clear authority.

Suggested readings: 2 Timothy 4:1-8 and Galatians 2:8-16.

APRIL 2nd

## CONCERNING THE VALUE OF TWO

One of the really high points in a marriage service is the giving of the wedding rings. As the rings are exchanged these lovely words have often been said: 'I give thee this ring as the pledge and memorial of our wedded love'. These words are polished smooth by much use, but they are also hallowed by thousands of sacred memories. The wedding ring is very important, perhaps especially for the bride; so if by some unhappy accident it is lost, it is most distressing. The wedding ring is a symbol of the strong and steadfast enduring love between two people.

Jean Hall tells that on her wedding day, her husband, Peter, gave her a ring which had inscribed on the inside: 'If one is down, the other will lift him up' (Ecclesiastes 4:10). How true that is in a blessed marriage: it is quite correct to say that sorrows are halved and joys are doubled within the compass of a loving and faithful marriage. Actually, the preceding verse on this subject is also quite telling: 'Two are better than one' (v9). This wise saying, of course, has a much wider reference than simply the marriage bond, and can equally well apply to two close siblings, friends, companions, colleagues or even business partners.

During the Second World War, Winston Churchill as Prime Minister carried an enormous burden of responsibility, often truly grievous, raising a key question: can one ever imagine making decisions where failure could mean the death of thousands of servicemen and women? He shouldered a load of responsibility which would have crushed most people, but a great deal of his strength and courage came from a deep and loving relationship. His wife Clemmie (as she was affectionately known) played a significant role in his life. He felt deeply the pressures of office: he faced criticisms from politicians, he made mistakes, he suffered some serious defeats which set him back but, as his soul-mate in life, she alone could lift him up.

How many politicians, business people, church leaders, medical personnel, statesmen and women have behind them a good partner who stands by in the hour of testing and crisis? Husbands can be a tower of strength, and wives can be a solid rock of faithfulness. In a true marriage, there is so much giving and receiving, through loyal companionship and support. Of course, some marriages sadly do break down, but it is good to remember with thanksgiving all the marriages which last a lifetime! It is a tragedy when there is abuse or neglect in such an intimate relationship, and it is vital that there is trust and respect on the part of both partners. One of the foundation stones of a successful marriage is a basic truth: 'If one should fall, the other helps him up' (Ecclesiastes 4:10 Jerusalem Bible). The heart of a stable, loving marriage is mutual caring and sharing, with faithful support and encouragement.

Suggested readings: Ecclesiastes 4:4-16, 5:1-7, 18-20 and 1 Corinthians 13:1-13.

APRIL 3rd

## A BELIEVER MUST CONTINUE TO LEARN

Many people have been grateful to use the programmes and facilities of the Open University in order to gain a degree. One of the interesting features of this pioneering educational institution is that numerous retired people, as well as working people, have taken the opportunity to do academic study; for so many, it is the fulfillment of a lifetime ambition. The plain fact is that we are never too old to learn, a truth that has biblical authority! All who profess to be Christians are disciples and that means being learners: car drivers can throw away their L plates after passing the driving test, but there is a real sense in which the Christian can never do that, for we surely remain learners all life long!

Dr. Graham Scroggie exercised a remarkable ministry as a Bible expositor: those who heard him at the Keswick Convention were always treated to a feast of good things. He used to tell theological students that he read the Bible through every sixty-six days, as he had a scheme by which he read one book of the bible everyday; Genesis, Exodus, Leviticus and Numbers were read in just four days! This meant he read the Bible through at least five times annually, yet despite his vast knowledge of the scriptures, he was always humble enough to acknowledge that he had so much more to learn. Life-long learning is for all Christians, too.

The Book of Proverbs has this verse: 'Give instruction to the wise, and they will become wiser still; teach the righteous and they will gain in learning' (Proverbs 9:9). In his work, Dr. Moffatt has translated the latter part in this way: 'Teach a good man and he will learn the more'. That is perfectly true: the good person is willing to learn from nature, from history, from others and, of course, from the Holy Scriptures, at the same time being willing to learn from mistakes, too! This memorable notice was seen outside a church: 'Mistakes are but ladders for thinking people'. It is indeed true that we can learn some of life's deepest lessons from our own mistakes!

Luke chapter 2 contains unique material which is not found in any other gospel. Significantly, we are given insight into Jesus' childhood. One story is of a visit Jesus made as a boy with his parents to the temple at Jerusalem. The story ends with this profound verse: 'And Jesus increased in wisdom and in years, and in divine and human favour' (Luke 2:52). We can cherish those remarkable words: 'Jesus increased in wisdom'. So should we all as we go on life's way; it's imperative to go on learning, and thus daily reading of scripture is not only worthwhile, but essential for those who are followers of Jesus.

Suggested readings: Proverbs 9:1-12 and Luke 2:41-52.

APRIL 4th

## A TIRELESS ZEAL, NOT SLUGGISHNESS, IS NEEDED

While few people would want to openly confess to a tendency to be lazy, there are many people who seem to be so. Strangely laziness often appears to be a special temptation to very gifted people: we all know of brilliant college students who have gained a lower degree than expected. Students who plod on with their studies sometimes obtain better results than their colleagues judged by others to be far more able. Laziness is considered a fault and, indeed, is challenged and rebuked in Holy Scripture. In the Book of Proverbs we read: 'A farmer who is too lazy to plough his fields at the right time will have nothing to harvest' (Proverbs 20:4 GNB).

Those who are lazy will often find a variety of excuses not to undertake a job: the weather is deemed too hot, or too cold, or the task is reckoned to be too boring or too complicated; or they simply have something more important to do! There is a humorous depiction of this attitude in Proverbs: 'The sluggard says, "There is a lion outside!"' (Proverbs 22:13). The sluggish person sees plenty of difficulties in the way, and most of them tend to be feigned or are wholly imaginary!

C. H. Spurgeon was a very powerful preacher of the gospel and could well affirm for himself the words of the psalmist. 'I have told the glad news of deliverance in the great congregation; lo, I have not restrained my lips, as thou knowest, O Lord. I have not hid thy saving help within my heart, I have spoken of thy faithfulness and thy salvation' (Psalm 40:9-10). The amount of work he did was staggering: he established a training college for ministers and the children's home, as well as writing and publishing numerous books, while also travelling around the country lecturing and more besides. Yet, even so, he openly testified that his great temptation was to be lazy, and it was an area where he fought a constant battle. However, by the grace and strength of God, he was able to persevere and to overcome sluggishness.

There are lots of people who are tempted to be lazy but they do not yield to it. However, many people do succumb, even professing Christians. Some people, it seems, want to enjoy the benefits of belonging to a church fellowship, but do little service in return. One apposite verse is found in the Epistles: 'And we do desire each one of you to show the same earnestness in realizing the full assurance of hope until the end, so that you may not be sluggish but imitators of those who through faith and patience inherit the promises' (Hebrews 6:11-12). Surely, a tireless zeal, not a weary sluggishness, should be the mark of the Christian! We have the example of those great figures of faith who have gone ahead, and Christ ever before us.

Suggested readings: Proverbs 20:1-13 and Hebrews 6:9-12.

APRIL 5th

## THERE IS A LIFTING MINISTRY

One of the great mysteries of the human body is that one day a person can feel fit and well, and the next day be laid low. Everyone who has experienced a fever knows how that, within a few hours, one can feel debilitated and exhausted. Fever has a sort of vice-grip and the whole body seems invaded and possessed! In Mark's gospel we are told the story of Peter's mother-in-law who was in the grip of fever. Jesus was told and Mark, recording the story with a lovely economy of words, says: 'And he came and took her by the hand and lifted her up, and the fever left her; and she served them' (Mark 1:31). With simplicity, these words give a picture of the ministry of Jesus Christ; it was indeed an uplifting ministry.

The last verse in this same chapter gives another glimpse of Jesus' ministry: '. . .and people came to him from every quarter' (v45). They all came with various concerns: physical, mental and emotional problems, together with spiritual problems and family troubles, even inheritance issues! Some were laid very low by their current difficulties, but then just a few moments spent with Jesus Christ lifted them up. The ministry of Jesus was uplifting, but challenging, too. We can pause today and recall the means Jesus used to lift people up: some kind words, a loving touch or a powerful intervention often made an amazing difference in their lives; people left His presence feeling lifted to a new and higher level of experience.

The testimony of generations of Christians is that Jesus has exercised this gracious ministry in every age. In every church fellowship that truly honours Jesus Christ, there are people who can gladly testify that they have experienced for themselves, the tender lifting power of the Saviour. A man had reached a low point (due to a series of disappointments and failures) and just when he felt like giving up, he experienced the lifting power of the Blessed Master. Just an hour of worship can be the turning-point in a person's life: the Holy Spirit uses music or a hymn, a prayer, a reading, or a sermon to raise someone's spirit to a new perspective. This happens every Sunday in organized worship, but the same ministry is going on every day of every week, year on year.

We all need to catch a glimpse of the possibility of sharing in this loving, caring ministry. There's a relevant verse in the Old Testament: 'Anxiety weighs down the human heart, but a good word cheers it up' (Proverbs 12:25). Every Christian should be willing to use kind words and loving deeds to help encourage someone else. The uplifting ministry is a healing ministry and this is still exercised by our Lord Jesus in the world today; we, too, can share in that ministry ourselves.

Suggested readings: Proverbs 12:15-25 and Mark 1:28-39.

APRIL 6th

## WE ALL NEED TO LOOK AGAIN

In John's gospel there's a story of a man born blind: 'As he passed by, he saw a man blind from birth. And his disciples asked him, "Rabbi, who sinned, this man or his parents, that he was born blind?"' (John 9:1-2). We might question if the blind man had overheard this question. If so, it means that in addition to his infirmity, he had to cope with the problem of implied guilt, too. There is no doubt that Jesus looked upon this needy man with great compassion: He dismissed the disciples' question very speedily, and then exercised power to heal the blind man. As we consider this story, we can be grateful that in our modern world, through the wonderful advance of medical knowledge and science, some people are fully cured of their blindness.

The story is told of a lady who had been afflicted with blindness for thirty years. Life had presented her with a whole series of problems and she could well sympathize with the man in the gospel story. Then, suddenly and marvellously, her sight was restored; it seemed almost too good to be true. With her restored sight she feasted her eyes upon the ordinary things around her: the blue sky, the green grass, the colourful flowers, the scenic trees and shrubs. It was all so wonderful and beautiful. One day, she remarked, she felt astonished that people did not stop each other in the street to say 'What lovely trees and pretty flowers' or 'How beautiful is that green grass'; it seemed they all took these sights for granted. It is very true that – so often – sighted people neglect to appreciate the beauty that is in the world of nature, and it takes a person with restored vision to make us think again!

There is a real sense in which all the seasons of the year have a magnificence of their own: spring, summer, autumn and winter each have their respective colours and glories. We can picture two delightful scenes: a ripened cornfield just waiting to be harvested or the splendour of an autumn day when the trees are dressed in their rich colours. All through the year there are scenes which are attractive, and if truly observed with a seeing eye, should be appreciated. It is sad that sometimes, we are too busy or unhappy or distracted to see the beauty of nature all around us.

In the Old Testament there is a verse which is well worth pondering for a few moments: 'Only fear the Lord, and serve him faithfully with all your heart; for consider what great things he has done for you' (1 Samuel 12:24). For those with eyes to see, there are countless reasons for gratitude, and for a spirit of praise at the wonder of creation and at what the Lord has done for us, and still does, as we are open to God every day of the year!

Suggested readings: Psalm 86:5-12 and John 9:1-11.

APRIL 7th

## GOD NEVER FORGETS

How forgetful we can be! A Christian man thought it was a good idea to write to an acquaintance in a London hospital who was facing a hip-replacement operation. He spent time wording the letter (adding a few Christian thoughts) hoping that it would bring some cheer and encouragement. He hurried to the postbox so that the letter would arrive by the weekend; on returning home, he suddenly realized that he'd forgotten to put a postage stamp on the envelope! He hurried back to the postbox hoping to correct his error but unfortunately, and to his dismay, he was just in time to see the postal van moving away, the fate of the letter uncertain!

Forgetfulness is a part of life and it happens every day of the year. We could name many common examples: a spouse forgets a wedding anniversary or a friend a birthday, a motorist forgets to fill up a vehicle with the correct fuel, a business person forgets an appointment, or children forget their school bags. The list is truly endless, since forgetfulness is an age-old shortcoming: generation after generation has faced this malady. In fact, the Old Testament suggests that wilful forgetfulness is the besetting sin of the people of God.

In Genesis chapter 40 we are told how, in Egypt, the royal baker and chief butler were imprisoned after offending Pharaoh: 'He put them in custody in the house of the captain of the guard, in the prison where Joseph was confined' (Genesis 40:3). In this time of humiliation, Joseph seized an opportunity to show kindness to the demoralised butler, and in conversation said: 'But remember me, when it is well with you, and do me the kindness, I pray you, to make mention of me to Pharaoh, and so get me out of this house' (Genesis 40:14). That sounds perfectly reasonable! Joseph had helped the chief butler and it was fair that he should receive kindness from him in return, when circumstances had changed for the better. The plain words of the Old Testament record the sequel: 'Yet the chief butler did not remember Joseph, but forgot him' (Genesis 40:23). It was truly a culpable error, something we are familiar with today, just as it was often a past failing of God's people.

Like the people of God of old, we also sometimes forget the God who has blessed us and delivered us from past troubles. There is a wonderful verse in Psalm 103: 'Bless the Lord, O my soul and forget not all his benefits' (Psalm 103:2). As with every new day, today is an opportunity. This very day, we might decide to take a little time to recall the blessings which our gracious God has granted to us: the whole sum of yesterday's blessings, today's gifts and graces, as well as all the promises in Holy Scripture as we look to the future ahead of us.

Suggested readings: Genesis 40:1-23 and Psalm 103:1-5.

APRIL 8th

## RIGHT EQUIPMENT IS ESSENTIAL

The Matterhorn is a mighty challenge for mountaineers to scale and it has been estimated that three thousand climbers attempt to conquer it each year. Yet, so many do not fully appreciate the real dangers involved; sadly, most seasons there are tragic deaths on this famous mountain. A few years ago, a search team found the body of a German climber who had fallen two hundred metres to his death. He had all the equipment such as crampons, ice axe and rope, but they were all packed away in his rucksack! He had the right equipment but – to his great peril – he had not used it.

In various places in the Bible, the Christian life is likened to a battle, and the sound advice of the apostle Paul is to use the right equipment. Paul says 'we wrestle not against flesh and blood but against principalities and powers' (Ephesians 6:12). Elsewhere we read likewise: 'Share in suffering like a good soldier of Jesus Christ' (2 Timothy 2:3). Similarly, he put it in a memorable expression: 'Fight the good fight of faith' (1 Timothy 6:12 AV). He was, of course, warning believers that they were facing a spiritual battle, and insisted that they must be prepared for it. Paul wrote: 'Be strong in the Lord and in the power of his might. Put on the whole armour of God' (Ephesians 6:10-11 AV).

How important it is to be properly equipped, and how dangerous it is to ignore this advice! Yet, in spite of these warnings, people sometimes have endeavoured to fight spiritual battles without the proper equipment, as it were, and have faced defeat through being ill-prepared. Just as a mountaineer who climbs a mountain with proper equipment packed away is unwise and ill-prepared, so also is the Christian who seeks daily to fight the battles of truth and righteousness over against darker powers, but fails to put on the whole armour of God. The apostle depicts, in Ephesians chapter 6, the detail of the spiritual armour, concluding it in this way: 'And take the helmet of salvation, and the sword of the Spirit, which is the word of God' (Ephesians 6:17).

The notion of the Word of God as a sword is a striking image: the dynamic Word of God, the sure living Word, is the sword of the Spirit. Rightly deployed, the Word has put to flight many foes and sustained many believers facing all kinds of adversaries and adversities. We may recall that John Bunyan, in the seventeenth century, studied this particular passage with great interest and reminded Christians in his seminal volume that there is no protection for the back. If we turn back, we are left unprotected as it were, in this battle. That's certainly something we should always keep in mind as we seek to live the Christian life.

Suggested readings: Ephesians 6:10-17 and 1 Timothy 6:1-16.

APRIL 9th

## PRAYER GIVES SPIRITUAL STAMINA

A group of children were playing the old game of hide-and-seek and there was much fun and laughter. Then one of them found an excellent hiding place and the others could not find her. They searched and searched to no avail: frustrated, one of them shouted 'I give up'. Within seconds, the other children joined in yelling, 'We give up'. Generation after generation have played this game: both children and adults have enjoyed it! Yet, actually, it is a real parable of life: some people get weary of seeking a resolution to a problem and, instead of persevering, they simply throw up their arms in defeat and give up as they lose their motivation to continue.

In Luke chapter 18, Jesus spoke concerning the efficacy of prayer – persistent prayer – and Luke records the reason: 'They ought always to pray and not lose heart' (Luke 18:1). The New International Version gives an interesting translation of this verse: 'They should always pray and not give up'. There are two key things we should note here: prayer does give strength, courage and endurance, but growing weary in prayer involves a downward spiral, 'a giving up'. In so many areas of life, there is a temptation to 'give up': the footballer feels weary because the team is losing by three goals and thinks there is so little time left in the match, so why bother now? So in business life, in political life, in family life and even in church life, there are moments when weariness sets in. In all these areas, problems can arise which can seem to us insurmountable, and the struggle saps us of strength and vitality. There is a startling verse in the Old Testament which provokes thought: 'The children of Ephraim, being armed, and carrying bows, turned back in the day of battle' (Psalm 78:9 AV). The record stands that this group of people 'turned back': this verse is a salutary reminder that men and women do give up and fail in their determination, sometimes, when they are most needed!

When John Bunyan was in Bedford prison 'for the sake of the gospel', he was acutely aware of the suffering his imprisonment was causing his family; they were paying a high price for his spiritual obedience and loyalty. If he had compromised and had promised not to preach, he could have been released and returned to his family. Yet, he would not give up, but remained faithful to Christ. As Bunyan well knew, prayer gives spiritual stamina; it also gives insight, fortitude and endurance. So let us continue on the pilgrimage with a steady persistence in faith and prayer. Indeed, as the Master urged believers, let us also continue to 'pray and not give up'.

Suggested readings: Luke 18:1-8 and Hebrews 11:23-27.

APRIL 10th

## BITTERNESS IS VERY HARMFUL

In Britain, lots of cars have failed the annual MOT safety test because of rust! Looking at the outside, a car can appear perfectly sound but, underneath, unknown to the owner, rust can be doing its deadly work and, unless checked, can do much damage. Accidents are sometimes the result of vehicles that are not roadworthy because of rust. In the realm of relationships, bitterness is like rust: it eats away in the mind and heart of a person and wreaks great harm. Whole families have been wrecked by one person's bitterness of spirit.

A.L. Rouse has been astonishingly honest and open about his childhood and youth. He tells how two members of his family quarreled over money: it was a quarrel that lasted for years. There was deep bitterness and other people became involved in it and, sadly, that is often true to life for so many. Bitterness can truly contaminate a person, as it were, and then it spreads to others, too. There is a verse in the Epistle to the Hebrews which speaks of the 'root of bitterness'. The writer of the epistle goes on to examine the issue and explain the problem: 'See to it that no one fails to obtain the grace of God; that no root of bitterness springs up and causes trouble, and through it many become defiled' (Hebrews 12:15).

The 'root of bitterness' is a fact of life. We can think of situations where people have been affected by it: couples involved in divorce proceedings, brothers and sisters at loggerheads over a will, societies where there is a power struggle between groups, home situations of domestic abuse or neglect, office life marred by a clash of personalities and even strife within churches, too. Bitterness is like rust which is harmful and potentially dangerous; it is possible to try to ignore it but that doesn't cure it, and so it goes on doing its deadly work, secretly and menacingly. When we think of health problems arising from such a bitter spirit and its repercussions, this malady proves so very costly!

In the Old Testament, we have the record of how the Children of Israel came to Marah: 'They could not drink the water of Marah because it was bitter' (Exodus 15:23). Moses then took a certain tree and threw it into the waters and, miraculously, they became sweet. That is like a parable, as we think of another 'tree' mentioned in the Bible. Countless souls have discovered that when their hearts are bitter – even for seemingly understandable reasons of sorrow or mistreatment – they may find peace within, as they approach the cross of Christ. This is an open secret: there is a deep spiritual healing to be found at the place called Calvary, so we can thank God for this gospel of healing and renewal which brings us life and hope.

Suggested readings: Exodus 15:22-27 and Hebrews 12:12-15.

APRIL 11th

## GOD SEES TRUE GREATNESS

Quite some time ago a book was published which had the simple title: *One Hundred Great Lives*. It is a fascinating book giving biographies of scientists and inventors, leaders and reformers, writers and poets, artists and musicians, soldiers and explorers, statesmen and women, together with many more. It must have been a very difficult task selecting just one hundred persons from world history to include in the book; it was bound to be highly selective, and also not truly inclusive or wholly representative. Interestingly, the well-known character from the Bible, John the Baptist, was omitted from the list. Yet, John the Baptist has an important place in history and in Luke's gospel we find the story of John's conception and birth (Luke 1:5-25). This story begins dramatically: Zechariah was about his priestly duties when he was interrupted by an angel who said: 'Your prayer is heard, and your wife Elizabeth will bear you a son, and you shall call his name John' (Luke 1:13). The angelic word included, also, this profound and very significant prophecy: 'Many will rejoice at his birth; for he will be great before the Lord' (Luke 1:15). John was destined to be very significant.

Supposing a university asked all arts and sciences students to compile a list naming their choice of the world's one hundred greatest lives; it is debatable how many would include John the Baptist. Yet, while he may not be at the top of the list of any human assessment of great achievements, he is certainly highly ranked on God's list, as it were! As we ponder the discrepancy between human judgement compared with God's, we may reflect on these words from Isaiah: 'For as the heavens are higher than the earth, so are my ways higher than your ways and my thoughts that your thoughts' (Isaiah 55:9). How true are those words!

As Christians, we are aware how often the way the world (with an emphasis on celebrity) may evaluate greatness is not how we are to think of others. Jesus once said to the disciples: 'But whoever would be great among you must be your servant' (Mark 10:43). The world sees 'great' people as those who are served by others; God sees 'great' people as being servants! John the Baptist served his generation by his boldness, courage and faithfulness, and he paid the ultimate price with his life. Jesus said of John, the one who had prepared the way: 'Among those born of women none is greater than John' (Luke 7:28). John, of course, was exemplary in his service of the Lord and duly pointed to Jesus as the promised Messiah, claiming: 'He must increase, but I must decrease' (John 3:30).

Suggested readings: Luke 1:5-19 and Mark 10:42-45.

APRIL 12th

## THERE ARE INVISIBLE SPIRITUAL RESOURCES

One of the hazards of being a prophet is the risk of offending influential people, especially those in authority. The true prophet often must speak uncomfortable words, indeed, words that shock or hurt. We read in 2 Kings chapter 6 that Elisha displeased the King of Syria, and so there was a powerful determination on his part to silence the prophet. This meant that Elisha and his servant (staying in Dothan) were in peril. The forces of the king, 'an army with horses and chariots', encompassed the city. The danger for Elisha was extreme. The servant of the prophet was gripped with fear and cried 'Alas, my master! What shall we do?' (2 Kings 6:15). Elisha's words to his servant are of outstanding beauty: 'Fear not, for those who are with us are more than those who are with them' (2 Kings 6:16). Though true, that seemed totally impossible; how could Elisha's servant believe the prophet's bold statement of faith? The prophet saw the fear and panic in the young man's face and prayed: 'O Lord, I pray thee, open his eyes that he may see' (2 Kings 6:17). This fervent prayer was wonderfully answered and the young man amazingly 'saw' the spiritual forces surrounding them, protecting Elisha. As the story is told, it was a revelation to him: there are mighty spiritual resources which are invisible but which, on some rare occasions, become as it were 'visible', offering us hope and calming our fears.

In the Epistle to the Hebrews, we have the marvellous passage named by Bible students as the 'chapter of faith': Hebrews chapter 11 tells of Enoch, Noah, Abraham, Moses and many others. In the verses describing the faith of Moses, we get these lovely words: 'He endured as seeing him who is invisible' (Hebrews 11:27). Moses truly believed in spiritual resources and unseen powers. He both believed in God and trusted in God. We have to acknowledge there are people who profess belief in God but, who in a strange and almost contradictory way, seem less sure of His willingness and His power to help them. However, through many centuries, countless people have experienced God at work in the world and in their own lives; some would confess, in a sense, the invisible forces had been made visible to them.

A minister dealing with a man with spiritual problems once said: 'Have you been to Australia? It exists whether you've seen it or not! Have you seen the Niagara Falls spectacle? It exists whether you've seen it or not!' So there are spiritual resources, which we may not readily see, but they are a great reality. God's unfailing presence is with us at all times, even when it cannot be glimpsed.

Suggested readings: 2 Kings 6:11-17 and John 20:26-31.

APRIL 13th

## THERE ARE GOOD AND BAD ESCAPE ROUTES

Every year numerous people go to the Cotswolds for their holidays: they are drawn as if by a magnet! It is an area of outstanding beauty, and people find a new sense of serenity and perspective as they enjoy the lovely scenery. The hills, valleys, little villages nestled deep in the countryside and the ancient towns all have an appeal of their own. For many, the Cotswolds bring a complete change of atmosphere; tourists visit this beautiful area from all parts of Britain and from overseas, too! There are a number of steep hills in the Cotswolds and motorists have to take extra care. Broadway Hill is one example: it is long and steep with sharp bends halfway down. It is quite easy for a motorist to get into difficulties, especially if the car brakes prove defective. Thus, halfway down this very steep hill there is an escape route – a slipway with lots of deep sand – so if any motorists should lose control they can make their escape. How important that escape route has been to numerous motorists! It is no exaggeration to say that some people owe their life to its existence.

As we live, there are times when life's tough demands, constant pressure and heavy burdens of responsibility, bring a longing to escape. The psalmist puts it perfectly: 'O that I had wings like a dove! I would fly away and be at rest' (Psalm 55:6). Most of us can remember days we've felt like that! We remind ourselves that there are escape routes which are good and wholesome, such as reading a fine book or hearing sublime music. Yet, there are other routes which are positively harmful and should be avoided, as it were, like the plague. We think of all the men and women who've tried these dangerous escape routes: drug-taking, indulging in bad habits with alcohol, gambling, or excessive consumerism or 'living it up'. Sadly, so many have come to grief – causing hardship to others – on these escape routes which, as we know in our hearts, prove to be no relief whatsoever.

Today, we thank God for those escape routes which are truly helpful and wholesome: a relaxing break or a therapeutic opportunity, a change of job or abode, a new friendship or relationship, an altered lifestyle and – most important of all – a fresh interest in spiritual matters. The 'wings of a dove' may take us to new and inspiring places, and we find real escape from our unrest, trouble or despondency. However, sometimes the Lord requires us to stay exactly where we are, and to see things through by His enabling grace. This can be tough, but it is very rewarding, too, as we experience afresh God's mercy and help; He leads us on safely (Psalm 78:53).

Suggested readings: Psalm 55:1-8 and Philippians 4:4-9.

APRIL 14th

## CONCERNING THE SAVIOUR'S GRACIOUS WELCOME

In the Book of Proverbs we find this thought-provoking verse: 'The mouth of the righteous is a fountain of life' (Proverbs 10:11). The New International Version of the Bible gives an added dimension by its rendering of the verse: 'The lips of the righteous nourish many', and how true we surely find that in our own experience! As we ponder the ministry of Jesus Christ, we see how his words were 'meat and drink' to the multitudes, as they were spiritually nourished. In the ministry of Jesus, there were words of outstanding comfort, words which have since been graciously and abundantly used by the Holy Spirit to bring assurance. We think of one important teaching: 'Anyone who comes to me I will never turn away' (John 6:37 REB).

A man with leprosy came to Jesus, according to the record: '. . . and kneeling said to him, "If you will, you can make me clean"' (Mark 1:40). The Blessed Master, moved with compassion, stretched out His hand and touched the leper and he was healed. This delighted man went about talking freely about it, spreading the good news of his cure so people flocked to Jesus, as Mark noted: 'People came to him from every quarter' (Mark 1:45). Within the compass of these few words we see a vivid picture of Jesus attracting and receiving a whole variety of people. He was not prepared to turn them away: anyone who came to Him was welcomed. Many artists have pictured Jesus standing with His arms wide open in invitation saying: 'Anyone who comes to me I will never turn away'. So countless men and women have indeed come to Christ: the respectable and despised, the wise and the foolish, the famous and the unknown. People of different races, classes and backgrounds have discovered Him as the Bread of Life. They have been welcomed and never rejected.

It could be said that this invitation of the Lord expresses the glory of the gospel of God's redeeming love. In a sense, the invitation of love has shone through the centuries like a bright guiding light offering hope and assurance. One of the most noted stars in the heavens at night (viewed in the northern hemisphere) is the Pole Star: it has played an important role in the realm of navigation. In fact, it is said that the darker the night, the brighter this particular star appears to shine. Over the centuries, it has guided many explorers, as well as travellers and mariners, safely on their way. So this faithful promise of the Saviour – 'anyone who comes to me, I will never turn away' – is, as it were, our spiritual Pole Star. No matter how dark and difficult a situation may seem, those who respond to the light of the Lord's gracious invitation and know His kindly welcome, will find hope and peace.

Suggested readings: John 6:26-40 and Revelation 22:16-21.

APRIL 15th

## CONCERNING GOD'S GLORIOUS GRACE

There are lots of ways in which people make an investment: some rich people invest in paintings and other works of art. This means that London auction houses have some truly spectacular sales! In April 1987, a record was broken: a Vincent Van Gogh painting called 'Sunflowers' was sold at Christie's for £23 million. The art world was staggered: it was expected that the painting would attract a good price but this amount was just amazing. The remarkable thing is that 'Sunflowers' is not a large painting, so its value works out at a massive figure per square inch of painting. Likewise, there are very special little phrases in Holy Scripture which have a truly extraordinary value: we can think of Peter's first epistle where he uses the phrase, 'The God of all grace' (1 Peter 5:10). What a priceless description of God!

God grants grace to forgive sin and to restore the sinner, grace to strengthen and to enrich the soul, grace to enable us to show endurance and perseverance. Yet above all, there is grace to redeem and to transform the heart. The apostle Paul knew from experience a tremendous amount about the grace of God; it literally turned him from being a religious bigot into a devout servant of Christ, a faithful proclaimer of the good news. So, in one great chapter in 1 Corinthians (a chapter where he defends key doctrines of the Christian faith), he testifies: 'For I am the least of the apostles, unfit to be called an apostle, because I persecuted the church of God. But by the grace of God I am what I am, and his grace toward me was not in vain' (1 Corinthians 15:9-10). The grace of God, in its many forms, had enriched and blessed him. Thus, his clear testimony, 'By the grace of God I am what I am', has been used by numerous people who have known a deep and an abiding spiritual transformation.

Paul had no doubt about the importance of grace in the salvation of men and women: 'For by grace you have been saved through faith, and this is not your own doing; it is the gift of God – not the result of works, so that no one may boast' (Ephesians 2:8-9). Of course, even as Paul rejoiced in 'the riches of his grace' (Ephesians 1:7), he also faced many difficulties. To the Christians in Corinth he wrote: '. . . a thorn was given me in the flesh' (2 Corinthians 12:7). The apostle prayed for divine deliverance from it, but the Lord's reply was simply reassurance: 'My grace is sufficient for you, for my power is made perfect in weakness' (2 Corinthians 12:9). Paul discovered God's grace and help even in trouble. So may we also keep on discovering this vital truth about God's grace: it is always available, unchanging and free.

Suggested readings: 2 Corinthians 12:1-10 and 1 Peter 5:1-11.

APRIL 16th

## GRACE CAN BE SEEN

Luke records that the church at Jerusalem heard the news of much blessing among the believers at Antioch, and so Barnabas was sent to investigate. Luke notes what he found: 'When he came and saw the grace of God he was glad' (Acts 11:23). Barnabas beheld the grace of God; he saw it in the face of the new converts, in their changed lives and in the rich fellowship of the believers. Surely, the grace of God can still be seen in our day, and often in the surprising actions of very ordinary people.

In November 1987, the town of Enniskillen was catapulted into prominence when, at the town's Remembrance Service, a bomb exploded killing eleven people and injuring many others. The violent incident shook the people of Northern Ireland and people around the world. The next day, the father of a twenty-year-old nurse, Marie Wilson, who was killed in the explosion, said: 'Last night I prayed for the terrorists and that God would forgive them'. These words moved the hearts of millions of people. Those who watched the television interview and saw this man of sure Christian faith expressing such unforgettable words, truly saw the grace of God.

Gordon Wilson was known in his area as a humble believer, a man who attended church regularly. Certainly, the words he humbly, and sincerely, uttered expressed his faith in action. One of the hardest commands in the scripture is this: 'Love your enemies and pray for those who persecute you' (Matthew 5:44). Some say it is impossible to do that! However, a very ordinary man, who would make no claim to great saintliness, prayed for the terrorist who killed his beloved daughter, and people saw in his loving response, the marvellous grace of God. No one can ever calculate how many people were influenced by Gordon Wilson's example in Northern Ireland in 1987.

Throughout the gospels, we are reminded that the grace of God was seen in Jesus Christ: His words, His deeds, His attitudes and His face. As John's gospel puts it: 'And the word became flesh and dwelt among us, full of grace and truth; we have beheld his glory, glory as of the only Son from the Father' (John 1:14). As followers of Jesus, we too, are to be bearers of grace and, in fact, we may observe grace at work in the lives of others. We see it in people bravely facing disappointment or sorrow, in people coping cheerfully with serious trouble or devastating poverty, chronic pain or serious disability, or in those who risk their lives to rescue complete strangers. Moreover, those who do not yet believe may observe God's grace at work in us and desire the knowledge of it for themselves. Thus, it is no surprise that the last verse in the Bible is, 'The grace of our Lord Jesus Christ be with you all' (Revelation 22:21). In Christ, God's wonderful grace is displayed for us all.

Suggested readings: Acts 11:19-26 and Matthew 5:38-48.

APRIL 17th

## GOD CALLS RELUCTANT PEOPLE

In the Good News Bible there is an interesting translation of Proverbs 10:7: 'Good people will be remembered as a blessing'. Such was Andrew Bonar, a truly good man who exercised a powerful ministry and brought rich blessings into many lives. He is remembered as a pastor, deeply sincere and humbly devout. One November day in 1877, he received notice that he was to be named as the Moderator of the Free Church General Assembly. He wrote in his diary 'I am nominated to the moderatorship and every letter that has come insists upon the call of God through the church to me. This is very trying to me: a real cross'. Bonar was very reluctant to take on the responsibility of high office. God's people are sometimes reluctant to respond to God: reluctant to obey God's call, or to follow God's will. Yet, sometimes, this reluctance may be provoked by a genuine feeling of unworthiness or inadequacy, as was the case with Andrew Bonar, for he was a truly humble man with a rich experience of spiritual things.

The Bible tells of others who shared his type of reluctance. In Exodus chapter 3, we see how Moses received God's call to leadership and responsibility and his response was: 'Who am I that I should go to Pharaoh, and bring the Israelites out of Egypt?' (Exodus 3:11). Moses was acutely aware of his own short-comings: he was not a perfect man and he felt very inadequate. Yet, the story recounts how the call of God was persistent, and so Moses relented and became the leader of God's people. A study of many leaders in the Old Testament era reveals that a good number of them were initially unwilling to serve, but they finally yielded under the insistence of God's persistent call!

Sometimes, people truly love to be 'up front', and actively seek the limelight; they might even have a passionate desire to display their leadership skills. Others might be shy and sensitive, and very reluctant to be leaders; when the call comes to them, as in the case of Andrew Bonar, they feel it to be 'a real cross' but they finally respond, and are greatly used by the Holy Spirit. Often, it seems, God has used the most reluctant people, and through them accomplished great things. So the apostle Paul stated his view: 'We have this treasure in earthen vessels, to show that the transcendent power belongs to God and not to us' (2 Corinthians 4:7). God can equally call, and use to His glory, the shy and retiring as much as the bold and extrovert! This call, even of the most unlikely persons, is a part of the mystery of the divine will and purpose. Reluctant people need, and also receive, God's special help in responding to the call to service.

Suggested readings: Exodus 3:1-12 and 1 Corinthians 1:25-31.

APRIL 18th

## GOD HAS MANY DIFFERENT WITNESSES

The shop had a large display of badges, a good number of them very brash or even rather saucy; however, there was one circular badge, a couple of inches wide, which had the words 'BORN AGAIN – ATHEIST'. One assumes – given the context – that the emphasis was on the final word! We have to acknowledge it is true that some people abandon the Christian faith and become atheists: if not exactly thinking, convinced atheists, then at least everyday, practical ones. However, the psalmist has some strong words on the subject: 'Fools say in their hearts "There is no God"' Psalm 14:1). Yet, even if a person claims to have no belief, God's Spirit can use some momentous event in anyone's life to trigger thoughts about life's meaning, and to prompt individuals to consider the things of God.

A television programme featured religious faith in Orpington, Kent, a town with a good number of churches. It showed how the town has a mix of devout Christians, ardent unbelievers and others who argue that they spend Sundays simply relaxing or in leisure pursuits. There was one married woman who gave her fascinating testimony: literally, a 'BORN AGAIN – ATHEIST', with the stress being on the first two words! She told of the days when she was an atheist, and quite happily so. To her mind, humankind could achieve so much and there was no need for God. She went up to university, gaining a degree in economics and there fell in love with a fine young man whom she married. One unforgettable day, she gave birth to her firstborn son; her joy, her awe, and her sense of wonder knew no bounds. Then, as she held her precious child in her arms, she knew there was more to life, and sensed a notion of the divine Maker. As she gazed at this tiny miracle of creation her thoughts turned heavenwards. In the months that followed, slowly but very surely, she was drawn towards worship in a church and eventually became a regular churchgoer and committed Christian. The birth of her baby had set her mind thinking about God, and she was literally a 'BORN AGAIN – ATHEIST'.

When the apostle Paul visited Lystra, he spoke about God's witnesses: 'In past generations he allowed all the nations to walk in their own ways, yet he did not leave himself without witness, for he did good and gave you from heaven rains and fruitful seasons, satisfying your hearts with food and gladness' (Acts 14:17). God has a large number of witnesses: sun, moon and stars, the seasons of the year, beautiful scenery, and maybe also newborn babies, too! Today, we give thanks to God for the many ways that God's love and grace are revealed!

Suggested readings: Psalm 111:1-10 and Acts 14:8-18.

APRIL 19th

## LOVE IS SUPREME

One morning George Thomas, one time Speaker of the House of Commons, received a special letter from the Archbishop of Canterbury. It was a thrilling letter because the Archbishop wrote to say that Prince Charles had specially requested that Thomas should read the lesson at the Royal Wedding in St. Paul's Cathedral in 1981. As a Methodist Lay Preacher, George Thomas had read this lesson namely, 1 Corinthians 13:1-13, in many churches, and before various congregations both small and large, yet this was really different! This time the lesson would be heard all over the world. He rejoiced in the privilege but, he also felt the magnitude of the responsibility, for this was a glorious opportunity to help others see the beauty of this lovely passage of Holy Scripture. He used the opportunity to the full, and Christians all over the world were profoundly grateful for the splendid manner in which he read the lesson.

This chapter, often referred to as a love poem, was written by a man of many parts: Paul was apostle, evangelist, pastor and writer of letters. Many people would subscribe to the view that this wonderful passage, with its surpassing beauty and truth, is the finest piece of writing ever composed, far surpassing the works of Shakespeare and all the rest! Did Paul ever imagine – even in his wildest dreams – that this passage would be studied and loved by so many people, or would be read at a Royal Wedding, listened to by millions of people around the globe? It is a remarkable composition and the moving words in it are very challenging.

This lovely passage on the supremacy of love has been read at countless weddings. It is good to read it in our own devotions: to read it slowly, and also in several modern translations. When we ponder Paul's letters, there are three dominant themes: faith, hope and love. We can just imagine that, when Paul was preaching to people, these same key notions would often be used and explained. These three spiritual ingredients are essential in the Christian life; yet Paul, blessed by the Holy Spirit's wisdom, went even further (as put in the old translation): 'And now abideth faith, hope, charity, these three; but the greatest of these is charity' (1 Corinthians 13:13 AV). The word 'charity' in the New Testament means something very special: it means real, self-giving love. Love is, indeed, supreme, above and before all else.

Suggested readings: 1 Corinthians 13:1-13 and John 13:34-35.

APRIL 20th

## NARROW ROADS CAN LEAD TO LARGE PLACES

In the town of Bedford, there is an ancient passageway which is both narrow and restricted, but it leads to the lovely riverside gardens. Surely, this is a parable of human life and experience. How often men and women have walked, as it were, through a long, restricted pathway, through illness, bereavement or disappointment, and there does not seem much 'largeness' in life. Then, by the goodness and mercy of God, the narrow path brings them out to a wide place of blessing! There is a marvellous verse in the Psalms: 'I called upon the Lord in distress: the Lord answered me, and set me in a large place' (Psalm 118:5 AV). There are lots of people who can testify that they have had a similar experience; how often a narrow or tortuous pathway has led to a large and beautiful place, thereby bringing much consolation after all the difficulty along the way.

Before he came to personal faith, John Bunyan, the seventeenth-century tinker from Bedford was, as he put it, 'in distress': his conscience troubled him and he felt a deep sense of guilt. He was in bondage and he felt as though he were travelling along a very restricted path, too. Then, in God's abundant mercy, he came to the 'large place' where he received God's forgiveness and blessing, knowing he was set free! How wonderful is the love of our Blessed God, and in the life of Jesus Christ, we see this love most clearly demonstrated and beautifully revealed. Bunyan rejoiced in God's deliverance and described his experience as knowing 'grace abounding'!

Every year many people travel to Cornwall for their annual holiday: a good proportion of these visitors delight to explore the quieter beauty spots. Sometimes one travels down a very narrow road which leads to a cove, then – bursting into view – there is a grand vista of the Atlantic Ocean; the narrow road has brought one out to a large place. So we think of other 'narrow roads' in life such as a student studying hard for a key examination, an author struggling to write a major work, a scientist or researcher painstakingly sifting through evidence, or a lone parent coping with the demands of young children. All these people may feel they are travelling a narrow road, but with God's help and by God's mercy, as well as a persistent and patient quest, eventually each may discover the wide vista of divine goodness. God's love can make every narrow path lead to joy. Perhaps this is why the prayer was offered by Paul: 'I pray that you may have your roots and foundation in love, so that you, together with all God's people, may have the power to understand how broad and long, how high and deep, is Christ's love' (Ephesians 3:17-18 GNB).

Suggested readings: Psalm 118:l-14 and 1 John 1:11-18.

APRIL 21ˢᵗ

## GOD DRAWS NEAR TO THE BROKENHEARTED

It began as a normal day but ended in deep despair. The newborn son was 'the apple of his mother's eye' and she held him with special joy and happiness. The prospects were exceptionally good and life seemed to be heaping joy upon joy, but then came the shock. In quiet and measured tones, the specialist said the baby would never develop. The mother was numb with shock: anger, despair, frustration, deep pain and self-pity swept over like large ocean waves. Yet, through that, in an experience of one of the deepest and strangest mysteries of life, she simply testified that she felt the nearness of God. This type of encounter with God is an awesome mystery, but it is a fact of life, that many have strangely experienced this divine presence. In the darkest moments of despair and brokenness, people have truly felt God's nearness. The psalmist put this remarkable truth in the clearest of terms: 'The Lord is near to the brokenhearted and saves the crushed in spirit' (Psalm 34:13). So we have this powerful witness that those caught up in the drama of life – pain, tragedy, loss and bereavement – often find that they're conscious, at such poignant moments, of spiritual forces. It is obviously not always so, but many hospital chaplains have come across this experience in patients, and can testify to its veracity.

In Luke's gospel, we have the exquisite story of two people, who both felt crushed in spirit, walking together on the Emmaus Road. The recent events at Jerusalem culminating in the arrest, trial and crucifixion of Jesus of Nazareth, had left them numb with grief. Yet, as they walked along the road in heaviness of spirit, a stranger joined them. At first, they had no idea it was the risen Lord, until it came to the meal and He broke bread with them: 'Then their eyes were opened and they recognised him' (Luke 24:31). In their sadness and brokenness, they found the closeness of the Saviour's presence which then became fully revealed. It seems that they, too, discovered this amazing truth: 'The Lord is near to the brokenhearted'.

There are days when we may feel crushed in spirit thinking, 'How can we face today?'. In those moments, however, we can recall the wonderful assurance: 'For we have not a high priest who is unable to sympathize with our weaknesses, but one who in every respect has been tempted as we are, yet without sin. Let us then with confidence draw near to the throne of grace that we may receive mercy and find grace to help in time of need' (Hebrews 4:15-16). Often in life, when things are most difficult, we may sense God very near; this is a real mystery of faith, but a glorious truth and a sure ground for confidence.

Suggested readings: Psalm 34:1-13 and Hebrews 4:14-16.

APRIL 22nd

## JESUS CHRIST IS THE DIVINE RESCUER

History abounds with fascinating stories of brave rescuers: people who have literally risked their lives to save other people. Today we recall lifeboat crews, firefighters, mountain rescue teams, coastguard and maritime services and many other brave rescuers after mine or cave emergencies or earthquake disasters. How often it would appear that when there has been a particularly brave rescue, even by just a brave member of the public as a bystander, our faith in human nature, as it were, is restored!

It is true that in our world there is so much greed, lust, violence, selfishness, hared or prejudice, but that is not the full story. There are still lots of ordinary people, quite apart from the professional rescuers, who are prepared to risk their lives for others. On 15th January 1982, in the USA, a large plane crashed soon after take off into a frozen river, the Potomac. The plane happened to crash near a bridge, and a motorist stopped his car and dived off the parapet into the freezing waters to rescue one of the passengers. She was a total stranger but he risked his life to save her, and so he was fêted as a hero. The incident was captured on film, and the hearts of millions of people 'gloried' in the drama and the courage of this brave man; it was a story of heroism which made people proud to belong to the human race.

We can hear again the words of Jesus Christ: 'No one has greater love than this, to lay down one's life for one's friends' (John 15:13). We are reminded today of all the brave men and women who have literally laid down their lives for others. Also, we remember the large number of people, like the hero at the Potomac, who proved willing, if necessary, to lay down their lives for other people. We thank God for gallant rescuers down the years who have risked their lives that others might live, and we see the demand of true care and compassion which is very often costly.

In John's gospel, Jesus is described in so many ways: Good Shepherd, Light of the World, the Way, the Truth and the Life; beyond those images we might add the 'divine rescuer'. For, in the letter to the Galatians, there is a lovely verse which describes our Lord's sacrifice in this way: 'Grace and peace to you from God our Father and the Lord Jesus Christ, who gave himself for our sins to rescue us from the present evil age' (Galatians 1:3-4 NIV). The Cross of Calvary remains a place of deepest mystery: books have been written, sermons preached, lectures given on the theme of the cross, but there remains an unfathomable mystery. However, with the apostle Paul, perhaps we can simply say: 'I live by faith in the Son of God, who loved me and gave himself for me' (Galatians 2:20).

Suggested readings: John 15:12-17 and Galatians 1:1-5.

April 23rd

## JESUS CHRIST RECEIVES SINNERS

It has been said that there are two ways to gain information about persons: listen to their friends and then listen to their enemies! In the gospels we are told that Jesus had His critics and some of them were very hostile; they wanted to find fault with Him and discredit His message! Some Pharisees noted that Jesus mixed with tax collectors and sinners and even had a meal with them. Luke records their reaction: 'This man receives sinners and eats with them' (Luke 15:2). Unwittingly, these critics were uttering a wonderful gospel truth! It was meant to be a severe criticism but it stands as a sublime compliment. Truly, we rejoice that Jesus gladly welcomed sinners!

In His ministry, Jesus gave a gracious invitation: 'Come to me, all who labour and are heavy-laden, and I will give you rest' (Matthew 11:28). It is worth noting what Jesus did not say: He did not welcome people on condition of their being worthy, faultless, or having reached a certain standard. The invitation was simply an open one: to all and sundry, He said, 'Come'. At the heart of the Christian gospel is the glorious truth that Jesus Christ did – and still does – receive sinful people. The Parable of the Prodigal Son tells of a young man who rebelled, who sinned and who hurt his loved ones, but his father received him back. The forgiveness was generously and gladly given. If that is true of a human parent, then how much more it is true of the heavenly Father.

The life and ministry of Jesus Christ displays a willingness to receive sinners. A young minister received a request from a young woman for Believers' Baptism and then church membership. The minister had some doubts about the wisdom of this, as something of her past was plainly known. In a close-knit community, failings are both well known and remembered so, if he decided to comply with her request, there would inevitably be certain criticisms. In his dilemma, he shared his problem with a colleague. There was silence, and then came quite a forceful comment in response: 'If the gospel isn't for sinners, we haven't got a gospel'. These words were like a prophetic utterance; timely, powerful, challenging and direct, 'as from the Lord'. It certainly settled the matter in question there and then.

Luke records that when 'Jesus was crucified, two thieves were crucified with Him, one on either side'. Acknowledging that Jesus had done nothing wrong, the penitent thief then petitioned the Master: 'Jesus, remember me when you come in your kingly power'. To him, Jesus gave a beautiful reply: 'Truly, I say to you, today you will be with me in Paradise' (Luke 23:41-43). Thus Jesus received sinners and we can be assured now that He still receives them!

Suggested readings: Luke 23:39-46 and Romans 5:1-5.

APRIL 24th

## REAL FAITH BRINGS SOLID ACHIEVEMENT

Countless people can testify that they have experienced important turning points in life that have changed their lifestyle and increased their happiness. These experiences come our way, sometimes invited but often not so: reading an inspiring book, meeting a new friend, visiting another region, or even discovering a programme on the television or radio. Another key turning point for many can be hearing the gospel preached, whether in church or on a broadcast. When the apostle Paul wrote to his friends at Thessalonica, he referred to their crucial turning point: 'You turned to God from idols, to serve a living and true God' (1 Thessalonians 1:9). They had found genuine faith, and he rejoiced in it. J.B. Phillips, in his wonderful translation, highlights their faith and sincerity: 'We are always thankful for you all, for we never forget that your faith has meant solid achievement, your love has meant hard work, and the hope that you have in our Lord Jesus Christ means sheer dogged endurance in the life you live before God, the Father of us all' (1 Thessalonians 1:2-3). Those few words 'Your faith has meant solid achievement' are truly beautiful. It is a reflection of all who have had a genuine experience of the Lord and persevered in Christ's service.

It was true of Paul himself, as His strong faith had brought about solid achievement: many came to faith under his ministry, numerous churches were established and nurtured, countless believers were encouraged and his remarkable letters were written. Real faith brings 'solid achievement', and this can be demonstrated from the Bible, and from Christian history, too. We think of Martin Luther and the other reformers who challenged the Church, John Bunyan, William Carey, John Wesley, who all witnessed to God's grace, as well as Elizabeth Fry in her reforming work, Florence Nightingale in her pioneering endeavours, Mary Slessor the missionary in Nigeria, and Mother Theresa of Calcutta in her work of compassion, besides many untold others.

Reflecting on the work of all of these Christian witnesses, we are reminded of the verses found in the Epistle of James: 'For as the body apart from the spirit is dead, so faith apart from works is dead' (James 2:26). Faith can have many different levels. Acknowledging this, surely we yearn for a deeper faith for ourselves and a richer experience for others, in order that it be said of us, and of others too, in the pilgrimage of discipleship: 'Your faith has meant solid achievement'.

Suggested readings: 1 Thessalonians 1:1-10 and James 2:14-26.

APRIL 25th

## WE SHOULD TRUST THOSE WHO HAVE FAILED ONCE

Paul and Barnabas made a wonderful team to serve God's Kingdom. In the opening verses of Acts chapter 13, we have the beautiful picture of the fellowship setting them apart for God's service. They were brave, sincere, and zealous, but also imperfect. We have a fascinating account of a nasty disagreement between them: 'They had such a sharp disagreement that they parted company' (Acts 15:39 NIV). They had experienced a very successful missionary tour, so such an argument was quite out of character; the incident with John Mark was the cause of their dispute.

Mark had been with them on their first tour but, at Perga, it seems he had abandoned the mission as indicated in the narrative report: 'And John left them and returned to Jerusalem' (Acts 13:13). For whatever reason, John Mark had somehow faltered; he had failed to live up to the great trust that had been placed in him, perhaps owing to a failure of courage. So later, when Paul and Barnabas planned a second tour, there was a disagreement as Barnabas wanted to take John Mark (who may have been kin to him), but Paul certainly did not agree! Luke records it thus: 'But Paul thought best not to take with them one who had withdrawn from them in Pamphylia and had not gone with them to the work. And there arose a sharp contention' (Acts 15:38-39). Paul had rather much less patience with Mark because he believed that he had somehow failed; but Barnabas disagreed, and took a different view, wishing to give Mark a second chance to serve with them.

There are various forms of trust: we can trust those who are just beginning in Christian work, and make the step of faith that they are sincere and will do well. Another form of trust is where one allocates Christian duties to people who have proved their worth in Christ's work and have done valiant service. One of the most difficult things in entrusting responsibility is accepting people who have failed once, but who are eager to try again! Barnabas was ready to trust John Mark and history records that he was right, too! It was a salutary gesture on his part.

A man came out of Norwich Prison and found a world of hostility awaiting him; he went for job after job but, as soon as the firms discovered he had been in prison, he was turned away. Then a Christian acquaintance accepted the responsibility to plead with a businessman to employ him: 'Please give this man one chance'. The person agreed to do so and, years later, he testified that the ex-prisoner was the best workman he had, one who had proved worthy of trust. It is so easy to write people off, or to take a harsh attitude towards those who have failed once before. Let us recall that Barnabas gave John Mark another opportunity for service and that proved right! As God has been merciful to us, so let us be full of compassion toward others.

Suggested readings: Acts 15:35-41 and 2 Timothy 4:9-13.

APRIL 26th

## THERE ARE DIVINE OVERRULINGS

Have you ever locked yourself out of your home? If so, you will know how annoying and frustrating it can be! One morning, Mr. Jarrold did this and he simply seethed with fury directed towards himself. With a deep sigh, he decided to go to the Public Library and sit out the time until his wife came home in the afternoon. The library was nice and warm and he enjoyed the facilities. Actually, there was a book sale on and he purchased an excellent biography for just 50p! Straight away, he knew that this particular book would give him hours of reading pleasure, but it was all the result of a mishap. Had he not locked himself out, he would not have visited the library that day! So the great frustration had ultimately yielded a profit which did not disappoint!

On a much higher level, there are people who can look back on some of life's bigger disappointments and see a blessing in them. Dr. Billy Graham has told the story of how he had a disappointment in romance: the girl he intended to marry opted for someone else. It was all very upsetting, but a little further down the road of life he met Ruth, and God had better things in store for him. In a significant way, 'the disappointment was God's appointment'. The world knows that the partnership between Billy and Ruth was so richly and marvellously blessed. Ruth exercised, in her own right, of course, a tremendous ministry, and on numerous occasions Billy Graham spoke of her spiritual worth and her vital contribution.

One Old Testament figure who suffered a bitter disappointment was Joseph: he was betrayed and unjustly treated by his brothers. One can imagine his feelings of distress, frustration and bitterness, too. Yet, by a remarkable turn of events, Joseph became significant in Pharaoh's household, as the seemingly impossible had happened. Genesis chapter 45 stands as one of the great passages of literature: it tells of the time when Joseph met his estranged brothers again and disclosed his identity in the words, 'I am Joseph' (Genesis 45:4). To say it was a surprise to the brothers is an understatement: it was a massive, stunning shock to see Joseph again, alive and well, years after they had abandoned him.

Then, there follows a moving testimony of faith, as Joseph addressed them: 'And now do not be distressed or angry with yourselves, because you sold me here; for God sent me here before you to preserve life' (Genesis 45:5). Thereafter we read some of the most remarkable words Joseph ever spoke: 'So it was not you who sent me here, but God' (Genesis 45:8). Joseph truly believed that another hand (an unseen divine hand) had been at work in his life. For Joseph there was no doubt that in his life, God had overruled. Seated on the throne, sovereign over all, God's wondrous purposes were coming to pass. We, too, can know God's overrulings.

Suggested readings: Genesis 45:1-9 and Philippians 1:3-13.

APRIL 27th

## PRIDE NEEDS ITS REBUKE

One of the momentous days in the ministry of Jesus Christ was when He sent out the seventy 'two by two' with the specific message: 'The Kingdom of God has come near to you' (Luke 10:9). These followers, commissioned by the Master, were to heal and to teach; after a most successful mission, they returned flushed with the knowledge of their achievements! Luke says: 'The seventy returned with joy saying, "Lord, even the demons are subject to us in your name!"' Put plainly, they were very conscious that a good work had been very successfully accomplished.

With firmness, the Blessed Master 'brought them down to earth' with this thought-provoking sentence: 'Nevertheless do not rejoice in this, that the spirits are subject to you; but rejoice that your names are written in heaven' (Luke 10:20). Jesus sought to shift the emphasis from what they had done for God to what God had done for them! How often people who have done church work for some years talk much of their own achievements. Typical comments include such claims: 'I was church visitor for years', 'I served in the choir forty years', 'I was church treasurer for decades', 'I worked among the young people until I was sixty!' Sometimes these things are said with glowing pride. How subtle and pervasive pride can be if we are not vigilant; it can even penetrate the hearts of faithful servants of Jesus Christ.

India will never forget William Carey, who arrived there with his wife, at the end of the eighteenth century. He was a loyal and faithful worker for the Kingdom, and served in numerous ways as pastor, teacher, translator, church planter and author. Towards the close of his life, Carey was visited by Alexander Duff, who throughout his visit, kept talking about Carey's victories and accomplishments. Carey very gently rebuked him: 'Dr. Duff, you have been speaking about Dr. Carey . . . Dr. Carey. When I am done, say nothing about Dr. Carey. Speak about Dr. Carey's Saviour'. In His service for Christ, Carey had carried an enormous workload and his successes were numerous, but his real joy was in what Jesus Christ had done for him, as His glorious Saviour! His was, indeed, an exemplary life of Christian service.

The psalmist exulted: 'The Lord has done great things for us; we are glad' (Psalm 126:3). That's the right spirit in thinking about our place before God: we rejoice that we are used in God's service, and that there are victories in His name. Yet, the greater cause for rejoicing is the marvellous love He has lavished upon us and the knowledge that our 'names are written in heaven'. Let us take care not to fall to the besetting sin of pride. Instead, we need to focus our thoughts aright: not on what we have done for God, but on what God has done for us.

Suggested readings: Psalm 126:1-6 and Luke 10:1-20.

APRIL 28th

## THERE IS AN ULTIMATE CERTAINTY

For many people around the world, earthquakes are a part of life, especially in certain areas of this planet. Sometime ago, one of the quality newspapers published a world map showing 'map-points' depicting the great earthquakes in history. Certainly there are periodically gigantic convulsions in certain areas which can devastate a region, and it is as if the hills and mountains are shifted, when the ground is subject to enormous subterranean stresses! Such earthquakes often bring in their wake awful destruction and terrible uncertainty about the future. The familiar becomes unfamiliar and parts of the landscape can be so distorted and radically changed as to be scarcely recognizable, in just a matter of seconds.

Sometimes, we speak of earthshaking events and, as we know, some families do experience these and feel overwhelmed by such life traumas as accidents, sudden illness, unexpected bereavement, the collapse of a business or the breakdown of a marriage. For those affected, there seems to be no solid, secure ground beneath their feet. However, those who confess faith in a gracious, almighty God acknowledge there is, indeed, some solid ground (or what scripture calls the 'Rock'); God's love remains eternal and never diminishes. As we read in the Book of Isaiah: 'For the mountains may depart and the hills be removed, but my steadfast love shall not depart from you, and my covenant of peace shall not be removed, says the Lord, who has compassion on you' (Isaiah 54:10). There is one great certainty, namely, God's steadfast love, which will never fail us.

One proud day, in April 1912, a famous ship left British shores and boasted that it was unsinkable; yet on its maiden voyage to New York City, it struck an iceberg and sank with a fearful loss of life. Skilled designers and shipbuilders had put their best skills into the work of building the Titanic and were justifiably proud. However, the ship proved to be vulnerable, and its sinking sent an awesome shock-wave around the world; people realised that our best plans can fail, our highest promises can disappoint, our greatest endeavours can collapse. Yet, as we are assured in Scripture: 'The steadfast love of the Lord never ceases, his mercies never come to an end; they are new every morning, great is thy faithfulness' (Lamentations 3:22-23).

In our modern world, it is a humbling thought that, in facing the reality of our situation, there natural forces which can devastate life as we know it, as well as man-made forces which could even destroy most of this lovely planet. However, despite all such concerns, this is the ultimate certainty we know in the Lord: nothing can ever thwart God's endless, boundless love, or separate us from it.

Suggested readings: Isaiah 54:1-10 and 2 Timothy 4:16-13.

APRIL 29th

## WE KNOW THE DOWNWARD DRAG AND THE UPWARD LIFT

It is a fascinating sight to see one of the mighty jet planes take off at a major airport: as we realise, some planes carry hundreds of passengers, with all their luggage, and the power required to 'lift off' is enormous. Considering the force of gravity, it is amazing how much effort and energy is required to overcome it. Rockets and planes are the obvious craft in mind, yet trains, trams, buses, lorries, cars all have to use much fuel to go uphill, while cranes, escalators and lifts use power to elevate people and objects. Watching a heavy vehicle struggling to get up a steep hill bears witness to the conflict between mechanical power and the force of gravity.

As we consider Holy Scripture, the truth dawns on us that there is another kind of gravity, as it were, in the downward pull which hinders people spiritually. The dark force which brought King David to adultery, which encouraged individuals such as Jonah to be disobedient, and which entered the heart of Judas to make him a traitor of Jesus, is powerful indeed. The downward pull is a great reality in the lives of so many of the great leading men and women in the biblical narratives who faced it, as did so many of the ordinary people in the story. It is abundantly clear from scripture, history, autobiography and personal experience that there is a downward drag, a sort of 'spiritual gravity'. The psalmist made this plea to God: 'If my soul cleaves to the dust, revive me according to thy word' (Psalm 119:25).

The aircraft needs power to rise up, and so do people! The testimony of the saints endorses the promises of the Bible: there is marvellous and wonderful spiritual power available from the Eternal One above. A number of texts speak about it, but one of the best known is found in Isaiah: 'But they who wait for the Lord shall renew their strength, they shall mount up with wings like eagles, they shall run and not be weary, they shall walk and not faint' (Isaiah 40:31). It has to be said, every day men and women struggle against the downward drag, and temptation is both very real and powerful. However, we are thankful that there is another, higher power, God's own gift of His presence, to draw us and lift us up, helping us rise to loftier things in life.

It is an awesome experience to travel in a plane high above the clouds and so in the bright sunshine. A few minutes before takeoff the plane at the terminal might be in dull, grey and wet weather; but then, by the marvels of modern engineering and science, the plane soars up high through the clouds into the sunshine. That is a true parable of the spiritual life, for we can experience being at the lower levels of life, even deeply conscious of the downward pull; then, by divine mercy, we can know a gracious power lifting us above the clouds of trouble or dismay into the glorious sunshine of God's love and faithfulness.

Suggested readings: John 13:21-30 and Colossians 3:1-14.

APRIL 30th

## THE LORD CAN CALM OUR HEARTS

Visitors to Papworth Hospital in Cambridgeshire are conscious that they are going to a place of miracles. This particular hospital is known throughout the world as a place where patients with serious heart conditions are given a new lease of life. However, in past times, one of the problems about Papworth Hospital has been in the parking of a car for, especially at busy times, it can be most difficult! On one occasion, a visitor found it exceedingly difficult to find a parking space; it must have been a record day for visitors as every nook and cranny seemed to be taken by cars! Eventually, he found a tiny space outside the electricity control room. His relief was palpable, as now he thought he could relax and visit at leisure. However, it was then only a moment before a spine-chilling siren sounded as an alarm went off! The driver panicked, wondering if he had triggered off some special alarm system, fearing the worst! People came rushing from all directions and the whole area became a hive of activity. As one of the hospital staff raced by, he shouted a curious comment: 'I bet it's those insects in the works again'! Apparently, that was the issue: not the parked car, but the interfering insects causing a malfunction of a certain system.

How important alarm systems are in today's world, but we recognise that they can be set off in error by a variety of means, even tiny insects. Life has equipped men and women with an efficient alarm system called 'fear'. If we ponder it, we see how fear plays a very important role in life, and seems to have a purpose of its own. As we all know, that personal alarm system can be activated by small things; it can be triggered needlessly and sound the alarm, as it were, unnecessarily! There is an old saying about 'crossing our bridges before we come to them', and maybe many of us have spent an anxious night doing so. Also, in a different respect, it is possible to let very small things really agitate us and, like 'grit in the shoe', make things pretty uncomfortable and cause us to be disturbed, setting that distress 'alarm' off again!

There is a verse in the Old Testament which can, indeed, help to calm our fears: 'For I, the Lord your God, hold your right hand; it is I who say to you, 'Fear not I will help you' (Isaiah 41:13). God can and will help us day by day, whatever our anxieties and difficulties. The New Testament reminds us that we need not be afraid: God's love is constant and boundless, so we can each let His perfect love cast out our fear (1 John 4:13). God's love is much greater than whatever the problem we have to surmount, no matter how paralysing our fears might seem to be for us! We need only to trust in the Lord daily and to rely hour by hour upon His divine help.

Suggested readings: Isaiah 41:8-13 and 1 John 4:13-21.

# May

I know that my Redeemer lives!
What joy the blest assurance gives!
He lives, He lives, who once was dead;
He lives, my everlasting Head!

He lives, to bless me with His love;
He lives, to plead for me above;
He lives, my hungry soul to feed;
He lives, to help in time of need.

He lives, and grants me daily breath;
He lives, and I shall conquer death;
He lives, my mansion to prepare;
He lives, to bring me safely there.

He lives, all glory to His name!
He lives, my Saviour, still the same;
What joy the blest assurance gives!
I know that my Redeemer lives

Samuel Medley (1738-99)

O Lord Jesus Christ, Wisdom and Word of God,
dwell in our hearts, we beseech thee,
by thy most Holy Spirit,
that out of the abundance of our hearts
our mouths may speak thy praise.

Christina Rossetti (1830-1894)

MAY 1st

## THERE IS A DIVINE SHEPHERD

The rear window of the car held a simple notice: 'I'm not a number. I'm a person!' A good reminder! We are all known by various numbers: whether those for National Insurance, the bank, building society or Post Office, other official records or forms of registration, including, of course, our individual tax reference! In an age of data on computer records, where so frequently our unique number takes precedence over our own personal name, sometimes this identification-by-number syndrome deserves to be challenged. So we protest: 'I'm not a number, I'm a person!'

Names are important! In the New Testament witness, Jesus Christ is known by a rich variety of titles: Teacher, Saviour, Lord, High Priest, Son of Man, Son of God and Shepherd. The passage which centres on this last theme is John 10, the chapter in which Jesus said: 'I am the good shepherd. The good shepherd lays down his life for the sheep' (John 10:11). In this wonderful chapter we are told that the shepherd looks after His sheep: He knows them each and calls them by name. To Jesus Christ, we are not just a number, but we are known individually by name as members of His flock. The parable is a reminder of God's care for every one of us as individuals.

There is another story in the Gospel of Luke which stresses, very powerfully, the value placed on each unique one. Luke records, in chapter 15, that Jesus told the story of a shepherd who had a hundred sheep: when he realises one is missing, presumed lost, he cares for that one. He leaves the ninety-nine safely in the fold and goes to search for that lost one and does not cease until he finds it (Luke 15:1-7). This parable shows how Jesus saw the importance of one: it is a short but beautiful story and the underlying truth is one of utmost importance. Individuals count in God's sight. So in the stories of the Blessed Saviour, He loves large crowds of people, as well as groups of friends and families, and yet, He also loves each one and cares for each person as a unique individual.

Unlike communication in our modern world which so often can have a rather impersonal tone, the Lord Jesus Christ showed concern for every person and, in so doing, revealed the character of God. For some people, God has been seen as rather remote from us: the Prime Mover or First Cause, as though some great impersonal Being or the unknowable, distant deity. For those who believe in Christ's message, God is very real, and very near. The Lord is like a shepherd who cares for all the sheep. As Psalm 23 affirms, our Lord God – as the shepherd who knows each of us by name – leads and guides us through every experience of life.

Suggested readings: Psalm 23:1-6 and John 10:1-13.

MAY 2nd

## HAPPINESS CAN COME AS A SURPRISE

One of the regular religious programmes which has been a great boon to listeners over many years is the Daily Service on BBC Radio 4 (LW). This is listened to by a wide variety of the British public: elderly shut-in folk, ones in hospital, care homes or in their own home, as well as people travelling by car, or at work. Some find the prayers particularly helpful, especially the items for thanksgiving and praise, which are inspiring and elevate the spirit to the things above. One very ordinary morning this little clause, within one of the prayers, was included in the thanksgivings: 'the happiness which takes us by surprise'.

In our modern world, happiness is sought in a whole set of diverse ways. The strange thing is that true happiness is so often a by-product; those who specifically seek it as an end in itself find it eludes them! However, thank God, there are times when happiness takes us by surprise. We may have been engrossed in work, or deep in thought, then – quite suddenly – we experienced the sweet taste of joy and delight which came as a 'bolt from the blue'. So, C. S. Lewis called his autobiography *Surprised by Joy*. Indeed, there are vast numbers of people who can truthfully testify that, in their own lives, some of their greatest joys have come as a complete surprise.

In Acts chapter 12, we are told that the Church was experiencing difficulties and Peter was put in prison: the chances of his release were slim, 'but earnest prayer for him was made to God by the church' (Acts 12:5). Then there was a dramatic intervention and amazingly Peter was set free! He went to the house of Mary where the believers were assembled; he knocked the door and initially received a rather strange reception! However, he persisted: 'But Peter continued knocking; and when they opened they saw him and were amazed' (Acts 12:16) They really did experience 'the happiness which takes us by surprise', and they rejoiced; their prayers had been answered a lot sooner than they had ever anticipated, and in an astounding way.

These surprising joys can come in different forms, be it through a phone message, a letter, a visitor, a chance meeting, an unexpected answer to prayer, an unusual spiritual encounter or just a remarkable awareness of the nearness of God. Most people, at some point in their life, have experienced sudden joyful, serendipitous, and happy encounters. Sometimes these occasions are very homely: the laughter of a small child, rediscovering an old friend, the colour or fragrance of a lovely flowerbed, the splendour of a beautiful sunset. We thank God for that inner joy which is always possible through a firmly rooted faith, but also for the unanticipated moments of elation, and 'the happiness which takes us by surprise'.

Suggested readings: Psalm 148:1-14 and Acts 12:5-17.

MAY 3rd

## TRUE FAITH GIVES BOLDNESS

Through the medium of television, multitudes around the globe have seen many remarkable things about our lovely planet. A variety of wildlife programmes enable us to see plants and animals in their natural habitat. We marvel at the skill and patience of the photographer, and the award-winning cinematography and accompanying commentary. One of the best nature films shown on British television, in the view of many, was the life cycle of the lion. It showed this fine animal in its various moods: its tenderness with its cubs, its loyalty to the group, its cunning in hunting and its resoluteness in the face of a threat. How fierce and strong the lion is by nature!

In the Book of Proverbs, we find this verse 'The righteous are bold as a lion' (Proverbs 28:1). Illustrations of the way a strong faith gives boldness of heart abound in the Old and New Testaments. We think of Moses facing the mighty Pharaoh, saying, 'Let my people go (Exodus 10:3), and David facing the giant named Goliath, saying 'You come to me with a sword . . . but I come to you in the name of the Lord' (1 Samuel 1:45). In the New Testament we know the stories of the women who courageously stood by the cross, and then were the first to go to the tomb on the third day. Luke records Paul standing before King Agrippa posing the challenging question, 'Why should it be thought a thing incredible with you that God should raise the dead?' (Acts 26:8). Also, in Church history, we find stories of men and women of great boldness and courage. One very well-known sixteenth-century reformer, Martin Luther of Germany, refused to recant of his beliefs and reputedly declared to the authorities: 'Here I stand, I can do no other'.

The decision to stand firm for the faith and to have 'boldness of heart' may also result in some dire peril, which potentially could rob us of peace and happiness. Yet, as the first disciples of Jesus discovered, true faith can overcome fear. We read in Acts that, a few weeks after the crucifixion and resurrection of Jesus, Peter and John were still to be found in Jerusalem which was a dangerous place. Even so, after Pentecost, they preached fearlessly that Jesus Christ was risen from the dead. On one occasion, they were arrested, and dragged before the authorities. Peter spoke out with great boldness, so we read these words: 'When they saw the boldness of Peter and John, they marvelled and they took knowledge of them that they had been with Jesus' (Acts 4:13 AV). So it has been through the centuries: men and women of strong faith have been 'bold as a lion' to challenge injustice, to speak out against evil practices and social ills, and to launch out on adventures of true obedience to the Lord.

Suggested readings: Proverbs 28:1-7 and Acts 4:7-20.

MAY 4th

## IT IS WISE TO GET A SECOND OPINION

Over a period of six months, Mr. Jarman had been visiting his doctor complaining of stomach pains: the doctor was kind and sympathetic, but the medication he prescribed did not cure the problem. After a very painful night, Mr. Jarman made the decision to seek a second opinion, and so a visit to a consultant was arranged: the routine examinations and X-ray checks were made, and the consultant made a new diagnosis which subsequently proved to be wholly accurate. While a solution to a problem is not always so easily reached, there are many experiences in life when it is useful to ask for a second opinion: someone purchasing a second-hand vehicle, a couple needing confidential advice, a person desiring to take legal action.

Second opinions are frequently very valuable and a wise person does not just 'go it alone', but listens to sound advice. Many people, faced with a particular crisis in life, have discovered that the Bible is full of wisdom and sound advice. Put plainly, it has offered many people who may have been looking at their situation from one perspective, an alternative view or a 'second opinion'. In a very real sense, consultation of the scriptures can help people to realise the paucity of their own previous way of thinking about a matter! Indeed, the Bible not only changes hearts and attitudes, but it opens minds which have been closed, also.

In the New Testament there are many stories which describe the way that people were attracted to Jesus Christ. We see how rich and poor, healthy and sick, educated and uneducated, religious and irreligious, ordinary folk and people in authority came to Jesus. In a sense, many found in Him a sound 'second opinion' and came to find healing. In John's gospel, there is a story about a man named Nicodemus, who came to Jesus to seek his advice. Interestingly, Nicodemus was a ruler of the Jews and was used to people consulting his wisdom, but he came to the Saviour for advice. According to the gospel writer, when they met, Jesus looked at Nicodemus and made a swift diagnosis: 'You must be born anew' (John 3:7). He meant, of course, that Nicodemus needed a radical change in his life; he needed to be born again, to be born anew (also, in a sense, 'from above').

One modern writer has said that no one can claim to be self-educated without having read the Bible, because it contains the profound wisdom of the ages and the holy wisdom of Jesus Christ. While reading the Bible can be disturbing and challenging, as well as comforting, it is certainly the place to go if we are in need of a 'second opinion', in order to find the true life with God.

Suggested readings: Psalm 119:97-104 and John 3:1-16.

MAY 5th

## THE CHURCH IS A PLACE OF DECISION

In the town of Bedford, there is a church which stands on a roundabout, or to put it more accurately, the church turns out to be the roundabout! St. Cuthbert's Church is a large and sturdy building used by the Polish Community for worship and fellowship. It stands in a commanding position and is part of an important road junction! As one approaches the church, a decision has to be made which road to take: there are six roads leading off the roundabout. So it is absolutely vital that, as you get near the church, you've made your decision! How true that is to life: people come to church and very important decisions have to be made. There are various alternatives: we can accept the challenge to seek to serve the Lord Jesus Christ and His Kingdom, or we can reject the call to follow Christ, and so take a different road which may lead to other pursuits. Some people, of course, may look for a road of neutrality which allows them to defer a decision as to whether they will either accept or reject Jesus Christ as their Lord and Saviour.

    The church on the roundabout is a parable of life as it is! The Christian message proclaimed within a service of worship in a Church should not only challenge us, but also help us make the right decision. People often come into a church with vital decisions to make: decisions about business, relationships, career or perhaps spiritual matters. Lots of vitally important decisions are made within the context of worship; sometimes a crucial decision is made during public worship and no one else ever knows about it. Indeed, a minister could feel a particular service had been unexceptional whereas, in fact, within the service, a person may have felt led by God to make a decision which turned out to be, as it were, the 'right road'.

    Psalm 122 has a very interesting beginning and ending. It begins: 'I was glad when they said unto me "Let us go into the house of the Lord"' (Psalm 122:1 AV). Then it ends with this remarkable testimony: 'Because of the house of the Lord our God I will seek thy good' (Psalm 122:9). Put very simply: we benefit when we go into the house of the Lord, and others benefit, too! The result of real and vital worship is a blessing to others; so often, within the context of a service of worship, decisions are quietly made which will have an impact to enrich the lives of others or, indeed, the wider community. We all have choices to make in life which not only affect us, but have wider implications. The church on the roundabout challenges us all to approach worship with a true desire to allow God to help us to decide aright as we journey onward in life.

Suggested readings: Psalm 122:1-9 and Hebrews 10:19-25.

MAY 6th

## KINDNESS MUST BE LINKED WITH CHEERFULNESS

How do you spend the time before a morning service begins? Some churches supply material or a display with suitable thoughts for quiet meditation and prayers; others supply a pew Bible and a worship sheet giving the references of lessons or noting prayers for the service. One Sunday morning, Jennifer arrived rather early for the morning service, and she quietly picked up the Good News Bible to read the appointed lesson. Suddenly, one verse seemed to leap out of the page: 'whoever shows kindness to others should do it cheerfully' (Romans 12:8 GNB). She found it challenging: kindness with cheerfulness! How often people can show kindness, though in a rather drab and dutiful way: 'professional' kindness is a fact of life we have all encountered. Yet, the Holy Scriptures remind us to show kindness with cheerfulness, reflecting the manner of our Saviour.

Actually, the Bible has a lot to say about acts of kindness and cheerfulness. We might ponder this verse: 'Now there was at Joppa a disciple named Tabitha which means Dorcas or Gazelle. She was full of good works and acts of charity' (Acts 9:36). The New English Bible translates one part of that verse in a beautiful way: '. . . who filled her days with acts of kindness and charity'. Here was a disciple who delighted in good things, who took pleasure in being kind and did it cheerfully. In the Book of Proverbs we read: 'A cheerful heart is a good medicine' (Proverbs 17:22). What a difference it makes when one is served by a cheerful, kind person!

Kindness is a universal language that is understood by people of different races and cultures, by total strangers, by people who are desperately ill or severely disabled, and even by animals, too. Cheerfulness – resulting in kindness – is a medicine which makes life so much easier to face day by day, especially when the going is rather tough! So we thank God for cheerful people we meet everyday: postwomen or men, as well as other delivery persons, bus or taxi drivers, domestic appliance engineers, doctors and nurses, receptionists, local officials, office staff, shop or library assistants, social workers and teachers, together with church leaders and many others. We remember, too, that as we seek cheerfully to show kindness, we are witnessing to the love and kindness of God, Who is always seeking our good. As scripture reminds us: 'For the mountains shall depart, and the hills be removed; but my kindness shall not depart from thee, neither shall the covenant of my peace be removed, saith the Lord that hath mercy on thee' (Isaiah 54:10 AV).

Suggested readings: Isaiah 54:1-10 and Ephesians 4:30-32.

MAY 7th

## IT'S THE PROOF THAT COUNTS

A church arranged to have an evangelistic mission to reach the 'outsiders' in the parish: there had been some criticism that the fellowship was too inward looking! At one particular Sunday evening service, the minister announced that there would be an after-meeting 'to prove Christianity'. This poses the vital question: how can our Christian faith be proved? Jesus gave an interesting answer to that question: 'By this everyone will know that you are my disciples, if you have love one for one another' (John 13:35). We can use all manner of meetings, seminars, lectures, as well as audiovisual or printed resources to defend the faith, but the best argument for Christianity is a loving heart, expressed in practical ways.

Sometimes, churches have not always 'proved' the faith – whether torn by division or simply too exclusive – and sadly, they have caused people to reject the Christian faith and to turn away from the Church. Yet, there are many passages of scripture which say, in effect, 'true love is the greatest argument'. We may recall that, as a young man, Albert Schweitzer made a simple resolution: 'I have decided to make my life my argument'. History records his dedication and labour of love at the hospital at Lambaréné, where his actions matched his words. He truly tried to follow the scriptural challenge: 'Little children, let us not love in word or speech but in deed and in truth' (1 John 3:13). Plenty of other people have also responded to that challenge, and their loving ways in selfless service have been a strong argument for the faith.

Mother Teresa has been known throughout the world for her devoted work in Calcutta showing love to the needy and the dying. On one occasion, she came to England and was interviewed on the television; her rugged, but kindly, face appealed to millions. Letters simply poured in begging that the programme should be repeated! Her love had truly struck a chord in many hearts. Over the whole of the Christian era, disciples of Jesus Christ have demonstrated love, and revealed the authenticity of the gospel: Dr. Barnardo, Dick Sheppard, Amy Carmichael to name but a few, as well as many other people not known to us, but known to God.

Throughout His life and ministry, Jesus revealed the truth that 'God is love'. On the Cross of Calvary, He revealed a love which was unconquerable by evil. So we, too, may now claim, in the words of the apostle Paul: 'He loved me and gave himself for me' (Galatians 2:20). The essence of Christianity is a loving spirit and a compassionate heart, reflecting the very nature of God as that has been revealed supremely in Jesus Christ. Such love – reflecting God's love – endures for ever: it is surely the most convincing argument for our faith.

Suggested readings: John 13:31-35 and I John 3:11-24.

May 8th

## FAITH IS AN ADVANTAGE AND MORE

It was a nice car standing in the street and, even a casual observer could see that it had a careful owner and was in pristine condition! Emblazoned on the passenger door was the single word 'ADVANTAGE'. We can ponder the ways this word is commonly used: it is an advantage to have a good education, or to live in the country, or to have employment that we enjoy, and so on. Adverts in the media and commercials on television, often stress the advantage of one product or service or other over the alternatives, whether washing powders or cars, insurance or investment options! The word 'advantage' is often used with a hint of superiority implying something of the very best in quality or value.

In Psalm 87, the psalmist expresses an ancient view of the advantage of being born in Jerusalem. His language is crystal clear: the Lord records as he registers the people, 'This one was born there' (Psalm 87:6). The psalmist had no doubt that the Lord had a special love for that city since he wrote, 'The Lord loves the gates of Zion' (Psalm 87:1). So, for the Children of Israel, it was seen as a privilege to be born in Jerusalem for it was a special place to count that city as their home. Indeed, the Old Testament speaks of the special covenant promises that were given to the people of Israel and the significance of the temple as a place of worship in Jerusalem.

Christians, of course, believe that in Christ, we have been called into a new community of faith. Being part of a fellowship of believers is an advantage or, perhaps better stated, a blessing. One person's story was this: she was very happily married, both she and her husband doing everything together, indeed living completely for each other. Then sadly he died and she was left desolate, feeling quite bewildered and devastated as she had lost her soulmate. She decided to start attending church, and there she made a pleasant discovery. Within weeks she had found new friends and much kindness was shown to her; the friendship and fellowship within the church helped her face the pain and distress of her bereavement. She found a new dimension to life through a personal faith, and she could give thanks to God who led her to a place where she experienced grace, forgiveness, encouragement, solace, and help. In short, her faith was not just beneficial; it was a rich blessing from God.

Real faith is more than an advantage, as it is a genuine gift from God! So, we give thanks today for fellowship in and through the gospel of Christ. Especially, we thank God for the life of the Church and for Christian friends who support and encourage us; faith is an advantage, and more! It is a blessing!

Suggested readings: Psalm 87:1-7 and 1 Timothy 4:6-16.

MAY 9th

## REGRET IS A PART OF THE HUMAN CONDITION

In October 1976, Jimmy Carter and Gerald Ford were competing for the Presidency of the USA. They appeared together on television and, it was estimated that one hundred million people watched the programme. The debate reached a hot-point when they spoke about Russian-dominated countries. Ford spoke a few sentences which appeared to underestimate the problem: it was a slip, and a notable slip, too. It brought forth howls of protest from the press, radio and television. Later the comment was made: 'If only he hadn't said those words'!

Someone has suggested that said together, the two saddest words in the whole English language are 'if only'. There are many stories in scripture which speak of human regret. In the Old Testament we are told how Joseph's jealous brothers planned to get rid of him: 'They took him and cast him into a pit. The pit was empty, there was no water in it' (Genesis 37:24). Shortly afterwards they modified their plans and sold him to some Ishmaelites for twenty pieces of silver; then with devilish cunning they took Joseph's coat of 'many colours', and stained it with blood, taking it home to their father. Jacob's response to this was immediate: 'It is my son's robe, a wild beast has devoured him, Joseph is without doubt torn to pieces!' (Genesis 37:33) The trick had worked perfectly! The brothers had covered their tracks! However, as they watched the grief and brokenness of their father, we may wonder if some of them felt remorse and perhaps, in their inmost being, uttered within, 'if only'.

Most people know how it feels to regret words or deeds: if only I had not made that decision, if only I had not said those words, if only I had not made that mistake under temptation, if only I had not quarrelled with that person. However, there is another more poignant cry we sometimes feel deeply within: if only I had kept faithful to the Lord Jesus. The Bible includes stories of those who must have had bitter regret: David, Jonah, Peter and John Mark to name but a few. Most people, looking back over their own experience, have reasons for sorrow and regret, consequently sighing, 'if only'. Yet, we may give thanks, because we read in scripture that God does not hold our mistakes or deliberate wrong-doing against us. Indeed, we read: 'If we confess our sins, he is faithful and just, and will forgive our sins and cleanse us from all unrighteousness' (1 John 1:10). So, while we acknowledge our regrets, we may also give thanks to God who is merciful and forgiving.

Suggested readings: Genesis 37:17-34 and 1 John 1:5-10.

MAY 10th

## WE CAN DEPEND ON DIVINE SUPPORT

The 'ACKNOWLEDGEMENTS' page, where people express thanks to others who have supported and helped them, has always been one of the interesting features of a local newspaper. Two typical examples are: 'Thanking all my customers for their support of my business during the last 30 years', or 'Thanking all our neighbours, friends and colleagues for their comfort and support in our sad bereavement'. The notices of thanks serve as a reminder that daily we depend on others. Indeed, that care and support may be received at many different levels: from receiving help with a repair in our homes to the literal 'life support' that some people require when they are in hospital. We all depend upon so many others in the world about us simply to live day by day.

While human love (such as of spouse, child, parent, sibling or simply a close friend) can be a marvellous strength, the psalmist reminds us of another kind of support, on which we depend as well. Crying out to God, the psalmist claimed: 'When I thought, "My foot is slipping," your steadfast love, O Lord, held me up' (Psalm 94:18). Genuine love is a wonderful support for each of us; especially divine love, which is so much greater and richer than we can ever imagine.

The psalmist's description of his foot slipping seems to express the way we are sometimes suddenly in desperate need of help. Most mountaineers can speak of a time when, as they climbed a difficult section of a mountain, their feet began to slip; surely a horrendous experience! However, they also speak of a rope which anchored them safely, so they were delivered from certain injury or death. In life, numerous people have times when, in a sense, their feet begin to slip and they are dreadfully afraid as they face misfortune, trouble, hardship, accident, bereavement or betrayal. It is at such times that people can testify to the Eternal One as the divine support, and to that anchoring divine love which does not let them go.

There are so many times when we know not only the support of others, but divine care. God surely holds us and provides 'life support' when we are in need! A lovely hymn contains these words 'But for thine upholding, where would strength be found?' We ponder David's words: '. . . but the Lord was my support' (2 Samuel 22:19). A newspaper once had an unusual acknowledgement included in the respective column, as a reader thanked the Holy Spirit for help received. It was perhaps a rather strange notice in the paper, but it was heartfelt and certainly is a reminder that as well as thanking others for their help, we should also acknowledge God's love and care which supports us at all times and in all places.

Suggested readings: 2 Samuel 22:1-25 and John 14:25-31.

MAY 11th

## SUPPORT TEAMS ARE IMPORTANT

When we think of the life of Jesus Christ, there are a number of questions that we don't normally ask, though curious children will do so at times! For example, they might ask: Where did He find the money for purchasing necessary clothing? Who did His laundry? Who provided His daily food and where did He wash or sleep? Of course, we know these are not the most fundamental questions, but they're worth asking because an issue is at stake! One thing we do know is that Jesus and His disciples had a loyal support team, and these faithful women are listed by Luke, as Mary, Joanna and Susanna, with many other unnamed women too, 'who provided for them out of their resources' (Luke 8:3). Luke's record implies that these women provided vital aid throughout the whole ministry of Jesus.

We can think of a church perhaps where the fellowship has experienced great blessing and seen much growth. People in the area might say: 'They've got a good minister, crowds of people, many youth, lots of activities, large collections or new building work'. Yet, that is never the whole truth: the minister has a faithful and loyal support team. We could never give an exhaustive list of such people but it would include key leaders and church officers, as well as others who work diligently behind the scenes. The ministry of a local church is always dependent upon people working together.

The last chapter of Paul's letter to the Christians in Rome is not an easy chapter to read, but it is well worth taking a few minutes to look at it because it shows that Paul, and the other leaders, depended on the support of others. There are some interesting anecdotes, of which this is the first: 'I commend to you our sister Phoebe. . .she has been a helper of many and of myself as well' (Romans 16:1). Her name is just one of a whole catalogue of the members who were active in the church. She was a faithful member of the support team and Paul deeply appreciated her work. In so many places in the New Testament epistles, Paul, whether wittingly or unwittingly, reveals his need of other people and he is quite open about the fact that he required their prayers, their service, their support and their practical help.

No matter how accomplished or acclaimed a person may be in the eyes of the world, she or he needs those who back up the work with solid support. The evangelist Dr. Billy Graham would be termed by many as possibly the most noted high-profile evangelist in the modern age, but he was always supported in all his endeavours by a team. So let us rejoice in this verse: 'For God is not unrighteous to forget your work and labour of love' (Hebrews 6:10 AV). We remember that, in the life of the Church, everyone has a part to play in the wider ministry.

Suggested readings: Luke 8:1-3 and Romans 15:22-16:16.

MAY 12th

## CHRISTIANS MUST BE PREPARED

Two men were members of the same church and enjoyed a lot of things in common. Their friendship had a spiritual basis and they were both concerned for the things of the Kingdom of God. Yet, in one particular area they differed: in the use of their cars! One of them had the boot of his car packed with items including tools, spare parts, bottles of oil and vital fluids, as well as plentiful supply of nuts and bolts just in case of breakdown. The other man used to say 'I don't even carry a spanner. If my car broke down, I just wouldn't have a clue what to do!' That's true in so much of life: there are those who are well prepared and others who don't bother with it at all.

The well-known motto of the Boy Scout and Girl Guide movements, 'Be prepared', is an excellent motto for life, since it is wise to be ready to cope with the unexpected. For some, that might mean having tools in the boot of the car, or at least subscribing to a breakdown organisation! In so many areas of life, preparation is essential: repairs to the roof of a house have to be done before the onset of the wind and the rain! The apostle Peter had another angle on this theme. In his epistle we read: 'Always be prepared to give an answer to everyone who asks you to give the reason for the hope that you have. But do this with gentleness and respect' (1 Peter 3:15-16 NIV).

Peter was reminding believers that they should be ready to speak to others about their faith. Nowadays, we might say that he was advocating an informed, open discipleship. They had to be prepared to tell others what they believed, and why! Sharing one's faith can be a daunting prospect for some people. Fortunately, there are many books and programmes which can assist us in our discipleship today. Hence, the contemporary Christian can be well-prepared to have some knowledge of the faith to be able to give such an account. Some Christians are keen to do so, and they spend time and effort to prepare 'to give an answer'. However, others unfortunately, for whatever reason, are not so diligent and remain ill-prepared and unsure as to how they might speak to others.

Wrestling with the truths of the Christian faith is not easy, but it is important to study God's Word and to try prepare ourselves always 'to give an answer' concerning faith, especially as we seek to relate it to life's challenges. For those who may be hesitant and want to know how to prepare, one approach is to read or hear, on a regular basis, portions of the Bible itself, both methodically and prayerfully. However, the best way to deepen and to learn spiritually is through fellowship with others, perhaps in Bible study in a local church, where insights can be meaningfully shared. Such sharing can equip us to share our faith more widely.

Suggested readings: Isaiah 44:1-8 and 1 Peter 3:7-17.

MAY 13th

## GOD MEETS US AT LIFE'S CORNERS

Hugh Redwood, a journalist and Christian writer, told his friends how he came to an important turning point in his life: he was under stress because certain decisions needed to be made. All this coincided with the fact that he was staying in a friend's house prior to speaking at a large assembly. His friend offered a room where he could rest: it was most acceptable! In the room there was a nice fire burning, a comfortable chair, and a small table with an open Bible on it. The Bible was open at Psalm 59 and someone had written an interpretation opposite verse 10. 'My God in his loving-kindness shall meet me at every corner'. It was just the assurance that Hugh Redwood so needed!

There are, of course, many 'corners' which must be navigated in life, literally and figuratively! In Switzerland, there is a mountain loved by tourists which has a road right to the very top. It has thirty-three corners and each one of them is potentially dangerous. Such is life for us each day. Just as when travelling by car or bicycle to a destination we may come across many deceptive and dangerous corners, so we may round a bend in life and find that we are facing great difficulty. The good news is that, however difficult the twists and turns may be, God still meets us there. Indeed, at certain points, we may even pause and look back over the road we've travelled and bless the Lord for His goodness toward us. In that loving-kindness, we have seen God there at every corner. Countless people can echo the words found in Genesis: 'I praised the Lord, the God of my master Abraham, who had led me on the right road' (Genesis 25:48 NIV).

As we read the Holy Scriptures, we see how numerous men and women came to a dangerous or important corner, as it were, and God met them. We can think of Noah, Sarah, Joseph, Hannah, Amos, Jeremiah, Daniel, Elizabeth, Peter, Mary and so many others. It is said, for instance, that Leo Tolstoy worked hard at his literary labours and, at forty-five years of age, he was both wealthy and famous. To the observer, Tolstoy had all that his heart could wish for in life, but he confessed that life had no meaning for him. It was a time of questioning, strain and tension and so proved to be a very dangerous corner. However, in the providence of God, it was the beginning of a crisis that led to his conversion to Christian faith. God met him at the dangerous corner. That can be our experience, too.

It is wonderfully true that God, in His faithfulness and mercy, helps us at life's turning points: the Lord is there for us whatever the day may bring.

Suggested readings: Psalm 59:1-10 and John 6:15-21.

MAY 14th

## JESUS CHRIST GUARANTEES GOD'S PROMISES

For two long years John had been saving hard to have money to buy a racing bicycle. His sixteenth birthday brought the extra money to make the purchase possible! As he hurried out of the door to go to the shop, already knowing which bicycle he was going to buy, his father called out: 'John, don't forget the guarantee'. Of course, such things are important. A guarantee is a promise that something will be, or will happen, as stated and, if there is a fault, it will be recompensed. On a whole range of goods a guarantee is a must: from cars to ovens, fridges to televisions, phones to watches, the guarantee is vital for peace of mind. Many people have been grateful to be able to invoke the guarantee because their purchase proved unsatisfactory.

Guarantees are not limited to products that we buy, but are included in Scripture, too. In the Old Testament there is an exquisite promise: 'Behold, God is my salvation, I will trust, and will not be afraid; for the Lord God is my strength and my song' (Isaiah 12:2). The apostle Paul also included assurances about the Lord Jesus Christ in his letters to the churches. He claimed: 'He is the image of the invisible God, the firstborn of all creation: for in him all things were created, in heaven and on earth, visible and invisible, whether thrones or dominions or principalities or authorities – all things were created through him end for him' (Colossians 1:15-16). Magnificent words indeed! Such words inspire the mind and cheer the heart. Alongside that, we can ponder the down-to-earth promise that Jesus Christ is the guarantee of the promises of God, in the words of the apostle: 'For all the promises of God find their Yes in him' (2 Corinthians 1:20). Jesus Christ is high and lifted up and we rejoice in such truths of His Lordship: the writings of the apostle give us splendid insight into His majesty and glory. However, we can also rejoice in this specific ministry of our Lord which guarantees God's ancient promises. As the psalmist rejoiced, so we, too, have no need to fear because the Lord is our strength and song.

A few years ago some shops were issuing guarantees which were so deviously worded that they actually limited one's consumer rights. This was brought before Parliament and the law on the 'small print' of guarantees was tightened up. We can say with absolute confidence that there is no dubious 'small print' about God's marvellous promises: Jesus is the 'Yes' or 'Amen', to God's promises. He is the sure guarantee! The New English Bible translates that verse thus: 'He is the Yes pronounced upon God's promises, every one of them'. Indeed, when we may be worried, troubled, or afraid, we can take another look at God's perfect guarantee and rejoice in the risen Lord in Whom we know great blessing and assurance.

Suggested readings: Isaiah 12:1-6 and 2 Corinthians 1:12-22.

MAY 15th

## UNBELIEF NEEDS PATIENCE AND PRAYER

Some of life's joys are deeply felt: they give a warm glow to the heart. There is a very special joy to Christian people when real living faith is found by a relation or friend; it is a glorious moment when one realises that a loved one has accepted Jesus Christ as their personal Lord and Saviour. So the Bible says 'I have no greater joy than to hear that my children are walking in the truth' (3 John 1:4 NIV). Yet, the sad fact remains that some Christian parents do not experience this special joy over their children because, occasionally for a time, they turn away from the faith of their upbringing.

Yvonne Stevenson was nurtured in a vicarage and her parents were hard workers for their church. For a number of years, she went along with the family's devotion and regularly attended church. After leaving home, in her upper teens, for a whole variety of reasons she came to reject the Christian faith and became an atheist. She recalls the long train journey home for the vacation knowing full well it meant facing her parents with the painful truth of her unbelief. After being at home a couple of days, she experienced the dreaded confrontation: 'I don't want to attend Holy Communion . . . I am an atheist now'. The atmosphere was indescribable: her father was visibly shaken and, for the first time in her life, Yvonne saw her mother red-eyed from crying. There was unavoidable real pain and deep hurt; however, she had to be herself. Many Christian parents have had to face this type of situation, and sometimes they feel a tremendous sense of guilt about their children's loss of faith; yet, we know all have to decide for themselves and grow up in their own way.

Faith is a deeply personal affair: no parent can make a child believe! They can set an example, and can encourage, inform and or even possibly gently persuade, as well as pray. Indeed the prayers of others can follow friends and loved ones into 'the far country' of disinterest and unbelief. In the face of such unbelief, it is no good arguing or even ranting! Kindly patience is required; constancy in love is absolutely essential. In the New Testament, there are so many beautiful pictures of Jesus Christ, and one of the finest is of the Saviour waiting: 'Listen! I am standing at the door, knocking; if you hear my voice and open the door, I will come in to you and eat with you, and you with me' (Revelation 3:20). Jesus does not bludgeon His way in or force an entry, or break down the door, or impose Himself unwanted. He is ready always simply to wait, exercising infinite patience as the One from the Father above Whose love is unending. If Jesus Christ exercises this kind of patience in dealing with those who would reject Him, so should we ourselves. We can recall today a striking verse from Proverbs: 'Patient persuasion can break down the strongest resistance' (Proverbs 25:15 GNB): that is God's way, and it ought to be ours, too.

Suggested readings: Lamentations 3:19-26 and Revelation 3:14-22.

MAY 16th

## TRUTH HAS A FINE ATTRACTIVENESS

Literally millions of words have been written about Dr. Martin Luther King and it is significant that in the USA there is a special day of the year when he is remembered. Like all great leaders, he had to face considerable criticism. However, Dr. King is remembered by people all over the world as a brave and courageous leader as well as a person of deep insight and wisdom. When Dr. King came to London, he was invited to preach at St Paul's Cathedral. All who attended the service were conscious that this particular preacher was living out his faith in difficult circumstances and was exposed to many dangers. The congregation listened with rapt attention. In his sermon he referred to the Parable of the Good Samaritan, and two sentences were memorable, the first being this comment: 'The priest and the Levite looked at the wounded man and asked themselves, what will happen to us if we stop and help?' Secondly, by way of contrast, the Samaritan asked himself a different question: 'What will happen to this man if I don't stop and help him?' After this service, Bishop Wand (a man miles apart from this preacher, ecclesiastically) said to him: 'I am an old man, Dr. King, but I am glad I have lived long enough to hear that sermon'. Many agreed that his sermon had the 'ring of truth'; his words seemed to transcend human barriers, and they had an undeniable authenticity. The truth evidently hit home for many, perhaps because it was so appealing.

As we ponder the need for speech to have the 'ring of truth', we are reminded that when men and women listened to Jesus of Nazareth, they often commented that his speech was different. In Matthew's gospel we read: 'And when Jesus finished these sayings the crowds were astonished at his teaching, for he taught them as one who had authority, and not as their scribes' (Matthew 7:28-29). One particular passage, which we know as the Sermon on the Mount, has survived the centuries and many people of various cultures and generations have pondered its message. Here Jesus spoke plainly about the need for people not to live to themselves, but to live for God and for others. This, of course, was also the message of the parable of the Good Samaritan which is recorded in Luke's gospel, and to which Dr. King referred memorably in his sermon preached at St Paul's Cathedral. In that parable, Jesus made it clear that our 'neighbour' is anyone who is in need, regardless of race, colour or creed. Having described the Samaritan's care for the man who was in need, the parable ends with this firm word to all who will listen: 'Go and do likewise'. The truth about God's call speaks volumes, and draws us each to accept it. Once we acknowledge the truth, there is no other way for us.

Suggested Readings: Luke 10:29-37 and Matthew 5:1-16.

MAY 17th

## HUMAN HANDS DO SPEAK

In recent years, the television authorities have designed programmes specifically for the hearing-impaired and these have brought enormous pleasure. It is quite fascinating to see presenters 'talking with their hands', conveying the verbal content, and visually explaining the content of the programme. Indeed, sign language is now one of the great blessings of life for many. Actually, the vast majority of people who who do not rely on sign language also talk with their hands! We know that within certain cultures, some people are very skillful in using their hands during an animated conversation.

Hands are very precious in human life. The hands of a surgeon, a concert pianist, a craftsman, a nurse, a therapist or beautician – to name but a few – express skill and care. One man particularly treasured a photo of his mother because, in a truly wonderful way, it was a perfect picture of her hands: those hands which had kept the home, reared children, helped others, and cared for the sick or dying, but which had also been clasped often in prayer.

The much-loved story in Acts chapter 9 is one of the most dramatic told by Luke, and Christians have often pondered the story of Paul's conversion on the road to Damascus. Much interest has been concentrated on the opening verses and sometimes this has detracted from the profound significance of the later verses! We recall the lovely passage which tells of the encounter in the city, at the Lord's bidding, between Ananias and Saul of Tarsus after the incident on the road. 'So Ananias departed and entered the house. And laying his hands on him he said "Brother Saul, the Lord Jesus who appeared to you on the road by which you came, has sent me that you may regain your sight and be filled with the Holy Spirit"' (Acts 9:17). We think of the touch of those welcoming hands: the renewal, comfort and healing bestowed. We can be sure that the hands of Ananias were indeed 'talking hands': Saul (later known, of course, as Paul) received the vital message, in part, by physical contact.

Numerous painters have sought to portray the Lord Jesus Christ, often taking great pains to depict His hands: those hands which were so strong and tender. One of the finest 'word pictures' in the gospels is where a person with leprosy came to Jesus for healing: 'And a leper came to him beseeching him, and kneeling said to him, "If you will, you can make me clean". Moved with pity, he stretched out his hand and touched him, and said to him, "I will; be clean"' (Mark 1:40-41). As we think of the 'talking hands' of Jesus, let us also ponder the words of the hymn writer: 'Take my hands and let them move at the impulse of love'. Actions speak louder than words, and quite often even more powerfully, memorably and eloquently than words.

Suggested readings: Mark 1:40-45 and Acts 9:10-19.

May 18<sup>th</sup>

## GUIDES SHOULD BE RELIABLE

The porter at the railway station was quite definite in his direction: 'That's the train you want'. So the lecturer boarded the train feeling confident that he would be able to keep his engagement and be on time. After a few miles, though, a nasty little doubt niggled at the back of his mind and it just would not go away: 'Is this the right train, after all?' It turned out it wasn't; a conversation with a fellow passenger dispelled all doubt. The porter had made a mistake and put him on the wrong train. The lecturer got off at the next station and began the task of finding how to get to Croydon on time: he was annoyed and angry that he had been misled by someone who should have known better, yet, in the end, he made it to Croydon just in time!

In the scriptures we have these words of challenge: 'I found it necessary to write appealing to you to contend for the faith which was once for all delivered to the saints' (Jude 1:3). The overwhelming majority of Christians would endorse the fact that one of the primary tasks of a Christian minister is to proclaim the gospel and defend the faith. Sadly, in this modern age, there are those who have written books, given lectures and made broadcasts on radio and television, which have undermined the faith as it is commonly held. Like the mistaken station porter, there are some who have pointed people in the wrong direction, leading them to go astray.

There are basic requirements for certain professional roles: any person should be reliably trained in the tasks that they undertake in their job. Ministers of the gospel and local church leaders should – by training and experience – know the gospel of God's redeeming love, and declare it in word and deed in Christian ministry with confidence and diligence. There is no doubt that Jesus Christ spoke severely about false prophets, giving a very serious warning: 'Beware of false prophets, who come to you in sheep's clothing but inwardly are ravenous wolves. You will know them by their fruits' (Matthew 7:15-16). Spiritual guides should be dependable.

Life's guides should be reliable, pointing out the right way, and that is especially true in all kinds of Christian ministry – through teaching and example – in the Church! We thank God for all the faithful men and women who have known the gospel, preached it, defended it, and shared it by their committed service. Of course, it is just possible the porter made only that one single mistake that day, but the story underlines the need for all who seek to guide, and all who follow the guidance of others, to exercise vigilance! For Christians, this means spending time in prayer and Bible study, and being ready to challenge teachings that do not seem to accord with the overall sweep of scripture as commonly interpreted.

Suggested readings: Matthew 7:11-20 and Jude 1:1-4.

MAY 19th

## OUR GOD NEVER FAILS

One fateful day, 28th January 1986, will be forever etched upon the memory of the people of the USA for, on that day, the Space Shuttle 'Challenger' exploded. Many people watched the launch and all seemed normal; then seventy-five seconds after lift-off, horrified spectators witnessed a massive explosion. The giant fireball in the sky was a powerful reminder that things can fail. This was the twenty-fifth launch and all should have been well, but there was a disastrous malfunction and precious lives were lost. This particular project was intended to be a symbol of human achievement; it had involved a massive investment of money and expertise, but it failed and seven brave astronauts perished.

We live in a world where failure is a possibility; machines large or small sometimes end up faltering. We know only too well, that people of all ages, races, and backgrounds also fail and we acknowledge it ourselves from bitter experience! How painful it is when someone we love fails to live up to our expectations of faithfulness and integrity: business relationships can be twisted and family ties in the home can be broken. Conflicts between business partners and marriage breakdowns can be extremely painful for all involved. Scripture acknowledges that even a mother's love can fail. The prophet Isaiah said: 'Can a woman forget her nursing child, or show no compassion for the child of her womb? Even these may forget, yet will I not forget you. See, I have inscribed you on the palms of my hands; your walls are continually before me' (Isaiah 49:15-16). The scriptures affirm that none of us is perfect; we are prone to failure all too easily, and often. Life as we know it includes elements of failure as, alliances and relationships fail, yet God remains faithful.

God does not fail, and will never let us down. The prophet Zephaniah bluntly stated how a city was rebellious and unbelieving, but then added: 'The Lord within her is righteous, he does no wrong; every morning he shows forth his justice, each dawn he does not fail' (Zephaniah 3:5). The solid foundation to our faith is that the God Whom we serve neither makes mistakes, nor fails. God's Word does not prove inadequate or unfruitful for His promises stand sure, His throne endures forever and His eternal love is unfailing.

When Jesus hung upon the cross, one of the taunts was, 'He trusts in God; let God deliver him now' (Matthew 27:43). The cross looked like failure, but God, in His mighty wisdom, brought light out of darkness; God's love won through and that boundless love still prevails in our lives, even though we sometimes falter.

Suggested readings: Zephaniah 3:1-5 and Romans 8:31-39.

MAY 20th

## OUR WELCOME CAN BE GOD'S INSTRUMENT

It is quite interesting to read the notices outside our churches: notices which advertise anniversary services, musical evenings, craft markets and other special events! They inevitably include the word 'Welcome'. However it is very interesting to see how this is interpreted by many of the church members! One couple recalled that on holiday they went to a church in Cornwall and, as they stepped inside the door, they were almost overwhelmed by the zeal of the church officer! A welcome can take so many forms and have varying degrees of warmth! Another couple elsewhere visited a church and sat down awaiting the commencement of morning worship only to be told that they were sitting in someone else's seat; then, a few moments after they moved places they were approached again and told they were in another person's seat so they moved yet again! The husband quietly whispered to his wife: 'The next time we move it will be out of the door'. It seems that for some, a 'welcome' is sometimes qualified by the word 'if': if you don't sit in someone's seat or if you think just as we do or if you conform to our way of doing things! The notion of a welcome can sometimes seem to include setting various conditions which must first be met, and that is not true to the spirit of the gospel.

Writing to the Christians in Rome, Paul gives some very practical teaching: 'Welcome one another, therefore, as Christ welcomed you' (Romans 15:7). We can each ponder the welcome of Christ; it is warm, loving, compassionate and accepting. Indeed, the New International Version translates this text using the word 'accept' in place of 'welcome'. It is truly a wonderful thing to be welcomed and accepted, as a true welcome naturally involves a full measure of acceptance! In the New Testament we read of numerous miracles: one of the greatest miracles – though often not included in our recollection perhaps – is that in the early Church both Jews and Gentiles worshipped together, welcoming and accepting each other. Yet, it was not all plain sailing in every fellowship, and some problems had to be ironed out so that the spread of the gospel was not impeded by intolerance or disunity.

There are lots of ways in which the gospel is shared; one of the finest instruments God can use is a loving and accepting fellowship, offering a warmth of welcome which is so vital that, when anyone enters the church door, they feel the presence of God. Our welcome should always be sincere, warm and accepting. Most of all, our welcome of others should be like the welcome we receive from Christ, always a genuine, most gracious one!

Suggested readings: Psalms 133, 134 and Romans 15:1-7.

MAY 21st

## CHRISTIAN FELLOWSHIP INVOLVES REJOICING AND WEEPING

It was a special joy for the minister to be visiting the maternity block of a hospital and see a new baby and to have the privilege of offering a prayer of thanksgiving. Ministers can readily testify that they usually receive a very warm welcome in a maternity ward and conversation is easy; the presence of newly born babies gives an air of joy and thankfulness. So, on this occasion the minister enjoyed the visit. However, his next pastoral call was to see a woman who had been tragically bereaved: one day she had been fine, but now she was in the depths of despair. Two pastoral visits, one to rejoice with a young mother, the other to grieve with someone in bereavement: such is the Christian ministry, to share in both joy and sorrow with others. Sometimes we share in words, but often simply in quiet waiting and silence.

In Romans 12, we have an ordinary person's guide to everyday practical Christianity. It is an amazing chapter! We can think of this down-to-earth verse: 'Rejoice with those who rejoice, weep with those who weep' (Romans 12:15). We should be under no illusion: this practical advice by the apostle Paul is for all Christians who want to honour and serve the Lord, not simply for ministers or others charged with pastoral care. There should be a willingness to rejoice with others in their positive relationships, in their family blessings, in their achievements, in their successes and in their celebration of particular triumphs, but also in their growth in grace. As we all acknowledge, it can be very hard sometimes to rejoice in another's success. Too many people have made important accomplishments and then found others, including their rivals or perhaps peers, even sometimes close friends, strangely silent on the matter! The apostle could be taken as implying that believers should have, as it were, a good supply of congratulation and best wishes cards!

The call to 'weep with those who weep' is a direct counsel here. Those who are open to the Spirit of God know it is possible to feel the pain of other people's sorrows and troubles; indeed, shared tears can prove to be a healing experience. Of course, personalities differ and some people may be inclined to cross the road, as it were, if they sense they are about to meet someone bereaved or facing problems. For whatever reason – perhaps because they do not know what to do or to say – some people try to avoid those who are in trouble. As we ponder the story of Jesus, we can see that He most certainly did 'Rejoice with those who rejoice, weep with those who weep'. What a wonderful divine Friend He is for us: indeed, a Friend for all seasons. So, if we are basking in the sunshine of blessing or shivering in the chill of sorrow, we can be assured the Lord is there just as He promised: 'Lo, I am with you, always . . .' (Matthews 28:20). Our task is to be there for others, by God's rich grace.

Suggested readings: Romans 12:1-15 and 2 Corinthians 1:1-7.

May 22nd

## STICKABILITY IS A CHRISTIAN VIRTUE

When, on 29th May1953, Edmund Hillary and Tenzing Norgay stood on the summit of Mount Everest, it was a moment of significant conquest. There were celebrations around the world and, in Britain, it gave added joy to the Coronation Day of Queen Elizabeth II. It was a mighty victory for sheer determination, a demonstration as it were, of utter 'stickability'. Few people knew at the time that, just before reaching the summit, they had come across an almost impossible barrier, a final approach which was as dangerous as it was daunting. However, they doggedly pressed on together and, with grim determination, reached the summit as they longed to do.

'Stickability' is a recognised virtue in so many areas: the researcher, the scientist, the inventor, the scholar, the author, the politician, the explorer and the reformer all need it. Watching the annual Oxford versus Cambridge boat race, it is so obvious that the principal quality of the rowers, beyond sheer fitness, is staying power, and so pressing on even when it hurts! The person of faith also, in a special way, needs staying power. As Elizabeth Goudge, the twentieth-century novelist, once wrote: 'The lover of God has glue in his veins'. Surely, the hallmark of a sincere and genuine faith is such endurance and perseverance.

On one occasion, Jesus told a parable about the seed falling into various places: 'As for what was sown on rocky ground, this is the one who hears the word and immediately receives it with joy; yet such a person has no root, but endures only for a while, and when trouble or persecution arises on account of the word, that person immediately falls away'. The New English Bible translates the key expression in the last phrase, 'no staying power' (Matthew 13:20-21).

How easy it is sometimes to want to give up! A new course of study, a new job, a new craft or hobby or learning a new instrument or language can all present difficult challenges, and as a result, it is tempting to feel like giving up. How many marriages would have been enduring if the couple had, like the climbers of Mount Everest, refused to surrender to the temptation to give up in the face of an obstacle!

Many well-known figures in the Bible – both women and men – had this particular quality to some degree. Yet, we see it supremely in the life of the Saviour as He humbly and obediently went the way of the cross. The gospel record puts it this way: 'He steadfastly set his face to go to Jerusalem' (Luke 9:51 AV). Jesus Christ refused to give up in spite of the fact that He knew that rejection and suffering awaited Him at Jerusalem; it was, indeed, a truly holy stubbornness. May God give us that same holy stubbornness, even as we seek to follow in the footsteps of Jesus.

Suggested readings: Matthew 13:18-23 and Luke 9:46-56.

May 23rd

## FAITH IS FOR EVERY DAY

One of the unforgettable days in the life of a missionary is the day of retirement for it often means leaving lifelong friends in an area and returning to the homeland. Such goodbyes can be terribly painful. The story is told of a missionary in Africa who, before his retirement visited his many friends, one special friend being a Christian tribal chief. This man had kept faith in spite of numerous difficulties, and offered this lovely testimony: 'Each morning at dawn, I watch the sunrise and say, "I believe in God"'.

Every Sunday, there are multitudes of people who stand in church and say the Apostles' Creed: 'I believe in God, the Father Almighty, Maker of heaven and earth'. These words: 'I believe in God' can be said in so many different ways. They can be said mechanically, carelessly, half-heartedly or with genuine warmth and enthusiasm'. Of course, we do not have to make this claim of belief simply as part of repeating the Creed, in the context of worship. Surely, for us too, a good start to each day might be to simply say: 'I believe in God'.

One of the most popular pieces of music in the Christian world is G. F. Handel's oratorio, *Messiah*: the 'Hallelujah chorus' gives a special thrill to the heart. Even those who have heard this sung (or sung it in a choir themselves) many times still find a special joy in the words. It has an enduring quality because it expresses enduring truth! It can be a deeply moving experience to hear a large choir singing these words: 'For the Lord God omnipotent reigneth!' Those six words have put hope and courage into countless hearts, and they remind us of the reason why we can affirm our belief in God.

As we think of the glory and majesty of our God who reigns supreme, we are reminded of an affirmation found in the first book of Chronicles: 'Thine, O Lord, is the greatness, and the power, and the glory, and the victory, and the majesty; for all that is in the heavens and in the earth is thine' (1 Chronicles 29:11). This is a glad and triumphant note of faith. We may readily acknowledge that life contains a 'mixed bag' of experiences for each of us; sometimes, life is hard and an uphill struggle and sometimes, we're in a glorious, joyful place. Yet, the Holy Scripture teaches us that we may go about our lives in quiet trust and confidence. As the psalmist reminds us: 'Trust in him at all times' (Psalm 62:3). Indeed, every day as people of faith, we may proclaim, 'I believe in God', and exult also, 'He shall reign forever and ever'.

Suggested readings: 1 Chronicles 29:10-19 and Psalm 62:1-12.

MAY 24th

## GOD'S SPIRIT 'WARMS THE HEART'

On 24th May 1988, there was a very special service in St Paul's Cathedral in London to celebrate the 250th anniversary of the conversion of John Wesley. It was a service attended by many distinguished guests including Her Majesty the Queen, Archbishop Runcie and Cardinal Hume, along with representatives from numerous denominations, faith traditions, and organisations. The singing was excellent and worthy of such a joyful occasion. Right at the close of the service, a group of people moved down the aisle carrying huge lighted candles and formed the shape of a heart at the West Door. The symbolism was vivid and dramatic, and it spoke volumes to people watching closely.

John Wesley's heart – as he testified – had been 'strangely warmed' and, as he testified, he personally experienced God's redeeming love through the ministry of the Holy Spirit. He wrote: 'Assurance was given me that he had taken away my sins, even mine'. Vital faith is a matter of the heart: John Wesley had, as it were, believed with his mind some years before his conversion; yet on 24th May 1738, truly for him, it became a matter of the heart. It was an experience of conversion which was to prove highly consequential because, in the providence of God, it was going to light a torch of faith which would be carried by multitudes of believers down the centuries. The Methodists, as those influenced by Wesley became known, have been widely influential and much involved in work for the Kingdom of God.

In Romans chapter 10, there are some key verses, which prove important as we ponder the experience of Wesley, as well as others: 'If you confess with your lips that Jesus is Lord and believe in your heart that God raised him from the dead, you will be saved. For one believes with the heart and so is justified, and one confesses with the mouth and so is saved' (Romans 10:9-10). The words remind us that faith is not simply a matter of accepting certain doctrines or believing 'in our heads', but true Christian experience is also a matter of the heart.

In the Letter to the Ephesians chapter 3 there is a beautiful prayer and it includes these words: '. . . that Christ may dwell in your hearts by faith' (v17). These are wonderful words to pray humbly in respect of fellow believers, for when Christ does really enter a human heart, as Wesley and so many others have testified, it is 'strangely warmed' and deeply blessed. God can use a person who has a living faith, which can readily speak of such a vital experience of the real presence of the Lord! Our faith is that God's Spirit warms the heart!

Suggested readings: Romans 10:8-17 and Ephesians 3:14-21.

MAY 25th

## HUMBLE BEGINNINGS CAN BE USED BY GOD

The House of Commons in Westminster is made up of a rich variety of men and women. Some have come from a privileged background of wealth, good education and friends in high places. Others come from a humble background and have won respect by their determination to succeed in overcoming all obstacles, and to serve their beloved country. One such member who received recognition from all political parties was George Thomas.

Thomas came from a humble home, his father then working as a coalminer. In common with lots of families in the Rhondda Valley, his family knew the struggle to live on a low income. So George developed a passionate desire to do something about conditions of poverty: he became a Member of Parliament and served with diligence, earning the respect of multitudes of people. Then came the great day when he was elected Speaker of the House of Commons. There is a verse in the Book of Job which seems to fit his life admirably: 'Though your beginnings were humble, your end will be great' (Job 8:7 NEB).

When we look at history, we see how often people from humble backgrounds have become great leaders and statesmen or women. The prime example in American history is, arguably, Abraham Lincoln who grew up in very humble circumstances, and then later rose to prominence and led the country during a very difficult period. In Britain, we might think of the life of John Bunyan who also had limited opportunities to gain an education when he was brought up in the small village of Elstow. Yet, later in the seventeenth century, he became a champion of the faith, and now has a truly honoured place in Christian history.

In the New Testament writings we have this splendid verse on the subject: 'God chose what is foolish in the world to shame the wise, God chose what is weak in the world to shame the strong, God chose what is low and despised in the world, even things that are not, to bring to nothing things that are, so that no human being might boast in the presence of God' (1 Corinthians 1:27-29). Of course, we should note the initiative of divine grace here, noting the repeated words: 'God chose'.

Jesus Christ was nurtured in the home at Nazareth; between them, Mary and Joseph had the tremendous responsibility of caring for Him. They belonged to the world's poor and life did not offer much comfort; however, they were both rich in faith and the grace of God was upon them. They humbly fulfilled their God-given task. Jesus of Nazareth was destined not only to be the greatest figure in world history, but the Saviour of the world: yet, this life began in such humility.

Suggested readings: Job 8:1-10 and 1 Corinthians 1:26-31.

May 26th

## CHRIST'S LOVE IS BEYOND CALCULATION

John's gospel chapter 13 recounts the remarkable story of Jesus Christ washing the feet of the disciples. It is a fascinating story and it has dimensions which are staggering: the perfect Saviour humbly ministering to imperfect disciples. The account portrays the Son of God – the One who was Prophet, Priest and King – offering a message of love as he revealed the Father's love, in His own life. This He did specifically, in stooping to do such a menial task of foot-washing.

The opening verse of the story is a marker for what follows: 'Now before the feast of the Passover, when Jesus knew that his hour had come to depart out of this world to the Father, having loved his own who were in the world, he loved them to the end' (John 13:1). Scholars, preachers and various church leaders, along with countless ordinary Christians have studied this splendid chapter. It has been used on many occasions as a significant study (especially in Lent) and there are many layers of truth to be discerned. The chapter speaks of sincerity, obedience, loyalty, friendship, humility and service with an emphasis above all, on love. So the New International Version translates the verse: 'He showed them the full extent of his love'.

A minister tells how he heard Bishop John Moorman preach at a cathedral service during Passion Week, an unforgettable experience for him: 'After twenty-five years, I can still hear that quiet but distinct voice, telling of how Jesus loved his disciples "to the end", "to the uttermost" spelling out that word deliberately'. It is surely our faith: Christ, the Saviour of the world, loved to the uttermost. No human mind can ever calculate the height, length, breadth and depth of that marvellous love, for He loved imperfect people, and that means all of us as sinners. Indeed, the voice of His critics is overheard in the gospel narratives: 'This man receives sinners and eats with them' (Luke 15:2). Thank God that such a criticism of Jesus was absolutely true! If Jesus Christ, the Son of God, showed His love in the washing of the disciples' feet, how much more did He reveal it on the cross, and in that divine love we find our assurance of God's acceptance.

In the Roman Empire, a cross was a symbol of shame and retribution for wrongdoing. Yet, two thousand years ago, the Saviour of the world transformed the cross on which He hung, with its unspeakable cruelty, to be a sign for something much deeper and richer. Thus, Calvary came to be affirmed as a place of glory, namely, ultimate love in self-sacrifice, that true loving 'to the uttermost'.

Suggested readings: John 13:1-15 and Luke 23:32-47.

MAY 27th

## TREASURES CAN BE LOST AND FOUND

Photographs and videos are an important feature at a modern wedding. It is a good and happy thing to have a permanent reminder of the great day! On one occasion in Suffolk, the photographer took many photos at the wedding of a young couple. Unfortunately, there was a gremlin, as it were, in the camera and all the photos were spoilt. The precious photographs were lost forever. The couple were deeply shocked and disappointed and felt that, in a sense, they had lost a treasure.

There are many treasures we can value in life: silver and gold, precious photographs, irreplaceable jewellery, priceless documents or special artwork. Yet, there is another treasure which we are sometimes in danger of losing: the confidence of our faith in the Lord. In the New Testament, much note is taken of the powerful ministry of John the Baptist, and four words seem to epitomise his ministry: he was dynamic, courageous, sincere and confident. His confidence is shown in this particular word to his critics: 'God is able from these stones to raise up children to Abraham' (Matthew 3:9). How confident he was in the power of God and his belief that Jesus was, indeed, the promised Messiah. It must have been difficult for him to remain confident, however, when he was arrested and put in prison. As the story is told, John sent word to Jesus by his disciples and enquired: 'Are you he who is to come, or shall we look for another?' (Matthew 11:2-3). Jesus' reply to John was firm and reassuring, though we may sympathise with John's plight and his questioning.

Many Christians who have faced difficult circumstances in life have had moments when their trust wavered. We think of the wistful words of the hymn by William Cowper: 'Where is the blessedness I knew when first I saw the Lord? Where is the soul-refreshing view of Jesus and His Word'. We might now ask ourselves, if events of life have ever shaken our confidence in the Lord. A question to pose to ourselves might be: 'Are we less sure of our faith now than some months or years ago?' The photos of that wedding could never be replaced; they were lost forever and the young couple had to come to terms with the sad fact. However, today we remind ourselves that hope and confidence in Christ can be restored; they need not be lost forever. Countless believers can testify that God, in His great mercy, restores men and women who seek, as Cowper put it, in that same hymn, 'a closer walk with God.' The promises of God are treasures we can know forever.

Suggested readings: Matthew 11:2-15 and John 21:9-19.

MAY 28th

## CHILDREN CAN HAVE GENUINE FAITH

A small team of zealous evangelists held a children's mission in a small village in Britain; their enthusiasm could not be faulted but their wisdom was questioned. After the campaign, a Sunday school teacher asked a young child, 'What did you learn?' Without blinking an eyelid, the little child replied: 'About hell'. That story makes us shudder, but it brings into focus the potential dangers in inappropriately seeking to foster faith in children, by using rather dubious methods and pushing for conversions! However, it can be acknowledged that there is a real need to communicate faith to children, but with the right methods and suitable subjects.

At the heart of the Old Testament, there is a specific command that children should be taught the faith: 'And these words which I command you this day shall be upon your heart; and you shall teach them diligently to your children' (Deuteronomy 6:6-7). It was the duty of successive generations of the Jewish people to pass on the faith: this was to be done by telling the ancient stories, and giving clear teaching as well as by example and loving encouragement. There is a lovely verse in the Psalms about young faith: 'For you, O Lord, are my hope, my trust, O Lord, from my youth' (Psalm 71:5). Indeed, faith can be nurtured in young hearts! Today, we praise God for the multitudes of people (many of whom are spiritual leaders and effective workers in church life), who can truthfully testify that as children they made their initial response to God's call.

Genuine faith is like an acorn that, when it is first sown, is so small, but can grow as a tree to incredible dimensions. In Luke's gospel, there is a special story about the childhood of Jesus: He was taken to the temple at Jerusalem. We have every reason to believe that this experience was one of the key moments in the early life of Jesus; no doubt it deepened His own stirrings of the mind and heart in growing up to be the obedient Son of God. Luke concludes the story with these words: 'And Jesus increased in wisdom and in years and in divine and human favour' (Luke 2:52).

Seeds of faith need to be sown in a child's heart by wise Christian parents, Sunday School teachers and leaders in mission among children and youth, through gentle instruction and loving encouragement. All who have this responsibility for the upbringing of children, are to fulfil their calling as directed: 'Instruct their children that the next generation might understand, that children yet unborn might rise and tell their children after them to put their confidence in God' (Psalm 78:6 Moffatt). That task is still the privilege and, indeed, the joy of all those who have the opportunity to nurture the young in faith; it is a holy duty to be undertaken gladly and wisely.

Suggested readings: Deuteronomy 6:1-12 and Psalm 78:1-8.

MAY 29th

## SOME MESSAGES ARE DEMONSTRATED

Jesus had the ability to speak profound truth about God to ordinary men and women. In Mark's gospel we read that 'the common people heard him gladly' (Mark 12:37 AV). His parables were listened to very attentively. He powerfully combined deep truth with eloquent simplicity, often with colourful stories drawn from everyday life. We can think how widely known are two teachings: the Parable of the Prodigal Son and the Parable of the Good Samaritan!

Many preachers and teachers, who proclaim the teachings of Jesus also seem to have a gift at skilled interpretation so they are able to speak plainly the profound truth of God's love for all people. Unfortunately, there are others who are skilled interpreters, but not dynamic preachers. Such was the case of Alistair McLemon. It is said that he had a brilliant mind and could think deeply about God and His Kingdom; yet, while he was devout and lovable, he was rather a dull preacher. It appears he was less able than some to put his message across in simple, winsome terms, though one day he did speak simply, but not in a pulpit.

The story is told that he was on a ship that was torpedoed in the Mediterranean, a dramatic and traumatic experience! An officer spoke to the crew and said that the lifeboat they were in was in grave danger of capsizing because it was overcrowded and, if that happened, they would all be lost at sea. At that point, Alistair quietly slipped overboard into the waters: he gave his life so that others could live. This was his finest hour, indeed, his greatest sermon! This good Christian man will be remembered for his noble deed and his self-sacrificing love, as his message was not spoken, but practically demonstrated. His selfless act of love was a demonstration of the stirring words of Jesus Christ: 'No one has greater love, than this, to lay down one's life for one's friends' (John 15:13). In a sense, he preached with his death as well as his life and, in so doing, he bore faithful witness to his Saviour, Whose ministry and sacrifice inspired his own.

Generation after generation of people have been challenged by the total self-sacrifice of the Blessed Saviour on the cross. The apostle Paul puts it succinctly when he refers to Jesus Christ: '. . . who loved me and gave himself for me' (Galatians 2:20). The cross has deeply exercised the minds of philosophers and theologians. Even so, the full truth is impossible to tell, but one thing is sure: Jesus gave Himself for others, dying so that all might come to live, and He now ever lives to bless us.

Suggested readings: John 15:12-14 and Romans 5:1-11.

MAY 30th

## WE MUST REMEMBER THE EMERGENCY SUPPLIES

Driving a car on a long journey can bring a number of hazards, whether a puncture, overheating of the engine, running out of fuel, mechanical failure or the breaking of a windscreen, to name but a few of the more common problems! There is wisdom in having a 'do-it-yourself' attitude to keeping the vehicle serviceable, and being prepared to cope with any such incidents should they occur.

Simon had been away in connection with his daily work, and it had proved to be a successful venture. As he calmly drove home alone on the Monday, he experienced the warm-glow of a weekend well spent. Then, suddenly, without any warning at all, the windscreen violently shattered into hundreds of pieces! Shocked and perturbed, he pulled into a lay-by and disposed of the majority of the glass, and then began the cold journey home: driving without a windscreen is a chilling experience! He lowered the speed, but the cold still came in with a numbing effect. On arrival, his wife made him a steaming hot cup of tea. Then, having heard the sorry tale, she turned and asked a simple question: 'Why didn't you use the emergency screen you always carry in the back of your car?' He was stunned and felt rather foolish since, for several years, he had carried the emergency screen in the rear of his car; yet, when he needed it, he had forgotten all about it. In the shock and drama of the moment, he had forgotten his supplies and spares in the boot!

Simon's experience is also very generally true in life itself; so easily, often in an emergency, we forget to stop and think about the resources available! So, in our difficult moments in life, when we are unsure or have experienced some less than welcome surprise, perhaps we need to have the psalmist's attitude: 'I will remember the deeds of the Lord; yes, I will remember your miracles of long ago. I will meditate on all your works and consider all your mighty deeds' (Psalm 77:11-12 NIV). The psalmist also urges: 'Wait for the Lord; be strong, and let your heart take courage; yea, wait for the Lord' (Psalm 27:14).

How often we tend to think that the best policy in a crisis is to do something; we rush 'hither and thither' and suppose we are solving the problem. It is very true that there are situations where it is best to sit still and think. There is a verse that, translated in the Authorised Version of the scriptures, says: 'Their strength is to sit still' (Isaiah 30:7 AV). Sometimes the best plan, may be first of all, to 'sit still', before seeking to determine the best way to proceed. Most of all, as we wait, we can be sure that God will provide us with the inner resources – both the strength and the courage – that we need to face even the most difficult situations in life.

Suggested readings: Psalm 27:1-14 and Philippians 4:19-20.

MAY 31st

## CONCERNING THE BREVITY OF LIFE

When people in Britain reach the age of one hundred years they receive special greetings from Her Majesty the Queen. Those who attain this important landmark are sometimes asked various questions by interviewers: 'What is the secret of your longevity?' or 'What is your philosophy of life?' Some of those who are questioned will often comment on the brevity of life, claiming: 'The older you get the quicker time passes'. Long before scientists discovered some of the secrets of the sun, moon and stars, the psalmist confessed awareness of the human span of life: 'Surely everyone stands as a mere breath' (Psalm 39:5). Realizing how quickly one's days pass, the psalmist also prayed: 'Lord, let me know my end, and what is the measure of my days; let me know how fleeting my life is' (Psalm 39:4). The psalmist, it seems, was reflecting not only on how quickly time sails by, as it were, but also wanting to make sure that life was lived well and to the full.

As we ponder 'the measure of our days', perhaps we should reflect on how every day of life is, in a sense, special. We may think of a day, as yet another ordinary day. However, even amid the mundane and routine activities of life, we may discover extraordinary treasures. In a lovely parish church in Staffordshire, the Church of the Good Shepherd, Rugeley, there is an unusual feature: an altar which incorporates a two hundred-weight (224 lbs) slab of coal! It is obviously a very sacred place of worship and yet, here we find something very ordinary: a slab of coal. It is a reminder of the ordinary things of life which we may sometimes take for granted: skill and labour, light and heat, business and industry. It also stands as a reminder of the 'treasures of darkness' (Isaiah 45:3). Deep in the earth, there are hidden treasures of gold and silver, oil and coal, minerals and diamonds as well as other precious stones.

Whatever, our age, as we each reflect on our own experience, we know there have been lots of very ordinary days but, in God's providence, each day also has a kind of sacredness to it. The psalmist seemed to be acutely aware of God's presence with him day by day, as he offered this affirmation: 'And now, Lord, for what do I wait? My hope is in thee' (Psalm 39:7). For us, too, each day is precious and it is a gift which will not be offered again. So let us make the most of every new day, ready to discover the sacred treasures in the ordinary encounters of daily life.

Suggested readings: Psalm 39:1-12 and James 4:13-15.

# June

O Thou who camest from above
The pure, celestial fire to impart,
Kindle a flame of sacred love
On the mean altar of my heart.

There let it for Thy glory burn,
With inextinguishable blaze;
And, trembling, to its source return
In humble love and fervent praise.

Jesus, confirm my heart's desire
To work and speak and think for Thee;
Still let me guard the holy fire,
And still stir up Thy gift in me.

Ready for all thy perfect will,
My acts of faith and love repeat,
Till death Thine endless mercies seal,
And make the sacrifice complete.

Charles Wesley (1707-88)

O Thou who art the light of the minds that know thee,
   the life of the souls that love thee:
   and the strength of the wills that serve thee:
Help us so to know thee that we may truly love thee,
   so to love thee that we may fully serve thee,
   whom to serve is perfect freedom;
   through Jesus Christ our Lord.

After St Augustine (353-430), Bishop of Hippo

JUNE 1st

## GOD LOVES IMPERFECT PEOPLE

She was terribly upset, as the finished job just would not do! During the week her house had been double-glazed and the problem was with the large window in the lounge. 'Look', she said, 'Can't you see it?' The friend peered and saw one tiny speck on the inside of the glass, though it was barely visible. For her, it just would not do! The next week, the men had to come back and take out this enormous window and remove the speck. Here was a seemingly over-fussy person in a world where millions were undernourished, thousands were homeless, countless numbers deprived and multitudes unemployed, concerning herself about an almost invisible speck! To meet this person at a shop or a library, one would not have known that she was a perfectionist, and rather obsessive over even minor things. Yet, if a perfectionist is a member of a congregation, issues are raised such as: the flowers on the communion table will not be quite right, the organist will play the hymns a little too slow or too fast, the new banner in the church will be slightly out of line with the colour scheme and, of course, the minister's attire could do with some improvement!

Thankfully, God loves imperfect people. The wonder of divine mercy is that God is patient, loving and forgiving for the Lord receives those who have been marked by shortfalls in life, as the scriptures affirm: 'But God shows his love for us that while we were yet sinners Christ died for us' (Romans 5:8). We are grateful that we do not have to be perfect before God accepts us; if God only accepted and used perfect people, none of us would ever qualify! So the apostle Paul wrote these beautiful and comforting words: 'For by grace you have been saved through faith, and this is not your own doing; it is the gift of God – not the result of works, so that no one may boast' (Ephesians 2:8-9).

J.B. Phillips, the British Bible translator, scholar, author and minister told how he was shaped by the influence of his father, who was a perfectionist. Phillips claimed that, very early in his life, the seed was sown in his mind that success meant being loved, but failure meant being 'outside the pale'. Phillips later discovered that this thought was being transferred to his relationship with God, and he sought professional treatment from a psychiatrist to help him. In fact, perfectionism cast a long shadow over much of Phillips' life and, at times, over his spiritual life, too. God loves imperfect people; that little statement sounds shocking, but it is the heart of the gospel! We can think of all the characters described in the Bible who were seen very clearly to be imperfect, but God took them each just as they were and, in His mercy, used them to His glory; so we can take heart, too!

Suggested readings: Psalm 5:7-8 and Ephesians 2:1-10.

JUNE 2nd

## WORDS HAVE A GREAT POTENTIAL

Memories can stir up a whole variety of deep feelings: anger, joy, remorse, satisfaction, fear, hope and more besides. There are lots of people who carry hidden scars: they recall bitter experiences, such as cutting words spoken to them as children. There is the schoolboy who remembers a teacher humiliating him in front of a class, a young girl who shockingly overheard her parents' conversation with a neighbour, 'We really wanted a boy'. Many counsellors can testify that they have encountered grown adults – sometimes in middle-aged or even older years – carrying sad memories of words spoken to them as children. Words can very painfully cut and deeply hurt!

Thank God it works the other way, too. Sometimes a young child hears a few words which remain as a precious memory for life. Yvonne Stevenson, the daughter of a vicar, recalled a time when she was very naughty and felt too ashamed to tell her mother. She claimed that her mother bent down and put her arm around her and said: 'It doesn't matter what you've done, I shall love you just the same'. This incident left a mark – a very good mark – on her mind and heart; she had experienced unconditional love. Years later, at a very traumatic period in her life, those words came back to her with tremendous force. The childhood memory had lived on and had been 'food and drink to her', as it were; to put it another way, those words of her mother had been like a living seed which had been planted deep within her.

As we consider the ministry of Jesus, we see that He recognised that words are like seeds. So, in the Parable of the Sower, the Master interpreted it Himself: 'Now the parable is this: The seed is the word of God' (Luke 8:11). Jesus told how some seed fell on the hard path, some on the rocky ground, some among thorns but some fell in good soil; while some seed on other ground proved in the end to be unfruitful, the seed sown in the good soil yielded an abundant harvest. That is a truth about the impact of God's Word. Yet, we know that our words also count.

How careful parents should be about how they speak to their children; how important it is to use positive, warm, and encouraging words. How deadly and damaging negative words can be! We must sow the good seed of God's Word in all our endeavours for the Kingdom. The work of the parent, teacher, the Sunday school teacher, or other Christian worker, is very important; of course, there may not be an instant harvest. Yet, our labours in sowing the seed may well bear fruit in later years; in that conviction of such a hope in God, we continue to serve the Lord day by day.

Suggested readings: Luke 1:5-15 and Ephesians 6:1-4.

JUNE 3rd

## MANY PEOPLE EXPERIENCE THE RESIDENT ATHEIST

Mr and Mrs Williams supplemented their income by taking in lodgers. Over a period of twenty years, they gave hospitality to many people and had some interesting experiences. One summer, they welcomed a middle-aged man to their home who turned out to be an atheist; he was friendly and co-operative, but he asked awkward questions. The Williams's were regular worshippers at the local parish church and were quite set in their ways and beliefs. They soon discovered that their new lodger asked, 'Why do you do this? Why do you do that?' It was a bit tiresome at times and their faith was challenged, but strangely, over time it came to be strengthened.

We can reflect on the fact that, in one sense, lots of people have such a lodger in the heart, as a sort of 'resident atheist'. How often people have been on a smooth path and received numerous blessings, so that they can say with the psalmist: 'The lines have fallen for me in pleasant places; yea, I have a goodly heritage' (Psalm 16:6). Then, quite suddenly, events take a dramatic turn: an accident or injury, a serious illness, a business loss, a bereavement or some other very difficult experience. From the deep recesses of the heart, the resident atheist asks some pointed and awkward questions: 'Why did this happen?' 'How come God allowed that?' Such questions start to arise, and even sincere Christians may feel challenged in believing unquestioningly just the same as they had done.

There are numerous Christian writers who say that a moment of crisis can prove to be a moment of growth, bringing an enlargement of faith. The psalmist endorses this: 'I was hard pressed, and thou didst set me at large' (Psalm 4:1 NEB). So often that is the case, but it is also true that some people discover that, deep down in their hearts, there is a form of atheism and this can be a most painful discovery. Dr. William Sangster used to tell of a man who was considered to be a 'pillar' of the church who went into hospital and showed a very different side to his nature, so much so that Sangster was shocked by the man's attitude and response to his trouble.

The story of the lodger speaks of the resident atheist sometimes within us, and the awkward questions raised; countless people in the hour of trauma and crisis, have truly felt the reality of it. The Bible includes many prayers (especially in the Book of Psalms), prayers which cover a rich variety of experiences. Today, we recall a small prayer in the New Testament which has been so helpful to generations of believers: 'Lord, I believe; help thou mine unbelief' (Mark 9:24). Actually, the New International Version gives a most helpful rendering: 'I do believe; help me overcome my unbelief'. This honest plea gives us a vital clue to real prayer from the heart.

Suggested readings: Mark 9:14-29 and 2 Peter 3:17-18.

JUNE 4th

## WE NEED COURAGE TO CHANGE OUR VOTE

One of the most important events in the life of the apostle Paul was the day he stood before King Agrippa and made his defence (Acts 26). In this chapter, we hear Paul's remarkable account of his conversion on the road to Damascus. It is worth noting that Paul spoke openly of his previous life without Christ: prior to his conversion, he had resolutely persecuted Christians. He confessed: 'I not only shut up many of the saints in prison, by authority from the chief priests, but when they were put to death I cast my vote against them. And I punished them often in all the synagogues and tried to make them blaspheme; and in raging fury against them, I persecuted them even to foreign cities' (Acts 26:10-12). He spoke of his pre-conversion days quite openly: 'I cast my vote against them'. Then, after his dynamic experience on the Damascus road, he changed his vote and gave a wholehearted vote for Jesus Christ and His Church. Paul had the courage, by the grace of God, to change his vote.

When well-known politicians appear to have changed their vote by leaving one political party and joining another, they are looked on with suspicion, criticism, and anger. Similarly, when Paul changed his vote from being against Christ to being for Christ, some were very angry indeed, as the record put it: 'The Jews plotted to kill him' (Acts 9:23). The world often despises the persons who change their vote, and that is why it is so hard and takes fortitude. Courage has many different faces such as the courage of the mountaineer, the bomb disposal expert, the lifeboat crew, the reformer, the missionary or simply the family member who devotedly cares for an elderly parent. Yet, in everyday life there is also the courage of one's convictions to change one's mind and one's vote! It needs courage to leave the world's side and join with Christ in serving the Kingdom of God; that is our calling to discipleship.

In the 1980s, when Dr. Billy Graham came to England for an evangelistic mission in London, a large number of people made a step forward and accepted Jesus Christ as their personal Saviour. These converts came from a variety of backgrounds, trades and professions, as they changed their vote, but many found it a costly business; they went home and then back to work to discover that some were very ready to express hostility to this newfound faith. Their change of vote was subjected to severe criticism or ridicule! Paul is noted for his stand for Christ: he displayed genuine courage in his service for the Kingdom of God. One of the finest ways that he displayed courage was when he first changed his vote for Jesus Christ. When we openly declare our intention to follow Jesus Christ we, too, will need the Lord's help to grant us courage, as our lives will inevitably be changed, and not everyone will approve of it. We thank God that, just as Christ promised, the Spirit comes to our aid.

Suggested readings: Luke 5:27-32 and Acts 26:9-19.

JUNE 5th

## THERE ARE BLESSINGS AT LOW TIDE

For a number of years the idea of a bridge over the River Orwell near Ipswich, in Suffolk, was discussed by the various authorities. It would be an important link with the road to Felixstowe docks and would relieve the traffic congestion in the area. It seemed a pipe dream, but on 17th December 1982, the people of Ipswich and the surrounding area rejoiced that a new bridge was officially opened; the dream had come true! It is a magnificent bridge so designed that, in spite of its length and size, it has a gentle curve in it: this massive structure has considerable aesthetic qualities and blends into the beautiful countryside of the area along the tidal estuary, a scenic site. Local people are justifiably proud of the Orwell Bridge and some even take their visitors to see the lovely views from it, especially the view at sunset!

The River Orwell is a tidal river and this governs the flow of ships into the docks with the time of the tide being vital; from the bridge, there are two distinct views, one when the tide is out, and quite a different view when the tide is in. When the tide is out, there are 'acres of mud' but this attracts thousands upon thousands of seagulls and other birds, as the incoming tide always brings new food for them. What a parable of life: how often, when the tide is out and things seem to be tiresome and difficult, men and women find, sometimes to their surprise and amazement, new 'food' which brings spiritual sustenance. Many can testify to this reality in life.

In Psalm 40 we have the story of the psalmist who experienced low tide: the tide was truly out and the problem was clearly voiced: '...for evils have encompassed me without number; my iniquities have overtaken me, till I cannot see; they are more than the hairs of my head; my heart fails me' (Psalm 40:12). A very low tide indeed! However, the psalmist finds, like many before, that when the tide is out there is spiritual food, and this truth is expressed in a verse of great honesty and beauty: 'As for me, I am poor and needy: but the Lord takes thought for me. Thou art my help and my deliverer; do not tarry, O my God' (Psalm 40:17). The psalmist, whatever the actual circumstance, had found spiritual sustenance at low tide. Actually, the Good News Bible adds an extra dimension in its translation of this important verse: '. . . but you have not forgotten me' (Psalm 40:27 GNB).

There are times when the tide is out and we see the desolate 'acres of mud' and we might feel depressed and fearful: it is at such times we need to remember that God does not forget us. There are blessings both when the tide is in, and when it is out! Our faith means we can know God very near at all times, and thus we find strength and hope for each new day, whatever the situation we face.

Suggested readings: Psalm 40:1-27 and James 5:7-11.

JUNE 6th

## CHRIST BRINGS ENRICHMENT OF LIFE

Often meeting another human being positively enriches a person's life. A young student goes to college and meets a tutor who has a real enthusiasm for a subject, or a young man with a reputation for aimlessness, meets a young woman who loves him and changes his attitude, or a parishioner who has lost direction meets a minister who gives encouragement and hope. One sensitive individual can bring radical changes into the life of another; care and friendship can be so transformative!

In the opening verses of 1 Corinthians chapter 1, Paul is in a thankful mood: 'I am always thanking God for you. I thank him for his grace given to you in Christ Jesus. I thank him for all the enrichment that has come to you in Christ' (1 Corinthians 1:3-5 NEB). We take special note of that record: '. . . all the enrichment that has come to you in Christ'. Paul affirms that Jesus Christ is surely the true 'enricher of life'. Paul had experienced this for himself: his life had been radically transformed and enriched by the Saviour of the world. So he could say: 'For me to live is Christ, and to die is gain' (Philippians 1:21). He knew the remarkable difference in himself.

In Luke's gospel there is a verse which gives us a timely reminder. Jesus said: 'The good person out of the good treasure of the heart produces good' (Luke 6:45). Actually, it is possible for us to look at that saying as an accurate piece of autobiography! How true it is that Jesus had – stored in His heart – a treasury of good things. He enriched the lives of so many different people, and He still does so. Many people of faith can testify to the reality of a conversion experience, and the discovery of the enrichment which Jesus Christ brings.

How sad it is that some have spoken of the Saviour as One who subtracts from life, as though He impoverishes human life! We think of the great claim made by Jesus Christ: 'I came that they may have life, and have it abundantly' (John 10:10). In the days of Christ's ministry, there were plenty of people living very impoverished lives suffering, as it were, from spiritual malnutrition. The coming of Jesus brought enrichment and new life. We may recall how He can enrich so many areas of life: our friendships, our relationships, our family life and our community life. He is just as much today the divine enricher for the world. Peter was a tough fisherman, very used to the hardships common to his trade; yet, after he met Jesus Christ and accepted Him as his Saviour, he testified with great feeling: 'Unto you therefore which believe he is precious' (2 Peter 2:7 AV). That was the testimony of those to whom he wrote, as it can be ours also. Millions of believers today can say 'Amen' to that!

Suggested readings: 1 Corinthians 1:1-9 and Luke 6:39-45.

JUNE 7th

## LISTENING TO JESUS CHRIST IS ESSENTIAL

Bible students readily acknowledge that the gospel records show that Jesus had an inner circle of disciples among the Twelve: Peter James and John. These three shared in unique experiences of the Lord. One of their most awesome experiences was to witness the Transfiguration of Jesus Christ: 'Jesus took with him Peter and James and John his brother, and led them up a high mountain apart. And he was transfigured before them, and his face shone like the sun, and his garments became white as light' (Matthew 17:1-2). To see their Master transfigured was a profound experience and, after seeing and hearing such wonderful things, the record narrates their response: 'They fell on their faces, and were filled with awe' (Matthew 17:6).

How often, in the study of the Transfiguration, people stress what was seen, but we ought to recall also what was heard! We read this amazing account: 'A bright cloud overshadowed them, and a voice from the cloud said: "This is my beloved son, with whom I am well pleased; listen to him"'(Matthew 17:5). Surely this verse takes us to the very heart of the story: the disciples (especially the inner circle) must listen to Him. Jesus Christ is very special, beheld as One 'full of grace and truth' so the fourth gospel affirms: He is indeed, unique, the 'only-begotten' Son of God, the Saviour of the world. The thrust of the gospel is that followers must listen to Him!

It is possible to be in a remote place and discover everything to be still and quiet; for example, at a beauty spot in Cornwall, when there is a stillness which is healing and inspiring. However, if one had a reasonably good radio, it would be possible, of course, in that very quiet, serene place to pick up voices and music from elsewhere in Britain, Europe or, indeed, the wider world. The air is full of voices! In a real sense, that is a parable of life itself as we are bombarded by voices and influences; daily we are told what to eat and drink, what to wear or carry, where to shop or buy, as well as how to plan or where to go. Yet, in the midst of so many things clamouring for our attention, if we are attentive, early in the morning, before the main rush of the city or town centre traffic, it is possible to hear all around us the song of the birds, even in the urban landscape. Just so, we should attend to Christ as we go through life.

The story of the Transfiguration of Jesus includes the vital instruction that we listen to Him. How important it is that Christians should fence off time daily to read the Holy Scripture and quietly listen to Jesus Christ. The best spiritual guides from mainstream Christianity stress again and again the absolute necessity to listen. The response which is pleasing to God is always an attentiveness to the Lord's voice that comes to us in many ways, as Samuel found: 'Speak, for your servant is listening' (1 Samuel 3:10). Listening is so very important: above all listening to the Lord Jesus.

Suggested readings: 1 Samuel 3:1-10 and Matthew 17:1-8.

JUNE 8th

## THE FAITH OF OTHERS IS A BLESSING

In the gospels we have a lovely story of Jesus staying at a house in Capernaum: 'And many were gathered together, so that there was no longer room for them, not even about the door' (Mark 2:2). This made it very difficult for four people who desired to bring a paralysed friend to Jesus. When they just could not get near to the Master their frustration provoked a bold plan! They decided to make an opening in the roof, and then lower their friend down into the presence of Jesus. At this point in the narrative, we read a very beautiful verse: 'And when Jesus saw their faith, he said to the paralytic, "My son, your sins are forgiven"'. The significant two words in that verse are 'their faith': Jesus honoured the faith of the four friends.

At one period in its history, the Metropolitan Tabernacle, London, had a minister by the name of A.T. Pierson. He was a good and faithful minister, loved by many Christians. However, he had one quaint fault in that, whenever he stood up to preach his sermon, he would announce his text, saying: 'This is a most remarkable text'. Of course, to him at that given moment, it was true: yet, the text could come from anywhere in the Bible and it would still receive just the same accolade! We can surely say, without any exaggeration at all, that this verse in Mark's gospel about Jesus seeing 'their faith' is truly most remarkable, for it refers to a significant point, namely, genuine faith which is shared.

Since the Reformation in the sixteenth century, in Christian circles, there has been stress on personal faith, and this is both scriptural and right. It is clearly expressed in John's gospel: 'But to all who received him, who believed in his name, he gave power to become children of God' (John 1:12). Personal faith is vital and warmly encouraged! However, this little verse in Mark's gospel speaks about 'their faith', meaning it included that of the four friends who, with great determination, carried the paralytic to Jesus. It preserves an important truth: the faith of others can be a blessing to us. This lovely verse is like a small window, through which we can see further vistas of God's love and grace. Personal faith matters, but it is always something we share with other believers.

In the Epistle of James we read: 'The prayer of the righteous is powerful and effective' (James 5:16). We recall the prayer and faith of parents, Christian workers, friends, ministers, counsellors and so on. A person who has been taken into hospital to have a serious operation is often heard to testify: 'I felt carried along by the prayers of others'. The four men truly carried the paralytic along in more ways than one! That is a vivid portrait of prayer for, and support given to, another in need.

Suggested readings: Mark 2:1-12 and James 5:13-20.

JUNE 9th

## CHRISTIANS MUST PRESS ON TOGETHER

In the Book of Ecclesiastes there are some very old wise sayings that are still relevant in this modern age. One example is this comment: 'If you wait until the wind and the weather are just right, you will never sow anything and never harvest anything (Ecclesiastes 11:4 GNB). The gardener and the farmer are fully aware that they must press on with their work, even when the conditions are very unfavourable. This is true of life in many different areas: the fisherman works in dreadful conditions, the Olympic runner races even when not feeling perfectly fit and well, the author plods on at times when there seems to be no inspiration, and the minister of the gospel sometimes takes services when there might be little motivation on a human level. On one occasion, the evangelist Dr. Billy Graham even preached at Wembley Stadium, in London, amid torrential rain! One of the facts of life is that people have to work in less than ideal conditions because, if they waited for them to be perfect, little would be done.

When Dr. Albert Schweitzer served in Africa, working in the hospital at Lambaréné, he performed many operations in conditions which simply appalled some people. He forged ahead, in spite of the criticisms, with his riposte to the critics being quite blunt: 'It is better to have half a cake than none at all'. Of course, he would have loved to have worked in far better conditions and have all the latest equipment, but that was not financially possible. So, he pressed on tirelessly, ably serving the community and bringing health and healing to many sick people; he didn't wait, as it were, until the wind and the weather were just right!

The glory of the New Testament is that the Saviour of the world (the sinless Son of God) called the Twelve to work with Him, along with others among His disciples. They were all imperfect, sometimes slow to understand or foolish, or even insensitive, and occasionally quite disloyal, but He worked with them. There is an ironic logic here: Jesus Christ was willing to work with imperfect people, under imperfect conditions, so why would we think of suggesting otherwise? We have to face the fact that all human beings are flawed and make mistakes, including ourselves, and so we have to learn to work alongside others, who will no doubt notice our imperfections, too! The basis for a realistic fellowship is to sow the seed and do our work for God trusting that, in spite of human frailties, the Lord can use men and women even when the wind and weather are not just right! We praise God for His patience and mercy towards us, and find our confidence in His grace.

Suggested readings: Ecclesiastes 11:1-6 and Mark 8:27-33.

JUNE 10th

## CONCERNING THE THREE-FOLD BLESSING

There are lots of preachers who still like to have three points to their sermons. It is an old method very much loved by Charles Haddon Spurgeon and other evangelical preachers, and it has often proved helpful to both the preacher and the hearers. Many years before Jesus Christ was born in Bethlehem, the psalmist spoke of three wonderful blessings in relationship with God and they still hold good for us now. 'Happy are those who live in your house' (Psalm 84:4). 'Happy are those whose strength is in you' (Psalm 84:5). 'Happy is everyone who trusts in you' (Psalm 84:12). Here we find three beatitudes in one psalm!

When we ponder these three Old Testament affirmations, we recognise that they wonderfully describe a man or woman of faith: there are three basic ingredients listed as the abiding in God's house, the drawing of strength from God and the placing of trust in God. This way of faith has been demonstrated in countless lives lived to the glory of God. Luke chapter six narrates the special moment in the life of the man with a withered hand, who entered the synagogue to see Jesus. On an ordinary Sabbath day, he went to worship, met Jesus Christ, and was instantly healed, so that life held new possibilities for him! Since then, many have found blessing in 'God's house': 'blessed', indeed, are all those who so abide in the Lord, and express that by setting aside time for prayer.

In 1961, John Freeman interviewed Dr. Martin Luther King Jr. on television. With simplicity, Dr. King spoke of the tension, suffering and fear that he, and other fellow African-Americans, experienced during the Civil Rights movement as they stood against prejudice. Yet, one thing came over clearly, namely, that Dr. King found strength in God as he knew the scripture: 'God is our refuge and strength, a very present help in trouble (Psalm 46:1). Generations of believing leaders, reformers, prophetic women and men, as well as ordinary Christians, have been able to say with the psalmist: 'Blessed are those whose strength is in thee'.

In recent years, deep-sea divers have explored sunken ships on the sea floor and recovered much treasure: such divers are immensely skilled and very courageous. They have to place their confidence in the ship above and in the colleagues working there; the diver has to be a person of trust. So likewise, people have trusted in God in the heights of joy and in the depths of despair, as well as during the long, dreary, humdrum stretches of their pilgrimage.

Surely the words of the psalmist are still true: blessed, indeed, are those who dwell with God. As we place our trust in God, we find the strength we need for each and every day, a blessing we know as God's gift of peace.

Suggested readings: Psalm 84:1-12 and Luke 6:6-11.

JUNE 11th

## GOD CAN TRANSFORM PAINFUL MEMORIES

Memories can be painful! Sometimes, they can be so terribly painful that people can hardly bear them. A television programme called 'Back to the Edge' showed U.S. soldiers returning years later for a tour of Vietnam; it revived very painful and disturbing memories. One man interviewed said simply, but very movingly: 'I lost something here'. He could not be specific, but Vietnam was the place where he felt that he had 'lost something' and, sadly, life could never be the same again. That experience is, in fact, so true to life as faced by many people. Men and women can return to a particular spot and reflect: 'I lost something here'.

For some people a place reminds them of lost opportunities, lost honour, lost friendship or lost peace of mind, but also, sometimes, of lost faith. There are men and women who survived the terrible concentration camps of the Second World War, but who found that for them, life could never be the same again. One survivor put it in these soul-searing words: 'Never shall I forget those moments which murdered my God and my soul and turned my dreams to dust'. For some, amazingly, the concentration camps strangely deepened faith; for others, their faith was so wrecked that it was all but destroyed, or even totally lost.

The narrative in John's gospel brings out a subtle truth about Peter's fall and restoration at the end of Jesus' earthly life. We read a charcoal fire was made in the High Priest's courtyard, because it was cold, and Peter stood by it (John 18:18). There, by the fire, he was challenged about his discipleship and denied it. Peter denied knowing Jesus, but then events moved fast as Jesus was condemned, scourged, mocked, crucified and buried in a tomb. However, on Easter Day, He was raised to life through the miracle of the resurrection! Soon after, we read of Peter standing by another charcoal fire, this time by the Sea of Galilee: 'They saw a charcoal fire there, with fish on it, and bread' (John 21:9). It was near that second charcoal fire that the risen Lord restored Peter, who reaffirmed his love for Him and devotion to Him. We take note that three times by a charcoal fire Peter denied Christ; three times by a different charcoal fire Peter confessed Christ. Surely, from that point on, Peter could never see a charcoal fire without vivid, indeed, poignant memories being evoked as he recalled his downfall and restoration!

The Cross of Calvary is a place of paradox: before it in quiet reflection, we can truly sense the wretchedness of our sin and feel heavily burdened. Yet, by God's grace our guilt is erased: the place of despair can be the place of hope! God can transform our memories of a place!

Suggested readings: John 18:16-27 and John 21:9-14.

JUNE 12th

## THERE ARE TIMES OF REFRESHING

We surely all thank God for flowers and plants, shrubs and trees! Besides gardening, lots of people find real pleasure in growing household plants, as it is both a rewarding and a fascinating hobby. Of course, the expert study of plants in their natural habitat yields very interesting discoveries. For instance, it is said that the Resurrection plant can survive for 100 years without water and, when immersed in water, comes alive to become a flourishing plant. From the study of this particular plant, medical research has made very important discoveries about blood-preservation. In the home, what a marvellous thing it is having seen a plant once looking old, withered and seemingly useless – then, placed in the right environment – blossoming into newness of life!

When speaking of the new life promised by God, the prophet wrote: 'The wilderness and the dry ground shall be glad, the desert shall rejoice and blossom; like the crocus it shall blossom abundantly, and rejoice with joy and singing' (Isaiah 35:1-2). While he was speaking of their hope of returning from exile, the words are also a reminder of what can truly happen when a person finds, or rediscovers, the Eternal One who is the Lord and Life-giver, and so comes to an experience of personal renewal of heart and mind.

Spiritual renewal can be experienced, not only by individuals, but also by an entire church community. A small church, whether in an urban or a rural setting, might experience many lean years with no one being drawn in, or obviously coming to faith, or evidently deepening spiritually, so that the people feel discouraged. At such a low point in the church's life, a Christian couple or family might move into the area and bring a new enthusiasm for God's work. Indeed, they may offer a new vision of what God could do in and through just a small fellowship, thinking positively and offering support, while serving humbly and praying faithfully. It might be said that such believers bring with them seeds of hope and a sense of expectancy that God will indeed bring a 'time of refreshing'. This can result in a season of refreshment as the seed, diligently and faithfully sown, by God's rich blessing, then comes to fruition; indeed, the desert has blossomed!

It is certainly the case that one truly 'on fire' Christian can (under God's guidance) bring renewed hope and blessing. Soon after Pentecost, Peter preached repentance: '. . . that your sins be blotted out, that times of refreshing may come from the presence of the Lord' (Acts 3:19). Openness to God is the way for us to find the newness for which we all long, deep down within us; as St Augustine put it, our restless hearts find peace, such as can only be found in God.

Suggested reading: Isaiah 35:1-7 and Acts 3:17-23.

JUNE 13th

## CONCERNING THE HEART OF THE GOSPEL

God has given many wonderful gifts for the upbuilding of the Church, and one of the most precious gifts is that of good biblical exposition: gifted proclaimers who can search the scriptures and faithfully expound it without fear or favour. Still today, lots of Christians feel thankful to the heavenly Father for the life and ministry of Dr. Martyn Lloyd-Jones, known to be a most powerful and effective expositor of the Bible. Indeed, he spent his strength preaching and expounding the Word of God; even in our day, his books and recordings of his addresses are still used throughout the world as a way of building up people in the faith. We recall that his life was punctuated by momentous decisions: for example, when he was on the way up to a very successful medical career, he felt called to be a minister of the gospel. He obeyed diligently and ended up paying the price for his obedience, too. Yet, there were also other big decisions too: in 1929, he had been preaching at Bridgend, South Wales, when a minister challenged him that the cross did not have a central place in his preaching. It was a powerful and faithful rebuke upon which he acted, and so Dr. Martyn Lloyd-Jones went to a bookshop and purchased two books: *The Atonement* by R.W. Dale and *The Death of Christ* by James Denny which he proceeded to read at home. As the story is told, much to the dismay of his wife, he ended up declining both lunch and tea that day, as he just kept on reading! Later, he came out of his study saying he had found the 'heart of the gospel', as he vividly put it.

After the apostle Paul discovered the 'heart of the gospel', he made the simple but profound resolution: 'For I determined not to know any thing among you, save Jesus Christ, and him crucified' (1 Corinthians 2:2 AV). So it was for Dr. Lloyd-Jones; he, too, proclaimed this essential message. His ministry at Westminster Chapel, London, was outstandingly fruitful: crowds of people (including hundreds of students) came to hear him expound the Holy Scriptures. Numerous men and women turned to God in repentance, received Christ as their own personal Saviour, found new purpose for living, and were transformed by the power of the Holy Spirit, some experiencing a deep and radical change from former ways.

True preaching of the Cross of Calvary – rightly heard – breaks down even stubborn hearts and gives hope to the sinful while revealing the glorious mystery and immensity of God's redeeming love. John Bunyan, the seventeenth-century dissenter imprisoned for his faith, wrote in *Pilgrim's Progress* how the troubled man lost his heavy load at the foot of the cross as the burden of sin and guilt rolled into the empty sepulchre. This was glorious imagery to express the heart of the gospel; so we thank God for it, and for the message of 'grace abounding' as Bunyan memorably put it.

Suggested readings: Isaiah 53:1-12 and 1 Corinthians 2:1-5.

JUNE 14th

## THE FAMILY LINE CAN BE INTERRUPTED

In recent years, there has been an increased interest in genealogy; for many people there is something very fascinating in tracing the 'family tree'! Clergymen have often received letters from all over the world asking them to look up old parish records to help trace details of people's forbears. On a different level, it is a thriving business for those firms that give specialist help in this type of research as records are made available. Some people have spent a small fortune tracing their family line!

Matthew's gospel begins with a genealogical reference: 'The book of the genealogy of Jesus Christ, the son of David, the son of Abraham' (Matthew 1:1). Biblical scholars have researched this record and have offered insights into the forbears of Jesus Christ. The list initially appears to be a rather tedious passage but, with deeper probing, it yields some interesting information. For example, we read one verse: 'And David was the father of Solomon by the wife of Uriah' (Matthew 1:6). Within those twelve words there are notable undertones and overtones; David's 'dark blot' stands in the records and is not erased. It was a most regrettable fact, but it was not omitted by Matthew when he gave close attention to the facts of Jesus' genealogy, it was set out in the preface to the gospel narrative.

When people research their family tree they make lots of discoveries, both pleasant and otherwise! Some have found a hero in the family, while others have found a scoundrel! One of the interesting things about a family line is that it can take a sharp turn towards spiritual matters. After a generation or more of unbelieving people, a conversion to the faith on the part of one can occur, which influences the family line towards Christ. Just one individual can bring an entirely new dimension to the family tree! So we need to think of evangelism beyond simply personal faith, to the wider perspective, even winning generations for the Lord Jesus.

A young person discovers faith in Christ and then in turn, upon marriage, may influence her or his spouse; when their children are born, the parents may nurture them in the faith and encourage them in Christian ways. One could argue that there has been (by that one coming to faith) an interruption in the family line; the gospel has started to work in one vital part of this family and it can continue for several generations. The Hebrew family traditions described in the Old Testament, involved a strong sense of kinship responsibility and intergenerational faith nurture. With regard to upholding the laws of God, the psalmist says: 'He commanded our ancestors to teach to their children; that the next generation might know them' (Psalm 78:5-6). This is surely an early version of family nurture in the faith, in order to guide, to encourage and to inspire generations yet to come!

Suggested readings: Psalm 78:1-8 and Matthew 1:1-17.

JUNE 15th

## OUR GOD IS RELIABLE

Every minister of religion is invited by businesses, institutions, organisations and government departments to give references for people seeking employment. Often, with someone who is familiar, it is very easy and the minister gladly supplies the necessary information, without any reservation, but at other times it is tricky! One question on a number of standard forms can often pose problems: 'Is the candidate reliable?' It should be a straightforward question to answer, but it is far from that in certain cases. We all know there are different personality traits in persons to consider in this respect: some people are very reliable in many aspects of life but, in a few areas (for example, with deadlines or punctuality), they are less reliable. One famous actor tells of an excellent assistant who was always late for appointments: ironically, one could rely on him being unreliable in this matter of timekeeping!

The testimony of Holy Scripture is that God is trustworthy; we can rely wholly on Him, for there is not a single respect in which He is unreliable. In the Old Testament there is the story of King Asa confronted by a strong enemy: it looked like certain defeat for him. We recall Asa's prayer to God: 'Lord, there is no one like you to help the powerless against the mighty. Help us, O Lord our God, for we rely on you, and in your name we have come against this vast army. O Lord, you are our God; do not let man prevail against you' (2 Chronicles 14:11 NIV). How moving it is to witness the faith of Asa when he prays: 'We rely on you'. It reminds one of the line in a popular hymn: 'Other refuge have I none, hangs my helpless soul on Thee'.

Witnessing a helicopter rescue of an individual in danger at sea is always dramatic. The pilot hovers the craft over the distressed person and a line is lowered: a skilled rescuer dangles from the line and seeks to manoeuvre into the correct position to grasp the individual to be winched up. At this particular point, both the person in distress and the rescuer have to trust the line: their lives depend on it. In a significant way, that can be a parable of the spiritual life: there are times when we get into serious difficulties and we know that it is impossible to extricate ourselves. At such times, we need another One to be our helper and so we discover, in a deeper way, that our God is truly our deliverer upon Whom we may rely. In one of his epistles, Paul tells how he and his companions encountered severe difficulties and he added his interpretation: 'This was meant to teach us not to place reliance on ourselves, but on God who raises the dead' (2 Corinthians 1:9 NEB). There are times when it is unsafe to place reliance upon ourselves or upon others; the only wise thing to do is to place our reliance upon God, Who is surely to be trusted. We thank God that we, and countless others, have found that God is absolutely reliable.

Suggested readings: 2 Chronicles 14:8-12 and 2 Corinthians 1:3-11.

JUNE 16th

## LOSERS CAN BECOME WINNERS

Mary Stott, speaking of her life, has been very frank about her childhood and describes herself as a plain child. With astounding honesty, she says that as a child she was a coward, a liar and a bad loser. Of course, plenty of children are bad losers and throw a tantrum if they lose a game; this kind of behaviour can be rather embarrassing for parents, and can even strain relationships with other friends. Actually, the sad fact is that some bad losers are adults who, in an immature way, can be terribly bad losers, and that's not just meaning poor sportsmen and women.

Each June, people from all over the world come to Wimbledon to watch first-class tennis at this most famous annual tournament; many of the games are quite breath-taking and the skill of the players is remarkable, but there are always a few really bad losers. Regrettably, there have been games when racquets have been thrown down, umpires subjected to verbal abuse, even with swearing and cursing, all before the eyes of the world! At a Wimbledon match some time ago, an idol of the tennis world lost his match – one he had been expected to win – and he was seen and heard leaving the court in a foul mood uttering a string of obscenities. He was a very bad loser, and it was a shameful scene.

At one point, the apostle Paul was definitely on the losing side, or that's how it appeared as he was in prison for his proclamation of the gospel. Here was a man who enjoyed his liberty as a Roman citizen, travelling far, often addressing large crowds concerning the Christian faith; yet, he ended up languishing in prison. It makes fascinating reading to see how he faced up to this difficult situation: 'I want you to know, beloved, that what has happened to me has actually helped to spread the gospel, so that it has become known throughout the whole imperial guard and to everyone else that my imprisonment is for Christ' (Philippians 1:12-13). He saw that by God's help, he could turn a loss into a gain! If he couldn't serve God in one way, he could serve in another, even using his imprisonment to the glory of God; in this instance, Paul was a triumphant loser!

Sometimes, we feel prayer isn't answered, or think that God is slow to act or our plans are thwarted and we seem to be losers, so we are unsettled. Even so, we can go on, for the apostle Paul wrote: 'We know that in everything God works for good with those who love him, who are called according to his purpose' (Romans 8:28). The crucial word there was 'everything'; it is such a firm confession of faith! This approach could turn loss into gain as Paul amply proved in his own experience. Losers can become winners, and Jesus Himself taught that the last would be first! That dynamic is the particular nature of life in the Kingdom of God.

Suggested readings: Philippians 1:12-18 and 1 Corinthians 16:5-8.

JUNE 17th

## CHRISTIANS NEED DISCIPLINED TRAINING

Countless people remember with gratitude the beautiful singing of Kathleen Ferrier: she was a world-famous contralto and her lovely voice gave pleasure and joy. How often a small child unwittingly reveals latent potential which is fully developed later: so it was with Kathleen! As a child she used to finger the piano and play a few notes. One day she sat at a piano and tapped out very haltingly a little tune then, all of a sudden, she burst into tears exclaiming: 'I want to play . . . I want to play . . . and I can't play properly'. So Kathleen had to learn an important lesson that training is a necessity! Her subsequent training was put to good use!

Jesus called people to be His disciples. Discipleship means learning and the gospels show us, with unmitigated honesty, how the disciples had to learn the ways of Jesus. Yet, they were sometimes slow to learn His ways! Disciplined training is hard work, but it brings its own reward and eventually, the harvest. Kathleen Ferrier knew the costliness of disciplined study and training, but finally she came to a position where her singing was a joy to herself and a blessing to others.

Training is essential in so many different areas of life, in ordinary work as well as in the professions of the teacher or pharmacist, the doctor or nurse, the engineer or pilot, the accountant or lawyer, or the athlete: all need thorough and disciplined training. We know the long years of study and practical work done by medical students before they qualify as physicians or surgeons. However, in the end, the hard work of study and practice in their training pays off. Of course, the word 'discipline' is not always very popular in our day! Some people want to be able to do what they want, or even undertake tasks before they've been properly trained. Even some Christians try to take short-cuts, too, so the apostle Paul urged believers to heed the value of discipline, and warned Timothy: 'Train yourself in godliness; for while bodily training is of some value, godliness is of value in every way, as it holds promise for the present life and also for the life to come' (1 Timothy 4:7-8).

Kathleen Ferrier had to learn that it was no good wishing to learn to play the piano unless she did something practical to achieve it. We live increasingly in a world of 'instant' products, whether tea or coffee, or photography, or communications, and so much more; our society seems to be developing an 'instant satisfaction' mentality. Perhaps a young or inexperienced driver, having just got his or her licence, ventures too soon into a difficult driving situation and ends up in real difficulty, or causing trouble for others. Impatience or inadequate preparation can result in frustration or heartache, and might even prove to be fatal. Likewise, in the spiritual life, Christians need disciplined training and encouragement.

Suggested readings: Matthew 11:28-30 and 2 Timothy 3:10-17.

JUNE 18th

## THE SUN DECLARES GOD'S GLORY

It is a good thing, sometimes, to look up into the sky, by day and by night, and to spend time thinking in quiet reflection! The psalmist says: 'When I look at your heavens, the work of your fingers, the moon and the stars that you have established; what are human beings that you are mindful of them, mortals that you care for them? (Psalm 8:3-4). There is no doubt that the sun, moon and stars have made a profound impression upon the minds of countless millions of people down all the ages. Generation after generation have looked up and pondered the heavens above. The person of faith affirms, as recorded elsewhere in the Psalms: 'The heavens are telling the glory of God; and the firmament proclaims his handiwork' (Psalm 19:1).

Some time ago an article was published concerning the power of the sun. Scientists are amazed at its magnitude! It is calculated that the sun loses millions of tons in weight every day. As we consider that astounding fact, we recall that the sun has been shining constantly since time began, and all life on earth depends upon it. In our daily lives, we recognise every harvest depends upon its power. Moreover, every living creature, every plant and flower, every human being depends upon its power to give light and warmth; we are reliant on the sun for its energy. With the psalmist of old we, too, can see how it reflects the glory of God; lots of people have looked up into the heavens and they have pondered the Creator of all. The majestic rising and the setting of the sun each evoke fascination and awe at the splendour of the colours! What grandeur there is so often for us to behold!

If the sun has such power, what might we say of the God Who created it? God our Father, we confess, is both Creator and Sustainer of the universe. The sun, of course, in spite of its magnitude to us, is a mere speck in the vastness of the universe! With the psalmist, we surely confess: 'Great is the Lord and greatly to be praised, and his greatness is unsearchable. One generation shall laud thy works to another, and shall declare thy mighty acts' (Psalm 145:3-4). As we think of the complexity and wonder of this planet, and of the universe itself, we are truly amazed; for many who think deeply and reverently, amazement turns into worship and praise.

In the Book of Deuteronomy we have these splendid words: 'O Lord God, thou hast only begun to show thy servant thy greatness and thy mighty hand, for what god is there in heaven or on earth who can do such works and mighty acts as thine?' (Deuteronomy 3:23). Over the centuries, the greatest minds have wrestled with the meaning of life and the universe, as we know it; if we do confess the reality of creation, we must realise we're only ever at the beginning of that quest!

Suggested readings Psalm 8:1-9 and Colossians 1:15-20.

JUNE 19th

## SELECTION IS VERY IMPORTANT

There was an important decision to be made! A small child was standing in a village shop with money to spend on sweets: she found it rather difficult to make the right selection and the shopkeeper was extremely patient. Making choices is a part of life from childhood right through life: choosing a partner, selecting work or study options, making lifestyle choices, settling in an area to live, deciding on purchases or investments. In so many dimensions to life, a decision has to be made at some point. While some choices prove immaterial, actually, in certain other choices, the selection is vitally important. It seems one key part of being a good landscape artist is the gift of looking at a scene, and then selecting what to draw or paint in that scene. So too, in all of life, making the right selection at certain times contributes significantly to the overall outcome; such choices can even determine the sum happiness of life.

Bible students have always been fascinated by the first chapter of Mark's gospel: it is something like a snapshot album with selected pictures: Jesus being baptized by John, Jesus being tempted, Jesus healing the person in the synagogue then healing others too, as well as taking time to pray, together with Him helping people who came from every quarter. In verses 16-20, there is the picture of Jesus selecting and calling four disciples; we see how He called and they responded. They were tough and unpolished fishermen, but the Blessed Master saw their hidden potential; another key factor in making choices is having an eye for likely potential!

In the work of the Christian Church, often a selection committee will be responsible for deciding upon the possible acceptance for training of men and women who have offered themselves for the Christian ministry. This task is not easy for those making the selection have a responsibility towards the candidate and towards the Church. They have to sift the available evidence regarding each candidate carefully and prayerfully going through all the various documents, as well as recommendations and interview observations. Sometimes, it is not only the best, but also, the kindest decision to turn the candidate down. It is hard because not only is the candidate disappointed but family, as well as the churches involved in the process of discerning a genuine calling to ministry, may feel deeply disappointed, too.

While the call to follow Jesus is offered to everyone, not all people have the same gifts. All of Jesus' disciples had different abilities and were of differing temperaments. Followers of Jesus were expected to use their particular gifts in the Lord's service. That is, indeed, the way God still calls us today.

Suggested readings: Mark 1:16-20 and Mark 1:32-39.

JUNE 20th

## THERE IS A MINISTRY OF STRENGTHENING

Sometimes a great deal of emphasis is put on bringing people to faith. Yet, in the Bible, there are many stories about people needing to be strengthened and encouraged. One lovely story, in the Old Testament, is that of Jonathan helping David (1 Samuel 23). In the New Testament, we see believers being strengthened by the apostles. Today, preachers and others, too, find an indescribable joy in helping people on the journey of faith. While bringing people to faith is important, we realise that conversion is just the beginning: then comes lifelong discipleship through daily fellowship with the Lord and here, we need to help one another.

The apostle Paul was a zealous advocate for the faith and he certainly 'preached for conviction'. He loved to see people make their first response to the Lord, but he never left the matter there. After much preaching on his missionary journeys, he came back at last to Antioch before leaving again: 'After spending some time there he departed and went from place to place through the region of Galatia and Phrygia strengthening all the disciples' (Acts 18:23). Paul saw that people needed to be challenged and converted to the faith, but they also needed to be helped, taught, encouraged and strengthened; disciples needed ongoing support! A striking example of this was when he went to Lystra and preached a powerful message: 'Turn from these vain things to a living God who made the heaven and the earth and the sea and all that is in them' (Acts 14:15). Some people stoned him and he was dragged out of the city, leaving him for dead. There was then the most remarkable sequel as the apostle and the others pressed on preaching valiantly: '. . . they returned to Lystra, then on to Iconium and Antioch. There they strengthened the souls of the disciples, and encouraged them to continue in the faith, saying, "It is through many persecutions that we must enter the kingdom of God"' (Acts 14:21-22).

This shows an outstanding example of courage, and it is evident that the believers at Lystra were truly strengthened by this brave deed. So Paul sought to strengthen the believers by proclamation, and his epistles, but above all by personal example. One striking idiom in the English language is when a person is described as being a 'tower of strength'. A family goes through times of crisis and say of a friend or neighbour: 'she (or he) was a tower of strength'. This exactly describes Paul's fine ministry, and we can all seek to be just that kind of support, as far as possible. We can give time and effort to encouraging new disciples, seeking to help them grow up and deepen spiritually. Every day, we can discover the opportunities to do this and so encourage others in their pilgrimage of faith; it is a joy to be able – with all due humility – to support others and to build up one another in our walk with the Lord.

Suggested readings: 1 Samuel 23:14-18 and Acts 14:19-23.

JUNE 21st

## CARELESS TALK COSTS LIVES

It had been a very moving service, one of those occasions when the hand of the Lord seemed to be at work with gracious power. Things seemed just right: a large eager congregation, good hymn singing, a timely message, and a blessed time of fellowship at the Communion Service. As the minister stood in the vestibule shaking hands with the attenders as they left, he noticed two people in deep conversation. The conversation was so animated that his curiosity was aroused and he caught just one fragment of it: 'Well, I always cook my sausages this way'. They were not talking about the worship or the fellowship, or the things of God, but about sausages! It was, for the preacher, a humbling and revealing moment, for when a person studies at a theological college in preparation for Christian ministry, much is made of the linkage between pulpit and pew. Here, it appeared that the message had not had the intended impact, and the minister's disappointment was inescapable.

A minister may prepare a service with the utmost care, and plan that all aspects of the worship blend together and focus on a set theme, but there is sometimes a 'disconnection' where distraction creeps in, and occasionally the whole point of the service is evidently missed! Sometimes, unwittingly, the hearty conversation which follows a service can do more damage than good: the laughter, the chitchat, the sharing of family and other news maybe totally innocent, but it can erode the real influence of a moving service. As many recall, during the Second World War, a stark warning notice appeared in many public places in Britain: 'Careless talk costs lives'. In a sense, that can ring very true in a spiritual sense, too.

In Matthew chapter 13, we have the famous story of the Parable of the Sower, and it contains numerous lessons, one being that of context: 'A sower went out to sow. And as he sowed, some seeds fell along the path, and the birds came and devoured them' (Matthew 13:3-4). That is true to life when the sharing of God's Word is thwarted by circumstances! A minister was particularly concerned about the spiritual welfare of one of his young people. After one service, there was a golden opportunity to have conversation with her. However, as they talked, a church member rather interrupted the conversation to enquire about some trivial matter, and the opportunity was lost. In the language of the parable, the seed was snatched away and nothing then came of that moment for nurture. Empty, frivolous, careless or inappropriate talk can be so detrimental, or even outright obstructive, to the work of the Kingdom. Yet, our speech, if wise and helpful, can surely bring glory to God.

Suggested readings: Psalm 145:13-21 and Proverbs 10:7-11.

JUNE 22nd

## WORSHIP GIVES PERSPECTIVE

A knotty problem, which has often exercised the minds of believers, is: 'Why do the wicked prosper?' In Psalm 73, a person of faith looks at life and sees that wicked people 'increase in riches' (Psalm 73:12); he also observes that, although he has kept his own heart clean, he has been stricken, and it all seems to be unfair! Then we get this remarkable verse: 'But when I thought how to understand this, it seemed to me a wearisome task, until I went into the sanctuary of God; then I perceived their end' (Psalm 73:16-17). It was entering the sanctuary that made all the difference.

Every week there are people who attend public worship and their heart is in a state of tumult: an inner civil war! There is profound unrest, dismay and annoyance over some puzzling situation where life seems so unfair. Then, at worship, in the quietness and peace of God's house, they find balance and perspective. A person might feel bitter towards another: a letter is going to be written and the pen will scorch the paper! However, between the inclination to write and the actual writing, the person attends a time of worship. During the service, the preacher quietly expounds the need to receive forgiveness and also to grant it. The letter is then abandoned as the ill will subsides. Quite unknown to the preacher, by the gracious work of the Holy Spirit, the words of proclamation of the gospel have transformed a situation from ugliness to harmonious living.

In that psalm, the expression '. . . until I went into the sanctuary', meant in so many words, '. . .until, in worship, I became conscious of the place of God in all life'. Think of the variations of this experience: 'I was troubled until . . .', 'I was angry until. . .', 'I was depressed until. . .' or maybe even 'I was anxious until. . .', A world of significance is contained in those words of the psalmist:'. . . until I went into the sanctuary'. In the Book of Proverbs, there is a lovely verse which speaks of the problem of being anxious: 'Anxiety weighs down the human heart, but a good word cheers it up' (Proverbs 12:25). Often, of course, the 'good word' is heard in the sanctuary, or at least in what that signifies, namely, in sincere fellowship and worship: in the reading of scripture, in the singing of the hymns, in the prayers and in the preaching. However, sometimes, the 'good word' comes through the still, small voice within the heart. Believers can testify thus: 'They that wait upon the Lord shall renew their strength; they shall mount up with wings as eagles; they shall run, and not be weary; and they shall walk, and not faint' (Isaiah 40:31). Very often in an encounter with God, as we gather in worship, we can specially receive the Lord's gracious blessings. Worship can, and often does, give people balance, perspective and hope.

Suggested readings: Psalm 73:1-17 and Isaiah 40:26-31.

JUNE 23rd

## CHRISTIANS SHOULD THINK DEEPLY AND DECIDE WISELY

The couple was standing in the middle of the pavement: the man was speaking earnestly and enthusiastically, but the woman was looking very thoughtful. As the man continued to talk, she punctuated the conversation with, 'I'll have to think about it'. Now every customer who has been in a shop and has been pressurized by an over-zealous shop assistant knows that this expression is a good delaying tactic! Shop assistants can identify customers who have been in and looked at many pairs of shoes, but who eventually say, 'I'll have to think about it'. Yet, these words can also be used positively, of course, for a much better purpose; and careful thought is at the heart of wisely living well. Many women can testify that the Girl Guide movement was real a blessing to them, and one of the things associated with the movement over the years has been its 'Thinking Day': a splendid idea to sow in the minds of these young people the place of careful thought and reflection.

In point of fact, we all need to have 'Thinking Days' as it were; times when we carefully consider decisions which will have an important influence on our family or circle of friends. We are all involved somehow in decision-making, ranging from major crucial decisions to relatively minor trifling matters. The surgeon ponders a delicate, possibly dangerous, operation, a jury considers a verdict which could literally destroy a person's career, young people consider their choices in education, training or career paths. All men and women have to make decisions which have an impact upon their own lives and the lives of others. It is a good thing, to be thoughtful, as the scriptures say: 'Take heed to the path of your feet, then all your ways will be sure' (Proverbs 4:26). The Authorized Version puts this verse simply: 'Ponder the path of thy feet and let all thy ways be established'. Pondering before a big decision is always a good thing!

However, there is a time when thinking has to give place to action and decisions must be made. We can recall the Old Testament story when Elijah gave a powerful challenge to the people: 'Elijah went before the people and said, "How long will you waver between two opinions? If the Lord is God, follow him; but if Baal is God, follow him"' (1 Kings 18:21 NIV). It is right to think, to ponder, but then we finally have make up our minds! There are people who come to church on a very regular basis but remain uncommitted: they seem to ponder the challenge of discipleship, but waver about making any firm decision. The path to the Cross of Calvary is a well-worn path: it has been the crossroads experience for many. It is there that we find ourselves either for or against Him, and there can be no neutrality: the time comes for us each to make our decision, after careful reflection.

Suggested readings: 1 Kings 18:15-21 and Philippians 3:7-14.

JUNE 24th

## FAITH CAN 'SEE' THE SOLID REALITIES

We thank God for holidays! It is a marvellous thing to be able to pack one's bags and leave one's familiar area and go on holiday to experience something new and to rest. For many people, their time away from home must include a 'good view' whether by sea or lake, hills or countryside. It is always such a pleasure to wake up in the morning and drink in the beauty of a lovely view. At such times, work pressures, life's problems, personal difficulties and the complexity of workaday life seem scaled down in perspective! So it was with the Brook family, as they went on holiday to Gloucestershire and they stayed in a small house overlooking a beautiful valley. There were trees and hedges, old stone walls and cornfields, cattle and sheep, and the rolling distant hills with exquisite scenery and colour. It was such a pleasure for them to draw aside the curtains those summer mornings and to see the outdoor world in its splendour, as they beheld a wonderful corner of 'England's green and pleasant land'.

One morning it was different! When the curtains were drawn back, they discovered the lovely view had completely disappeared! As if by some magic, the whole beauty spot had been obliterated by a thick mist that had filled the valley. The view was eerie and strange, but the family knew the beauty was still there, and it was just temporarily hidden from sight. That experience, is, of course, true of life itself. Sometimes, life is exceedingly pleasant: we get up in the morning and feel 'everything's going my way'. Life is beautiful, and with true understanding we can repeat the words of the psalmist: 'The lines have fallen for me in pleasant places; yea, I have a goodly heritage' (Psalm 16:6). All seems well, but then one day the 'mist' descends, everything looks rather different, and the prospects seem entirely changed! These mists might be experienced in different ways: illness, disappointment, loss, bereavement or frustration. The beautiful outlook we rejoiced in then seems to be obliterated, and even God can seem to be hidden. Such experiences are both painful and bewildering.

However, in our moments of quiet reflection, we know that the ultimate realities are still there: God is still our heavenly Father and His Kingdom stands secure. In the deep places of the heart, the believer knows the mist will eventually disperse, even though it might seem a distant prospect of once again rejoicing in God's love. If we feel depressed and defeated, or things have taken a nasty turn to alarm or disturb us, we can still be sure of this assurance from the Lord: 'This is the victory that overcomes the world, our faith' (1 John 5:4). The mists do descend around us in life from time to time, but by the eye of faith, we may perceive that God is as faithful as ever, for God's throne is sure and His grace abides forever.

Suggested readings: Psalm 16:1-8 and 1 John 5:1-5.

JUNE 25th

## GOD'S LOVE IS OCEANIC

In the Old Testament we have the story of Nebuchadnezzar, a king who had dreams; and 'his spirit was troubled, and his sleep left him' (Daniel 2:1). Lots of people are fascinated by how repetitive or varied dreams can be! There are dreams which alarm or excite, puzzle or amuse; quite often they can seem utterly bizarre or nonsensical. Sometimes, dreams appear to give a clear message on the state of things for us, and we do not really need any interpreter to assist us, as the meaning is quite plain.

One night Alan went to bed really troubled in spirit: it had been a bad evening and things had simply 'gone wrong'. He climbed into bed with a burdened mind and heart; so much so he quite expected sleep would be elusive. However, he did fall asleep and had a lovely dream: he dreamt that he was reading a modern translation of the Bible and came across a verse which included the two words, 'oceanic love', signifying God's love. He woke up and quickly realised that there was no such translation as far as he was aware using those two words, yet the dream left its mark. We can smile at the story of the little boy of five who had a lovely dream and called out to his older brother: 'Quick . . . Quick . . . share this dream with me'! In one sense that is impossible, of course, and yet we can share in Alan's dream of God's glorious love, and we can each discover it daily as a reality.

Those words 'oceanic love' stuck in Alan's mind; for him, in a wonderful way, the dream was a gift, as a spiritual message of assurance and comfort. God's love is truly oceanic and no person can measure its breadth or plumb its depths. One of F.W. Faber's fine hymns says: 'There's a wideness in God's mercy, like the wideness of the sea'. Truly, the love and compassion of God are oceanic and, through many centuries, men and women have rejoiced in the abundant grace of God. Paradoxically, people often experience the reality of God's love at life's low points.

In proclaiming this love, the prayer of the apostle Paul was heartfelt: 'That you, being rooted and grounded in love, may have the power to comprehend with all the saints what is the breadth and length and height and depth, and to know the love of Christ which surpasses knowledge' (Ephesians 3:17-19). Jesus Christ fully demonstrated and proclaimed the love of God: the Cross of Calvary is both a mystery and a revelation, for there divine 'oceanic love' was made manifest. We think of the words of Jesus as He hung in self-giving on the cross: 'Father forgive them; for they know not what they do' (Luke 23:34). The realisation of such wide and deep divine love 'vast as the ocean' is an astounding thought, for which there are no words. Little wonder it is the image used in many hymns and songs in praise of God.

Suggested readings: Ephesians 3:14-21 and 1 John 4:7-12.

JUNE 26th

## GOD SEES THE WHOLE PICTURE

We thank God for the gift of sight but we are always mindful that in our world there are numerous people who have limited vision; they are not totally blind but their eyesight is severely restricted and they can move about only with extreme care. These people often show much fortitude with their determination and cheerfulness, often surprising others by what they achieve. However, for many, their disability – depending on its severity – does often prove to have a considerable dominance in their thoughts and plans, and they have to think twice, as it were, in planning ahead!

There is, of course, a sense in which all human beings have limited vision for we do not know what the future will bring; actually, the scripture is quite definite about this: 'Do not boast about tomorrow, for you do not know what a day may bring forth' (Proverbs 27:1). All of us know a day may begin on a humdrum level and yet end dramatically. One of the parables of Jesus tells of a man who found a treasure in a field (Matthew 13:44). From being an ordinary day, in the story, the day ended on a note of excitement! We have days which bring unexpected sorrow or joy. The one big certainty about life is its uncertainty; our experience surely bears that out.

The subject manner of life's uncertainty raises the issue of guidance. The golden rule is this: if our heavenly Father can see the whole of the way ahead, then it must be wise to seek His help and look for His guidance. We may not see one day ahead; yet, knowing how the Lord can see the whole picture, we entrust ourselves to God. In the Psalms, there is a very important verse which helps us in our thinking about guidance: 'I will instruct you and teach you the way you should go; I will counsel you with my eye upon you' (Psalm 32:8).

Perspective, of course, is vital: there is all the difference in the world to viewing a city from the steps of the City Hall and viewing it from a helicopter! The aerial view has an entirely different perspective: it has a shape and a wholeness about it. So, with all reverence, we can say God's view upon our world and our life is different, for the Eternal One can see the whole of the picture. John Bunyan spent twelve years as a Dissenter in Bedford prison, during the years 1660-72. It was a source of deep sorrow to him that his imprisonment 'for the sake of Jesus Christ' caused his own family suffering. Yet, he trusted wholly in God, and believed that God's perspective was greater than his own. He was convinced the gospel would finally triumph, and that God would work out His purposes. Bunyan recognised that he had a limited view, but he believed that God saw the whole picture, and so he went on courageously, and eventually this bore remarkable fruit in his legacy to us.

Suggested readings: Psalm 32:1-11 and Acts 16:6-15.

JUNE 27th

## GOD'S WORD HAS QUICKENING POWER

When we think of the apostle Paul travelling as a missionary, preaching and writing, we must remember that he did not have a reference Bible as we would know it. What he did have was his schooling in the faith of the Hebrew people but more than that, a message in his heart concerning Jesus Christ. He knew the story of Jesus, the Son of God, including something of His ministry and teaching, His perfect life, His betrayal and rejection, His sacrificial death as the sinless One on the cross, as well His glorious resurrection from the dead and being taken into heaven. Furthermore, Paul proclaimed that this same Lord Jesus would ultimately return in power and glory. People listened to this preaching and recognised it as the Word of God, as he himself later acknowledged in his epistle: 'When you received the word of God that you heard from us, you accepted it not as a human word but as what it really is, God's word, which is at work in you believers' (1 Thessalonians 2:13).

God's Word does work in the heart of believers. Jesus had used the analogy of the power of yeast to express the way of God's Kingdom and, in a related sense, it applies also to the proclamation of the gospel. In the baking of bread, a small quantity of yeast permeates the dough and so brings about the leavening of the whole loaf. God's message acts in a similar way and, like yeast, influences the life of the believer. The letter to the Colossians notes this essential element: 'Let the word of Christ dwell in you richly, as you teach and admonish one another in all wisdom, and as you sing psalms and hymns and spiritual songs with thankfulness in your hearts to God' (Colossians 3:16). The indwelling Word is vital, informing our whole being.

The story is told that about two hundred years ago, dozens of ships sailed to North America, to see the New World. Those ships were crowded to the extreme and each family was allowed to take a tiny bit of luggage. It is interesting to note that three books took pride of place: the Holy Bible, Shakespeare's works and *Pilgrim's Progress*. People took the Bible as they knew in their hearts that it gave hope, strength and life; like yeast in the bread, the Word of God quickens the human heart.

So Paul, writing to his fellow Christians, spoke of 'God's word, which is at work in you believers'. The writer to the Hebrews puts it in another form: 'For the word of God is living and active, sharper than any two-edged sword, piercing to the division of soul and spirit, of joints and marrow, and discerning the thoughts and intentions of the heart' (Hebrews 4:12). The Word penetrates us to probe our deepest inner selves. The Word of God in Scripture is, indeed, a quickening power in our lives. It is surely unfailing and redounds to God's glory.

Suggested readings: 1 Thessalonians 2:13-20 and Colossians 3:12-17.

JUNE 28th

## CONCERNING THE RICH GENEROSITY OF GOD'S LOVE

We are all grateful to God for generous people! In Suffolk there is a beautiful Baptist Church which was the generous gift of a man in memory of his mother. Generosity with money in wider society takes many different forms: gifts to colleges, gifts to churches, gifts to charities, gifts to hospitals or clinics, gifts to organisations and so on, bringing much financial aid. Often large gifts to charitable organisations and churches are anonymous. Every year countless generous gifts are made day by day (many very quietly and secretly), and as a result of this benevolence, multitudes of lives are enriched and blessed. Generosity brings happiness to the giver and to the receiver, as the Book of Proverbs says: 'Those who are generous are blessed' (Proverbs 22:9).

There are numerous verses in the Old Testament which tell of the generosity of God. The books of the law, the writings and the prophets, together with the psalmist, proclaim the lavishness of God's love, the inexhaustibility of His mercy. One verse sums it up: 'They shall pour forth the fame of thy abundant goodness, and sing aloud of thy righteousness' (Psalm 145:7). A similar vein runs through the New Testament: 'The grace of our Lord overflowed for me with the faith and love that are in Christ Jesus' (1 Timothy 1:14). So much scripture points to the faith that our God is rich in generosity and abounding in love.

One of the parables of Jesus (in Matthew 20) has been much misunderstood. It is the story of the labourers in the vineyard who began work at different points of time during the day, but who all received the same wages for their work! Some look at this parable and see only the landowner's unfairness but the whole point of the story is his generosity! The landowner is a kind and generous man and the parable points to the amazing generosity of God. One of the basic lessons that can be drawn from this particular parable is that people come into the Kingdom of God differently, and may seem at different levels of commitment as they come along, but God is equally generous toward them. This indicates the wonder of God's abundant love and mercy drawing us all on in our journey of faith.

One key verse which has been used by ministers and evangelists is very clear: 'For God so loved the world that he gave his only Son, that whoever believes in him should not perish but have eternal life' (John 3:16). How much meaning can be discovered in that little word 'so'! There is no possible way to calculate the generosity of divine love: God gives without measure, so we can be thankful and rejoice.

Suggested readings: Matthew 20:1-16 and Philippians 4:13-19.

JUNE 29th

## JESUS CHRIST IS UNIQUE AND PRECIOUS

There are multitudes of people all over the world who can testify sincerely, from the heart, that Jesus Christ is precious to them: in their lives He has proved Himself a precious friend, guide and above all, Saviour. Charles Haddon Spurgeon, the famous nineteenth-century Baptist preacher, rejoiced in Christ and proclaimed to crowded London congregations the preciousness of his Saviour and Lord. It is well worth remembering the very first occasion he preached a sermon: it took place in a little thatched cottage in Teversham in Cambridgeshire. The congregation consisted of a few farm labourers and their wives, and he preached on a key verse: 'Unto you therefore who believe, he is precious' (1 Peter 2:7 AV). This set the tone for his future ministry for, again and again, in his powerful pulpit ministry in London, he preached on the preciousness of Jesus Christ.

There is a striking image in scripture, that of the quarried stone. We might picture a quarry near Jerusalem; many work there to quarry stone for various building endeavours in the city. There is one particular stone which is constantly ignored by the builders; over and over it is by-passed and rejected, until a builder comes along looking for just the right cornerstone and his eyes alight on it as precisely the one needed. So the rejected stone becomes the cornerstone, and it is that reality, says Peter, which is the truth about Jesus Christ: 'To you therefore who believe, he is precious. . . "The very stone which the builders rejected has become the head of the corner"' (1 Peter 2:7). Today, millions of people will be thankful for the life of the apostle Peter, the man who saw the shame of the cross and the glory of the resurrection; Peter knew what he was talking about! Peter knew the preciousness of Jesus Christ in his own life and in the lives of many others, so he proclaimed it, and this truth is affirmed in the epistle that bears his name.

When we think of Jesus Christ on the cross, we recall the words of the Old Testament: 'He was despised and rejected of men; a man of sorrows, and acquainted with grief' (Isaiah 53:3). The nails in His hands, the crown of thorns on His head, the mockery and the taunting all speak of His rejection. Yet, we affirm that God raised Him from the dead, as we read the apostle Paul's words: 'Therefore God also highly exalted him and gave him the name that is above every name, so that at the name of Jesus every knee should bend, in heaven and on earth and under the earth' (Philippians 2:9-10). Indeed, the 'stone which the builders rejected' has become the chief cornerstone. So Jesus Christ is exceedingly precious to vast numbers of people, ones willing to live and to die for Him. Peter the fisherman became Peter the apostle, and what he said about the Saviour is marvellously and gloriously true!

Suggested readings: 1 Peter 2:1-10 and Philippians 2:8-11.

JUNE 30th

## THE LORD PUTS THINGS INTO THE HEART

During the course of our lives, we all receive a number of promptings, whether from our partner, our family or friends, our colleagues at work, our minister or others in the fellowship; yet, occasionally, it seems to come directly as though from the Lord. In the Old Testament, we have an interesting letter sent by a king to the prophet Ezra: it tells of great generosity towards the temple at Jerusalem (Ezra 7:11-26). Ezra was delighted and his joy knew no bounds: 'Blessed be the Lord, the God of our ancestors, who put such a thing as this into the heart of the king, to glorify the house of the Lord in Jerusalem' (Ezra 7:27). Ezra truly believed that this generosity was no coincidence – no stroke of luck – but God had directed the king's heart. The New English Bible translates the verse beautifully: 'God . . . has prompted the king thus to add glory to the house of the Lord'. It was, indeed, divine prompting.

Scripture teaches that God does prompt men and women to do specific things in His service; divine prompting is a real experience and many have felt it quite clearly and responded! We recall the story of Solomon building the first magnificent temple: the first Book of Kings gives specific details of the material used and the dimensions, a fine building taking seven years to build. It is interesting to read of Solomon's recognition of that divine prompting when he resolved to build the temple: 'I purpose to build a house for the name of the Lord my God, as the Lord said to David my father, "Your son, whom I will set upon your throne in your place, shall build the house for my name' (1 Kings 5:5).

God, in His wisdom, has put into the hearts of men and women numerous unselfish plans which have served the Kingdom of God and brought glory to the Lord. Such divine prompting has inspired many and varied people to do extraordinary things for God, often undertaking service for the Kingdom in seemingly unpromising circumstances or in 'impossible' areas, or even just praying fervently and giving generously! One of the lovely comments which Paul uttered in defence of his life and service was his testimony: 'I was not disobedient to the heavenly vision' (Acts 26:19). He heard God's call and obeyed that prompting, and generations of Christians have been blessed because of his dedicated life and the ongoing witness in his epistles. Thus, day by day, there are lots of humble folk, even ordinary servants of God with, as it were, just the 'one talent', who respond to God's promptings with heart and mind to serve God. Yet, whether we feel we have 'ten talents' or 'one talent', we are all prompted to serve to God's glory!

Suggested readings: Ezra 7:11-28 and Acts 26:19-20.

# JULY

Love divine, all loves excelling,
Joy of heaven to earth come down:
Fix in us Thy humble dwelling,
All Thy faithful mercies crown:
Jesus, Thou art all compassion,
Pure, unbounded love Thou art;
Visit us with Thy salvation,
Enter every trembling heart.

Breathe, O breathe Thy loving Spirit
Into every troubled breast;
Let us all in Thee inherit,
Let us find Thy promised rest:
Take away the love of sinning;
Alpha and Omega be;
End of faith, as its Beginning,
Set our hearts at liberty.

Come, almighty to deliver,
Let us all Thy grace receive;
Suddenly return, and never,
Nevermore Thy temples leave.
Thee we would be always blessing,
Serve Thee as Thy hosts above,
Pray, and praise Thee without ceasing,
Glory in Thy perfect love.

Finish, then, Thy new creation;
Pure and spotless let us be;
Let us see Thy great salvation,
Perfectly restored in Thee;
Changed from glory into glory,
Till in heaven we take our place,
Till we cast our crowns before Thee,
Lost in wonder, love, and praise.

Charles Wesley (1707-1788)

O Lord God of time and eternity,
    who makest us creatures of time
that, when time is over,
    we may attain thy blessed eternity;
with time, thy gift,
    give us also wisdom to redeem the time,
        lest our day of grace be lost;
            for our Lord Jesus' sake.

Christina Rossetti (1830-94)

JULY 1st

## HIGH WALLS CAN BE OVERCOME

The Lord our God can grant us aid in so many different directions; one wonderful truth is the affirmation that God can help us overcome the high walls – the obstacles – that life presents. In the normal run of life, most people find that there are various obstacles to face and barriers to overcome, so we need stamina and grace to surmount these obstructions along the way. The psalmist puts it in a quaint way 'By my God I can leap over a wall' (Psalm 18:29). Put plainly, by the help of our gracious God, serious troubles can be overcome. There is a cherished verse in the New Testament, echoing another of the psalms (Psalm 118:6), which needs to be etched upon the minds and hearts of all believers: 'What shall we say to this? If God is for us, who is against us? He who did not spare his own son but gave him up for us all, will he not also give us all things with him?' (Romans 8:31-32). One old preacher used to say 'You can cross out the "if" in that verse'. The truth is that God is for us, indeed, on our side, and the cross stands as God's pledge of divine grace to help us in time of need.

The Olympic Games bring much excitement and true sporting pleasure to people who watch the various competitions throughout the world. One of the solo athletic competitions which always proves to be a great spectator sport is the high-jump. It is thrilling to watch first-class athletes pitting themselves against the force of gravity and jumping so high over the seemingly insurmountable bar. Men and women who succeed in this sport have to work very hard to prepare their bodies for the mighty effort required; their success is not a matter of chance! It is the same in facing life's struggles. We cannot succeed by our own efforts, of course, but truly by God's aid we can find a way through.

Obstacles test our mettle; one woman faced the shock that her husband had been hurt at work, sustaining serious, life-threatening injuries. When the case was later heard in court, several of his colleagues, out of fear for their own position, gave a false version of the event, which resulted in much lower compensation being paid out. This great injustice deeply wounded them both, especially the woman, who then felt terribly let down and bitter. She had a big obstacle – a high wall – to overcome and there was only a single way to victory: that was to seek God's help and strength to be able to go on in life, which she wisely did. As we know, bitterness is like an acid that eats away within the heart, and ultimately brings only havoc and self-destruction. The words of the psalmist are applicable here: 'By my God I can leap over a wall'. When feelings of bitterness, grievance or deep disappointment present themselves as obstacles to us along life's way, truly by God's grace alone, the victory can be won!

Suggested readings: Psalm 18:16-32 and Ephesians 4:25-32.

JULY 2nd

## LIFE MUST HAVE EMERGENCY STOPS

How important it is to be able to make an emergency stop in a vehicle! When someone in Britain is taking a driving test, they have to be prepared to make a safe emergency stop, and an inability to do this means failing the test. How essential it is because, in the normal course of driving, there is always the possibility of a sudden emergency through a vehicle, cyclist, pedestrian or animal unexpectedly getting into the way. One afternoon, two ministers were travelling to a conference centre and lost their way, caught up in the mysteries of a town's one-way system. After much confusion, and going round in circles, the passenger in the car said with some authority 'That's the way'. The driver took his advice, but within seconds knew with mounting alarm, that he was at that point driving the wrong way down a one-way street. Safety demanded an emergency stop!

The potential for needing a sudden stop is one of the hazards of being on the road, but the principle of the 'emergency stop' is true to life, too. There is a verse in the Book of Proverbs which says it plainly: 'There is a way which seems right to a person, but its end is the way to death' (Proverbs 14:12). The Good News Bible translates the verse quite succinctly: 'What you think is the right road may lead to death'. Lots of people have come to experience this realisation and they know that the wise counsel here is quite accurate in giving us this very clear warning.

In a sense, Saul of Tarsus was forced to make an 'emergency stop', on the Damascus road. He then had to change direction spiritually: Saul of Tarsus became a new person, known as the apostle Paul. The most vital and important change about him was his completely new orientation in life. The risen Lord – whom he dramatically met – transformed him, but it all began with an 'emergency stop'. We can think of people who have been travelling on the wrong road and have had to brake hard: the drug addict or alcoholic, the married person drifting into an illicit relationship, the office worker tempted to 'cook the books', or the professional trying to defraud the system. How easy it is to begin to slide downhill in wrongdoing and feel things getting out of control! It is then time to make an 'emergency stop', and to reconsider the right way forward in truth.

Actually, one of life's temptations is to forget what really matters in life. Perhaps, we ourselves need to stop and reflect on our priorities and choices. The words found in the Old Testament, 'Stop and consider the wondrous works of God' (Job 37:14), are good advice. Sometimes, if we pause in the midst of life, we find an opportunity with God's help to renew our faith and trust in God afresh. In fact, such an 'emergency stop' may lead on to a wholly new outlook on life.

Suggested readings: Job 37:1-16 and Mark 8:34-38.

JULY 3rd

## THE IMPORTANCE OF ONE LIFE

Every year there are numerous appeals for money from charitable groups. One international organisation produced an appeal which had these challenging words written on the envelope: 'You can make a difference'. While it was designed to catch the eye of the recipient, it is, of course, very true indeed. One person can make an important difference in the quality of life for a family, an organisation, a community, a church, a nation or even the world.

Malcolm Muggeridge told how he was once in New York's Times Square, and he saw rows of paperbacks on sale; the covers saddened his heart as so many were lurid, lewd, even sadistic. Suddenly, he noticed that amongst all these trashy books, there was a book on Mother Teresa, *Something Beautiful for God,* a book he had written! That book seemed to be a symbol: there is always light in the darkness, purity amongst impurity and good amongst evil. The story of Mother Teresa is well known. The streets of the Calcutta that she knew were a disgrace to humanity: lying there were the sick, the needy, the homeless and the dying. Mother Teresa decided to do something about it! The story of her labour of love has been told often over radio and television; to the special delight of countless Christians, she received recognition by her being awarded the Nobel Peace Prize. This faithful woman believed, that with God's help, she could make a difference and she did so, humbly and effectively.

'You can make a difference', as a principle of living well, is seen often in Holy Scripture. It is recorded that, at twenty-five years of age, Hezekiah came to the throne: 'He did what was right in the eyes of the Lord' (2 Kings 18:3). With commendable zeal, he challenged evil practices of his day, seeking to foster better ways and higher standards. He trusted in the Lord and so brought about change: one person's determination to challenge evil had a profound influence. The old saying proves true: 'It is better to light a candle than curse the darkness'. Sometimes, there are situations where things get dark – so terribly wretched – that it seems impossible to do anything to bring relief. Yet, so often in history, men and women have responded to such a challenge and, against all odds, have done something positive.

We can think of William and Catherine Booth, with their ministry shared in 'darkest England' in the nineteenth century; latterly, there was the courage of Mary Whitehouse in her valiant fight against the pernicious incidence of pornography and vile films. So many faithful believers have not simply accepted the fact that a dire situation is impossible to change, but they have instead lit a candle in the darkness, even as individual campaigners. As has been proved many times in the Church's life, one dedicated Christian can make a difference: that is the challenge to each of us.

Suggested readings: 2 Kings 18:1-8 and Colossians 4:12-13.

JULY 4th

## HUMBLE OBEDIENCE IS FRUITFUL

What a big difference one word can make, such as the word 'but' in the description of someone. In the Old Testament, we read how Naaman was the commander of the Syrian king's army and won an important victory. The scripture puts it this way: 'Naaman, commander of the army of the king of Syria, was a great man with his master and in high favour, because by him the Lord had given victory to Syria. He was a mighty man of valour, but he was a leper' (2 Kings 5:1). An extraordinary description: he was powerful, 'but . . . a leper'. His condition was something which – for all his military prowess – cast a long shadow over his life. Naaman then received advice that the prophet Elisha could help so he came to the prophet's house: Elisha had a powerful and distinguished visitor! The scripture makes it quite plain that the prophet was not exactly overwhelmed by the presence of Naaman. He simply sent a messenger to tell him: 'Go and wash in the Jordan seven times, and your flesh shall be restored, and you shall be clean' (2 Kings 5:10). Naaman was furious! He thought the prophet would come out and call on the name of his God and wave his hand over the leprosy, or at least send him to a better river for cleansing! His initial reaction is recorded: 'So he turned and went away in a rage' (2 Kings 5:12). Naaman's servants, presumably when his rage had calmed down, suggested he think again: 'If the prophet had commanded you to do some great thing, would you not have done it? How much rather, then when he says to you, "Wash, and be clean"'(2 Kings 5:13). Those words struck him forcibly, and he accepted them; he simply obeyed what Elisha directed and was duly healed. A reflection on this passage shows that there is a real sense in which Naaman's servants spoke the healing words; they spoke to him wisely but also bravely, because it was no small thing to rebuke a commander of the Syrian army!

When, during the 1980s mission to England, Dr. Billy Graham preached at Portman Road Football Stadium, Ipswich, scores of people responded to the challenge of the gospel. Among them was one woman who had been sitting high in the stands and came forward some time after others; she claimed that it took her time to come forward because 'it was a long way down'. That is very true to life; sometimes, from our position of pride or self-assurance it really is a long way down to a position of obedience. Naaman eventually discovered this himself, and he found that humble obedience to God brings much blessing. All believers realise that such humble dedication in glad devotion to God is, indeed, the golden rule for truly fruitful living! If we so open our hearts in obedience to the Lord, then we may know rich blessing, and we can each become a channel of blessing to others, too.

Suggested readings: 2 Kings 5:1-14 and 2 Corinthians 7:13-16.

JULY 5th

## CLEAR SEEING GIVES A SENSE OF PROPORTION

What a happy thing it is to take holiday snapshots! During the long winter months, these photos remind us of sunny days and times of relaxation. When the Bushby family went on holiday in Cornwall years ago, the weather was perfect: every single day brought hours of warm sunshine. One special day, Mr. Bushby went to St Ives and spent most of the day taking snapshot photographs of the spectacular scenery. It was a very happy summer's day, and so the trusty camera was constantly in use in the picturesque town. He and his wife decided to have the film developed at a local 'one hour film developing service' shop. Eagerly, they awaited the results, but on returning to the shop, the assistant handed over the envelope which had two words written on it 'film failure': not one of the photographs had come out properly! Mr. Bushby was annoyed and frustrated: the photographic record of that glorious, happy day on holiday was lost forever.

Just as he was nursing his grievance, he observed a man whose vision was evidently impaired. The man was carrying a white stick and trying to wend his way through the throng of holidaymakers. Suddenly, something clicked deep within Mr Bushby! What was the loss of a film with some photographs compared with the loss of one's sight? Here was a man, on a beautiful summer's day, unable to see the trees and flowers, the blue sky, golden sand and shimmering sea, let alone the faces of his loved ones. With a jolt, Mr. Bushby realised how small his trouble actually was compared with the disability of this other person; ashamed at this realisation, a sense of proportion returned.

How easy it is for life's disappointments to be seen as mountains of difficulty, or for us to be thrown off balance or to get a jaundiced view of things! Luke's gospel tells the story of a woman who had an infirmity for eighteen years: 'She was bent over and could not fully straighten herself' (Luke 13:11). The Lord mercifully addressed her, his heart full of compassion: 'Woman, you are freed from your infirmity'. The gospel story continues: 'And he laid his hands upon her, and immediately she was made straight, and she praised God' (Luke 13:12-13). However, not everyone was happy about this healing, as the narrative tells of the reaction: 'But the ruler of the synagogue, indignant because Jesus had healed on the Sabbath, said to the people "There are six days on which work ought to be done; come on those days and be healed, and not on the sabbath day"' (Luke 13:14). Jesus remarked that this leader was not rejoicing that a woman had been released from her infirmity, but was instead carping about keeping the rules! Clearly, Jesus had a very different perspective on the real needs of the situation and reached out to the woman who was healed.

Suggested readings: Psalm 150:1-6 and Luke 13:1-17.

JULY 6th

## LISTENING IS VERY IMPORTANT

How often God brings together two people who are so very different! Such was the meeting between Peter and Cornelius: a fisherman and a soldier, a Jew and a Gentile, a Christian and a 'righteous man'. It was an encounter between those of vastly contrasting status and class. They were so different, but Acts chapter 10 tells the fascinating story of how, by God's leading, these two figures were brought together under the same roof to fulfil God's wider purposes. As we think of Cornelius, Peter and the others assembled together, we note the laudable words of Cornelius in being wonderfully open to the Lord: 'Now we are all here in the presence of God to listen to everything the Lord has commanded you to tell us' (Acts 10:33 NIV). In a splendid way, these significant words tell us of the right attitude when we assemble for worship and fellowship. As we gather together, mindful of God's presence, we have to recall these things: (1) we are all sinners needing forgiveness, (2) we all need to hear God's Word, (3) we all require power to live truly on a spiritual level, (4) we all need openness to receive new light and truth from God.

One Sunday, at a friend's suggestion, a churchgoing young woman attended worship at a different church, and it proved to be an unforgettable experience. She testified: 'Even before the service began, I felt the presence of God. This service was something different! I desired to have the kind of faith these people possessed'. Often a believing community can communicate the faith even before the minister mounts the rostrum or the preacher enters the pulpit! Vibrant faith brings its own powerful message and can really be 'felt' by others there. Sometimes, when we attend a place of worship there is an air of routine: the minister, other leaders and possibly the choir can seem to be just 'going through the motions'. We know we cannot judge by appearances, but it is plain which type of service encourages faith: God is not glorified by merely routine worship or, indeed, thoughtless devotion.

As we gather with others for worship in the presence of the living God, surely there should be rising up within us, a sense of anticipation and openness to God. Cornelius, though a good man, wanted to know much more, and Peter was led to both teach and preach, while Cornelius was willing to listen and to respond. According to Luke, Cornelius said: 'Now we are all here in the presence of God to listen'. This wise comment sums up the right approach in which people ought to assemble for worship. Drawing on an Old Testament truth from the prophecy of Isaiah, the apostle Paul wrote on 'hearing' as he addressed the Christians in Rome: 'So faith comes from what is heard, and what is heard comes by the preaching of Christ' (Romans 10:17). True listening is vital for any Christian, as we gather for worship, or indeed, as we meet for fellowship or sharing together outside the church building!

Suggested readings: Psalm 70:1-5 and Acts 10:1-33.

JULY 7th

## GOD USES HUMBLE INSTRUMENTS, TOO

The prophet Amos was making himself a nuisance! The message he was giving was causing quite a disturbance, and the priest on duty at Bethel in the northern kingdom of Israel wanted him cease speaking and to go away. The meeting between this particular priest and Amos was tense, and the rural shepherd-turned-prophet from the southern kingdom speaking at this key shrine made his humble defence: 'I am no prophet, nor a prophet's son, but I am a herdsman and a dresser of sycamore trees, and the Lord took me from following the flock, and the Lord said to me 'Go, prophesy to my people Israel' (Amos 7:14-15). How significant and profound are those simple words of indisputable testimony spoken by this person of faith! Amos had no doubt that, 'The Lord took me'.

One of the fascinating things about the Old Testament is to see how God used unexpected methods and unexpected people! Amos had humble origins and made no attempt to conceal that fact, but he was sure that God had called him to exercise a spiritual ministry. Others could point out his lack of credentials, but he could simply testify to the reality of his calling: 'The Lord took me from following the flock'. This plain fact gave him courage and boldness, and so his ministry was a powerful and disturbing challenge to a society which had many social ills and which permitted evil ways, thus becoming a society which had failed God!

The beautiful words, 'The Lord took me', indicate a divine initiative which has been demonstrated over and over again in so many lives. The Lord took David from keeping sheep, took Joseph out of prison, took Peter from his fishing boat, took Matthew from the seat of custom, and used them all to His glory. The whole of Christian history provides numerous illustrations of how humble people were taken by the Lord and used in the service of the Kingdom of God. For example: who would ever dream that John Bunyan (a humble tinker in Bedfordshire) would be led by God to write a world-famous book? The book *Pilgrim's Progress* has been translated into many different languages and loved by people all over the world. God used a humble man to do a magnificent work for the Kingdom.

In so many cases God uses the unexpected person. The apostle Paul put it this way: 'For consider your call, brethren; not many of you were wise according to worldly standards, not many were powerful, not many were of noble birth. But God chose what is foolish in the world to shame the wise, God chose what is weak in the world to shame the strong' (1 Corinthians 1:26-27). God seems to delight in using humble instruments; many such people are serving God today and most of them will never be in the spotlight of publicity, but God is glorified in their lives.

Suggested readings: Amos 7:14-15 and 1 Corinthians 1:26-31.

JULY 8th

## OUR DECISIONS INFLUENCE OTHER LIVES

When Gerald Priestland was 37 years of age, he was offered the job as the BBC's chief correspondent at the Washington Office; it was considered the top post in his profession but there was a problem! He was deeply perplexed as to how he could break the news to his widowed mother, fearing an unfortunate reaction. When he did tell her, she was visibly shocked. Just two days before his flight to take up the post in USA, he visited her again and tried to cheer her up, but instead, in his presence she died, before his very eyes! Priestland commented later: 'But all I could do was sit at the bedside and stare first in pity, then horror. She was dead. I had solved my problems, gained my freedom, killed my mother by breaking her heart'. The doctor took a much kinder view. A variety of medical phrases included on the death certificate actually told another story; nevertheless, Gerald Priestland still felt an enormous sense of guilt about the whole situation.

Undoubtedly, Priestland was hard on himself, but this moving story underlines the apostle's dictum: 'We do not live to ourselves, and we do not die to ourselves' (Romans 14:7). We can all recognise that our mistakes, our failures, our disobedience, our selfishness and our lack of godliness can influence both our friends and our family; yet, we can thank God it works the other way, too! Our obedience and our active service can greatly influence other people, but also even our quiet witness to Christ can encourage others themselves to know and serve the Lord.

As we all know, sometimes decisions are very hard. Gerald Priestland was 'the right one for the right job': his experience in radio and television had prepared him, but it was still a hard decision. So, there are people who receive a call from God and their decision impinges immensely on their family. Think of a young person with brilliant qualifications set to be a successful professional, say in law or medicine, and then a decision is made (after a significant Christian experience of the Lord's call) to abandon such career plans, and to go into the Christian ministry in Britain or overseas. Those who, perhaps, have supported the person financially feel let down that so much was invested in education and training, but it would appear it is being thrown away. One wonders, when Peter (with his brother Andrew) gave up the successful fishing business and followed Christ, did his mother-in-law feel he was totally irresponsible? Did she suffer from a fever of anxiety, only then to discover the reality of Jesus' ministry for herself? Some decisions to be faithful, loyal, honest and obedient can prove to be very hard but, of course, there is no option in the matter!

Suggested readings: Mark 1:14-20 and Mark 1:29-39.

JULY 9th

## LIFE IS LIKE A GAME OF CHESS

One popular table game is chess and, at an international level, competitions have even gained the attention of television cameras! The game demands skill, concentration, patience and foresight: the good player watches every move, carefully analyses the strategy, and looks far ahead. In fact, the ability to anticipate, to foresee moves and seize opportunities is the major part of the game. In the Book of Proverbs, the wise teacher advocates a philosophy of life which is very straightforward: 'The simple believe everything but the clever consider their steps' (Proverbs 14:15). The Good News Bible puts it in crystal clear language 'Sensible people watch their steps'; in other words, they truly look where they are going!

In Holy Scripture there are scores of verses which refer to walking; in fact, over 300 verses make some allusion! There are various admonitions: these take various forms as we are urged to walk by faith, and also to walk in the truth, in the light, in wisdom or, indeed, in 'newness of life'. The apostle Paul advised: 'Look carefully then how you walk'. Both Old and New Testaments stress that wise people of faith always carefully look where they are going.

On one occasion, a minister of the gospel spoke about the journey of life; it was likened to an obstacle race. That seems an exaggeration, but actually men and women do encounter many and varied obstacles: these might include debris in the way, dangerous drop-offs, narrow passes, unforeseen pitfalls and slippery patches, to name but a few. Even journeying on a bright sunny day can bring its own dangers, too, with the dazzling sun low in the sky ahead! The Highway Code gives the rules of the road for travel which are all extremely important. However, one of the most vital rules is paying close attention to what is around one and carefully looking ahead. Not only is it vital for the chess player or the driver to concentrate and anticipate; that imperative applies also to those on the journey of life, at all stages along the way.

The prudent person looks ahead and prepares to take necessary action. This has been put in a somewhat humorous way: 'It is a good thing for the spiritual man [or woman] to use binoculars!' How many mistakes would have been avoided if people had spent time thinking and looking ahead in thought and prayer! Over the years, many people have walked from John O'Groats to Land's End (a journey of some 891 miles), in order to raise money for charity. It is quite clear that no person does that on the spur of the moment: the long journey – however it is undertaken – demands much thought and preparation in looking ahead. Like a game of chess or a journey, it is imperative, by God's guidance and strength, to consider our next moves as we go on in life, doing our best, as we are able, to plan each step with prudence!

Suggested readings: Proverbs 14:6-17 and Ephesians 5:7-17.

JULY 10th

## REMEMBERING CAN SET PEOPLE FREE

It was a low-key interview on the radio, but suddenly this thought-provoking sentence was spoken: 'To remember means to be liberated'. It came like a brilliant ray of sunshine on a very dull afternoon. Indeed, it is a truth which is as solid as a rock: remembering can and does set people free. As we look at Holy Scripture, we observe that there are numerous verses which challenge us to remember, and two of them are the following: 'You shall remember all the way which the Lord your God has led you these forty years in the wilderness' (Deuteronomy 8:2) and 'Remember the wonderful works he has done' (1 Chronicles 16:12). We acknowledge here that remembering can provoke many different feelings: we can remember and be grateful, or we can be bitter, ashamed or even fearful. We thank God, especially, that we can duly remember and so be liberated! In one of the psalms, we read this poignant prayer: 'Deliver me from my persecutors; for they are too strong for me! Bring me out of prison, that I may give thanks to thy name!' (Psalm 142:6-7). No doubt, we have all known what it is to feel constrained in some way, but remembering can set us free.

We may think of moments of being in the prison of fear, anxiety or guilt. It may be that a person has done wrong and has a crushing burden, day by day, feeling the weight of guilt. Then, one unforgettable day, God's offer of forgiveness becomes clear, perhaps for the first time and, once it is acknowledged, there is the experience of being set free, liberated indeed. The words of the Old Testament are like a liberating angel: 'He does not deal with us according to our sins, nor requite us according to our iniquities . . . As far as the east is from the west, so far does he remove our transgressions from us' (Psalm 103:10,12). For us to remember God's boundless love and generous forgiveness is a truly liberating experience.

We ponder those comforting words in the Epistle to the Hebrews: 'For I will be merciful toward their iniquities, and I will remember their sins no more' (Hebrews 8:12). To be cleared of guilt through being forgiven, is to be set free. One minister who exercised a fine pastoral ministry used to have a special word for those people overwhelmed by serious difficulties: 'Remember God dealt with a much larger problem yesterday'. How comforting and encouraging that thought can be! So the psalmist puts it very concisely: 'I will remember the deeds of the Lord; yes, I will remember your miracles of long ago' (Psalm 77:11 NIV). When we remember that God has answered prayer, has given guidance, has bestowed strength and has worked out His purposes, then we can rejoice and know freedom, for the Lord is faithful and good; we can be sure that God will never let us go, yet also longs for us to be free.

Suggested readings: 1 Chronicles 16:7-24 and Hebrews 8:10-12.

JULY 11th

## THAT LETTER WRITING IS A MINISTRY

We thank God that the apostle Paul wrote his epistles! He must have been one of the busiest of the leaders of the churches, toiling tirelessly as pioneer evangelist, church planter, preacher, theologian, pastor and counsellor as well as friend; yet he found time to write letters, too! One of the letters, which has been loved by generations of Christians, is Philippians. In the last chapter, he gives insight into his own simple philosophy of life: 'I have learned, in whatever state I am, to be content' (Philippians 4:11). He gives powerful testimony concerning his confidence in God's sufficiency: 'And my God will supply every need of yours according to his riches in glory in Christ Jesus' (Philippians 4:19). This one short letter includes so much encouragement; it has been a blessing to countless believers down the centuries.

Untold numbers of people have been blessed through the writings of Dr. F.W. Boreham. In one of his fine essays, he writes of the 'ministry of the postage stamp': he skilfully underlines the fact that one letter can be of great value. A moment's reflection reminds us that a single note through the post – or by some other means – can change a person's situation, or at least his or her outlook: a letter can bring much comfort, assurance or encouragement. Just a short letter, or one judiciously timed note or card, can redirect the course of a whole life!

Volumes have been written about C.H. Spurgeon and his powerful ministry in the nineteenth century at the Metropolitan Tabernacle, London, as he preached to vast crowds Sunday by Sunday. However, behind his very visible public ministry, there was a lovely Christian woman: Susannah Spurgeon took it upon herself to write many hundreds of letters! She had a special concern for Christian workers and she showed it by writing letters to encourage them. Her husband inspired people by his mighty proclamation of God's Word: she, in turn, inspired many by her thoughtful and timely letters.

The splendid thing about this ministry is that it can be done when we are unable to intervene in any other way. In our public libraries there are numerous books which come under the heading 'Life and Letters', as if the life and letters were bound together; it was certainly so with Paul! His life and letters were bonded together in a remarkable way, and generations have gained insights and inspiration through them as he was used of God. It is just possible that God is calling us each to share also, as we are able, in this humble but very effective ministry of writing letters or sending some other kind of timely greetings. Many of us can simply, but faithfully, be engaged in the incredibly valuable 'ministry of the postage stamp': it can be surely used by God to bring great blessing and encouragement.

Suggested readings: Philippians 4:4-23 and 2 Timothy 1:1-7.

JULY 12th

## THE MIND'S FOCUS IS IMPORTANT

The human mind has amazing powers and, although the human body is confined by illness and physical limitations, the sound and focused mind can roam to other places or times, or to a myriad different situations, as well as soar to higher, loftier realms or probe to the depths, to deeper thoughts and issues! Someone can be travelling through Scotland on a train reading a daily newspaper, but his mind can be in Australia remembering friends and relatives. A woman can be shopping in a busy store or speaking to a neighbour, but her mind be centered on a loved-one having a special interview at that very time on the other side of the globe.

The mind has free range, but there is also a need for focus. In Isaiah, there is a verse which serves as a reminder that the focus of the mind's attention is important and shapes attitudes. The prophet says: 'Those of steadfast mind you keep in peace – in peace because they trust in you' (Isaiah 26:3). We acknowledge that the mind can centre on fears, problems, difficulties and various loathings, and these disturbances to our peace can bring deep anxiety and distress. Alternatively, the human mind can centre on positive, good and wholesome things, and this can bring happiness and blessing. Throughout Church history, men and women have stressed the importance of last thoughts at night and first thoughts in the morning. What we choose to focus on – and also what we decide to blot out of our minds – is very significant for our mental, emotional and, indeed, spiritual health.

Dr. Norman Vincent Peale is well known because of his books on positive thinking and, in his ministry of pen and pulpit, he advocated beginning the day by reminding oneself of some of the great texts from the Bible. It is one thing to start the day saying, 'Oh dear! Yet another day at the office'; it is quite another thing to truly ponder, 'The Lord is on my side to help me' (Psalm 118:7). How important it is to let the mind think about the goodness of the Lord. How wonderful it is to think of His love, His power, His mercy, His grace and His faithfulness. A few moments spent thinking about our gracious God can enliven and strengthen the heart!

A ship needs a good location for safe anchorage, and so does the human mind. We can let our minds be anchored in the troubled waters of life's difficulties and problems, or we can anchor our minds in the still waters of God's grace. One of the great verses says: 'His mercies never come to an end; they are new every morning; great is thy faithfulness' (Lamentations 3:22-23). It is a wise thing to let the mind dwell on the positive and the good; it is even wiser to let it focus on the God of grace Whom we serve and adore.

Suggested readings: Isaiah 26:1-9 and Lamentations 3:21-27.

JULY 13th

## JESUS CHRIST CAN STILL THE STORM

One of the most frightening experiences is to be caught in a storm at sea. Life seems to lose all its certainties! The boat tosses at sickening angles and one is both disorientated and afraid. As we know, a number of the first disciples of Jesus were seasoned fishermen: they had, no doubt, each experienced many storms on the Lake of Galilee. However, this storm was different! Mark tells us about it in his gospel (Mark 4:35-41). This storm's wildness and ferocity was enough to strike terror into the bravest heart. The simplicity of the words underlines the crisis: '. . . a great storm of wind arose, and the waves beat into the boat, so that the boat was already filling' (Mark 4:37). The disciples urgently sought help from Jesus and we read these marvellous words: 'He awoke and rebuked the wind, and said to the sea, "Peace! Be still!"' And the wind ceased, and there was a great calm' (Mark 4:39). With His sure word, Jesus demonstrated He had power over the forces of nature and this truth is captured in the astonished response: 'Who then is this, that even the wind and sea obey him?' (Mark 4:41). There is little doubt that the disciples had their eyes opened on this dramatic occasion as they witnessed His ability to calm the storm, but furthermore, to still the tumult in their hearts.

Many Christian people have discovered that Jesus Christ can still storms, particularly the tempests in the human heart. We can think of the storms that can rage there: the storms of anger, sorrow, frustration, disappointment, anxiety or shame, possibly even regret. These particular storms may terrify us with their ferocity and violence, but Jesus can – in His grace – still the storms within the human heart. Countless people have proved this true and they have found in Him, 'the peace of God, which passes all understanding' (Philippians 4:7). Some people, like the disciples on Galilee, have been wonderfully 'shocked', as it were, at the ability of Jesus Christ: in His amazing power and mercy, He has surpassed their highest expectations.

The disciples witnessing this awesome wonder said, 'Who then is this?' That is a good question! He is the Saviour of the world and millions of people have found in Him true peace. It is possible that we, or someone very close to us, is presently caught in the centre of a violent storm, feeling anxious or even very afraid, but the good news of Christ remains ever the same: 'Take heart!' This same Jesus, as the risen Lord, can help anyone so beset by storms within: He still rebukes the storms of life, saying with gracious authority, 'Peace! Be still!', and so we can trust Him.

Suggested readings: Mark 4:30-41 and Philippians 4:1-9

JULY 14th

## SOMETIMES MEN AND WOMEN SAY, 'NO LORD!'

It is commonly said that 'confession is good for the soul', and many would agree with this maxim. Sometime ago, a magazine invited a number of well-known people to write about some deed of which they were ashamed, meaning some action they would have preferred to forget. The resulting article was fascinating: one had made a deception in a relationship, another had cheated in an examination, one had lied to a friend and one woman even confessed that she had kicked her husband so hard that she broke her foot! It was most revealing of human nature. The fact is, of course, that just about all men and women have said and done things which they've regretted afterwards.

Simon Peter has always been a much-loved character in Church circles: his personality is so poignantly revealed in the New Testament and people 'feel at home' with him! What a blended character: strong but weak, wise yet foolish, quick though slow, devout while frail. He was a mixture of a personality and that's why people so appreciate the way he is portrayed! He had his memorable high points, but moments of shame, too. In Acts 11, Luke records how Peter declared that the Lord came to him in a vision to prompt him to act in an unexpected manner, and he had replied, 'No, Lord' (Acts 11:8). Evidently, Peter had definite ideas about ritual purity, and also about Gentiles: to him, as a faithful adherent of the law, they were different, even 'unclean'. Now he had to learn, as a disciple of Christ, that the truth of God's mercy was deeper and broader than that: God loved both Jews and Gentiles. One of the key verses here, as the story of Peter's own further 'conversion' is related – giving the reaction on the part of the Jerusalem church to his account – reads as follows: 'Then to the Gentiles also God has granted repentance unto life' (Acts 11:18).

The story is told of a young man who felt he had received a clear call from God to serve on the mission field as a missionary. For personal reasons, he declined the call of God and, like Peter, said 'No, Lord'. Years later, at a missionary meeting, this man confessed his disobedience, and urged the young people present to say 'Yes, Lord'. There are many Christians who can testify (with great shame and regret) that they have said 'No, Lord'. Our disobedience may not be known to others, but it is known to God. The psalmist prays: 'But who can discern his errors? Clear thou me from hidden faults. Keep back thy servant from presumptuous sins' (Psalm 19:12-13). If we have ever said, 'No, Lord', or if we have ever been deliberately disobedient to the known will of God, we can trust that God is merciful and forgiving, always ready to accept us and to grant a new beginning.

Suggested readings: Acts 11:1-18 and Psalm 19:7-14.

JULY 15th

## PATIENCE BRINGS FRUITFULNESS

How foolish it would be for a farmer to be impatient about the harvest! It is no good sowing the seed and expecting a harvest at the end of the month! The farmer has to plough the field, sow the seed, tend the ground, and then wait. One of the best-known stories of Jesus is the Parable of the Sower: it underlines the fact that the seed falls in different places with varying results. Right at the end of this beautiful and instructive parable, we get these words 'And as for that in the good soil, they are those who, hearing the word, hold it fast in an honest and good heart, and bring forth fruit with patience' (Luke 8:15). Patience can bring forth fruit; that's a fact of life!

One very active schoolteacher has long taken delight in doing giant jigsaw puzzles, the type that lots of people possess but never get round to doing! This particular lady thinks nothing of spending a whole winter season (in her few spare hours!) to get a giant puzzle completed. She lives a busy life and is engaged in a whole variety of activities, and yet slowly but surely the jigsaw is done. Finally, she sees the fruit of her patience. In so many areas, patience produces fruit in the form of a good outcome with genuine results. We can ponder the roles of the farmer, the fisherman, the detective, the craftsman or woman, the artist or the horticulturalist, among many others. We know the patience of the rose-grower who seeks to develop a special rose: it may take years to cultivate the new rose so that it has the required colour and fragrance but, in the end, horticulturalist's patience will be handsomely rewarded.

In the Book of James, we have this striking verse: 'See how patient a farmer is as he waits for his land to produce precious crops. He waits patiently for the autumn and spring rains. You also must be patient' (James 5:7 GNB). There is so much in Holy Scripture which encourages the belief that patience is productive in the end. One of the supreme examples of patience is the Blessed Master. How slow His disciples were to learn the basic truths and to begin to understand His way. In the end, His patience brought forth fruit as the Church began to flourish.

We can think again of the apostle Paul's testimony: 'And I am the foremost of sinners; but I received mercy for this reason, that in me, as the foremost, Jesus Christ might display his perfect patience for an example to those who were to believe in him for eternal life' (1 Timothy 1:15-16). The New International Version translates the words 'perfect patience' as 'unlimited patience'; the Saviour's unlimited patience produced much fruit, and so we rejoice in the Lord's goodness.

Suggested readings: Luke 8:11-15 and 1 Timothy 1:12-17.

JULY 16th

## CONCERNING THE MINISTRY OF KIND WORDS

Standing at a bus or railway station waiting to travel, it is interesting to see the looks on people's faces. It appears that quite a large proportion of people have an anxious look; of course, there are numerous reasons why anxiety grips the human heart. Just a few obvious ones are domestic problems, relationship conflicts, stress at work or difficult decisions, fear of redundancy or of debt, or illness within the family, not to mention national crises or worrying world events. The scripture includes this simple but profound remark: 'Anxiety weighs down the human heart, but a good word cheers it up' (Proverbs 12:25). The ministry of good words, kindly interest and timely encouragement can be well used in the service of God's Kingdom.

One of the most lovable characters in the New Testament is Barnabas, so well known for his kindness! When the newly converted Paul first came to Jerusalem 'he tried to join the disciples but they were all afraid of him, not believing he really was a disciple but Barnabas took him' (Acts 9:26-27). Barnabas accepted him and came forward to speak kindly words in Paul's defence. It is a salutary thought how much the Church owes to this kindness shown by Barnabas! The story goes on to reveal that all this kindly support gave new courage and confidence to the new convert. Good words can cheer the heart, kind words can give sure encouragement; indeed, the Spirit of God can powerfully use our words to bring hope and peace.

In Ephesians, there is lofty teaching about God's plan and purpose, but the apostle also gives a hefty measure of practical Christianity: some sections of the letter could be entitled 'How to live the Christian life in everyday situations'. The advice is quite clear: 'Let all bitterness and wrath and anger and clamour and slander be put away from you, with all malice, and be kind to one another, tender-hearted, forgiving one another, as God in Christ forgave you' (Ephesians 4:31). One of the important means of living this way is to show kindness through good words. We think of the story of the man with leprosy coming to Jesus (Mark 1:44-45). We can picture the scene and consider Jesus' gracious thoughts, His gentle touch and the kind words.

Amazingly, kind words break through the language barrier! Everyone seems to know when kindly words are spoken. There is a Japanese proverb which says, 'One kind word can warm three winter months!' That is obviously an exaggeration, but if we carefully consider the importance of kind words, we see much that rings true in the very suggestion that winter can be somehow shortened. Kind words can be used by God's Spirit to set individuals on their first steps towards the Kingdom. Thus, we can always be about the task of envisaging what our kind words, by God's rich mercy, might do in the lives of others, and so seek to reach out in ways to help, to console, to encourage or to inspire!

Suggested readings: Proverbs 12:24-28 and Acts 9:26-31.

JULY 17th

## LIFE DOES HAVE MIRACULOUS ESCAPES

Plenty of people use the words of the Bible without even knowing it! After a close shave with catastrophe, if someone has a very narrow escape, say, after a high-speed crash or a dangerous fall, colleagues relating the incident describe it as missing death 'by the skin of their teeth'. Those actual words are in the Old Testament: 'I have escaped by the skin of my teeth' (Job 19:20). Narrow escapes feature a great deal in the Old Testament: Sarah, Joseph, Rahab, David, Daniel all faced such risky episodes. The apostle Paul had numerous narrow escapes. In Acts 27, we read a dramatic account of a storm at sea with the awful tempest leading to despair: 'all hope of our being saved was at last abandoned' (Acts 27:20). After fourteen nerve-wracking days, the sailors suspected they were near land, and so once the morning light proved them right, an order was given: 'those who could swim to throw themselves overboard first and make for the land, and the rest on planks or on pieces of the ship. And so it was that all escaped to land' (Acts 27:43-44). It was quite an extraordinary escape in the midst of such danger, and the apostle attributed it to God's aid.

There are numerous people who can testify that they have had narrow escapes: sailors, mountaineers, servicemen and women, coal-miners, pilots, explorers, bomb disposal experts, divers, emergency service personnel and countless others. It is a dreadful thing to be trapped and often a truly surreal experience to manage to escape! Psalm 124 is very short, but it contains a powerful verse about God's people escaping: 'We have escaped as a bird from the share of the fowlers; the snare is broken, and we have escaped' (Psalm 124:7). Then the psalmist gives voice to their moving testimony about God: 'Our help is in the name of the Lord, who made heaven and earth' (Psalm 124:8). People of faith sense God's aid in their miraculous escape! Some people of the world talk in general about a 'lucky escape', but people of faith who have sensed the Lord's aid in a crisis, speak reverently of divine deliverance.

Sometimes, when a person has a dramatic escape, it leaves an abiding impression on the mind: so it was with John Wesley. One never-to-be-forgotten day, the Epworth Rectory caught fire and, at the height of the blaze, the boy John Wesley appeared at an upstairs window. He was rescued, a dramatic escape from certain death, 'by the skin of his teeth'! This episode left an indelible mark on the mind and heart of Wesley and, in his own words, he was 'a brand plucked from the burning'. This gave him a deep sense of purpose and destiny. Although, he was especially associated with Methodism, there is a deeper sense in which his great ministry belongs to the whole family of God. God used that experience of escape to good effect and, as an adult, John Wesley was mightily used to God's glory!

Suggested readings: Psalm 124:1-8 and Acts 27:33-44.

JULY 18th

## GOD STEPS IN

On the occasion of the Jubilee of the World Evangelization Crusaders, a book was published with a fascinating title *Then God Stepped In*. In the introduction, Leonard Moules made the comment that most Christians can recall occasions when God came to them and gave aid 'in timely and remarkable ways'; the book includes a series of testimonies concerning God's intervention and deliverance. It is a salutary reminder that God does step into events and circumstances, and works His sovereign will in and through us, or even despite us! The Holy Scriptures contain numerous stories of God's deliverance in what was felt to be a dramatic way; in fact, there are many passages in scripture which could be prefaced with the words 'then God stepped in'.

One of the most incisive speeches recorded in the New Testament is Stephen's address to the Sanhedrin. He spoke boldly of the God of glory acting in sovereign power to form His people; in the opening part, Stephen spoke of God's dealings with Abraham and Joseph. The passage about Joseph's amazing deliverance is significant and tells of God's intervention: 'And the patriarchs, jealous of Joseph, sold him into Egypt; but God was with him, and rescued him out of all his afflictions, and gave him favour and wisdom before Pharaoh, King of Egypt, who made him governor over Egypt and over all his household' (Acts 7:9-10). To him it was plain: God rescued Joseph, by stepping into the situation, in order to work out His purposes! The story of Joseph, as it is told in the Book of Genesis, is a great illustration of how the Lord can redeem situations to His greater glory.

Actually, it is a fair assessment that a large part of the Old Testament is about God's intervention in situations: God stepping into the lives of people and into the life of one nation. However, the most wonderful story of God's intervention is demonstrated in the life of Jesus Christ. We know how He was rejected by His own people and died a painful and humiliating death on a cross, forsaken by the world. This shocked the disciples, and they were left feeling absolutely desolate, as the situation seemed beyond hope! Yet, death did not have the final word. God 'stepped in' as Jesus Christ was raised from the dead. In the bleakest moment of history, when it seemed that evil had won final mastery, God 'stepped in' and proved that love could not be conquered by hate. The apostle Peter, addressing his own people with the gospel, put it this way: 'And you, with the help of wicked men, put him to death, by nailing him to the cross but God raised him from the dead' (Acts 2:23 NIV). God does 'step in' and intervenes so that lives are transformed and people find new hope.

Suggested readings: Genesis 45:1-7 and Acts 2:21-24.

JULY 19th

## LIFE IS A PRECIOUS GIFT

In the Old Testament, we read how King Hezekiah became dangerously ill 'and was at the point of death' (Isaiah 38:1). The extremity of the situation was underlined by the advice given by the prophet Isaiah: 'Set your house in order for you shall die, you shall not recover' (Isaiah 38:1). It was a very direct, rather blunt, message from the Lord and, unsurprisingly, it upset Hezekiah. The king turned his face to the wall and wept. The only thing left to remedy the situation was prayer! Power, riches, status, comfort, regal office and its privileges were all put in perspective since nothing could be done except pray, and so prayer was indeed offered. Then comes an important twist in the story, for the same prophet who had predicted death was sent by the Lord with another message: 'I have heard your prayer, I have seen your tears; behold, I will add fifteen years to your life' (Isaiah 38:5). So Hezekiah was brought back from the precipice as he was given the most unusual – but exceedingly precious – gift of fifteen more years of life. It was, no doubt, the best gift he had ever received, and the scriptures narrate how he used them well.

What is life, and how might it be portrayed or depicted? Artists, sculptors, musicians, poets, psalmists and hymn writers, theologians, philosophers, not to mention scientists, have all tried to explain. Life is a gift, and every day, every hour, every minute is a gift, and so the psalmist made this plea: 'So teach us to number our days that we may get a heart of wisdom' (Psalm 90:12). Of course, people do number their days marking birthdays, wedding anniversaries, and other annual reminders of special life events! So, in Britain, if a married couple reach their diamond wedding anniversary after sixty years of marriage, or if someone reaches the ripe old age of one hundred years, a special greeting is received from the Queen. All this underlines the fact that life is so very precious, and to be highly cherished as a wonderful gift.

Sometimes, we meet people who have been brought back safely, as it were, from the brink. As in the case of Hezekiah, an experience of being delivered from a life-threatening illness, or near certain death in an accident, can be transformative. There may be a new dimension to life and often a new delight is taken in the simple pleasures of home and family; there is a fresh appreciation of the everyday joys of life in the world. The Holy Scriptures always urge us to count our blessings, and live fully each new day, finding joy and satisfaction in each day's good things; even an ordinary day can be overflowing with lovely things. As believers, we can be mindful that God gives us each day as a gracious gift: so we are to live in gratitude.

Suggested readings: Psalm 90:1-12 and Isaiah 38:1-5.

JULY 20th

## THE HEAVENLY FATHER CAN BE TRUSTED

Our human capacity for memory is marvellous! It can be used of God to provoke present faith, as well as to rekindle recollections of trust from the past. Malcolm Muggeridge, a writer and broadcaster, spoke of lovely childhood memories of going for walks with his father. Sometimes their walk would be over rough ground, or up a steep hill, or on marshy ground, however, none of this ever worried the young Malcolm. He had confidence in his father and relied on him to arrive back safely. He trusted that his father could cope with the difficulties on the way! This memory spoke to him of the heavenly Father and of His ability to handle situations and to see us safely through rough paths.

Not all, but many people thank God for truly good fathers who were formative in their upbringing! One elderly lady loved to speak of her happy childhood memories, one being a Christmas tradition. At the festive season her father would secretly give her a nice sum of money so that she could purchase Christmas presents for others, and those 'others' included both parents! This generous and considerate deed remained in the memory for her for decades. Her father's loving generosity was never forgotten and it was a cause for thanksgiving. Sadly, not everyone has fond memories of a father's love and care; yet, for all who have had a positive experience of parental care, and who are willing to ponder over spiritual matters, it can remind us of the far more gracious and glorious ways of our heavenly Father with us all.

The Bible speaks often of God's love being like a parent's love for a child. Indeed, Jesus prayed to God using the Aramaic word, Abba, translated into English as 'Daddy'. It is a way of expressing the intimacy of relationship with God. Moreover, one of the finest thoughts about the life of Jesus Christ is expressed in this short expression: the heart of God revealed. In John's gospel we read that Philip made a request: 'Lord, show us the Father, and we will be satisfied' (John 14:8). The Blessed Master gave an astonishing reply, treasured by believers: 'Whoever has seen me has seen the Father' (John 14:9). We glimpse God fully in Jesus Christ.

As we reflect on the great love that God has shown to us in Jesus, we know that wherever life may take us, we may experience the love of God in Jesus Christ. Christian faith teaches that the believer need have no distressing fear for the heavenly Father is absolutely faithful, and His generosity beyond all comprehension. In all circumstances, we may trust our heavenly Father. With the psalmist we may claim: 'This I know, that God is for me' (Psalm 56:9). Thanks be to God!

Suggested readings: Psalm 56:1-13 and John 14:8-11.

JULY 21st

## GOD'S GREAT WORD IS 'WHOSOEVER'

A man who had studied the scriptures for over forty years and freely testified that the modern versions had given him wonderful help said: 'But, when I have my own Quiet Time with God I use the Authorised Version: because its grace and beauty still grip my mind and heart'. It is very interesting to note that, often at great cathedral services, this version is still used! Even some avowedly contemporary, progressive people have a particular love for it. One of the lovely words used in the Authorised Version is the word 'whosoever', and it is found in three of the finest texts of the Bible, which are fully inclusive despite the older archaic rendering: 'For God so loved the world, that he gave his only begotten that whosoever believeth in him should not perish but have everlasting life' (John 3:16), 'And it shall come to pass that whosoever shall call on the name of the Lord shall be saved' (Acts 2:21), 'Let him that is athirst come. And whosoever will let him take the water of life freely' (Revelation 22:17). What gloriously open and gracious promises to us all!

This lovely word 'whosoever' tells of the height and breadth, the length and depth of God's marvellous love. It speaks of love which includes people from all backgrounds, of every age and generation: people around the globe are drawn from North and South, East and West to experience this wonderful love and mercy. The word 'whosoever' has been on the lips of sincere preachers, teachers and evangelists, as well as all who seek to broadcast the faith authentically. It is special as it reminds people that God's love is beyond all human calculation and is wholly inclusive. As we recall these three special verses, the heart of the Christian faith is revealed: our God loves people and the Lord's invitation is to 'whosoever'. We can ponder the great proclaimers down the recent centuries who have used this great word: John Wesley, George Whitefield, Charles Spurgeon, Billy Graham, but also less well known men and women have always witnessed to a God who offers grace to 'whosoever'. As a result of the faithful witness of ordinary believers and noted proclaimers alike, many people have responded to God's loving call: 'Believe in the Lord, whosoever you are!'

Millions have found courage to come to God for forgiveness and mercy because of the inspiration given by the word 'whosoever'. Jesus challenged religiosity ridden with exclusiveness, and instead spoke of God's love and its availability to all the world. Astronauts have viewed the planet Earth as a tiny ball in space and have spoken about how special the world looked, different from anything else in sight. Human love is wonderful, yet the word 'whosoever' declares God's eternal self-giving love for this world, a love for us all which is unique and beyond compare.

Suggested readings: John 3:1-16 and Revelation 22:16-21.

JULY 22nd

## THE BIBLE HAS HIDDEN TREASURE

Some fifty years ago, a woman went to a house sale and, on impulse, purchased an old oak desk; her parents were displeased because they had sent her to buy something entirely different! However, there is a very pleasant twist to the story. About forty years after the purchase, Jane decided to give the desk a thorough 'tidy up' and she took out the old draw linings and put them in a bin. At this point she spotted that some of the linings were old manuscripts and, on closer inspection, noticed something very important: one manuscript bore the signature of Sir Edward Elgar. It was shown to the Elgar Foundation and they were absolutely thrilled with it. Eventually, this valuable document was handed over for a four-figure sum, then a very large amount. The purchase had been more than vindicated as, quite unforeseen, the old oak desk had yielded up a treasure!

This reminds us that, in so many homes today, there is one treasure – a copy of the Holy Scriptures – which is often neglected, undiscovered, and even forgotten. However, from time to time, there are people who suddenly discover its worth: they find the Bible is a precious book and it brings a radical change into their home. The records of the Bible Societies contain numerous accounts of this kind of discovery. Sometimes, people find a helpful passage in scripture, apparently quite by accident. However, believers refer to such instances, not as a chance occurrence, but as an example of the gracious ministry of the Holy Spirit. The discovery that the Bible is important can be life changing since it often brings radical transformation of life and home. Many stories would confirm that, and so it is, indeed, a good thing to discover – or perhaps to know afresh – the value of the Bible. In fact, very often a different translation can help such discovery!

Sometimes, in the ancient world people stumbled on hidden treasure: a farmer could be ploughing a field and suddenly discover a rich hoard and, of course, this has happened in modern times, too. One of life's big discoveries is to find the richness of God's promises: 'I rejoice at your word like one who finds great spoil' (Psalm 119:162). 'Rich treasure' is how the Good News Bible translates it. Jane purchased an old desk and found a treasure; so, men and women can purchase a Bible at low cost and then discover its riches. Sometimes, a Bible is purchased and not actually read by the purchaser for decades, but then its true worth is discovered. One person once testified that she went through life for years facing all kinds of troubles and then opened her Bible and found this promise: 'God is our refuge and strength, a very present help in trouble' (Psalm 46:1). The discovery of this truth was one of the best discoveries she had ever made, and it can be known by us, too.

Suggested readings: Psalm 46:1-5 and Psalm 119:144-162.

JULY 23rd

## CHRISTIANS CANNOT CHAIN JESUS CHRIST

One of the most humiliating experiences a person can face is to be put in chains. People who have actually experienced this have spoken of their distress and horror. Comedians crack jokes about the 'ball and chain', but the reality is truly horrible. So we read with dismay the opening words of Mark chapter 15: 'As soon as morning came, the chief priests, having made their plan with the elders and lawyers in full council, put Jesus in chains then they led him away and handed him over to Pilate' (Mark 15:1 NEB). They put Jesus, the Blessed Son of God, in chains.

As we ponder the story of the last week in the earthly life of Jesus, we know that He was mocked and jeered, falsely accused and scourged, put on a cross and crucified. However, we recall what happened at the beginning: He was put in chains. If we ponder this, we know that, at the deepest level, paradoxically, Jesus was truly free but – in reality – they were chained! They were bound by hatred, prejudice and spiritual blindness; Jesus Himself was physically chained, but spiritually free. They were physically free, but in spiritual chains! It is a glorious affirmation that nothing keeps Jesus Christ in chains: that is one of the powerful lessons of the gospel story.

Over the centuries, people have endeavoured to keep Jesus, as it were, in chains and, at times, even Christians have tried to do it! We can think of those who have sought to 'chain' Jesus in an exact and precise formula or category; they very foolishly feel they have the Saviour of the world 'taped and measured'! Yet, this is impossible. As John's gospel reminds us: 'But there are also many other things which Jesus did; were every one of them to be written, I suppose that the world itself could not contain the books that would be written' (John 21:25). Jesus is greater than any category we can imagine! He is greater than our highest thoughts and finest words! Who is He for the world? He is Shepherd, Saviour, Friend, High Priest, Messiah, Lord, King, and so much more: words cannot fully describe all His glory!

As we reflect on how a disciple 'grows in the grace and knowledge of our Lord and Saviour Jesus Christ' (2 Peter 3:18), we realise that the Lord is majestic, glorious and wonderful in His splendour; we could never chain Him with our poor estimation! The computation used for the most sophisticated systems in our world could never calculate His love 'which surpasses knowledge' (Ephesians 3:19). The words of the hymn are fitting: 'Hallelujah! What a Saviour!' We rejoice in a Saviour Who is far greater than any language could possibly describe, but Whose love is available to the meek and the humble, and welcoming to even the least and lowliest. No chains can hinder the Lord's gracious way or impede His welcome.

Suggested readings: Mark 15:1-15 and John 21:24-25.

JULY 24th

## CHRISTIANS ARE CALLED TO BE DIFFERENT

She was strutting through the shopping centre: confident, upright, sprightly and with a jaunt in her steps. In her hand was a carrier bag with these words boldly inscribed: 'Entirely Different'. One is used to seeing carrier bags emblazoned with various retailers' well-known brand names, but this caught the eye: 'Entirely different'! Whoever thought of the name of that clothing brand had a touch of genius! Some women and men like clothes that make them stand out and feel unique. No one wants to arrive at a special reception or party and see several people in exactly the same outfit!

In his lectures, Dr. William Barclay stressed that the root of the word holy is 'different'. Thus, when we speak of a holy place, we are speaking of a 'different' place; when we speak of a holy day, we mean a 'different' day. The people of God are called to be holy, in fact, to be different. So we read: 'But as he who called you is holy, be holy yourselves in all your conduct; since it is written, "You shall be holy, for I am holy"'(1 Peter 1:15-16). The disciples of Jesus are to be different: showing different standards, attitudes, perspectives and values, arising from a different spirit and lifestyle, too.

Over the centuries, preachers and pastors, teachers and spiritual guides alike, have underlined this aspect of the Christian life: believers' ways need to be different from the worldly standards prevailing. Yet, one might question: 'entirely different'? Very few men and women – even if they profess to be mature Christians – would dare to make that claim! Conversion, or coming to new faith, might have brought about big changes in their lives, but still the work is not yet complete. Paul's conversion on the Damascus road brought a radical change of life: the persecutor of the gospel became the proclaimer of the gospel. In so many ways, he was very different and he gave the glory to God: 'By the grace of God I am what I am, and his grace toward me was not in vain' (1 Corinthians 15:10). He was honest, and too much of a realist to believe he was faultless, so he openly testified: 'I have not yet reached perfection, but I press on, hoping to take hold of that for which Christ once took hold of me. My friends, I do not reckon myself to have got hold of it yet. All I can say is this: forgetting what is behind me, and reaching out for that which lies ahead, I press towards the goal' (Philippians 3:12-14 NEB).

Unfortunately, at times many Christians do not appear to be different. It is wise to remember that Jesus Christ challenges His disciples to live in the world, yet to be different, while also humbly pressing on toward the goal set before each one of us! To do that, without looking down upon others or being proud, is a challenge, indeed.

Suggested readings: Psalm 1:1-6 and Philippians 3:12-16.

JULY 25th

## WORSHIP HELPS US TO SERVE OTHERS

One of the most thrilling moments in the life of the Hebrew people was when they went up to the temple for the first time; taking part in the worship there was something very special and Jerusalem had a unique place in the life of the nation. So the psalmist wrote: 'I was glad when they said to me, "Let us go to the house of the Lord!"' (Psalm 122:1). We can imagine the excitement of the first-time worshippers and how they would store up memories to bring back to friends and loved ones. The last verse of this beautiful psalm reminds us that worship must not end in self-satisfaction, but with a practical aspect: 'For the sake of the house of the Lord our God, I will seek your good' (Psalm 122:9).

There are people who seem to go to worship only to receive. Yet, the broad sweep of Holy Scripture teaches us that worship should deepen our openness to God and increase our love and concern for others. We can be thankful that in countless Christian lives this is what happens! There have been people living completely outside the church who – on the journey to faith – have been changed by the work of the Holy Spirit. Some testify that, for many years their thoughts did not turn to God. Then they became more aware of God and of others, too. Worship gave them a new dimension of thought; with the psalmist they can now affirm, 'For the sake of the house of the Lord our God, I will seek your good'. Worship always continues after the service ends: devotion leads to action.

People who do door-to-door visitation for their church are aware of one of the defensive answers given by unbelievers: 'I don't go to church, but I'm as good as those who do. I never do anybody any harm'. In that context, it might be difficult not to reply: 'But do you do anybody any good?' Could it be that a defensive answer might be an excuse for merely selfish living? Sometimes, those who claim to be 'good', but appear to have no time for God, are in fact, living only for themselves.

Reading the prophets in the Old Testament, the abiding impression is that real worship is linked with practical good, and sincere devotion diminishes selfishness! In the New Testament, we read these challenging words: 'Let each of you look not to your own interests, but also to the interests of others' (Philippians 2:4). Significantly, this verse is in a passage which then depicts the ministry of Jesus Christ, the self-giving 'man for others'. Sincere worship directs our eyes upwards to God and outwards to others, and so worship does not ever cease, but rather it is demonstrated in true self-offering to the Lord. Countless blessings are bestowed because believers have proved faithful in worship and dedication to Christ, the Son of God and Saviour of the world, and so live out that devotion in service to others day by day!

Suggested readings: Psalm 122:1-9 and Philippians 2:1-13.

JULY 26th

## GOD SEES THROUGH ALL THE CAMOUFLAGE

One of the places which is well known in Bedfordshire is the old RAF station at Cardington. Thousands of men and women have been stationed there over the years so it is a household name throughout the country. At Cardington, there are two massive sheds which were used in the past to make and to house the large airships like the R101, the early giants of the sky. In latter years, smaller airships have operated from there, used for both business and industry. In the Second World War, those two huge hangars were skilfully camouflaged as they had to be, or else they could have been clear landmarks for the enemy. Many gallons of paint were used to give them a totally different appearance from the air. Camouflage is a dire necessity in wartime with buildings, vehicles, tanks, gun-sites and even service men and women being camouflaged in an attempt to reduce the degree of visibility and risk! It might be said that, in a sense, a kind of camouflage is used in peacetime, too! The cosmetic industry is a multi-million pounds business in our country and around the globe.

Of course, people use another kind of camouflage, too: the mourner 'puts on a brave face', the nervous person shows 'a bold front', and many a smiling face conceals an aching heart deep within. We give a lot of credit to people who can successfully hide their real feelings of sadness, disappointment, betrayal or even shame. However, there are types of superficial appearance – like camouflage – that Jesus challenged, especially, the spiritual one where the fault is that of hypocrisy. One instance is in Matthew 15, which is not comforting to those so living a lie. It contains the stern words of the Saviour to describe such falsity, quoting from the prophet Isaiah: 'This people honours me with their lips, but their hearts are far from me; in vain do they worship me, teaching human precepts as doctrines' (Matthew 15:8-9). We all know that it is possible for a person to be in God's house singing hymns and apparently listening very attentively to the sermon, and even giving generously in the offering but, in fact, to be far from God in everyday life.

There are verses in scripture which teach that God knows us through and through: the Book of Common Prayer contains the prayer which uses these words: 'From whom no secrets are hid'. The Lord sees through all the pretence: His searching gaze pierces through all the outer camouflage. It is when we fully realise this awesome reality that then the comforting truth dawns upon us: we are all saved by grace and not by works. He Who sees the heart is merciful! A great prophet of the Old Testament declared: 'He delighteth in mercy' (Micah 7:18-19 AV). Surely that assurance in scripture is the bedrock of our faith in the eternal Lord God.

Suggested readings: Psalm 139:1-14 and Matthew 15:1-9.

JULY 27th

## THE HOLY SPIRIT HELPS SOLVE PROBLEMS

Many young people in this modern age make their T-shirt their notice-board! It is quite amazing what words are displayed, and one is sometimes more impressed by the courage of the wearer than the actual words themselves. One glorious July day, a young man was seen walking in the town of St Neots with two words boldly inscribed on his T-shirt: NO PROBLEMS. One might argue that on some summer days in Britain when the weather is warm and sunny, nature is in full bloom, and people are in holiday mood, there seem to be no problems! However, we all know that is not true! It is interesting to sit on a train crowded with commuters or a local bus in the rush hour, and to study people's faces: they doze, talk, read, listen to music, play or work on some device, or do puzzles in the newspaper, and their faces wear a whole variety of expressions. Yet, during these unguarded moments, it is possible to see that some are worried or seem to have real problems. The man or woman who says 'No problems' is living in an unreal – indeed, rather selfish – personal world, and is arguably, quite oblivious to the wider problems in society and on the planet!

In the Book of Daniel we are told how King Belshazzar gave a great feast for a thousand of his nobles. In the middle of the celebrations 'the fingers of a man's hand appeared and wrote on the plaster of the wall' (Daniel 5:5). The king's reaction was quite dramatic and is starkly recorded in the Bible: 'Then the king's colour changed, and his thoughts alarmed him; his limbs gave way, and his knees knocked together' (Daniel 5:6). One urgent issue was: who could interpret the writing and its message? The queen had an answer and told him of a man who had a keen mind, with deep knowledge and understanding, as well as the ability to interpret dreams, explain riddles and solve difficult problems: 'Call for Daniel, and he will tell you what the writing means' (Daniel 5:12 NIV). He did so, and Daniel, gifted as he was, explained to the king the meaning of the graphic message with its dire warning.

We think of Daniel, and many others, thanking God for the army of problem solvers, about whom we read in the Bible: the host of men and women, then and now, who have close fellowship with God, possess deep spiritual wisdom and show remarkable insight, with the ability to help others. Within the Christian Church, there are lots of people today who have this ability to help people solve problems, and they are used by the Holy Spirit. In our lives, we know that while the Spirit works graciously by inspiring and strengthening women and men, bringing untold blessings, one of the most cherished blessings is our experience of the Spirit as the problem solver. Myriads of people have known the reality of the Spirit's guidance and enabling, leading us into all the truth, the truth which, as Jesus said, sets us free.

Suggested readings: Daniel 5:1-12 and John 16:7-14.

JULY 28th

## EYEWITNESSES ARE EXTREMELY IMPORTANT

It was Easter Sunday morning, and a large congregation had assembled for worship. Many young people and children were also in the congregation. There was an air of expectancy: once again the singing would be joyful and hearty, and the minister could be expected to bring an inspiring message. However, not one person in their wildest dreams could have anticipated what they would witness that morning! The minister came down from the pulpit to speak to the children; he knelt down and stood on his head. The congregation was shocked, amazed and also quite bewildered! After a few seconds, the minister reversed his position, stood on his feet and said: 'Children, when you go home someone may say "What did the minister do today at church?"' He paused for a few seconds and continued: 'Tell them he stood on his head and, if they don't believe you, tell them you saw it with your own eyes!' Then, with great skill, the minister told how – on the first Easter Sunday – a wonderful thing happened, and the disciples beheld the Lord arisen from the dead, so that they could say: 'We know it is true for we saw the risen Master with our own eyes!' In a similar way, in the second epistle which bears his name, Peter claimed: 'We were eyewitnesses of his majesty' (2 Peter 1:16 AV).

The earliest disciples were privileged to see Jesus Christ during His ministry and after the resurrection. They saw Him risen from the dead as He appeared to them: they knew that Jesus had been raised from the dead, because they saw Him with their own eyes on Easter Day. One of the finest passages defending the 'Easter experience' of knowing Christ raised from death, is Paul's recitation of the early tradition in 1 Corinthians 15: '. . . that he was raised on the third day in accordance with the scriptures, and that he appeared to Cephas, then to the twelve. Then he appeared to more than five hundred brothers and sisters at one time, most of whom are still alive' (1 Corinthians 15:4-6).

There were many eyewitnesses: one study of the Bible contends that about 517 people must have seen the risen Jesus. Hence, we can say with some clarity that the story of the risen Christ is not a cunning tale, nor just a beautiful story, but is the truth of what happened, though human language breaks down to express it adequately. Those children in church saw something they would never forget as it was imprinted indelibly on their minds; the early Christians saw something, indeed Someone, they could never forget, namely, Jesus Christ in His risen power. We thank God for those faithful early eyewitnesses of the resurrection, and yet, we also recall how we, too, as modern day of followers of Christ, are blessed to have a similar testimony to tell of our risen Lord, Who is now present with us, just as He promised.

Suggested readings: Matthew 28:1-10, 18-20 and 1 Corinthians 15:1-10.

JULY 29th

## THERE IS A MINISTRY OF THE LOUD VOICE

It was a lovely, quiet Sunday morning and people were strolling by the river in Bedford. That particular morning, the River Ouse was flowing swifter because of a recent spell of heavy rain. All was tranquil and peaceful, until suddenly there was a piercing yell, as a man by the riverbank was shouting at the top of his voice! He was shouting at a group of youngsters in a boat and the peace of the morning was rudely shattered. The youngsters had foolishly boated too near the weir which had a treacherous overflow from the river, and their boat was being sucked into deadly waters. The man yelled instructions and slowly, painfully, they managed to manoeuvre the boat away from the danger zone, to get into safer waters. The bellowed warning had shattered the peace, but had potentially saved five young lives! Sometimes the ministry of the loud voice is essential.

When we consider John the Baptist preaching in the region of Jordan saying, 'Repent, for the kingdom of heaven is at hand' (Matthew 3:2), we know that his voice was strong, insistent and urgent! He could see that men and women were being sucked, as it were, into the whirlpools of selfishness and sinfulness; he lifted up his voice with power as 'the voice of one crying in the wilderness' (Matthew 3:3). Some people might have even been embarrassed by such a brazen word uttered with urgency and forcefulness, but it was one of the key elements of his vital ministry.

There is ample evidence in the New Testament that the Blessed Master had a wonderful voice, one of calm gentleness and true peace, such as when He gave the gracious invitation: 'Come unto me all ye that labour and are heavy laden, and I will give you rest' (Matthew 11:28 AV). Yet, when Jesus stood outside the tomb of Lazarus and faced the fact of His friend's death, we read 'He cried with a loud voice, "Lazarus, come out"' (John 11:43). Jesus used the ministry of the loud voice! A great miracle happened that day: lifeless men don't respond to gentle voices! Lazarus was then restored to life, but it was through the bold summons of the Lord.

A parent discovered that his own son was dealing with drugs and reported him to the police; a controversy raged about this action and one newspaper called it 'hard love'. The sequel to this story is that this particular son 'came to his senses' and, recognised the 'tough love' of his father. He kicked the drug habit and all that went with it. His father had spoken with a bold, insistent voice, a voice that could easily have been misunderstood by others and, indeed, his own son. We all need wisdom to know when to use the soft and persuasive voice, and when to use the firm voice of determination, sometimes even indignation. In the right manner, and in appropriate circumstances, both quiet and loud voices are important.

Suggested readings: Matthew 3:1-12 and John 11:38-46.

JULY 30th

## TRUSTWORTHINESS IS A GREAT VIRTUE

Down the years, it has always been interesting to ponder the 'SITUATIONS VACANT' pages of a local newspaper and see what is required of applicants! Employers stress the need for skill, self-motivation, honesty, enthusiasm, experience and reliability. The vast majority of employers explicitly seek people who are trustworthy and reliable. As we read the Holy Scriptures, we see how these two virtues – inextricably linked – are extolled, and one verse puts it in a nutshell: 'It is required of stewards that they be found trustworthy' (1 Corinthians 4:2).

In the Book of Nehemiah, we are told of a large-scale building project going on in Jerusalem. When the wall was rebuilt, it was essential to have the right people with a deep sense of responsibility to take charge, and this is recorded: 'I gave the charge of Jerusalem to my brother Hanani, and to Hananiah, the governor of the citadel, for he was trustworthy and God-fearing above other men' (Nehemiah 7:1-2 NEB). The governor was a man 'head and shoulders' above the rest as he was faithful, dependable, a man of integrity, and this is how one translation puts it: 'He was a truly reliable man' (Nehemiah 7:2 Moffatt's version).

We are all on the lookout for reliable people: a reliable partner in life as well as dependable friends, but also reliable doctors, dentists, opticians, lawyers, financial advisors, builders, mechanics and engineers, not to mention a reliable minister. So the Christian Church needs women and men who are wholly trustworthy. We thank God for all the faithful people we have known within the fellowship of the local church: pastors, leaders, Sunday school/Junior church teachers, youth and other outreach workers quite beside all the ordinary members working behind the scenes. However, sadly, that is not the full story, as there have been examples of superficial or shoddy service for the Kingdom which sadly mar the overall ministry of the Church.

The apostle Paul dedicated himself to Christian service, but he wrote often of his dependence upon trustworthy helpers, too: 'Epaphras, our dear fellow-servant, a trusted worker for Christ on our behalf' (Colossians 1:7 NEB) and 'Tychicus, our dear brother and trustworthy helper and fellow-servant in the Lord's work' (Colossians 4:7). How important it is to have reliable colleagues in whatever sphere, be it government, politics, commerce, education, health care and social work, as well as in the maintenance of law and order! It is especially so in church work and other areas of the voluntary sector. Trustworthiness is a real virtue and, along with numerous other qualities of character, it yields truth in relationship and brings a rich harvest to God's glory. It is the Spirit of God who can graciously fashion us to be trustworthy and faithful, while being effective in the Lord's service.

Suggested readings: Nehemiah 7:1-6 and 2 Thessalonians 3:1-5.

JULY 31st

## JOY WILL EVENTUALLY REPLACE THE TEARS IN SOWING

In Holy Scripture there is considerable teaching about sowing. Our Saviour spoke of the sowing and the waiting, and only thereafter, the harvest: 'The kingdom of God is as if someone would scatter seed upon the ground, and should sleep and rise night and day, and the seed would sprout and grow, he does know how. The earth produces of itself, first the stalk, then the head, then the full grain in the head' (Mark 4:26-28). We must be under no delusion that sowing time can be awkward and sometimes, downright difficult! The weather, the state of the ground, the availability of workers, can all make the time of sowing disheartening. However, in His parables, Jesus claimed that, in spite of all the difficulties of sowing seed for the Kingdom, the patient worker will in time reap a fruitful harvest. The mystery, but also the certainty of that process of fruition, is in mind here.

There is a marvellous note of confidence in Psalm 126: 'They that sow in tears shall reap in joy' (Psalm 126:5). Many of God's servants have been encouraged and inspired by that beautiful promise! Sometimes, believers have found the time of sowing very hard and have feared the prospects of a good harvest to be slender. However, in God's good time, they have experienced the joy of harvest and all the effort and labour has proved to be worthwhile. It is well known that when William Carey went to India, for years he did a tremendous amount of sowing, working long – often hard – days. The harvest was long delayed, and some of his supporters began to lose interest, yet eventually, after some years, the harvest did come.

The text 'They that sow in tears shall reap in joy' perfectly fits the case of William Carey and his colleagues in the 1790s; it no doubt describes the experience of many others down the centuries. A whole host of other Christian workers have sown the seed with much difficulty, and yet gone on to discover that the ancient promise is true. The harvest surely comes eventually – by God's unfailing mercy – and it is abundant! The Book of Ecclesiastes gives this sound advice to would-be sowers: 'He who observes the wind will not sow; and he who regards the clouds will not reap' (Ecclesiastes 11:4). There is a real need to press forward in spite of obvious difficulties. God's promise holds fast: 'They that sow in tears shall reap in joy'. That is a magnificent reason for confidence, and a tremendous encouragement to keep looking forward and pressing ahead with our labours for the Lord!

Suggested readings: Mark 4:26-29 and Psalm 126:1-6.

# AUGUST

Away with our fears,
Our troubles and tears:
The Spirit is come,
The witness of Jesus returned to His Home.

The pledge of our Lord
To His heaven restored,
Is sent from the sky,
And tells us our Head is exalted on high.

Our glorified Head
His Spirit has shed,
With His people to stay,
And never again will He take Him away.

Our heavenly guide
With us shall abide,
His comforts impart,
And set up His kingdom of love in the heart.

The heart that believes
His kingdom receives,
His power and His peace,
His life, and His joy's everlasting increase.

Charles Wesley (1707-88)

O Eternal Son of God,
who camest from the Father, the Fountain of light,
to enlighten the darkness of the world: shine thou upon this day,
that whatsoever we shall do or suffer
we may be acceptable to thy Divine Majesty;
for thy Name's sake. Amen.

Jeremy Taylor (1613-1667)

AUGUST 1st

## THE HALF HAS NEVER BEEN TOLD

Reports are often exaggerated! In recent times, with many travelling abroad, there are the occasional scandals about certain holiday resorts abroad: people have read glossy brochures about the hotels, chalets or other lodging places with all their facilities, and have booked holidays, but have then been terribly disappointed, as the descriptions proved to be grossly untrue! It seems that, at times, descriptions of certain places are 'over the top' or at the least, misleading, and – when the truth is discovered – things are not quite so impressive or spectacular.

Sometimes, of course, reports which may seem to be exaggerated, turn out to be true. For instance, the Old Testament tells us a lot about King Solomon and claims that: 'King Solomon excelled all the kings of the earth in riches and in wisdom' (1 Kings 10:23). The fame of the king spread abroad and attracted the curiosity of many, including the Queen of Sheba; we're told that she came to Jerusalem to see for herself, and she was impressed by Solomon's wisdom, his palace, his food and his many servants! She stated: 'The report was true which I heard in my own land of your affairs and of your wisdom, but I did not believe the reports until I came and my own eyes had seen it; and behold, the half was not told me; your wisdom and prosperity surpass the report which I heard' (1 Kings 10:6-7).

In the New Testament, Jesus Christ is affirmed to be greater than the temple, greater than Jonah, greater than Solomon! Matthew's gospel has this verse referring to that queen's visit: 'She came from the ends of the earth to listen to Solomon's wisdom, and now one greater than Solomon is here' (Matthew 12:42). We can cherish that majestic word, and we can ponder the greatness of Jesus Christ: His Wisdom, His Power, His Grace, His Love, His Glory are all beyond our human calculation. Over many centuries, scholars have attempted to describe Him, but words are inadequate. Artists have tried to portray Him in pictures and sculptures, but someone has rightly said, in this respect: 'Every painting of Jesus Christ is a failure'. That is inevitably so, because of His all-surpassing greatness, splendour and majesty. It's true that 'the half has never been told'!

One of the great affirmations in the New Testament is that the Holy Spirit of God opens the hearts and minds of people to behold the truth, and to glimpse something of the glory of Jesus Christ. This gracious ministry of the Spirit of the Lord has enabled Christians not only to 'see' for themselves, but also to convey to others, something of the greatness of the Saviour. However, there are always more depths to be probed and heights to be scaled for the truth to be fully discovered, and that is surely no exaggeration! Far beyond our comprehension is the glory of Christ.

Suggested readings: 1 Kings 10:1-13 and Matthew 12:38-42.

## AUGUST 2nd

## GOD REQUIRES FAITHFULNESS IN SMALL THINGS

Some might say how relatively easy it is to cope with the big things of life, or at least that's how it seems sometimes. Lots of people can face trouble and tackle major crises with seeming calm and dignity, but then get very disturbed and alarmed about petty mishaps. J.B. Phillips claimed that his father was a strong man with a powerful personality facing life as a whole but, if a slate came off the roof, the situation was regarded as disastrous! Sometimes, of course, it is the little things in life that count the most. Rather than stumble from crisis to crisis, a real part of discipleship is learning to live faithfully, trusting in God, even as we deal with the normal stresses and strains of life on a daily basis. In this respect, it has been suggested that one Christian discipline might be the willingness to do small tasks such as writing letters or filling out forms for others, or running errands for the housebound, visiting the sick, helping the frail or the lonely and so on.

Some of the greatest saints have offered the lowliest service to God, and the hallmark of their piety was willingness to do dismal and boring tasks to God's glory! The point is that nothing is too humble a task for those who are seeking to be on pilgrimage as followers of Jesus. One verse in the scriptures is very relevant here: 'Whoever is faithful in a very little is faithful also in much' (Luke 16:10). So often the small, even tedious matters, and how we cope with them, reveal our character! We remember, with thanksgiving, the faithful people who serve the Kingdom of God with enthusiasm and joy, all quite prepared to accept God's call to do, even the lowly and menial tasks including roles which are often quite hidden from sight. They are prepared to be faithful in the small things of the cause of Christ. It is evident how much the Church owes to these hard-working Christians quietly serving.

All over the world, there are Christians who have rejoiced in the ministry of John Stott as a preacher, scholar, leader and author, admiring the stand he took for biblical, indeed, evangelical truth. His scholarly, but eminently readable, book *The Cross of Christ*, made its mark in the theological world as an important evangelical study. It is fascinating to observe that he dedicated the book to his secretary, Frances Whitehead, for her thirty years of outstanding loyalty and efficient service. We thank God for the whole army of faithful people who can tackle the big things and also undertake the small details, too. So now, as in all the centuries of Church history, there are believers who never actually come into the spotlight, but their faithful service for the Kingdom of God, often in unobtrusive, quiet and unspectacular ways, proves to be essential. For all this faithful service, we give hearty thanks to God.

Suggested readings: Luke 16:1-13 and Philemon 1:1-7.

AUGUST 3rd

## GOD'S SPIRIT GIVES STRENGTH

The disciples, Peter and John, would not stop talking about their faith in the risen Lord! The authorities in Jerusalem were upset: 'They were annoyed because the two apostles were teaching that Jesus had risen from death' Acts 4:2 GNB). So they arrested them and put them in gaol! The next day at the trial before the Sanhedrin, the members of Council were amazed at the apostles' ability – even as uneducated men – to speak persuasively. The leaders were also aware of the volatility of the situation, so they gave the two apostles a solemn warning to speak no more before releasing them! With haste, Peter and John returned to the fellowship, sharing the bad news about the threats, and they all prayed fervently. What a prayer meeting! Luke records: 'They lifted their voices together to God and said, "Sovereign Lord, who didst make the heaven and the earth and the sea and everything in them . . . look upon their threats, and grant to thy servants to speak thy word with all boldness"' (Acts 4:24,29). Their prayer was plainly answered as the sequel indicates: 'They were all filled with the Holy Spirit and spoke the word of God with boldness' (Acts 4:31). The dangers were real, but they were given courage and boldness to keep speaking.

The Holy Spirit has a multi-faceted ministry: the Spirit of God convicts, convinces, converts, comforts, interprets, gifts and equips believers, as well as strengthening all those open to God's presence. 17th October 1943 was a dark day for John Leonard Wilson: he was the Bishop of Singapore and was arrested by the Japanese authorities and then experienced three days of questioning and torture. The torture was so brutal that he remained in a semi-conscious state for three weeks. When he 'came to', he found himself locked in a small cell with a tiny, barred window. Then, in God's mercy, three things happened: he heard the song of a bird; he could see the top of a church, he remembered spiritual words and his soul was wonderfully fed. He was 'strengthened within' and lived to witness boldly, to forgive heartily and to love sincerely. His faith took on a new dimension: he will always be remembered as one made bold by the Holy Spirit and equipped to serve the Lord in a remarkable ministry.

One of the loveliest prayers in the Bible is found in Ephesians chapter 3, and one part of it is expressed as a deep longing: 'I pray that, according to the riches of his glory, he may grant that you may be strengthened in your inner being' (Ephesians 3: 16). Paul wanted his friends to have inner strength and that is the need of every believer. The Holy Spirit strengthened the early followers of Christ, and we can be thankful to God that the Spirit still inspires and strengthens! Our part is to be open to the Spirit of God, even as we support and pray for others, too.

Suggested readings: Acts 4:19-31 and Ephesians 3:13-21.

AUGUST 4th

## TRUE CHRISTIAN MARRIAGE IS A STRONG BOND

Whatever our circumstances in life, we can all thank God for the companionship and joy in a truly Christian marriage! What a lovely thing it is to see a Christian couple coming to their place of worship to make their vows in the presence of God. The old words in Genesis come to mind in the formalising of such a partnership before the Lord: 'It is not good that the man should be alone; I will make him a helper fit for him' (Genesis 2:18). Over the centuries, people have rejoiced to be pledged together in marriage and have experienced the joy of such commitment. In the Book of Ecclesiastes we read: 'Two are better than one, because they have a good reward for their toil. For if they fall, one will lift up the other' (Ecclesiastes 4:9-10). It is quite obvious that this wise saying has a much wider reference than the marriage bond, but it is surely applicable to it, as well as to other kinds of friendship bonds. When two people are truly committed in marriage, they are a strong team and face life together, with all its ups and downs. If one falls ill, the other nurses, if one feels depressed, the other encourages, if one trips over a tricky problem the other lifts up; this is true partnership which surely finds its summation in holy matrimony.

While we rejoice that there are millions of couples who are happily married, sadly, that is not the full story. Around the globe, there is the increasing incidence of separation and divorce, quite apart from the vast number of broken homes, and homes where there is domestic abuse or neglect. Why is this so? There are lots of reasons behind the breakdown of a relationship and many factors can be involved: social, moral, emotional, sexual and spiritual. The big question in society is: how can this trend be slowed down or reversed? One answer to the problem must surely be a renewed spiritual awareness. There is an old saying: 'people who pray together, stay together', and there is much truth in that very simple word of wisdom.

We may ponder another verse from Ecclesiastes: 'A threefold cord is not easily broken' (Ecclesiastes 4:12 Moffatt). Whatever the original intention of that saying with regard to relationships, it most certainly applies to Christian marriage. When a couple make their vows and exchange their promises along with the rings, there are three involved: the Bride, the Bridegroom and the Lord. While even committed Christians sometimes find that their marriages do not last, many Christians find that the bonds of commitment are 'not easily broken', and they share through all the 'ups and downs' in a lifelong relationship. For persons of faith, the foundation of their relationship is Christ, who binds them together.

Suggested readings: Ecclesiastes 4:1-12 and Ephesians 5:21-33.

AUGUST 5th

## WITNESS WITHIN THE HOME IS ESSENTIAL

In Mark's gospel, there is a verse which has inspired many, as it relates words of the risen Lord: 'And he said unto them, "Go ye into all the world, and preach the gospel to every creature"' (Mark 16:15). This powerful challenge has inspired dedicated service and has motivated believers to witness in all types of situations. It is thrilling to hear how many people are in training even now to be ministers and missionaries in order to proclaim the gospel in many contexts. Jesus Christ still challenges people to accept responsibility to speak and work for the spreading of the gospel, and verses such as this one prove foundational to their sense of calling. The gospel is spread in diverse ways: preaching and teaching, pastoral work and counselling, as well as the modern media of television and radio, books, films and other means. However, it is also spread personally, and it is said that a living faith can be 'caught' as much as 'taught'! One of the vital places of influence is the Christian home: a godly father and mother can (by life, attitude, speech and example) pass on their faith to another generation. God has greatly used parents and grandparents, but also other relatives and close friends, to spread the good news of Jesus Christ.

When George Thomas (one-time Speaker in the House of Commons) celebrated his eightieth birthday, he was interviewed on the radio concerning his life and his faith. His story is quite remarkable! He grew up in Wales amid lowly conditions but, by hard work, was elected a Member of Parliament and had a distinguished political career. Eventually, after many years of service in the House of Commons, he was selected to be the Speaker, a very great honour. On the radio, he gladly testified about the influence of other people upon his life, especially his mother. He said: 'She had faith like the Rock of Gibraltar, and I'm a chip off the old block'! George Thomas never forgot his roots. In the great moments of triumph, when he was honoured by society, he kept the faith which he had witnessed in the life of his wonderful mother. A Christian mother can exercise such a powerful influence but, of course, this also applies to good and godly fathers, too!

We think of a wonderful mother in the Old Testament, Hannah, the mother of Samuel: 'For this child I prayed; and the Lord has granted me my petition which I made to him. Therefore I have lent him to the Lord; as long as he lives' (1 Samuel 1:28). In the New Testament, we read of Mary, the one woman in history entrusted to bear and to nurture the Son of God, born as the infant Jesus. Much has been written and said about her, and she is widely acknowledged as having had a unique role. She was a woman of faith, a devout mother and a faithful witness. In our lives, witness at home is vital and can prove to be a source of much blessing.

Suggested readings: 1 Samuel 1:10-28 and Luke 2:51-52.

AUGUST 6th

## THERE IS A NEED FOR PATIENT WAITING

Not many people enjoy waiting, at least not for very long! Lots of people find it both frustrating and annoying to be kept waiting and they readily show their impatience. One of the funniest assignments for a 'candid camera', as it used to be on television, was the filming of antics of people waiting for their turn to use a public facility such as a telephone kiosk or a ticket machine. We can recall that the Bible has quite a lot to say about waiting and often those passages stress the advantages of it. One of the best known verses on this subject is found in Isaiah: 'But they who wait for the Lord shall renew their strength, they shall mount up with wings like eagles, they shall run and not be weary, they shall walk and not faint' (Isaiah 40:31).

Right at the end of His earthly ministry Jesus Christ gave special instructions to the disciples: 'Go therefore and teach all nations, baptizing them in the name of the Father, and of the Son, and of the Holy Ghost' (Matthew 28:19 AV). However, we also recall that, in another context, He uttered these words to the disciples: 'But stay in the city, until you are clothed with power from on high' (Luke 24:49). There was so much to be done and so many people to reach, but Jesus commanded the disciples to wait patiently for the promised power of the Holy Spirit. We remember that waiting time need not be wasted time! So the disciples obeyed Jesus, their Blessed Lord and Master, and in God's good time, the Spirit came upon them, and they experienced a new power for service to obey Jesus' command to go and proclaim.

How often younger Christians feel the urge to do missionary work and yearn to go out to serve immediately, but it is vital for them to receive essential training and language study, or sometimes, just gain more experience of life. This 'waiting time' is crucial: we have to note that Jesus of Nazareth waited thirty years for His life's work to begin. So much waiting, followed by just three years of service, but what wonderful years they were as they bore witness to the necessity of waiting on God's time. The truth enshrined in the waiting time which Jesus underwent, speaks to every generation of those who just want to 'get on with it'!

Numerous people have to wait: the business person who invests time and money in a project, a farmer who plants seed in readiness for next year's harvest, and the preacher or teacher of the gospel who steadily sows the seed! We read in the Epistle of James: 'The farmer waits for the precious crop from the earth, being patient with it until it receives the early and the late rains' (James 5:7). Waiting is an essential part of living and we must learn to cope with it. The person who shifts about impatiently in a queue by a bank cash-point or parking ticket machine doesn't get to it any quicker! There are many things we can do in waiting time: pray, think, praise, or simply be still and ponder that which is good.

Suggested readings: Luke 24:44-53 and James 5:7-16.

AUGUST 7th

## SOME FOOLS ARE REALLY WISE

One of the strongest instincts within men and women is the herd instinct: it is developed usually during childhood and often continues as a powerful influence throughout adult life. The pressure is to conform, to do what others do and to say what others say! If a person breaks loose from accepted patterns, she or he is often considered an oddity, an erratic one who seems to be a fool! In the early history of the Church, Christians broke away from the usual lifestyle of their age and were different; from the outset many, though perhaps not all, dared to be different! They largely challenged accepted standards of behaviour and many were reckoned by their peers in society to be fools. One of the most striking passages on this theme is 1 Corinthians 4: here the apostle Paul speaks in uncompromising terms about the cost of his discipleship and testifies, 'We are fools for Christ's sake' (1 Corinthians 4:10). We can well imagine some of his former friends and colleagues talking about him and his conversion to the Christian faith, deriding him as a fool.

Albert Schweitzer was a very gifted man with exceptional skills: he was Doctor of Music, Doctor of Philosophy, Doctor of Theology and a Doctor of Medicine. He could just have lived for his own betterment and enjoyed a comfortable living in the country of his choice becoming a wealthy man, relishing his status. However, by deliberate choice, he turned his back on 'accepted standards' and worked terribly hard to establish a hospital in Lambaréné in Africa. The work demanded long hours, costly commitment and sheer hard work plus real sacrifice. Some people thought he was crazy: a fool throwing away his life in poverty-stricken Africa when he could have been a renowned, wealthy man enjoying a professional life with all its privileges! Another example of such a fool for Christ was Dr. Stanley Browne, a man with high qualifications in the medical world and with promising career prospects: he decided to be a medical missionary and a campaigner against the prevalence of leprosy. What a dedicated life he and his wife lived in the cause of the Kingdom. We can thank God for such so-called fools!

Christ's teaching may seem unacceptable to lots of people: the challenges to 'take up your cross and follow', 'to seek first the Kingdom of God' and 'to go the second mile' appear foolish to those closed to the Kingdom! Yet, it is true, as the apostle Paul rightly claimed, that there is a wisdom not of this world: 'For the foolishness of God is wiser than human wisdom, and the weakness of God is stronger than human strength' (1 Corinthians 1:25).

Suggested readings: 1 Corinthians 1: 8-25 and 1 Corinthians 4:6-13.

AUGUST 8th

## PEOPLE MUST SPEAK FOR JESUS

There are some lovely sounds which remind people of England's green and pleasant land: one such is the sound of church bells! One of the most satisfying experiences is to be in the English countryside on a beautiful summer's day and hear the sound of distant church bells. As we hear the bells, believers can reflect that in some parish churches, people have met for worship on the site for hundreds of years. A report made by the Central Council of Church Bell Ringers recorded at one time that one third of church towers remain silent because of a lack of bell ringers in the area. The lovely sound of bells is not heard because of a lack of interest in parish church life, and it gives cause for reflection. There are some who would be terribly upset if they knew their ancient parish church was going to cease having services, and yet they don't give the church regular support or show any interest in the faith.

The prayer of the prophet comes to mind: 'I pray thee, open his eyes, that he may see' (2 Kings 6:17). In this modern age, when so many things are just taken for granted (especially the village chapel or church), there is a great need for people to have their eyes opened; opened not just to practical realities but also to the spiritual realities in life. It is right that people of faith speak up for the Lord; indeed, their lives, as much as their words, must tell of His greatness and of the authenticity of the Christian faith, in transforming empty or broken hearts, and bringing hope to the world. It is, indeed, a privilege to speak for Jesus.

In the Book of Psalms, we read these challenging words: 'O give thanks to the Lord, for he is good; for his steadfast love endures for ever! Let the redeemed of the Lord say so' (Psalm 107:1-2). It is obviously sad when fine, ancient church bells remain silent without ringers; it is even sadder that some Christians remain mute on their faith. We recall that the Saviour of the world, at His ascension, challenged the disciples: 'You shall be my witnesses in Jerusalem and in all Judea and Samaria and to the end of the earth' (Acts 1:8). Christians are called to bear witness: we can testify by life, by words, by service and in a whole variety of other ways.

However, 'ramming' religion down people's throats is not recommended! In fact, some zealous Christians have done much harm. Yet, in contrast to that, there ought to be a willingness to speak when the opportunity presents itself. Wise is the Christian who knows the right time to speak, and the right time to keep silent for a while, in offering effective witness to the Saviour! One older believer testified that his mother's words always stayed with him, 'Son, speak a good word for Jesus Christ'; it's a challenge for us all! We thank God that the Spirit prompts us to speak a timely word, and gives us divine aid as we do so.

Suggested readings: Psalm 107:1-8 and Acts 1:1-11.

AUGUST 9th

## THERE IS JOY IN FACE-TO-FACE MEETING

The modern age has brought us scores of advantages and blessings, especially the 'mod cons' so many of us take for granted in the home, whether the humble washing machine or fridge-freezer, or the high-tech car, device or computer. Multitudes around the world readily testify that the telephone is one of life's greatest boons: through gadgets and sophisticated telecommunications, we can keep contact with most of the world. How wonderful it is that, within a few seconds, we can speak to someone thousands of miles away. However, we readily acknowledge that meeting in person is infinitely superior. When a loved one has been far away or overseas for a long time, how splendid it is to welcome them back and talk with them: a personal greeting and encounter is surely better than a thousand telephone calls, as there is such joy in face-to-face meeting.

The apostle Paul, having been separated from some of his friends, wrote: 'As for us brothers and sisters, when, for a short time we were made orphans by being separated from you – in person, not in heart – we longed with great eagerness to see you face to face' (1 Thessalonians 2:17). Paul, like others in the early Church, yearned to have close fellowship with his friends.

In Luke chapter 15, the Parable of the Prodigal Son tells of the wayward son leaving home to seek pleasures in the far country, after which there was no contact with his father at all. However, the story tells of the dramatic moment when he returned and met his father face-to-face: 'And he arose and came to his father. But while he was yet at a distance, his father saw him and had compassion, and ran and embraced him and kissed him' (Luke 15:20). That vivid portrait of their meeting expresses the essence of the gospel hope that, when an individual returns to the heavenly Father, there is a welcome, an offer of forgiveness and a new beginning.

One of the most moving face-to-face meetings in scripture is that between the risen Lord and Thomas in the Upper Room. On the first Good Friday, Jesus had been rejected, unjustly treated, crucified and buried, and all hope seemed lost: Thomas was in the grip of devastating sorrow. Eight days after the resurrection, the risen Lord Jesus met Thomas: it was a genuine face-to-face meeting and, overwhelmed, Thomas exclaimed: 'My Lord and my God' (John 20:28). Down through the Christian centuries, people have – in their own way – had a vital experience of encountering Jesus Christ and have been richly blessed. We know from the scriptures that, on one glorious and unforgettable day – in the mercy of God and by His gracious timing – we, as believers, shall no longer simply rely on faith, but shall see the Lord face-to-face and rejoice abundantly forever in His eternal abode.

Suggested readings: 1 Thessalonians 2:13-20 and John 20:19-31.

AUGUST 10th

## GOD IS GREAT AND GENTLE

It is interesting to note that in some chapters of the Bible we get sharp contrasts. For example, Isaiah 40 says: 'The Lord is the everlasting God, the Creator of the ends of the earth' (Isaiah 40:28). Yet, in the very same chapter, we read these moving words about God's gentleness: 'He will feed his flock like a shepherd, and will gather the lambs in his arms, he will carry them in his bosom, and gently lead those that are with young' (Isaiah 40:11). The prophet saw that the Lord God is both great and gentle. How strange it is that some preachers stress the greatness in their preaching and teaching, but rarely speak of His gentleness! Occasionally, it is the reverse but, to be true to scripture, we need to keep these two wonderful truths in balance.

We can see a similar truth in the lives of certain great people in history. In some circles, Winston Churchill has been described as 'the man of the century': he has been recognised throughout the world as an outstanding leader and statesman in the twentieth century, having played an important role on the world stage. As Prime Minister of Britain during the Second World War, he was known as a tough leader: he could be bold and determined, sometimes almost ruthless, in pushing forward plans to win the war. On his shoulders rested tremendous responsibilities; in fact, he had to make 'life and death' decisions which had awesome consequences. Of course, he had vociferous opponents! Many were afraid of him and some were jealous, but millions admired him and later applauded him for his wisdom and toughness. Yet, this rugged character had a side to him which was so very different: he loved Clementine, his wife, with a lover's warm tenderness. Jack Fishman's book *My Darling Clementine*, is a revelation of that strong marriage which had deep love and much tenderness, as well as a remarkable gentleness, too.

While we ourselves may have known relationships of care and gentleness, scripture reminds us that there is a gentleness to God which is beyond any human description. The prophecy of Isaiah gives both sides of God's wonderful character. Two verses from the book of Isaiah convey the same truths: 'Thus saith the Lord, "The heaven is my throne, and the earth is my footstool"' (Isaiah 66:1) and 'As one whom his mother comforteth, so will I comfort you; and ye shall be comforted in Jerusalem' (Isaiah 66:13 AV). With the help of the Holy Spirit, we may discover more and more of both the greatness and the tenderness of the Eternal One Whom we worship and adore. A sad fact of Christian history is that sometimes one truth has been stressed and the other, regrettably, rather neglected. Yet, the truth is that we may know God's mighty power and God's gentle loving-kindness, and so we rejoice in the holy, majestic and glorious ways of the Lord.

Suggested readings: Psalm 71:1-21 and 2 Corinthians 1:1-4.

AUGUST 11th

## THERE ARE SPIRITUAL TREASURES

All of us have treasures! It is quite astounding what a vast variety of things are described as treasures. Elizabeth Goudge tells of her experiences in the Second World War when the German planes streamed over her house on their way to bomb Plymouth. Her mother was never really afraid but, in the times of danger, she loved to have her jewellery case close to hand: her mother truly loved and cherished her few pieces of jewellery. In life, we all have treasures of some sort or another, whether a unique heirloom, a special piece of furniture, an old picture or a rare piece of china, a nicely bound old book or even a bundle of letters! We cherish such treasures and long to keep them safe.

There are other treasures, too. For many centuries, Luke chapter 2 has been very special: the first part tells of the birth of Jesus, the second part narrates an account of the Presentation of Jesus at the temple; the third records the one and only story from the boyhood of Jesus. We have this priceless verse: 'He went down to Nazareth with them and was obedient to them. But his mother treasured all these things in her heart' (Luke 2:51 NIV). Mary and Joseph had very precious and lovely memories, and Luke has recorded a few of them for us. We can ponder some of life's treasured memories: the day of our engagement, the day of our marriage, the day a baby was born, the day we passed an important examination or qualified for a position, to name but a few! The story is told of a father who had been away for a few days on important business and big changes were ahead of him! As he returned home, his mind was racing with all the possibilities: a new job, in a fresh area, with a different house, new colleagues, as well as additional responsibilities. As he stepped off the bus and walked towards home, his young son came rushing to meet him. The true treasure for this parent was then very evident. They met in a whirl of love and greeting: the little child was both innocent and trusting. It was a precious moment of love and comfort: the experience made a lasting memory!

There are special treasures which can be stolen or damaged, but there are treasures of the heart which endure for ever, for they are part and parcel of our being as Christ's own. At the close of His earthly ministry, the risen Saviour promised the disciples: 'And remember, I am with you always, to the end of the age' (Matthew 28:20). Surely, that precious promise is a real treasure for all believers! The words of the risen Master, given to the restored disciples just before His final departure from them, have been cherished by succeeding generations of Christians; indeed, they're like priceless jewels! We can treasure this promise and all of God's promises.

Suggested readings: Luke 2:39-52 and Matthew 28:16-20.

AUGUST 12th

## GOD CHALLENGES PEOPLE TO UNHESITATING OBEDIENCE

Hesitation is something that grips us all from time to time: before signing an important document, before booking an appointment, before purchasing a costly item, before accepting the offer of a new job or moving home, and maybe even before seriously thinking about marriage. Much of this hesitation is natural and right but, sometimes, it is an expression of our reluctance or unwillingness to obey God! Indeed, it could be said that there are many people who belong, as it were, to 'the order of hesitation'.

In Acts chapter 10, we read how God dealt with Peter's reticence to consider accepting Gentiles into Christian faith. As a Jew by birth, he had natural reservations about the gospel's relevance to the non-Jew (the 'uncircumcised'), and he received a vision which left him 'inwardly perplexed' (Acts 10:17). The narrative tells how three men came to Peter's lodging as part of God's unfolding plan, and Peter was then divinely challenged: 'Rise and go down and accompany them without hesitation for I have sent thee'. It was without hesitation, to Peter's credit, that he obeyed and, as the story is told in Acts, God's plan was seen to be fulfilled, in that Peter did preach the gospel to Cornelius and his friends. All this led to the glorious testimony at Jerusalem: 'Then to the Gentiles also God has granted repentance unto life' (Acts 11:18). It proved to be a milestone in the Church's life.

Guidance sometimes comes slowly in life! Lots of sincere believers can testify that in facing some choices they have agonised in spirit to know the right decision before the Lord. So we, too, can probably testify that certain major decisions have been made after much time spent in prayerful consideration. Yet, it is equally true that there are times when God's Spirit has really challenged Christians to make a decision promptly and to act upon it 'without hesitation': sometimes, the urgency is part of the response called forth. We thank God for all the courageous men and women who have served with glad obedience. Of course, often very sincere Christians may have struggled to give such unhesitating obedience and have wrestled with what it might mean to seek God's way and purpose for their lives.

The Old Testament scriptures tell us quite clearly that some of God's finest servants were, at first, reluctant to respond in faith and obedience to God's call to service: we can think, among others, of Sarah, Moses, Gideon, Jeremiah and Jonah. When Peter recounted his experience to the mother Church in Jerusalem, he included these words of testimony 'And the Spirit told me to go with them without hesitation' (Acts 11:12). It is always worth pondering our 'hesitations' and our readiness before the Lord! We are called to be those who gladly respond in a fitting way.

Suggested readings: Acts 11:1-18 and 1 Peter 1:1-7.

AUGUST 13th

## OUR BELIEFS HAVE BEEN BUILT UP SLOWLY

There are over thirty magnificent cathedrals in England and each year they attract a wide variety of tourists as well as pilgrims. It is fascinating to remember that some of these sacred buildings have been places of prayer and devotion for eight or nine centuries or even longer. They seem to be a link with the past, as well as a link with the 'spiritual'. These splendid buildings were built and adapted over a long period, and numerous generations contributed to the architecture and craftsmanship. Likewise, there is a similar sense that God did not grant us all the profound and glorious doctrines of the Christian faith in one single gift; rather, like the great cathedrals, these magnificent elements of our faith were built up over a long period of time.

Certain biblical commentators, theologians and scholars, especially some of the classical scholars, have spoken of 'progressive revelation'. The tenets of our faith did not come overnight, but God revealed Himself down the centuries to successive generations in many and varied ways though, of course, the supreme revelation was in Jesus Christ, and since His coming there has been a deepening appreciation of what He came to make known of God. We revere what the Holy Scriptures call, 'Your most holy faith' (Jude 1:20), and know that it is the serious responsibility of Christians to guard it and defend it, as well as to proclaim the whole message. The unfolding revelation of God's being and character is at the heart of our most glorious – but also ultimately, unfathomable – faith. Christians rejoice in the certitude of salvation, and knowledge of the Saviour, but we also have to recognise the true, wondrous mystery of our faith, too.

In Psalm 64, we get this lovely verse: 'They will tell what God has wrought and ponder what he has done' (Psalm 64:9). There are many ways in which lessons are taught: history, nature, scripture, and the lives of the saints. We also learn by our fellowship with others and our quiet individual meditation on the truth of God, too. So the New English Bible translates the above verse in a fine way: 'This is God's work'. It continues with the rendering: 'They learn the lesson from what he has done'. Our understanding of faith is built up gradually, as it were, and that verse in Jude applies it to our individual lives shared together: 'But you, beloved, build yourselves up on your most holy faith; pray in the Holy Spirit; keep yourselves in the love of God' (Jude 1:20). We also thank God for all those who have reflected on what God has done and who have testified to it. As we grow in our understanding of faith, it is important that we, too, open ourselves to God's truth, so that in the words of the hymn writer, we may, 'Ponder anew what the Almighty can do . . .'

Suggested readings: Psalm 66:1-12 and Jude 1:17-25.

AUGUST 14th

## PEOPLE CAN DISAPPOINT THE LORD

We all know how life has its disappointments! The person who purchases a new car and discovers it has numerous faults, the young person who sits university examinations and is utterly dismayed by the published results or the young couple who upon marriage find they are quite incompatible. We know people can be disappointed with their work colleagues and even with their family members! In our day, there are numerous parents who feel deep anguish because their children have refused to live sensibly and well, according to their accepted values and standards.

God has His disappointments, too. In Isaiah, there is a masterpiece of a parable: 'My beloved had a vineyard on a very fertile hill. He dug it and cleared it of stones, and planted it with choice vines; he built a watchtower in the midst of it, and hewed out a wine vat in it; and he looked for it to yield grapes, but it yielded wild grapes' (Isaiah 5:1-2). Likening the people to the vineyard, this parable tells us that they had disappointed the Lord. The Old Testament reveals that, in a variety of ways, the people of God disappointed Him by their stubbornness, their forgetfulness and their waywardness. This fault is as ancient as the story of humankind: men and women have often failed and disappointed their Creator, as we know today, too.

About three hundred years ago, Matthew Henry wrote a telling comment concerning this particular passage: 'God expects vineyard-fruit from those with vineyard-privileges'. As we think of the blessings which the heavenly Father has bestowed upon us, we should bear fruit to His glory. The lovely words of Jesus found in John's gospel remind us of the secret of spiritual fruitfulness: 'I am the vine, you are the branches. He who abides in me, and I in him, he it is that bears much fruit, for apart from me you can do nothing' (John 15:5). This is borne out in our lives: it is possible to see lives that are evidently in vital relationship with Jesus Christ because of the good fruit borne to God's glory.

All four evangelists record how Peter denied his Master, not once but three times. The story goes on: 'And the Lord turned and looked at Peter' (Luke 22:61). People have been fascinated by that verse: 'What kind of look was it?' It must have been one of sorrow and disappointment, yet also of deep compassion. It is a sober reflection that those who profess Jesus Christ to be their Saviour and Master often disappoint Him; we can all, in a sense, disappoint Him by failures and lack of fruitfulness. However, we can thank God for His mercy toward us. God's love is as sure as the dawn and as fresh as a new day! Peter experienced the restoring power of Christ, and God's love is still known today by all who turn to Him.

Suggested readings: Isaiah 5:1-4 and John 15:1-11.

AUGUST 15th

## GOD IS OUR STRONG TOWER

There are special times in life when we need a strong friend; a friend who is truly understanding and sympathetic, but also strong. We all know that fear is very contagious, it can spread faster than influenza, yet we thank God that courage is contagious, too! In times of uncertainty, danger or sorrow, a friend can be a marvellous source of strength. Often we refer to such a good friend as a 'tower of strength'. There are verses in Holy Scripture which speak of God as our tower: '. . . for thou art my refuge, a strong tower against the enemy' (Psalm 61:3). In the Book of Proverbs there is another lovely verse on this theme: 'the name of the Lord is a strong tower' (Proverbs 18:10). In times of danger and hostility, the people of Old Testament days put their trust in a strong tower; it gave them security, confidence, protection and hope. So God was (and still is for us) a tower of strength in the storms of life that threaten us.

In various places, we can still see some of the strong towers used by our forebears; there are numerous such towers still standing in Britain. These towers, and the ramparts of castles, have weathered many storms: the walls are thick and formidable and some of them have stood for centuries. The remarkable thing is that some of the finest towers show little sign of decay, but we know that they will disintegrate eventually as time and weather do their relentless work! Yet, our 'spiritual tower' – our mighty and eternal God – will endure forever. God has been a tower of strength to many generations of believers and His faithfulness always endures. God's love, grace, mercy and power remain undiminished by the passing of the centuries and the sorry mistakes of human failings. So, in a world where strong towers crumble and decay, where reliable friends pass away into God's eternal presence, our God remains. The Lord God Almighty is the great tower of strength enduring for all eternity: this is the great hope and confidence of all believers.

The sixteenth-century reformer, Martin Luther, felt called to challenge people of his day: it was a difficult and highly dangerous task. At certain periods of his life, he was literally surrounded by hostile people, but he found great comfort in the thought that God was a strong tower. For him, this profound truth gave him renewed confidence and hope. He loved the words of Psalm 46: 'God is our refuge and strength, a very present help in time of trouble' (Psalm 46:1). He wrote a noted hymn on this theme. Understandably, when we are besieged by difficulties, there may be a measure of panic in the human heart: at such times let us remember the sure strong tower, the eternal Lord God who is our true, dependable helper.

Suggested readings: Psalm 46:1-11 and Proverbs 18:4-10.

AUGUST 16th

## IT IS A GOOD THING TO GIVE THOUGHTFUL ANSWERS

We live in a world that quite often demands quick answers! Television quizzes or competitions give contestants a few seconds to reply, politicians interviewed by the press are expected to give direct and swift answers, investors are expected to decide promptly on options available, and people facing various tests or examinations to qualify have timed questions. So often speedy replies are expected! In that context, we remember that the Holy Scriptures have much to say about thoughtful answers, namely, replies which have been duly weighed in one's mind. In the Book of Proverbs, there are numerous verses which refer to the foolishness and wisdom of human speech. We think of some of them: 'To make an apt answer is a joy to anyone, and a word in season, how good it is!' (Proverbs 15:23). Later, in the same chapter, we read these significant words: 'The mind of the righteous ponders how to answer' (Proverbs 15:28). We thank God for those people with authority and responsibility who refuse to speak merely 'from the top of their head', but who seek to give answers that have been properly considered. These people 'weigh their words'! In point of fact, the New International Version translates Proverbs 15:28 as 'The heart of the righteous weighs its answers'. Time to reflect before speaking is so important: it is the thoughtful answer that means the most and is usually the wisest.

On 15th April 1989, a football match was due to be played at Sheffield; actually, just six minutes were played. There were such large crowds that when crowd control went tragically amiss, scores of Liverpool fans were crushed to death. The game was stopped and the football pitch looked like a battlefield, with the wounded and the dying lying around as the emergency services struggled to cope with the scale of the disaster. The city of Liverpool was overwhelmed by sadness and the sporting world was stunned: How could this have happened? 'Why?' Leaders, politicians, local officials and the police, as well as clergy, were bombarded with questions. The popular press began supplying ready answers, and these were often not fair or accurate, and such answers caused almost intolerable pain and hurt. Yet, to their credit, many of the religious leaders – almost without exception – gave duly 'weighed' answers. There are never any easy answers to tragedies and problems that people face. It is always best to stop and offer a far more considered and thoughtful answer, rather than to reply too easily. There is all the difference in the world between a quick reply and a considered answer: it is always wise to think before speaking, just as Jesus did!

Suggested readings: Proverbs 15:22-33 and Luke 8:19-21.

AUGUST 17th

## TESTING IS A NECESSARY EXERCISE

Many work in the business of testing. We can ponder the things which have to be tested to meet with stringent safety and performance standards: vehicles or machinery, electronic products or building materials, drugs and pharmaceutical products. Some things (such as steel and similar materials) are tested to breaking point. Testing is a vital part of modern life: if it were not so, life would be very dangerous. Of course, in our lives we are tested, too! Sometimes, our patience is tested to breaking point; examples might be dealing with difficult people, or rather awkward relatives, or simply finding home life rather hectic in school holidays! In another sense, testing can be protracted: some get through a qualifying exam or their driving test first time; yet, for others, being tested, takes multiple attempts. In numerous ways that is a commentary on life, as we know it; that is particularly the case for many believers. Various individuals suffered different trials and testing in the Old Testament stories, but Job – a long-suffering man – had problem upon problem: he struggled as it seemed that he had far more than his fair share!

In the Book of James, there is a most challenging verse: 'My brothers and sisters, whenever you face trials of any kind, consider it nothing but joy, because you know that the testing of your faith produces endurance' (James 1:2). That goes remarkably near to saying that testing is good for the soul, and actually, of course, it is often so. We may think this hard teaching, but it is absolutely true that a measure of testing can be spiritually productive. In fact, the New International Version says 'The testing of your faith develops perseverance' (James 1:3 NIV). In Psalm 119 there are two verses about affliction which grip one's attention: 'Before I was afflicted I went astray; but now I keep thy word' (Psalm 119:67), and also, 'It is good for me that I was afflicted, that I might learn thy statutes' (Psalm 119:71).

Over the last few decades, lots of mountaineers have sought to climb Mount Everest: it has been conquered numerous times, but it still presents a very tough challenge to dedicated mountaineers. The men and women who endeavour to climb this high mountain must adopt a rigorous training schedule. Some train by walking long distances with heavy weights so that they develop good muscle power! The Book of James stresses the great need for perseverance: 'Indeed we call blessed those who showed endurance. You have heard of the endurance of Job, and you have seen the purpose of the Lord, how the Lord is compassionate and merciful' (James 5:11). The plain truth for all believers is that testing produces fortitude, endurance and perseverance and often, in the end – by God's mercy – brings a very special blessing.

Suggested readings: Psalm 119:57-72 and James 1:1-4.

AUGUST 18th

## OUR GOD FORGIVES GRAVE SIN, TOO

More and more people are becoming concerned about the pollution of this lovely planet Earth. Each year brings its own catalogue of pollution problems and serious damage is done to life and property. In March 1989, news came through which shocked countless people throughout the world: a large oil tanker carrying over 50 million gallons of oil ran aground on a shallow reef and eleven million gallons of oil spilled into the sea! A black wave of death and destruction swept along the Alaskan coast doing massive damage to marine life: birds, animals and fish were terribly affected along the coastline. Lots of people were angry, and the subsequent enquiry revealed that the tanker's captain was not on the bridge at the time of the accident and even hours after the event, he was still over the blood alcohol limit; naturally, he was punished.

Of course, we all make mistakes, and the majority of them are small and insignificant. However, some mistakes are like a giant oil slick that contaminate. When King David committed adultery, he cried in anguish: 'For I know my transgressions, and my sin is ever before me. Against thee, thee only, have I sinned, and done that which is evil in thy sight' (Psalm 51:3-4). He sinned against God but the contamination spread like a massive oil slick and others were injured; it caused great pain, heartache, and suffering. It was a grave sin of huge proportions, and he knew it, but he believed in divine mercy and was able to receive God's forgiveness, and he experienced freedom from his profound sense of guilt.

It is quite impossible to imagine how deeply that ship's skipper, Captain Hazelwood, suffered because of his huge mistake: it is pretty certain that he felt the pain and shame of his foolishness, plus the hostility and bitterness of others. However, as we contemplate any error of judgment, we may ponder the vital question whether God truly forgives our sins, and especially what we might consider serious misdeeds. While we think of sin in terms of degrees of gravity and severity, with variations of any impact upon others, the Bible tells us quite plainly that the mercy of God is greater than our sinfulness. David, Jonah, Mary Magdalene and others such as the woman taken in adultery, and even the apostles including Peter and Paul, all experienced the greatness of God's mercy and forgiveness. So at Antioch in Pisidia Paul spoke to the people about their sin, but then he went on to say: 'Let it be known to you therefore, brethren, that through this man forgiveness of sins is proclaimed to you . . .' (Acts 13:38). It is at the foot of the cross of Jesus that we discover the boundless and generous love of God: there, in Christ's outstretched arms, we see the heart of God revealed. There are many people who – as ones much forgiven – can testify that they know from experience the marvellous loving-kindness of the Lord.

Suggested readings: Acts 13:26-38 and Romans 5:6-11.

AUGUST 19th

## RIPENESS OF CONVICTION IS A POWER FOR GOOD

It is a lovely sight to see an orchard where the apples are ripe for harvesting. The fruit has known a variety of weathers – cool, breezy nights, hot sunny days, as well as rain and mist – but now it is ready for picking. The orchard is a pretty sight for those who see it, but it brings deep satisfaction to the fruit grower! There is a quality about ripeness which is truly beautiful. In fact, it is used in a prayer for the early believers. Alluding to this prayer, the apostle Paul wrote of, 'Epaphras, servant of Christ, who is one of yourselves. He prays hard for you all the time, that you may stand fast, ripe in conviction and wholly devoted to doing God's will' (Colossians 4:12).

Ripeness certainly depicts the experience of a disciple of Christ full of the joy of the Lord and testifying to God's love with zeal and true earnestness. It is heartening to see a Christian going forward, and enduring trials with fortitude. Surely, one of the loveliest sights is to see a man or woman who has reached Christian maturity and is 'ripe in conviction'. These people trust their Lord with a steadfastness which is both attractive and challenging. So Epaphras, himself a wonderful Christian, prays for others that they should become 'ripe in conviction'. Ponder the long-serving Christian minister who had experienced the closeness of a small fellowship and also the great burden of responsibility of ministering to a sizeable church in a large town. With growing wisdom, he had shared the life of his people – deep joys, distressing sorrows, complex problems – and he carried in his heart the secrets of many people. To those acquainted with him, he was well known as a man 'ripe in conviction'. Strangely, this man was a person of few words; and even showed a reluctance to speak! However, whenever he spoke at a committee meeting, a pastoral session or an important regional meeting, people really listened. There was no need for him to raise his voice; people were always very attentive to him.

Some new converts to the faith can, in their enthusiasm, 'rush in where angels fear to tread': their zeal can have a grating effect on others like 'spiritual sandpaper'. How different is the person who is 'ripe in conviction'! He or she ponders meaningfully, listens to others and makes thoughtful decisions. There is a relevant verse in James: 'You must understand this, my beloved: let everyone be quick to listen, slow to speak, slow to anger, for your anger does not produce God's righteousness' (James 1:19). The person who is truly 'ripe in conviction' knows that God will work out His purposes when the time is right. Sometimes, an unwise or even unworthy feverishness in Christian service seems to underestimate the powerful work of the Holy Spirit: yet, we have the assurance of faith that God is ever at work. We are called to be those who live faithfully on the basis of that assurance.

Suggested readings: Colossians 4:10-18 and James 1:16-25.

AUGUST 20th

## BELIEVERS CAN BE CHANNELS OF BLESSING

The story of the feeding of the five thousand (Matthew 14:13-21) provides us with many topics for reflection! One theme is the amazing distribution of the food, once Jesus had multiplied the limited resources: 'Then he ordered the crowds to sit down on the grass; and taking the five loaves and the two fish he looked up to heaven, and blessed, and broke and gave the loaves to the disciples, and the disciples gave them to the crowds' (Matthew 14:19). Clearly, as the disciples obeyed Jesus, they were channels of blessing. The whole of the Bible testifies that God blesses people, so they can be a blessing to others. Illustrations of this abound! The promise given to Abram (and so also to Sarai) was: 'I will make you into a great nation and I will bless you; I will make your name great, and you will be a blessing' (Genesis 12:2).

We remember, of course, that God does not wait for people to be perfect before using them. A closer look reveals that some of the people of faith like Abraham and Sarah, Joseph, David – and no doubt Rahab and Ruth, too – as well as Peter, Paul and others in the early Church, all had one thing in common: they were imperfect people. Yet, in His wisdom and mercy, God used them and they were channels of blessing to others. Our hearts rejoice in their work for the Lord. If God's servants had to be perfect first, the Kingdom of God would be greatly short of workers! However, God's purpose did include One Who was perfect: Jesus Christ, the sinless Son of God, through Whom we know abundant blessing.

When J.B. Phillips went up to Cambridge as a student, he was an atheist and never attended college chapel. Then he met a group of men who had a glowing faith. Right up to this point in his life, he had never met people to whom Christ was a living reality. This group made a great impression upon him and in due time he came to a living, personal faith. If a person has a real faith and a true devotion, he or she is going to be used as a channel of blessing. So, as a matter of historical fact, Phillips himself (through his preaching, teaching, and writing) became a channel of blessing, too. His translation of the Bible (the full New Testament and part of the Old Testament) enriched the minds and hearts of many Christians.

We recall the fine words of testimony that Laban spoke to Jacob: 'I have learned by experience that the Lord hath blessed me for thy sake' (Genesis 30:27 AV). What a testimony! Actually, those words can be used concerning lots of God's faithful servants. Just one Christian in a family, an office, a shop, a class, a factory, a sports team, or a business group, can be a tremendous channel of blessing to others. So, also, our prayer should surely always be: 'Make me a channel of blessing'.

Suggested readings: Genesis 12:1-8 and Matthew 14:13-21.

## AUGUST 21st

## LIFE IS LIKE A JIGSAW PUZZLE

One of the pleasures of life for many people is to work on a good jigsaw puzzle: some families have been known to be so keen that they reserve a table in the winter months for this activity! We all know that certain parts of a jigsaw are easily put together, but other parts are extraordinarily hard, especially a large expanse of one dominant colour such as sea, sky, or landscape scenes with extensive ranges of mixed colours. In many ways, putting the pieces of life together is a bit like completing a complicated jigsaw puzzle, and sometimes it can prove to be puzzling or bewildering.

The many parts to life are often revealed in biographical works. So often autobiographical books have fascinating titles: *In Search of Myself*, D.R. Davies; *You are My God*, David Watson; *Changeful Page*, William Wand. Occasionally, the title consists of one word. Sybille Bedford wrote a biographical novel that she called *Jigsaw*. For her life had been like a complicated jigsaw! In a sense, the life of every individual consists of many pieces, so to speak: daily work and leisure, relationships and responsibilities, interests and hobbies, citizenship and political allegiance, prejudices and partialities, friendships and community life and, of course, faith or the lack of it.

As we think of the life of the apostle Paul, we realise how complicated it was: his life consisted of many different pieces, a bit like a gigantic jigsaw puzzle. Sometimes, when we read of all the things he did and the numerous places he visited, we are astounded that one individual did so much for the Kingdom of God. He accomplished a lot even in often very trying circumstances! He also knew much about pain and suffering 'for Christ's sake'. Yet, he still offered this positive affirmation of faith: 'We know that in everything God works for good with those who love him, who are called according to his purpose' (Romans 8:28). He realised that God knew all about the jigsaw puzzle of his life and that the final sovereignty in every situation was always God's alone. That can be our experience as believers, too.

When – after all the hard work of much trial and error – the last piece of a jigsaw puzzle is put in place, there is real pleasure and satisfaction at the sense of the work being complete as a whole. Of course, life can be a bit more complicated and at times we may feel we've come across a really tricky section of the overall puzzle. We may think of the psalmist's words: 'I wait for the Lord, my soul waits, and in his word I hope; my soul waits for the Lord more than those who watch for the morning' (Psalm 130:5-6). A quiet waiting upon the Lord can bring refreshment and then, in the mercy and goodness of God, we come to see the Lord at work and may discern how the pieces might fit together. Yet, even when we cannot see the puzzle complete, we trust God is still working out His purposes and leading us on safely.

Suggested readings: Psalm 130:1-8 and Romans 8:26-30.

## AUGUST 22nd

## TALKING TO OURSELVES IS REVEALING

It's undeniable that many, if not most, people talk to themselves: whether it's the motorist who sees someone driving dangerously, or a baker making a very special cake, or a craftsman or woman or artist facing a challenging task, or a delivery person who has just done a tiresome round, or a writer trying to get just the right wording. Actually, talking to one's self reveals a great deal! In Luke's gospel we're told how Simon invited Jesus for a meal: it was a golden opportunity for this Pharisee to have Jesus present and to study Him at close quarters, and to ask Him some questions, too. As they sat at table, there was an interruption! Luke tells how a woman came in and showed her deep devotion towards Jesus: '. . . kissed his feet, and anointed them with ointment' (Luke 7:38). Simon was upset by the woman's actions and Luke records: 'Now when the Pharisee who had invited him saw it he said to himself, 'If this man were a prophet, he would have known who and what sort of woman this is who is touching him, for she is a sinner' (Luke 7:39). Even without hearing Simon's dialogue with himself, Jesus knew the whole situation.

It appears that Simon had a grievance which he nursed in his own heart. He didn't say a word out loud, but his face no doubt said it all. We might say that he talked to himself! Numerous people talk to themselves and it happens at many levels: a couple see neighbours in expensive outfits and inwardly comment, 'Who do they think they are?' or a young person is rebuked and mutters under his breath, 'Leave me alone'. In the gospel story, Simon had an unspoken, but conspicuous, condemnation of Jesus' approach to the woman who was reckoned by others to be a sinner and therefore not acceptable. Luke suggests that Jesus was fully aware of what was going on in Simon's heart and mind. So He told a parable about forgiveness, contrasting two people who were forgiven debts on vastly different scales (Luke 7:40-43).

In the Parable of the Prodigal Son we have another illustration of a man talking to himself. When the prodigal found himself in serious difficulties, he spoke to himself 'I will arise and go to my father, and I will say to him, "Father, I have sinned against heaven and before you"' (Luke 15:18). While the wayward son had been foolish, he finally came to show some wisdom, too! He was wise enough to reflect, to talk within his own heart and then to return to the father. Sometimes, in life, we may find ourselves in the position of 'talking to ourselves': it could be mulling over some past failure, nursing some old grievance, or crying out for help. Yet, there is always a sense in which this inner conversation might actually help us as individuals to arise and to return, as it were, knowing that the heavenly Father is more ready to forgive us, than we are even to seek forgiveness. God has such love for us!

Suggested readings: Luke 7:36-50 and Luke 15:17-24.

AUGUST 23rd

## CURIOSITY IS A GIFT FROM GOD

One of the most interesting things about children is their insatiable curiosity: they want to know all sorts of things, especially about how things work! They certainly ask plenty of questions! Actually, in the story of humankind, curiosity has been vital in the quest to discover more and more. We know some of the tales of the explorers who were immensely curious about vast tracts of untravelled territories, the highest mountains or the depths of the oceans. Scientists have wondered about space and have even explored the surface of the moon. Some of these conquests in discovery were a feat of both daring and human ingenuity! The day two astronauts first stood on the surface of the moon in July 1969 was a triumph for human exploration.

The word 'curiosity' does not occur in the Bible as such, but there is plenty of evidence that it often abounded! We think of Zacchaeus, the tax-collector, who was so keen to see Jesus for himself, that he let his curiosity have free rein: 'And he sought to see who Jesus was, but could not, on account of the crowd, because he was small of stature. So he ran on ahead and climbed up into a sycamore tree to see him, for he was to pass that way' (Luke 19:3-4). What a strong inquisitiveness Zacchaeus must have had to do such an unconventional thing! In order to satisfy their curiosity, men and women have done some very strange things. We may be amused at how some keen naturalists have to put on camouflage and hide away for hours, so that they can get a closer look at birds, insects and animals in their natural habitat!

It is a simple fact of life that humankind has always been curious about the world and – beyond our planet – the whole realm of space; indeed, the world of nature has excited deep curiosity and much time, energy and money has been expended exploring it. The cost of the missions to discover more about the moon and the planets, or outer space – or even to probe the earth's farthest bounds and the ocean depths – has seemed exorbitant to some, but it does give a clear indication of the human desire to pursue such exploration. That curiosity is a God-given capacity to seek truth. We recall words found in the Book of Job: 'As for me, I would seek God, and to God would I commit my cause; who does great things and unsearchable, marvellous things without number' (Job 5:8-9).

People in successive generations have been curious about life's meaning and purpose. If it is true to say that curiosity has sometimes brought people to strange places, it is also true to say it has brought many to discover God. Men and women have sought, and so often have found, the reality of God; or, as some might put it, God found them! We remember the words of the prophet: 'Seek the Lord while he may be found, call upon him while he is near' (Isaiah 55:6). That's life's deepest quest.

Suggested readings: Job 11:1-8 and John 1:35-42.

AUGUST 24th

## APPEARANCES CAN BE MISLEADING

If a person observed a couple travelling and noticed that the husband was letting his wife carry the most awkward luggage, one might make assumptions and wonder as to his sense of decency! However, one could be very wrong, indeed, not knowing the actual circumstances, as was the case in this instance, where Michael, did exactly that. Knowing the actual situation of his ill health, suffering from a heart complaint and having been warned not to carry anything heavy, one would understand the reason for this odd behaviour. Michael found this instruction of his doctor very difficult to obey, especially when travelling on holiday, as he imagined people muttering: 'Fancy him letting his wife struggle with that heavy case!' Happily, Michael and his wife then came to a satisfactory answer: when they went on holiday, he carried a suitcase but it was always empty. Perhaps it sounds bizarre but, by this subtle deception, he could keep up appearances! Agatha Christie could have written an interesting mystery story entitled, 'The man with the empty suitcase'.

This tale of the empty suitcase can be used as a parable: how many Christians (including Church leaders and ministers), give the appearance of diligent service for the Kingdom, but in reality it is much different. Ultimately, it is not for us to judge, of course, but how many might appear to be carrying, as it were, the 'empty suitcase'? This is shown in a variety of ways, when worship services seem unprepared, or the church building looks rather unkempt, or even in little ways, such as still having the Harvest poster on the notice-board in January, or an old Christmas poster still displayed in Holy Week. Sometimes, sadly, the disorder is rather more deep-seated and serious! Outward, superficial appearances are not the full story.

In one of his letters, the apostle Paul reflects back on his ministry: 'I have fought the good fight, I have finished the race, I have kept the faith' (2 Timothy 4:7). Paul knew that he could never be accused of slovenly work: he had a burning zeal for the Kingdom. However, he also knew deep disappointment: 'For Demas, in love with this present world, has deserted me and gone to Thessalonica' (2 Timothy 4:10). Demas, a colleague of Paul, somehow, had 'emptied his suitcase' of genuine Christian commitment, returning to the pre-occupations of this world. In the Church's history, this is a pattern which has recurred many times. It might be considered by each of us, whether we still really 'carry the suitcase' in bearing the load of Christian service through sincere commitment to Jesus Christ, or whether, in reality – despite outward appearances – our suitcase is, as it were, empty. We recall what Jesus said: 'The good person out of the good treasure of his heart produces good' (Luke 6:45).

Suggested readings: Luke 6:41-46 and 2 Timothy 4:6-18.

AUGUST 25th

## THERE IS A FIRM FOUNDATION

Every year a large number of people go to Devon for their holidays: the hills and valleys, the beaches and rivers, the villages and beauty spots have a strong attraction. There are some people who would never dream of going anywhere else for their holidays: Devon has so captured their hearts that they return year after year to relax and to explore the area. One small town which is a particular favourite, especially for photographers, is Kingsbridge. It has a lovely estuary and people stand on the town's bridge to take photographs of the boats, swans and other points of interest.   One of the things of great interest to Christians is the large rock which stands in the waters of the estuary; it has a fascinating history. Over three centuries ago, when some Christians in the area were persecuted for their faith, they could not worship freely without interference. So, these Dissenters decided to go and worship in seclusion on the rock. This meant that Sunday services were governed by the time of low tide in the estuary! The Lord's people met on the rock amid the estuary waters and were therefore able to worship God 'without let or hindrance'; the reason was that they were secure on the rock. They shared in fellowship and worshipped together on the rock: it was a safe and sound place where they could gather in fellowship freely.

Surely, this is a parable: the Holy Scriptures teach us that we must abide on the 'rock of ages' which is the Lord Jesus Christ, the very truth of God. So we are reminded of the graphic parable which Jesus told of the two builders: one building on the rock, and the other on the sand. When the storms came, the house on the sand collapsed but the house on the rock stood firm. So Jesus said: 'Every one then who hears these words of mine and does them will be like a wise man who built his house upon the rock; and the rain fell, and the floods came, and the winds blew and beat upon that house, but it did not fall, because it had been founded on the rock' (Matthew 7:24-25). There is security and strength on the rock of His teaching.

One of the great prayers recorded in the Old Testament is found in Psalm 61: 'Hear my cry, O God, listen to my prayer; from the end of the earth I call to thee, when my heart is faint. Lead thou me to the rock that is higher than I for thou art my refuge, a strong tower against the enemy' (Psalm 61:1-3). Countless generations of believers have confidently prayed the psalmist's prayer. They have found true refuge and real security on the 'Rock'. We might imagine that, in ages past, the dissenting Christians of Kingsbridge cherished that prayer in the opening verses of Psalm 61. They could certainly identify fully with the ancient psalmist's longings! We, too, by trusting in Jesus and His Word, can know that firm foundation in life.

Suggested readings: Psalm 61:1-8 and Matthew 7:24-29.

AUGUST 26th

## WE SHOULD REMEMBER THE LORD

How often, when people commence a good work, it seems to attract opposition and criticism; true reformers are at times, very unpopular people! There are numerous people who just cannot stand any kind of change or suggested improvement. In the Book of Nehemiah, we learn of the determined effort to rebuild the walls of Jerusalem. The story is told that they worked 'from the break of dawn till the stars came out' (Nehemiah 4:21). However, the opposition was fierce: 'But when Sanballat heard that we were building the wall, he was angry and greatly enraged, and he ridiculed the Jews' (Nehemiah 4:1). This burning anger attracted support and a plan was soon hatched to spoil things: the mood of hostility was very strong. At this point, God's servant Nehemiah spoke comfortingly to the nobles, the officials, and to the people as a whole: 'Do not be afraid of them. Remember the Lord' (Nehemiah 4:14).

As we consider the sound advice given by Nehemiah, we realise that it is wisdom for all generations! There are times when people need to shift their gaze from the opposition and look to the Lord: to remember the Lord God Who delivered the Hebrews from the clutches of Pharaoh and his armies by working the miracle at the Red Sea, the God Who provided for His people in the wilderness, and the God Who brought them to the Promised Land. In essence, it is the same word for us today: remember the Lord, for God does not change! God's power, love, and faithfulness are still the same. God worked to save His people yesterday and, even now, God works today. How often – in times of fear or daunting challenge – we need to remind ourselves of the words of Nehemiah: 'Do not be afraid of them. Remember the Lord'. Recalling God's help, we can go onward in life with confidence day by day.

Sometimes, we are caught up in situations which are very dark and threatening: the opposition seems well organised and tremendously strong. At certain times, our hearts 'quake with fear' and we are truly alarmed. On those occasions, we should pause, be still, take a few deep breaths, look upward, as it were, and – above all – remember the Lord, the God of our forebears. Situations change, problems change, dangers change, but the Lord God does not! In New Testament days, there were times when it was dangerous to be a Christian. So the writer to the Hebrews counselled: 'Let us run with perseverance the race that is set before us, looking to Jesus the pioneer and perfecter of our faith' (Hebrews 12:1-2). When we are afraid or facing strong opposition, and it is not easy to go on, we can find rest as we know solace in these timeless words: 'Do not be afraid of them. Remember the Lord'.

Suggested readings: Nehemiah 4:1-20 and Hebrews 12:1-2.

AUGUST 27th

## GOD REMAKES LIVES

Two children were playing happily together in the lounge. All was well and mother and father were relaxing by the lovely fire in the fireplace: it was a scene of peacefulness and tranquillity, but not for long! Suddenly, heated squabbling shattered the peace of the lounge: a toy had been broken, and so had the peace! In the commotion a child's voice was heard to say: 'Why is it so easy to break things?' A good question, as so often in life things are broken: broken promises, broken relationships, broken homes, broken hearts, broken friendships and broken systems or organisations. It is so easy to break things, but we remember that, at the heart of our Christian faith, there is a belief that God can heal our brokenness: the brokenness we know in our world and in our community, as well as in our individual lives.

In Jeremiah chapter 18, we're told how the prophet received God's prompting to go down to the potter's house and he was promised: 'There I will let you hear my words' (Jeremiah 18:2). So, obediently, Jeremiah went and he found the potter busy at his craft. As the potter was making a certain vessel, it was spoilt, 'so he made it again' (Jeremiah 18:4 AV). As the prophet saw the potter take the same clay and make a new vessel, Jeremiah was inspired: 'The word of the Lord came to me: "O house of Israel, can I not do with you as this potter has done?" says the Lord. "Behold, like the clay in the potter's hand, so are you in my hand, O house of Israel"'(Jeremiah 18:5-6). If a potter can take a piece of clay and remake it, how much more can the divine potter take a broken people, as well as broken lives, and remake them as the master craftsman! This is a word summoning us to trust in God.

We rejoice that God can bring joy out of sorrow, light out of darkness, victory out of defeat, and wholeness out of brokenness. It is absolutely imperative to remember that the things which are impossible for us, are possible with God! The resurrection of Jesus Christ from the dead provides us with evidence that our God is a God Whose love knows no bounds. Whatever we face in life, however broken we feel, we may be sure that God is ever at work in our lives. Of course, sometimes we are not only broken, but we know that we are responsible for the brokenness in the lives of others. However, God, Who raised Jesus from the dead, stands ready to forgive us and give us a fresh start. Scripture says that Peter failed Christ near a charcoal fire in the High Priest's courtyard by denying his Lord; yet, John's gospel tells how it was again by a charcoal fire – this time on the Galilean beach – that Peter was restored as a true disciple! God forgave him and God will forgive us, too.

Suggested readings: Jeremiah 18:1-10 and John 21:11-19.

AUGUST 28th

## PEOPLE CAN CHOOSE A COLLISION COURSE

The English Channel is one of the busiest shipping lanes in the world and sometimes there are near misses! Two ships on a collision course have to take swift evasive action. The expression, 'They're on a collision course . . .' is an integral part of spoken English and is used in a wide variety of ways. The expression can be used to describe the potential breakdown of a relationship or business partnership, the friction between groups within a community, or factions within an organization. Of course, in another sense, it might be observed that some people by their actions, words and attitudes can seem to be on a collision course with God.

One of the strenuous tasks given to the prophet Jeremiah was to warn his own people of the error of their ways: he spoke to them of divine judgement and appealed to them to accept a change of lifestyle: 'Turn now, all of you, from your evil ways, and amend your ways and your doings' (Jeremiah 18:11). Yet, that plea ended up being rejected by most of the people! C.S. Lewis has pointed out that the path downward is a gentle slope, and we know the truth of that comment. One could say waywardness is like a large ball rolling downhill that gathers momentum, and then is hard to stop. So as the prophet discovered, the people were terribly stubborn. We read in scripture their attitude: 'But they say, "It is no use! We will follow our own plans, and each of us will act according to the stubbornness of our evil will"' (Jeremiah 18:12). Jeremiah saw that the people were on a collision course, indeed.

This waywardness still occurs today, and sometimes people prove unfaithful to one another and to God. For example, there was a woman who became infatuated with a young man: she had a family, with a loving husband and children but she continued this flirtation at work. One day, she simply eloped with her lover, leaving her husband and children sad, dismayed and bewildered. A friend of the family found her and pleaded fervently for her to remember her responsibilities, and to have second thoughts for the family's sake. Her reply was direct and final: 'I've made up my mind'. Sadly, nothing would budge her from that attitude of selfishness and disregard for those closest to her. In this respect, one modern version of Jeremiah 18 is very apt: 'Things are past hope. We must stick to our own plans, each of us follow the promptings of his wicked and stubborn heart' (Jeremiah 18:12 REB). That woman was on a collision course and refused to turn aside, so lots of people, including herself, were badly hurt. There is a law built into the fabric of life: you cannot build your happiness on the foundation of someone else's unhappiness. Surely, many people might have taken decisive action to steer clear of the collision course if they had known and heeded that one simple rule of life!

Suggested readings: Jeremiah 18:11-18 and 1 Corinthians 10:11-13.

AUGUST 29th

## PEOPLE CAN BE RICH SPIRITUALLY

During the course of a normal year, Her Majesty Queen Elizabeth II has numerous public engagements where she meets world figures: Kings, Queens, Presidents, Statesmen and women, Prime Ministers and other governors. Sometimes, the Queen meets someone who is completely different, as in 1983, when she met Mother Teresa of Calcutta. They met in the grounds of the Presidential Palace in New Delhi, and the Queen gave her the insignia of the Order of Merit, an honour which was applauded by millions who respected the work done by 'this little lady'. One photograph which was published, showed Her Majesty presenting the insignia to Mother Teresa and underneath were these thought-provoking words: 'The richest woman in the world in the world pays tribute to one of the poorest'. When we think of the possessions and lifestyles of these two women, we realise that in their meeting, two different worlds met! Her Majesty would, of course, be one of the first to acknowledge this fact. Thinking of that meeting, an important question arises: 'Was it correct to view Mother Teresa as really poor?' Certainly, it has always been acknowledged that she was one rich in friendships, truly blessed in her service and so loved by many! She has always been seen as one who was 'rich in faith' and 'rich in good works'.

The epistles of the apostle Paul and of James, respectively, remind us of the nature of true wealth, and give counsel: 'They are to do good, to be rich in good deeds, liberal and generous, thus laying up for themselves a good foundation for the future' (1 Timothy 6:18) and 'Listen, my beloved brothers and sisters. Has not God chosen the poor in the world to be rich in faith and heirs of the kingdom that he has promised to those who love him?' (James 2:5). Down the years people looked on Mother Teresa as exemplifying these attitudes, and recognised her spiritual riches, acknowledging her true worth. Indeed, her quiet witness has spoken volumes!

When we ponder the life of Christ, we know that He did not have an abundance of possessions; in fact, history records Him as one of the world's poorest. Yet, the apostle Paul had a profound perspective on this subject: 'For you know the grace of our Lord Jesus Christ, that though he was rich, yet for your sake he became poor, so that by his poverty you might become rich' (2 Corinthians 8:9). So Mother Teresa, following the Lord's example in her poverty, brought enrichment to hundreds of poor people in Calcutta. Some of the world's rich people are actually quite poor in many ways, while paradoxically, some of the world's poorest and lowliest ones are – in a strange sense – gloriously rich in spiritual terms!

Suggested readings: 1 Timothy 6:11-21 and James 2:1-8.

AUGUST 30th

## GOD'S FAITHFULNESS REACHES TO THE CLOUDS

What a thrill it is to have a perfect summer's day in our part of the world! It is a thoroughly satisfying thing to wake up and hear the weather forecast: 'Today, it will be sunny, warm and dry in all areas, which is good news for all holidaymakers!' Rain on previous days will have made the countryside green and fertile, refreshing the land, so the sunny day has a perfect setting; most would agree that there's nothing quite like a glorious summer's day. Indeed, to speak of a 'blue sky' symbolizes contentment.

We may also reflect on 'blue sky' days in terms of the spiritual life. Most Christians have experienced times when, spiritually, they have felt as though it has been like a beautiful summer's day. However, life gives us variety, and there are also days when clouds gather overhead: the day begins with bright sunshine, but the evening brings ominous storm clouds. For instance, a couple might experience an illness, an accident, a tragedy or a bitter hardship, which seems to put their relationship under threat. It is as if a storm cloud is right overhead, dark and menacing. Perhaps, the couple go to church with despair in their hearts and the minister announces the text for the Sunday worship: 'Thy mercy, O Lord, is in the heavens; and thy faithfulness reacheth unto the clouds' (Psalm 36:5 AV). It comes to them as a powerful Word from the Lord and speaks to their hearts, touching their brokenness and reminding them of God's enduring faithfulness to all, whatever any of us may face each day.

In the Acts of the Apostles, Luke tells the story of the Ascension: the moment when the risen Lord was taken up from their midst. The record tells of the disciples quizzically watching: 'As they were looking on, he was lifted up, and a cloud took him out of their sight' (Acts 1:9). Yet, God's faithfulness reached to that cloud, too! As the story is told, the disciples gazed upon that enveloping cloud and saw Jesus' physical withdrawal from them. However, at that moment they could not comprehend how God would faithfully continue to work through the Holy Spirit. William Cowper's hymn, 'God moves in a mysterious way', includes this lovely verse:

Ye fearful saints, fresh courage take;
The clouds ye so much dread
Are big with mercy, and shall break
In blessings on your head.

There are days when the storm clouds gather and we feel apprehensive or afraid, but even on the stormiest days, as the psalmist put it, God's faithfulness does, indeed, reach to the clouds! So, trusting in God, we can live with confidence day by day.

Suggested readings: Psalm 36:1-12 and Acts 1:1-11.

AUGUST 31st

## GOD DOES NOT FORGET OUR LABOUR FOR HIM

There is an important verse in Hebrews which has given enormous encouragement and comfort to Christian workers: 'God is not unjust; he will not forget your work and the love you have shown him as you have helped his people and continue to help them' (Hebrews 6:10 NIV). Very sadly, men and women do forget our Christian service: occasionally there are aged Christians who, having served many years, then seem to be side-lined or overlooked. Indeed, if rendered housebound, they may miss out on support, even from the church where they served! However, God never forgets: our Blessed Lord has a sure memory! With complete confidence, we can rely on this promise that God will never forget the work we've done for His Kingdom; the knowledge that God honours such faithful work is a great comfort to many!

In 1988, a very special service was held in Bedford to commemorate the three-hundredth anniversary of the death of John Bunyan, the seventeenth-century tinker who refused to be silenced by the persecuting authorities of the day. In the presence of a large congregation at Bunyan Meeting, leaders of various denominations shared in the worship: Roman Catholic, Anglican, and other Christian bodies joined in the occasion, along with the Baptists and Congregationalists of that fellowship. The Archbishop of Canterbury, Dr. Robert Runcie, preached the sermon and unveiled the lovely memorial window. John Bunyan suffered at the hands of the Establishment and the Churchmen of his day: his faithfulness in preaching God's Word, resulted in twelve years of imprisonment. Ironically, three hundred years later, the Establishment was there to honour him, giving thanks for his writing and ministry! God had kept His promise: God had not forgotten John Bunyan's costly sacrifice and his many resolute labours through his steadfast devotion to the Saviour. In the service, God was praised by those of all backgrounds for the gift of Bunyan's life and witness there. This was quite a poignant moment of reversal!

We can remember with gratitude and thanksgiving, all those committed people in Christian history who rendered faithful service for God, but were despised in their day and generation. We know for ourselves that so often the world's judgement is badly defective: the ancient words of the Lord spoken by the prophet still ring true: 'For my thoughts are not your thoughts, neither are your ways my ways' (Isaiah 55:8). God's measure of true greatness is so very different from worldly standards! The Son of God was Himself, despised and rejected, but then was vindicated and glorified. When we think perhaps, that our service is not duly recognized, we take solace in the knowledge that God never forgets! So we thank the Lord who always upholds us.

Suggested readings: Ephesians 6:1-9 and Hebrews 6:1-12.

# September

The King of love my Shepherd is,
Whose goodness faileth never;
I nothing lack if I am His
And He is mine for ever.

Where streams of living water flow
My ransomed soul He leadeth,
And where the verdant pastures grow
With food celestial feedeth.

Perverse and foolish oft I strayed;
But yet in love He sought me,
And on His shoulder gently laid,
And home, rejoicing, brought me.

In death's dark vale I fear no ill
With Thee, dear Lord, beside me;
Thy rod and staff my comfort still,
Thy cross before to guide me.

Thou spread'st a table in my sight;
Thy unction, grace bestoweth;
And O what transport of delight
From Thy pure chalice floweth!

And so through all the length of days
Thy goodness faileth never;
Good Shepherd, may I sing Thy praise
Within Thy house for ever.

H.W. Baker (1821-1877)

Lord, make me an instrument of your peace.
Where there is hatred, let me sow love;
where there is injury, pardon;
where there is doubt, faith;
where there is despair, hope;
where there is darkness, light;
and where there is sadness, joy.

O Divine Master, grant that I may not so much seek
to be consoled as to console;
to be understood as to understand;
to be loved as to love.
For it is in giving that we receive;
it is in pardoning that we are pardoned;
and it is in dying that we are born to eternal life.
Amen.

St Francis of Assisi (1182-1226)

SEPTEMBER 1st

## LIFE CAN BECOME TOO FULL

We all have experiences that are irritating and embarrassing! For example: we borrow something and it is then damaged, we promise to meet a friend and the car breaks down, or we have planned to have the whole family together for a celebration meal and the cooker fails! Such experiences are surprisingly common. One student, who had won a place at a college was told to arrive at a specific time. He planned to travel by long-distance coach but, as he stood at the coach stop, his plans suddenly went awry as he watched the coach sail past because there was no more room for other passengers! It was annoying, but it also brought home a lesson about life.

Life may, at times, appear to be something like an overcrowded coach. As we move along, we collect interests: our work and family life, our hobbies and sports, our friendships and community activities, and so life becomes very full leaving no more space at all! Sometimes, it seems that there is little time for spiritual matters: activities associated with the inner life are wholly left aside, including times for prayer, reflection on scripture and corporate worship. Perhaps the psalmist was aware of this predicament when he wrote: 'there is no room for God' (Psalm 10:4 NIV).

On one occasion, while visiting a parishioner, just as the minister was about to leave, the woman said 'You know I would like to come to church but just don't have the time'. The minister was taken aback and replied directly, 'But that is ridiculous: if you were ill, you would have to find time; if you had to go into hospital, you would have to find time!' Those simple yet frank words of honest rebuke were accepted and bore fruit. The woman said: 'I'll be in church next Sunday', and she duly attended! As a result, she and her husband began coming to church on a regular basis and found a new start: they found room for God in their thoughts and in their lives.

There are lots of people who have no room for spiritual things: they exclude God from their plans, their home, their life and their thoughts. Life is cluttered up with so many different things which are good in themselves, but still there seems to be an aching inner void. The Good News Bible translates the verse in Psalm 10 in a striking manner: 'In his pride, he thinks that God doesn't matter' (Psalm 10:4 GNB). God comes pretty low on the list of priorities for so many; perhaps they may 'doff their cap' to Him by attending a service at Christmas or Easter, but otherwise God is given no place, excluded from their lives. Of such vanity or self-centred pride, the New Testament offers this warning: 'God opposes the proud but gives grace to the humble' (1 Peter 5:5). It is surely perilous to crowd God out of our lives!

Suggested readings: Psalm 10:1-14 and 1 Peter 5:1-5.

## SEPTEMBER 2nd

## OUR GOD CAN BE TRUSTED

When Elizabeth Goldsmith wrote the story of her Christian pilgrimage, she chose a very simple title: *God Can be Trusted.* The person who really believes those four important words honours God, and probably has a wholly different outlook on life. Indeed, if we believe God can be trusted, then life has a different perspective. In one of the small churches in Cambridgeshire there was an elderly church officer who could neither read nor write. In the evenings, his wife would read him a passage of scripture so he could ponder it. He truly delighted in God's Word and had a real hunger for it. He believed that God could be trusted and that was the level on which he lived. He could say with the psalmist, 'My flesh and my heart may fail, but God is the strength of my heart and my portion for ever' (Psalm 73:26), as well as the further affirmation, 'But for me it is good to be near God' (Psalm 73:28).

Jesus said: 'Blessed are those who hunger and thirst for righteousness, for they shall be satisfied' (Matthew 5:6). Thank the Lord for all the men and women who've had a real hunger for the things of God and who place their trust in God. In Acts chapter 13, we have a fascinating story of Paul's visit to Antioch in Pisidia: the rulers of the synagogue gave him opportunity to speak and he took it. He gave them a history lesson with a spiritual application. Luke reports: 'As they went out, the people begged that these things might be told them the next sabbath' (Acts 13:42). They were hungry to hear the things of God – nothing could have pleased Paul more! The next Sabbath a vast number assembled to hear the message; and, in spite of opposition from certain Jews, Paul and Barnabas spoke the message boldly. Then we read this wonderful verse: 'When the Gentiles heard this they were glad and honoured the word of the Lord' (Acts 13:48 NIV). How did they honour it? In three ways: by listening to it, by rejoicing in it and by believing it. Of course, our honour for the word of the Lord should be expressed in both word and deed. One missionary who served in India told how, in certain churches, there is a custom where every worshipper is encouraged to bring a light to the church: the result being the more people, the more light! There is a deep sense in which the more people trust in God and seek to honour God's Word, then the more light and truth will abound.

We rejoice that in Antioch there were people who trusted and so honoured the Word of the Lord; we rejoice even more that, in succeeding generations, there have always been such people. Indeed, today, we recall the confession of faith made by Elizabeth Goldsmith, who grew up in China where her parents served as missionaries: God can be trusted. Let us give thanks to God that such an affirmation is true to our experience, too. We can live knowing God as One wholly to be trusted.

Suggested readings: Psalm 119:25-32 and Acts 13:42-52.

SEPTEMBER 3rd

## CONCERNING THE BREVITY OF LIFE

On 3rd September 1939, the Prime Minister of Britain, Neville Chamberlain, broadcast the news over the radio that Britain was in a State of War with Germany. It was a Sunday morning and the broadcast was made at 11.00 am, a time when millions of people were at church. That Sunday, Hitler seemed so strong, so cunning and such a dynamic personality; in fact, a large number of the people in Nazi Germany, thought he was a powerful leader, and even idolized him! The psalmist spoke of an example of such power in this way: 'I have seen the wicked in great power, and spreading himself like a green bay tree' (Psalm 37:35 AV). By ordinary reckoning, Hitler seemed poised to win decisively and many people understandably feared him.

In a small village church that Sunday morning, a minister of the gospel preached a quiet, but very effective sermon on a rendering of the text in Job 38:11, 'He shall go so far but no further'. Very sincerely the preacher told the congregation that this evil time – indeed, this wicked force – would pass away eventually! How true that message proved to be. However, the conquest came at great cost and after terrible suffering and heartache. Empires rise and fall, monarchs come and go, powerful figures strut on the world's stage and then are no more; even the most powerful people live but relatively short lives. What is sixty, seventy, eighty or even one hundred years, on the timescale of history? Life is short: that is our common human lot. Our season on earth is but brief, as we are well reminded by the words of the psalmist: 'Lord, let me know my end, and what is the measure of my days; let me know how fleeting my life is!' (Psalm 39:4).

In the Book of Hosea, the prophet speaks of a people who have turned to idols and rebelled against the true God. Hosea spoke a word of judgement which includes this dire prophecy: 'Her king will be carried off, like a chip of wood on water' (Hosea 10:7 GNB). What a picture! We can recall children watching floating objects in a fast-flowing stream. The prophet claims that the life of Israel's king (in spite of all his vaunted power and authority) is like a woodchip bobbing on running water. Surely, that image, somewhat comically, catches the spirit of the Bible teaching that all human life is brief and transitory: even the longest life is quite short.

As we reflect on this particular theme, we recall that in many scriptural passages, we are told that our God endures forever: God remains as the faithful One. Generations come and go, as life hurries on at a great pace, with situations often changing radically, but God prevails in His power and glory, His love is everlasting. Christians worship the eternal God, and when our lives are offered to this Lord of all, we come to share – as incredible as it seems – eternal life as His gracious gift.

Suggested readings: Psalm 39:1-13 and James 4:10-17.

SEPTEMBER 4th

## THE QUALITY OF THE HARVEST IS UNPREDICTABLE

It is most interesting to witness the growth of the garden centre business. A visit to a local garden centre gives insight into the rich variety of seeds, plants, flowers, shrubs and trees, together with all the paraphernalia which assist their cultivation! Gardening provides plenty of spiritual lessons, in that a lovely garden does not just happen, but requires the constant discipline of work and the persistent quest of promoting fruitful cultivation. That goes for the Christian life, too: a person doesn't just drift into being a good Christian, but it comes about through being disciplined and focused.

Seeds fascinate many gardeners, especially, those who have, as it were, 'green fingers'. How wonderful it is that a tiny seed develops by germination, and grows according to an inbuilt programme and natural dynamism: an acorn produces an oak, from a cherry stone, we have a cherry tree, and so on. We know the seed has the potential for life and growth and, once sown, germinates and plants spring forth from the tiniest shoots. Yet, there is still an element of mystery to keep us in awe of the whole natural process, even with all our scientific or botanical knowledge and horticultural understanding! We recall the words of Jesus Christ: 'The kingdom of God is as if a man should scatter seed upon the ground, and should sleep and rise night and day, and the seed should sprout and grow, he does not know how. The earth produces of itself, first the blade, then the ear, then the full grain in the ear' (Mark 4:26-28).

The story is told of a couple settling into their new home: an intrepid relative (presumably marking the occasion) set two peach stones near one of the walls. After a considerable time, there was rather spindly growth; then year-by-year they produced a blossom. One year, to their delight, some peaches appeared! There was some excitement but Mother Nature still had a surprise for the couple, as one tree later went on to produce a splendid crop in abundance!

In life, too, there are years which are quite ordinary, then along comes a particularly extraordinary year when everything seems to happen for better or for worse, before life returns to being more mundane again. Christian workers know this sequence, too. They have known lean years when the 'spiritual harvest' has been very sparse; then comes a glorious year when there is an abundance of people won for the Kingdom. There is a verse in the Book of Psalms which has been a great comfort to many spiritual leaders and Christian workers 'They that sow in tears shall reap in joy' (Psalm 126:5 AV). So we serve with hope in our hearts remembering that our God is Lord of the harvest, and will not fail us; our part is to stay diligent and faithful.

Suggested readings: Psalm 126:1-6 and Mark 4:26-29.

## SEPTEMBER 5th

## THERE ARE GROUNDS FOR CONFIDENCE

One of the favourite stories in the Old Testament is the fascinating story of David and Goliath. Its appeal reaches down into the deep recesses of the human heart: we love to see the mighty fall and the underdog win! The whole world loves a story where the odds are stacked against a person who eventually wins out, and this is what makes the competitive world of sport so interesting. Sometimes, in a legal case even lowly workers win against a large firm: it may take several years for the processes of law to rule in their favour, but it is a huge victory for the complainants to savour in the end. The story of David and Goliath takes many different forms in our day and age!

If we consider the grounds of David's confidence to face Goliath, we note that Saul was not at all certain about David's ability: 'You are not able to go against this Philistine to fight with him; for you are but a youth, and he has been a man of war from his youth' (1 Samuel 17:33). On a human level, Saul's assessment of the situation was correct since David did not stand a chance. However, David's confidence was grounded in God's ability to help him: 'The Lord who delivered me from the paw of the lion and from the paw of the bear, will deliver me from the hand of this Philistine' (1 Samuel 17:37). He was sure that God would help him.

Martin Luther King Jr. will be long remembered as one of the outstanding twentieth-century men. He was deeply versed in scripture and he drew inspiration from the record of God's faithfulness and delivering power. As he took up the Civil Rights campaign in the USA, he was – quite literally – a young David fighting a very powerful Goliath. The campaign song, which was sung on so many occasions, was 'We shall overcome one day', and he really believed it, too! What gave him such confidence? He believed in the ability of God to deliver those striving in the cause of right; this was the ground of his boldness and confidence.

In the Holy Scriptures there are passages which give testimony to God's delivering power. In Psalm 107, for instance, we are granted insights into, and given memories of, God's enduring faithfulness, ending on a fine note: 'Let those who are wise give heed to these things, and consider the steadfast love of the Lord' (Psalm 107:43). The New English Bible translates it: 'Ponder the record . . .' God has a wonderful reputation for delivering men and women! In it lies our calm assurance of faith as we live in trust day by day. Indeed, we might 'ponder the record' as we consider that, down the centuries, God's people have experienced God's willingness to help them. As the psalmist put it: 'For this God is our God for ever and ever' (Psalm 48:14 AV). Surely, we too, can go in life, each day confident in God's help.

Suggested readings: 1 Samuel 17:31-46 and 2 Corinthians 1:1-11.

SEPTEMBER 6th

## PEOPLE'S EXPECTATIONS ARE A CHALLENGE

In New Testament times, a beggar needed to find a suitable – indeed, profitable – place to beg: the Gate Beautiful leading to the temple at Jerusalem was one such place. Luke tells of a man 'lame from birth' who was carried there daily 'to ask alms of those who entered the temple' (Acts 3:2). One ordinary day, he saw two men, Peter and John, approaching the temple gate: 'he fixed his attention upon them, expecting to receive something from them' (Acts 3:5). While the man had often received gifts from people, unbeknown to him, on this day, he was to receive something far exceeding his expectations: 'Peter said to him "I have no silver and gold but I give you what I have; in the name of Jesus Christ of Nazareth, walk!"' (Acts 3:6). According to the story, a miracle occurred as the man was healed and then entered the temple with them, 'walking and leaping and praising God' (Acts 3:8). He no longer sat outside in his needy condition; rather, he was quite able to enter the temple as a worshipper himself, on what must have been a most unforgettable day for him. Truly it was a gift beyond his expectation.

Expectations of others are faced by each of us, and for those of us who profess faith, this is especially true. Believers and unbelievers alike, expect a Christian to be kind, truthful, loving, patient, honest, generous and trustworthy. In this story, Peter and John exceeded the man's expectations by far, and that reminds us of an important passage in the Sermon on the Mount where Jesus spoke of going the 'second mile'. In every generation since the earliest days of the Church, there have been believers who have done precisely that: men and women who have exceeded people's expectations of them, willingly going 'above and beyond' in service.

One morning, a Christian man was strolling along a street and was stopped by a lorry driver who asked for directions. The pedestrian found it almost impossible to give clear directions. Instead, he said: 'I've got half-an-hour to spare. The route is so complicated I'll come with you'. So he clambered into the cab and did more than was expected, as a kind deed. One of the challenging things about people's expectations is that individual Christians can make it harder or easier for others to believe in God. People's high expectations are often rather a challenge, but then the life of the believer requires effort. Faithfully obeying Christ is always a challenge! As the saying goes, people don't climb mountains by sitting in armchairs! The challenge to believers is keep on in faithful resolve – whatever others might make of us – and gently to encourage fellow pilgrims along life's way, where possible, nurturing others in being open to God. Thankfully, we always have God's help in our service for Him.

Suggested readings: Acts 3:1-16 and Romans 15:1-6.

SEPTEMBER 7th

## PEOPLE CAN BE SWAYED BY OTHERS

Sometimes, the people who were hostile to the Lord Jesus during His ministry spoke words of truth without knowing it! In Mark's gospel we are told how people were sent to 'trap him in his talk' (Mark 12:13). They came with smooth talk and very clever flattery because they wanted to ask a difficult question and ensnare Him. They began: 'Teacher, we know you are sincere, and show deference to no one' (or as another version put it, 'You aren't swayed by men'). Then the flattery continued: '. . . because you pay no attention to who they are; but you teach the way of God in accordance with the truth' (Mark 12:14). High sounding words – flattering words – but they happened to be true! Jesus Christ was so strong mentally and spiritually that He was not swayed by fear or favour. He did not submit to the persuasive powers of hostility or evil and, in the struggle to overcome falsehood, Jesus stood His ground!

Alas, the story of the human race is so different, for men and women are so easily swayed. How many tragedies happen because of the persuasive powers of others! On a windy day, we can see the trees being swayed by powerful gusts and, although the winds are invisible, we observe even strong tree limbs moving in the wind, sometimes causing the whole tree to topple over! So the strong winds of fear, passion, anger, jealousy, greed and infatuation can sway or even topple the greatest men and women. We think of the story of King David which tells how he fell into the sin of adultery, as the strong wind of unrestrained passion carried him into sin and he grieved the Lord. It's that kind of powerful force which can lead an apparently quiet person into trouble. After a football match, a normally reserved lad gets in with a rowdy crowd. In the tension and drama of the moment, he is swayed by others into unfamiliar ways, assaults a police officer, is arrested and charged. His parents are shocked beyond belief. How could their quiet and usually well-mannered son have assaulted a police officer? It was unbelievable, but it happened after the subtle – but strong – influence of an unruly gang swayed him and led him in wrong paths.

Both young and old alike can be swayed by others and, even respected people of decency, may be pressured by their peers. A student may be less conscientious at college in order to keep in with the crowd, an adult member of a team may be led into unethical behaviour, and children may imitate the bad example of others. However, good influences are also very powerful! In several places in scripture, the Holy Spirit is described as being like the wind: the holy 'Breath' of life from Almighty God. As the strong 'Wind' of the Spirit of God is felt among us, people are enlivened, influenced, formed, shaped and empowered. We thank God for the good influence of sincere Christian men and women who are led by God's Spirit.

Suggested readings: Mark 12:12-17 and Acts 2:1-11.

SEPTEMBER 8th

## OUR GOD IS THE GOD OF MIRACLES

The Old Testament and the New Testament both testify that the God Whom we worship is able to do great things. We can recall just a few instances: a group of slaves in Egypt became an influential nation, the Red Sea divided and the Israelites crossed in safety, the walls of Jericho came down and Rahab – of all people – had a key part to play. Similarly, Moses and Jeremiah were both reserved in nature, but served God with fortitude, Sarah and Hannah each had a son with a critical role, though neither had previously been able to conceive. In the New Testament, aged Elizabeth gave birth, and Mary bore a child through the agency of the Spirit of God. Jesus performed His amazing miracles, and then signs and wonders were known in the earliest Church as God worked through the apostles! Some of the most amazing miracles, or signs, were not so much acts of individuals but occurrences beyond all human expectation, such as Saul's conversion to follow Christ (as Paul the apostle), or Jew and Gentile being united as one in Christ Jesus. Of course, the supreme miracle was that of the resurrection of Christ, heralding the new creation in Him.

There have been miracles throughout the Christian era; indeed, it could be argued that the survival of the Christian Church is a miracle! The fact that we have the Bible as God's Word to us in scripture is a miracle of providence! The glorious reality that men and women have come into leadership at the right time and place is a miracle of divine grace! In our time, the vibrant Church in the great land of China is an instance of God's miraculous power. There was an era when the Christian Church there experienced tremendous hostility: missionaries were expelled, churches were closed, believers were harassed, and powerful opposition threatened the very existence of Christian congregations. Yet, the glorious fact is that the Church in China has survived and prospered. To believers this is, indeed, a mighty miracle of God's grace and power at work in transformation, beyond all human telling.

Someone who came to faith once testified: 'There is nothing possible for me now except to believe in the impossible'. Paul was confident that God worked miracles, convinced as he was, of the reality of Christ's resurrection: 'If Christ has not been raised our preaching is useless and so is your faith' (1 Corinthians 15:14). Later, he added: 'If Christ has not been raised, your faith is futile; you are still in your sins' (v17 NIV). The resurrection of Christ was key for him and his attitude was that, if you believe in the resurrection of Christ from the dead, then you can believe in the God of miracles. The truth of Easter is vital for every day of the year because it reminds us of God's miraculous power and love. In the annals of Church history, there are countless stories of people who have gladly testified: 'You are the God who performs miracles; you display your power among the peoples' (Psalm 77:14 NIV).

Suggested readings: Psalm 145:1-7 and Mark 3:1-11.

SEPTEMBER 9th

## SUFFERING CAN PRODUCE GOOD FRUIT

People who have faced a sudden bereavement – such as the loss of a family member in an accident – have been astounded to receive many letters of condolence. It is a difficult time and can prove to be a highly sensitive, even perilous, moment for the mourner. Well-meaning people occasionally write letters of sympathy, giving explanations of God's will – in their perception – and there is a frequent reference to much misunderstood texts, including, 'All things work together for good' (Romans 8:28) and other similar quotations. Some of the letters (intended for good) actually cause harm, or even more anguish and pain. Sincerity is not enough: one needs wisdom, as well as a deep empathy with people in such a vulnerable position.

Those enduring pain or loss need extra care: words intended to be helpful, whether written or spoken, need to be chosen carefully. However, there are numerous passages in the Bible which testify that suffering – in certain contexts – can, indeed, have a purifying, even chastening and renewing influence. Peter wrote to believers facing suffering under persecution, giving some challenging teaching on hardships endured: 'Their purpose is to prove that your faith is genuine. Even gold, which can be destroyed, is tested by fire: and so your faith, which is much more precious than gold, must also be tested' (1 Peter 1:7 GNB).

Similarly, in the Book of Revelation, there is a deeply moving passage where John seems to point to both the suffering of Christ and His glory. He envisages this worship scene: 'Then I looked, and I heard around the throne and the living creatures and the elders the voice of many angels, numbering myriads of myriads and thousands of thousands, saying with a loud voice, "Worthy is the Lamb who was slain, to receive power and wealth and wisdom and might and honour and glory and blessing!"' (Revelation 5:11-12). Here, John is reminded that Christ wore the crown of thorns placed on His head by wicked hands, before He then triumphantly wore the crown of glory, acclaimed by the hosts above. So, too, it seems that from John's perspective, for those who are in Christ, both suffering and glory go hand in hand.

Over the centuries, in the Christian Church, many people have borne pain and suffering faithfully, but have also known the joy of serving Christ. Strangely, they have also discovered, as the apostle Paul wrote, that, 'Suffering produces endurance, endurance produces character, and character produces hope' (Romans 5:3-4). Later, Paul reminds us again that while we do not understand our pain or the suffering in the wider world, our hope is based on the assurance that nothing can separate us from God's love in Christ. By divine mercy, even suffering may be used within God's purposes to bring new beginnings and so, redound ultimately, to God's glory.

Suggested readings: Romans 5:3-4 and 1 Peter 1:3-9.

SEPTEMBER 10th

## 'CAUSE AND EFFECT' ARE GREAT REALITIES

In September 1988, there was very serious flooding in Bangladesh resulting in death, disease and homelessness for lots of people. It was a disaster that shook the world, and many Christians, as well as others who had a special interest in this particular area, were stunned by the awful news. Questions arose: 'Why did God allow this?', 'Where is God?' and 'Is our faith futile?' As with all natural disasters, on reflection, these probes for meaning raised searching, even disturbing, questions! At that time, a television programme showed that these floods were largely a direct result of deforestation. Over a hundred miles away, the mountainside had been stripped of thousands upon thousands of trees and this resulted in the silting up of riverbeds. The waters had rushed down the mountainside taking tons of soil which was deposited in the riverbeds; hence, the rivers had a greatly reduced volume capacity and so overflowed in floods. Here, there was a direct cause and effect: so it seemed nonsensical to blame God for something which was directly attributable to human foolishness in denuding the mountainside of trees. This particular incisive television programme made the situation very clear, perhaps more so than many sermons!

For those people who take time to think and reflect on life, there is so often a vital link between cause and effect. Actually, many harmful events have an interpretation which is very different from first observations. How true this is in personal relationships: for example, Joseph was betrayed by his brothers who 'sold him to the Ishmaelites for 20 shekels of silver; and they took Joseph to Egypt' (Genesis 37:28). The story of his brothers' jealousy, intrigue, hatred and cruelty is shocking. Yet, it appears that the jealousy was the result of favouritism which was shown to Joseph by his father, Jacob. The Genesis account reads: 'Now Israel loved Joseph more than any other of his children, because he was the son of his old age; and he made him a long robe with sleeves. But when his brothers saw that their father loved him more than all his brothers, they hated him, and could not speak peaceably to him' (Genesis 37:3-4). What we can see from the story is that cause and effect are realities of life: what Jacob did had wide and deep repercussions. In the end, paradoxically, Joseph was able to confess that he realised how God was seen to be at work through the situation of his rejection and vindication. Yet, the story is a grim reminder that our foolish actions can bring pain, even for future generations. This is true in personal relationships, as well as in our approach to this planet itself. The New Testament reflects this profound truth: 'Do not be deceived; God is not mocked, for you reap whatever you sow' (Galatians 6:7). It is true, there is real 'cause and effect'.

Suggested readings: Genesis 37:1-4 and Galatians 6:1-10.

SEPTEMBER 11th

## SOMETIMES JESUS CALLS US TO CROSS OVER

In the House of Commons, the two main parties have for a long time, vied as the Government and the Opposition, and normally, Members of Parliament show loyalty to their own party and vote accordingly. However, there are occasions when matters of personal conscience arise on issues such as capital punishment, abortion, Sunday trading or licensing laws, and a member might cross over to boldly vote according to the dictates of conscience, rather than his or her own party's policy. This 'crossing over' requires courage and stamina: the criticism levelled against such action of not 'towing the party line' can be very severe unless, of course, the party leadership has given a free vote on the matter, according to conscience, as sometimes happens.

There is a story in Luke's gospel about a literal 'crossing over' of a lake which brought Jesus' disciples into difficulty. Luke claims: 'One day he got into a boat with his disciples and he said to them "Let us go across to the other side of the lake"'(Luke 8:22). They obeyed and set out across the lake but were caught up in a fierce storm. However, the story ends well as Luke tells of the action of Jesus Who 'rebuked the wind and the raging waves; and they ceased, and there was a calm' (Luke 8:24). Meditating on this passage, we are reminded that following Jesus may sometimes require us to step out in faith and 'cross over', so to speak, in a costly way.

The story is told of a Sergeant Major in the British Army: he was a strong character, described by friends and rivals as 'tough as nails', living a life of utter selfishness, being both worldly and ungodly. One day, this hard character heard the gospel in a striking way and was soundly drawn to faith. In essence, he crossed over to a whole new life. In obedience to Christ, he crossed over from death to life, from darkness to light and from worldliness to godliness. However, in 'crossing over' the storm soon raged as he lost friends, was both misunderstood and derided, and found himself estranged from those who could not accept it! Even so, he was convinced in his faith so – in spite of the tempest he faced – he experienced wonderful blessings and he knew, in a very real way, true joy in the presence of the Lord.

Often, following Jesus Christ means that we are confronted with the challenging command, 'Let us cross over', and obedience to Christ can occasionally bring us into a storm. Sometimes, the call for us to cross over is from a rather nominal faith to a deeper faith, from halting service to sustained service, or from half-hearted obedience to full commitment. At times, we are also called to take a firm stand on an issue that may differ from the viewpoint of our friends or family members. Yet, even in the midst of the storm, we can know the help of the Lord Who has the power to calm every storm, and to bring us safely through trouble.

Suggested readings: Luke 8:16-25 and 1 Timothy 1:12-17.

SEPTEMBER 12th

## DETERMINATION IS A CHRISTIAN VIRTUE

When John Bunyan wrote his famous book *Pilgrim's Progress*, he revealed to the world that he knew a great deal about human nature! He gave some fascinating character-studies, such as 'Mr. Facing-both-ways'; every thoughtful person can recognise that particular character! Such people are in offices, industry, education, commerce, political life and in some churches, too. We can all testify to those who first say one thing and then later another. 'Mr. Facing-both-ways' is real, and causes lots of headaches. As we consider the people that God has used in remarkable ways, we might observe that they had one thing in common: a steadfast determination to serve with firm resolve once they had said 'Yes' to God's call.

Countless women and men have made that commitment, and among them we may recall, Moses, Hannah, Elijah, Amos, Jeremiah, Mary, the mother of Jesus. At the outset of the gospel story, we read of John the Baptist who, like the others, displayed enormous courage and determination; these people of faith 'set their face' to obey, as Luke would later say of Jesus. Luke's gospel records of Jesus that He ' . . . steadfastly set his face to go to Jerusalem' (Luke 9:51 AV). There was in the heart of the Blessed Master determination, and courage which made it an overriding priority for Him to go forward in obeying the Father's will and loving purposes.

There are various hindrances to our steadfastness to pursue what we believe to be God's call: friends can seek to change our plans, opponents can attempt to frighten us, relatives can seek to influence us, and simply natural fears can erode a person's determination. Yet, as we see in the life of Jesus, He moved resolutely forward, and no friend, disciple, relative, enemy or fear could divert Him from the way charted for Him. In Jerusalem, there would inevitably be rejection, injustice, mockery and crucifixion, but He did not flinch. We read: 'He steadfastly set his face to go to Jerusalem'. When the apostle Paul wrote of the Saviour's work, he put it this way: 'Christ Jesus came into the world to save sinners' (1 Timothy 1:15). So we acknowledge that the Master did not pursue an easy path, nor did He seek to save His own life, but He pressed forward with a holy steadfastness.

We thank God for good, determined people who did not give up in the past, and for those today who will not be deflected from their resolve to follow Christ. Even today, many stand so committed, while others might falter. The New Testament bids us gaze upon the Saviour: 'Looking to Jesus the pioneer and perfecter of our faith' (Hebrews 12:2). When courage is failing, it is necessary to look to Him and to find our inspiration in Him as our Master and as the glorious Lord of all.

Suggested readings: Luke 9:46-56 and Acts 23:6-11.

SEPTEMBER 13th

## OUR GOD DOES INTERVENE

Older ministers of the gospel have acknowledged over the decades that Dr. Moffatt's translation of the Holy Scriptures has been instructive and helpful. Some of his translated verses flash like diamonds and attract the attention of the preacher! For example, his translation of Psalm 138:8 reads: 'The eternal intervenes on my behalf'. In other words, divine intervention is affirmed as a reality! That is the experience of many men and women who, in faith, confess that the Lord has been shaping their lives, sometimes – but not necessarily often – in dramatic ways. A difficult situation arises and then, wonderfully, God intervenes in a way one might not have ever dreamt to be possible, and certainly not felt to be deserved. We praise God for those interventions which – by faith – are seen to have revealed His love and faithfulness.

In Daniel chapter 6, the narrative tells of a prophet in exile, elevated to a position of power and authority in the king's court. According to the story, there was jealousy on the part of powerful ones who then hatched a plot against him. They were determined to undermine this 'man of faith' and to see him out of favour with King Darius. Their treachery succeeded, and Daniel was put in a den of lions; surely, this would be the end of Daniel. Yet, as the story portrays it, God intervened. The next morning, Daniel was still alive and said to the king: 'O king, live for ever! My God sent his angel and shut the lions' mouths, and they have not hurt me, because I was found blameless before him . . . I have done no wrong' (Daniel 6:21-22). This much-loved dramatic story depicts Daniel as the prophet who knew the glorious truth that God had intervened on his behalf and wrought a dramatic deliverance. So, through many centuries, men and women have testified that they have had an experience of God's delivering power.

Of course, in the coming of the Lord Jesus Christ, we see God 'interrupting' history in the most extraordinary way, dividing the human eras into BC and AD. The incarnation changed history: it was love breaking into the circle of evil, like light shining in the darkness or water coming to a thirsty land. The apostle Paul graphically puts it this way: 'But when the time had fully come, God sent forth his Son, born of woman' (Galatians 4:4). At the right time, God intervened. This is a reminder to us that we can look at a situation and make our predictions, but then God acts in the situation and graciously recasts it for good. These truths about our God give us courage to go on even when the way ahead seems impossible. The experiences of God's people in the past, and the records of God's ways in the scriptures, still stimulate hope and faith, for we know the Lord in our midst.

Suggested readings: Daniel 6:1-28 and Acts 2:22-24.

SEPTEMBER 14th

## THE HOLY SPIRIT IS THE GREAT ENCOURAGER

We thank God for modern translations of the Holy Scriptures! How often we read a familiar verse in a new translation and it seems to glow with a fresh light. In the Acts of the Apostles there is one particular verse which describes an important aspect of the Holy Spirit's ministry: 'The church was strengthened; and encouraged by the Holy Spirit, it grew in numbers, living in the fear of the Lord' (Acts 9:31). The Holy Spirit encouraged the people of God: what a good insight that gives into the ministry of the Holy Spirit within the Church. We associate other aspects of the Christian life with the work of the Holy Spirit Who convicts of sin, points to the Saviour, transforms the human heart and brings the things of Jesus Christ to remembrance. The Holy Spirit brings about the miracle of conviction and conversion in an individual, yet we also think of the Holy Spirit of God as the divine 'Encourager'. God's Spirit is consistently encouraging individuals, families, churches and whole communities.

As we all know, there are times when a particular church might seem to be, as it were, 'in the doldrums': times when effort is not evidently matched by positive results. At such times, there is the ploughing, sowing, tending – to use another analogy – but the harvest seems to be delayed. Then, in God's time, there is much encouragement: a new worker or two, or possibly a family, or more helpers full of zeal for the Kingdom of God, coming onto the scene. They bring other gifts and skills and, with their energy for mission, they set to work in the fellowship, bringing a renewed sense of expectancy. Prayers for fresh growth are answered as doors begin to swing open, new initiatives are implemented, and the church receives positive encouragement. This is a work of the Holy Spirit, Who not only prompts, inspires, guides and equips, but also encourages.

On one occasion, a church leader was giving an Annual Report and spoke openly of disturbing difficulties: in fact, a number of churches in that area were experiencing severe problems. It was a report which caused both concern and alarm to those who heard it, but they could never forget his final words: 'But remember brothers and sisters we have the Holy Spirit'. It was a timely message for that moment. When faced with problems, we do well to remember that there is always the Holy Spirit of God to aid and encourage us. The work is God's, the Spirit is not thwarted: God is the God of new beginnings and we do not ever serve alone. We can rejoice today in the sure, constant, gracious work of God's Spirit, Who is ever the divine 'Encourager' for us all.

Suggested readings: Acts 9:10-31 and John 14:15-27.

SEPTEMBER 15th

## THE CLOSE VIEW IS OFTEN DIFFERENT

Many people enjoy a stroll by the Great Ouse river at Bedford. The embankment, at any season of the year, has a beauty of its own and the riverside gardens are beautifully kept. One particular year it looked extra special – just a riot of colours – reds, yellows, whites, and shades of blue, along with the lush green grass. It continued to look lovely for many weeks and attracted hundreds of visitors; even in late September it all looked in a magnificent condition from a distance. However, as you moved closer to the gardens, it was possible to see some wilting flowers, for such is life! There is an old saying: 'Distance enhances beauty' and that is very true! A river can look really beautiful from a distance, but then a closer look reveals all the rubbish in it. A country church can look absolutely exquisite standing in a village setting until, close up, one can see all the renovation that needs to be done. In another sense, individuals, groups, communities and even fellowships may not be as they first appear. A closer observation is important because it can reveal the truth.

One of the certainties of human life is imperfection: statesmen and women, politicians, leaders of the Church, influential broadcasters, renowned journalists or other high profile figures, including reformers, might look truly inspirational from a distance, but their close friends and relatives are conscious of frailties and weaknesses. So Cardinal Heenan entitled one volume of his autobiography, *Not The Whole Truth*; in point of fact, no biography or autobiography ever tells the full story! It has been known for a bitter spouse, family member or friend to fill in a few details missing from an official biography; then, even taking account of the motivation, enough is implied to reveal that there is another side to the account first given. The Holy Scripture says: 'All have sinned and fall short of the glory of God' (Romans 3:23). The writer, John, upheld a similar truth to what Paul wrote: 'If we say we have no sin, we deceive ourselves and the truth is not in us' (1 John 1:8).

While we may never see the perfect spouse, or manager, or secretary, or colleague, or agent, there is one perfect individual, our Lord Jesus Christ, the sinless Son of God. The life of Christ has been subjected to the closest scrutiny: scholars, poets, theologians, philosophers, artists and other learned critics have examined His life and ministry, but the verdict of history stands in agreement with the words of Pontius Pilate: 'Behold, I bring him forth to you, that ye may know I find no fault in him' (John 19:4 AV). The Church is made up of imperfect people: there is no such thing as a perfect Christian or a perfect church, but as we take a closer look, we can rejoice in a perfect Saviour Who ever lives and pleads for us as our great High Priest.

Suggested readings: John 19:1-15 and Romans 3:21-28.

SEPTEMBER 16th

## 'REVIVAL BY SUBTRACTION' IS A VITAL TRUTH

A Christian worker was very interested in the subject of spiritual revival and so read a number of books on the subject. Like lots of other people, he thought of revival in terms of addition: new converts or church members, new financial resources or enhanced outreach projects. However, one day in his reading, he came across a very provocative sentence: 'Revival often begins by subtraction'. We might reflect on the truth of those five words: how often it happens that a church fellowship can move forward – for various reasons – after one person, one family or one group has left. Sometimes, depending on the circumstances, the element of 'subtraction' has been strangely beneficial to the fellowship, and a new day of spiritual awakening has dawned, bringing revival which had been stymied by the routines of previous days.

All four gospels have one story which some Christians find rather surprising: the 'cleansing' of the temple toward the end of His ministry (though the event is narrated earlier in the fourth gospel). The story shows that while Jesus was truly the gracious teacher, healer and friend, He could act with a prophetic, righteous anger. The facts are these: at the temple in Jerusalem, the Court of the Gentiles was a hive of activity. At this place, the money changers exchanged money into the correct currency for the purchase – in the same location – of various items required for sacrifice. There was no doubt an element of corruption, profiteering and exploitation, besides the disruption of the worship in that part of the precincts open to all comers. So we read that when Jesus entered the temple, 'he drove out all who sold and bought in the temple, and he overturned the tables of the money changers' (Matthew 21:12). Then, alluding to words spoken by Isaiah the prophet (Isaiah 56:7), Jesus spoke these very challenging words: 'My house shall be called a place of prayer; but you make it a den of robbers' (Matthew 21:13). Clearly, in this situation, 'subtraction' was needed!

In this episode from the ministry of Jesus Christ, we remember that there was prophetic symbolism in His action in order to drive home the message in a stark way. The Court of the Gentiles often became very busy and crowded as it was so commercialised in this way, so much so that it actually interfered with the pilgrims' primary objective, to worship the true and living God. In one sense, therefore, when Jesus Christ cleansed the temple, He exercised a 'ministry of subtraction' by removing what was deemed unworthy and seen as an obstacle to the worship of God. It can, indeed, be right to show indignation at what is less than wholly true or honourable or worthy in the service of God. It may be that there are for us things which are crowding out our true commitment to Christ. If so, maybe there is a need – in some sense – for 'revival by subtraction' even in our own personal lives!

Suggested readings: Matthew 21:12-17 and Ephesians 4:25-32.

SEPTEMBER 17th

THOSE WHO HAVE LOST FAITH NEED OUR LOVING PRAYERS

Every Sunday a multitude of people around the world recite the Apostles' Creed which begins with the great affirmation: 'I believe in God. . .'. Of course, there are various levels of belief: there is the old saint who has a deep and abiding faith, the middle-aged person who holds faith in some tension, and the young believer who has recently placed trust in the Lord. Furthermore, faith, like the word 'love', has many different connotations! The searching question prompted by reciting the Creed is: 'How many people who recite the wonderful words of the Creed truly believe them and stake their lives upon the Lord to Whom the Creed bears eloquent testimony?' Undoubtedly, some who have had soul-shattering experiences find it difficult to say the familiar Creed very meaningfully, though perhaps most believers would offer the Creed as an aspiration to faith or, perhaps, in a genuine quest for piety.

Penelope Mortimer tells how her father, a clergyman in the Church of England, served in the First World War and his faith was badly shaken, to the point that he no longer believed in God. He returned to St. Mary's Church, Chilton, in Oxfordshire and resumed his duties, presiding at services: he said the prayers, recited the Creed, offered litanies and preached sermons, but no longer believed. We have to ask: 'Is there a sadder sight in the whole world than a person standing in the pulpit preaching sermons without personal faith?' Many would hasten to condemn this seemingly hypocritical conduct claiming he ought to have resigned, having lost his real sense of purpose in ministry. However, others, who have tasted the deepest depths of tragedy, might feel an overwhelming sense of compassion and empathy towards this man and others, who through unimaginable suffering, have lost faith.

We have to ask ourselves a probing question: 'If a person is seriously injured in an accident and we rally round to express love and concern, can we do any less for those who have been seriously damaged on the path of faith?' To have a rich and mature faith is cause for humble thanksgiving. Yet, to have had one's faith ship-wrecked through adversity is cause for reflection on the deepest things of life, and the best counsel is surely the biblical command, 'Be still . . .' (Psalm 46:10). One Psalm of David has a poignant prayer: 'Restore to me the joy of thy salvation, and uphold me with a willing spirit' (Psalm 51:12). Surely, that is a prayer for each of us.

The familiar parable of Jesus in Luke's gospel (Luke 15:3-7) reminds us that the shepherd searches for the lost sheep 'until he finds'. Such is always God's way with us in this world, and so we endeavour to keep on trusting in the Lord. At the same time, we also pray for, and encourage, those people who in the troubles and tragedies of life, have lost their faith, or had their faith depleted; our prayer is that they remember that God never abandons us whatever we face or we have done.

Suggested readings: Psalm 51:9-15 and Luke 15:1-10.

SEPTEMBER 18<sup>th</sup>

## 'WITHERED HANDS' CAN BE RESTORED

It was shocking to hear of the horrific fire at King's Cross Underground Station in November 1987: it will long be remembered as a night of terror. Millions of people travel on the London Underground each year, and this particular episode brought home the truth that what is accepted as routine, can have its dangers. Lots of stories can be told of that night, but a particularly poignant one is especially worth consideration: the guitarist who suffered horrific burns on his hands. He was a man who loved his instrument and, in the previous fourteen years, had played it daily. In the awful blaze, his hands received terrible injuries, but he survived. The loss of the proper use of his hands was a living nightmare. However, he continued on in hope.

One of the stories in the gospels is the healing of a man's hand. There are two threads of truth, as it were, woven into the story: the gold thread which tells of the love and compassion of Jesus, and the darker thread which tells of the hostility of some in the synagogue. The man with a 'withered hand' came to the synagogue on the Sabbath: Luke tells us the detail that it was his right hand which was afflicted. Jesus, moved with compassion towards this needy man, said 'Stretch out your hand' (Luke 6:10). He did so and the 'withered' hand was restored. We realise that a person can have a 'withered hand' because of a congenital issue or due to later disease or injury which, in each case, might cause great difficulty. In Luke's story, it was a physical hand which required healing. However, on another plane, we may think in terms of the 'withered hand' of friendship, or that of loving care and support, or even of Christian fellowship. We could think of a couple at their marriage who stand in the sanctuary before God rejoicing in each other's love: they stand there, hands clasped in sincere love, as a sign of intimacy. After some years, dissension comes into their home as they quarrel over matters, usually quite petty in nature, and their hands of care and mutual companionship 'wither' as their love for each other grows cold. There are people who have given long service to a church and then 'grow weary in well-doing' (Galatians 6:9), and their hands of devoted service 'wither', so to speak, as these Christians grow cold in the work of the Lord. There are so many ways in which hands of love and devotion can become quite ineffectual.

The injured guitarist in London needed the skill of the medical world to restore his hands. There is a divine physician who can restore the spiritual hands that have withered: the Blessed Master performed a miracle in the synagogue and our faith is that He still heals 'withered hands'. We do well to ask ourselves about how we continue to share in God's service; maybe we can all listen to the divine physician lovingly inviting us, 'Stretch out your hand'. So we may find ourselves inspired and equipped for renewed work in the wider Church's ministry.

Suggested readings: Luke 6:6-12 and Galatians 6:1-10.

SEPTEMBER 19th

## THE CHURCH CAN EXPERIENCE 'HESITATING JOY'

One of the great stories of Christian patience and perseverance is the saga of William Carey, the pioneer missionary. In April 1793, he sailed to India with the burning ambition to preach the gospel and win converts to the Christian faith. However, it did not take him long to realise that this task was going to be very tough indeed. In fact, Carey had to wait for seven years before he could rejoice in someone being brought to faith, after a long stretch of diligent service. When the breakthrough finally came, God's blessing was experienced in a wonderful way, and Carey could amply see the grace of God at work. The time came when Carey was officially dismissed from his church at Leicester so he could form a small church at Madnabati. The newly formed church consisted of five members, a tightly-knit fellowship of believers. They knew together the joy of the Lord and testified to their experience of His grace and power. When Carey wrote about this small fellowship, he said: 'We receive each newcomer with a hesitating joy'. It was initially 'hesitating joy', because there were so many things at stake: there was a real necessity that each church member should be committed to Jesus Christ and strong enough to withstand hostility and persecution. What he really meant was that each church member was very evidently a marked person, and so the failure of one could reflect badly on the whole fellowship.

These two words 'hesitating joy' could be meaningfully applied to the story of Saul of Tarsus! He was converted on the Damascus road, but there was a hesitation on the part of the early Christians to accept him, and it needed the intervention of a welcoming individual: 'Barnabas took him and brought him to the apostles, and declared to them how on the road he had seen the Lord who spoke to him, and how at Damascus he had preached boldly in the name of Jesus'. The persecutor of the Church had become a preacher! So Paul, as we know him, was received with 'hesitating joy' after understandable reservations at the outset, before the recognition that God could totally change such a harmful man!

These two words, 'hesitating joy', can be used of many different situations: a couple see their son or daughter off to begin college life, a couple welcome their newly adopted child, grand-parents see their grandchildren beginning school, a young person sets off to become a missionary far away from home. All these momentous situations have a real joy, but there is hesitation because of the question whether he or she will cope with the responsibilities and pressures of the new life. One of the lessons of life is to trust someone and to see them grow in the awareness of our support. Despite our initial hesitancy or apprehension, there is much joy in seeing new disciples grow in faith. As we thank God for the abounding grace offered to us all, let us also pledge ourselves in trust to commit every experience of life to Him.

Suggested readings: Acts 9:13-31 and Galatians 1:21-24.

SEPTEMBER 20th

## GOD USES A WIDE VARIETY OF METHODS

A comment is made: 'We've never done it like that before'. How many times these words have confronted the new leader or minister of a church or a Christian organization? This one remark could be a genuine concern for the work of the Kingdom, or it could just be a real stumbling block to progress. It is a truism that old ways are not always bad, and new methods are not always good! It is absolutely necessary to consider carefully the methods used and to recall that God is not bound to one particular style; in His providence, God can use a variety of people and methods. The story is told of how, in one particularly dry season in the New Hebrides, there was a shortage of water and a missionary, John Paton, began digging deep down into the ground. The indigenous people seemed to greet this work with derision, as they knew that water came down from above and not from deep in the earth! However, Paton was not dismayed or discouraged, but kept on digging until he found water. In that rather determined way, he demonstrated that there are other methods and, by his dogged persistence, convinced the islanders and so broadened their perspective on water supplies.

One of the thrilling things about the Kingdom of God is that the Lord uses so many different people and a wide variety of methods. We read the explanation the apostle Paul gives to the Christians in Rome: 'Now there are varieties of gifts, but the same Spirit; and there are varieties of service, but the same Lord' (1 Corinthians 12:4). We might reflect on the sheer variety of persons God has used: Christina Rossetti, Frances Havergal, John Newton, William and Catherine Booth, Gladys Alyward, Charles Spurgeon, William Temple, Tom Rees, being just a tiny selection. Some people find renewed faith in a rich liturgical service, some in the exuberance of a Salvation Army meeting; some are at home in a quiet, plain service of worship while others, alternatively, in a contemporary service complete with a band! God used a rich variety of methods in the Holy Scriptures and, we profess, still does today.

When Paul began his work he was very quick to use the good offices of the local synagogue service, where he reasoned with his fellow Jews that Jesus Christ was their longed-for Messiah. We might imagine some of the worshippers exclaiming – rather as they had done in the ministry of Jesus – that what he brought was new, in fact, unheard of! However, Paul was a chosen vessel used by the Holy Spirit of God, and his service was richly blessed, for many people came to faith through his dedicated ministry. His approach was (in various ways) an innovation that prevailed as the Church grew further field. God does work through new methods as well as old; in the end, both can be used as the means to extend the work of the Kingdom.

Suggested readings: Acts 18:1-11 and 1 Corinthians 12:1-6.

SEPTEMBER 21st

## OF A MERCY SO ABUNDANT AND A LOVE SO GREAT

The day began with a problem! James, in the words of the prophet Isaiah had a 'spirit of heaviness'. It was a Sunday morning and he decided to go to church. In the minutes prior to the service beginning, he picked up one of the church Bibles and quietly began to read. Suddenly, he came across a verse which was outstandingly beautiful: 'But God's mercy is so abundant, and his love for us is so great, that while we were spiritually dead in our disobedience he brought us to life with Christ' (Ephesians 2:4 GNB). How important that little word 'so' proved! James had gone to church feeling quite weary and unworthy, but God's Word which struck him then – even before the service began – had provided a double blessing: mercy so abundant and love so great. It completely changed his outlook on life that day.

In John's gospel there is a verse which is well known because preachers and Christian workers are constantly using it: 'For God so loved the world that he gave his only Son, that whoever believes in him should not perish but have eternal life' (John 3:16). God so loved! We can never understand the fullness of that little word 'so'. It has brought comfort and encouragement to countless millions of people. We recall that the apostle Paul prayed a profound prayer for his friends: 'To know the love of Christ which surpasses knowledge' (Ephesians 3:19). On this day, Christians all over the world will be remembering St Matthew the apostle: he was one who shared in the mercy and love of God. The Lord called Matthew to service in an incredible way, as he personally, discovered divine mercy.

On numerous occasions, Malcolm Muggeridge confessed that he felt a deep sense of unworthiness: he grew very weary and tired of old sins and failings. That could be the testimony of many people! Sometimes, on a day when everything is lovely, and we enjoy the company of loved ones and friends, there steals over the heart a feeling of guilt or unworthiness – which at the time and given the circumstances – seems strangely out of place. On such days, we need an inner assurance of a mercy so abundant and a love so great. The apostle Paul knew a spiritual remedy for 'heaviness of spirit': he knew that the human heart ached until it could find deep healing in the experience of divine grace made known in Christ. He wrote: 'But God's mercy is so abundant, and his love for us is so great'. That is the gospel in a nutshell, in which we wholeheartedly rejoice.

Suggested readings: Ephesians 2:1-10 and 1 John 1:5-10.

SEPTEMBER 22nd

## GOD USES MARRIAGE

Bible scholars have always indicated the importance of the ministry of John the Baptist. Luke recorded the words of announcement given by the angel Gabriel to Zechariah: 'He will be great in the sight of the Lord . . . he will be filled with the Holy Spirit. He will turn many of the people of Israel to the Lord their God' (Luke 1:15-16). History records that this remarkable prophecy was fulfilled; John the Baptist has an honoured place in the memory of God's people. Significantly, he was brought up in a home of deep faith and of humble prayer, and a place where holiness of life was the accepted standard. Luke describes the parents, Zechariah and Elizabeth, who nurtured John: 'Both of them were righteous before God, living blamelessly according to all the commandments and regulations of the Lord' (Luke 1:6). The translation of this verse given by the Good News Bible is simplicity itself: 'They both lived good lives in God's sight and obeyed fully all the Lord's laws and commands'. They were a devout couple open to all God would call them to undertake.

How often God has used couples to His glory: we think of Abraham and Sarah, Jacob and Rebekah, Mary and Joseph, Aquila and Priscilla. So, in every generation, God has used devout couples to do the work of His Kingdom. There is enormous strength of purpose when a couple is united in faith and service. God has used marriage and, through it, much blessing has flowed into other lives. William Booth was a strong personality, but both his life and his ministry were greatly enriched by his beloved, Catherine. Dr. Billy Graham expounded God's Word to untold millions, but he always gladly testified to how much his wife, Ruth, contributed to the enrichment of his life and ministry.

Surely, one of the loveliest descriptions of marriage is found in the first epistle of Peter: 'You are joint heirs of the grace of life' (1 Peter 3:7). The New English Bible translates it simply: 'You share together in the grace of God'. It is a joy to witness a Christian couple using their marriage and home to be a channel of God's blessing to others. There are couples engaging in many shared Christian ministries – both within and beyond the Church – as well as many others in different ways working together supporting, counselling and helping in all sorts of respects, to the glory of God and the furtherance of Christ's Kingdom. Some give of themselves in offering hospitality, quite apart from their official duties of offering pastoral care or organisational oversight. Many believers can look back with thanksgiving at knowing the special character of a Christian home, and being brought up in the 'nurture of the Lord'. A truly Christian marriage brings great blessing beyond just the home.

Suggested readings: Luke 1:15-17 and Acts 18:1-8.

SEPTEMBER 23rd

## WE MUST LOOK TO GOD'S SUFFICIENCY

One of the districts which attracts the attention and love of many people, including tourists to Britain, is the area of the Cotswolds: its hills and valleys, rivers and streams, hamlets and villages have a beauty which is lovely to behold, and most satisfying to mind and heart. The ancient parish churches, in their scenic and peaceful settings, have a splendour which reminds people of God. Such a place is Snowshill: the tranquillity of the glorious church with its quiet beauty, amid the pretty cottages, is truly wonderful. It is a place where it is possible to feel the presence of God in a special way, a haven hallowed by centuries of worship and prayer..

The experience of one visitor is quite telling. For a long period, he had been burdened with important responsibilities, especially in the counselling ministry. The problems, burdens, sorrows and perplexities of lots of people had been brought to him, and he was exhausted. As he stood in this magnificent little church at Snowshill, he had a quiet, but significant spiritual experience. Two marvellous sentences from the scriptures came to mind in the stillness there: 'Who is sufficient for these things?' (2 Corinthians 2:16 AV) and 'Our sufficiency is of God' (2 Corinthians 3:5 AV). As he later noted, looking back with thanksgiving, it was a moment when 'time stood still'. It was a time which would be long remembered because of the deep sense of assurance which he experienced that day.

How often men and women feel quite inadequate to face the responsibilities of life: this sense of inadequacy lurks in so many hearts. Even people who appear outwardly to be strong and quite self-sufficient have deep feelings of inadequacy on the inside! The businessperson or director, the teacher or student, the artist or author, the governor or politician, the councillor or administrator, even the preacher or Christian worker, can all, at certain times, feel inadequate, as can parents, too. Even God's prophets of old had perilously low feelings at certain periods.

In the first Book of Kings, there is the moving story of Elijah: he had won a signal victory and proved himself a man of great spiritual valour and determination, faith and courage, but now it was different. Scripture records: 'But he himself went a day's journey into the wilderness and came and sat under a broom tree; and he asked that he might die, saying, "It is enough; now, O Lord, take away my life, for I am no better than my fathers"'(1 Kings 19:4). He had to learn again the reality of God's provision and support. That is an issue for us all, everyday, if we face up to the truth as it really is for us. If we ever feel the task is too great for us, or the responsibilities too heavy, we do well to recall the apostle Paul's comforting words: 'Our sufficiency is of God'. Truly, we can see how the Lord undertakes for us.

Suggested readings: 1 Kings 19:1-8 and 2 Corinthians 3:14-4:5.

## SEPTEMBER 24th

## THERE IS A MINISTRY OF HEALING

Luke, traditionally, has been thought to be a physician so it is perfectly natural that his gospel takes a keen interest in the healing ministry of Jesus. There is no doubt that the four gospels give abundant evidence that Jesus performed miracles of healing; Luke's narrative records them in a special and fascinating way. It is worth reading this gospel at a measured pace, to sense the manner in which Luke handles the stories of healing. One verse in particular stands out: 'And all the crowd sought to touch him, for power came forth from him and healed them all' (Luke 6:19). Jesus Christ demonstrated that He had great authority, including the power to heal! He also sent forth His disciples with a two-fold task: to preach and to heal.

Countless people have engaged in this twin ministry. Undoubtedly, in the Christian era, there have been men and women imbued with the gift of healing by the grace of God. Yet, we also acknowledge that healing comes through medicine and surgery, as well as the extraordinary ministry of prayer. If you look at a medical directory, the number of surgeons, consultants and doctors who are listed is astonishing! In this country alone, there are many thousands of people engaged in medical or therapeutic work of some kind or another, in addition to all the support and administrative staff. The wide-ranging work of healing is quite amazing; and, indeed, on a world scale, the total number involved in such work is staggering. We thank God for all who truly care in this way. Of course, not all physicians are believers, but even so they can be channels of divine healing and restoration through their good medical care. Whether a person is cured through normal medical intervention such as drug therapy or surgery or, occasionally, through prayer with the laying on of hands or anointing, both types of restoration are through the healing which God graciously bestows.

However, there are other situations of healing, too. How often quiet conversation with a thoughtful minister, chaplain or counsellor, or hearing the living Word preached by ministers or expressed by Christian workers (as well as sharing with others in therapeutic encounters), brings healing and restoration in body, mind and spirit. Surely, to know one's sins are forgiven is healing, as is the knowledge that we are all accepted by the heavenly Father just as we are, warts and all! Many such healings take place in churches and counselling rooms, as well as people's homes or community locations, day by day. It is wonderful if, when someone comes with a broken heart or troubled spirit, they find solace by the mercies of the Lord, and know 'the peace of God, which passes all understanding' (Philippians 4:7). Thank God, the healing ministry of Jesus Christ still continues today in many and varied ways.

Suggested readings: Luke 6:12-19 and 1 Corinthians 12:4-13.

SEPTEMBER 25th

## THAT GOD'S WORD HAS TRANSFORMING POWER

Over the decades, Britain has experienced some quite crippling strikes by workers, but there was one strike which really hit the public in quite a different way: the bakers' strike during the 1970s! It was quite unbelievable that you could walk down a street and see no bread on sale and the vast majority of British people found it a big shock. However, from that time, a number of people made a discovery: they could quite easily bake their own bread. In doing this, they also realised, perhaps for the first time, the importance of yeast. Though used in only very small quantities, it can turn dough into something delicious to savour: the smell of freshly-baked bread must be one of the loveliest of all!

Seeking to describe the way God is at work in the world, Jesus once told a parable about yeast. He said: 'The Kingdom of heaven is like this. A woman takes some yeast and mixes it with forty litres of flour until the whole batch of dough rises' (Matthew 13:33 GNB). Jesus was saying that just as the power of yeast working unseen in the dough can leaven the flour and make it rise to produce a loaf, so the work of God's Kingdom may seem at times to be small and hidden from our sight, yet it is growing and developing, bringing forth abundant results.

There are many other examples of the secret growth of things that are seemingly unseen: the farmer sows seed into the ground and then secretly it sprouts to becomes an ear of corn, or the surgeon sews up a wound after an operation and the hidden forces of nature take up the healing process. In a sense, it is the same with the preacher who sows the good seed of the gospel, so it can then quietly develop in minds and hearts. Truly, the Word of God is like yeast in the dough: it works mysteriously and powerfully. So, too, with doing acts of kindness; we may find that one small act has a much larger impact on an individual or community. While initially, the work of Christ may seem to have little effect, we have the assurance, as the apostle Paul wrote: 'And let us not grow weary in well-doing, for in due season we shall reap, if we do not lose heart' (Galatians 6:9).

In the summer of 1970, one of the Baptist churches in Suffolk made a terrible discovery: dry rot in a wall of the chapel. As the workers took away the plaster, they saw the devastation. For many months, the deadly process had been at work – secretly and powerfully – and the congregation was astounded and dismayed at the amount of damage done. This reminds us of the fact that destructive forces can be at work undetected, bringing untold harm. However, the love of God made known in so many ways is also working – often quietly and unobserved – producing a wonderful outcome, bringing hope and joy in the lives of people.

Suggested readings: Mark 4:26-29 and 1 Thessalonians 2:9-13.

## SEPTEMBER 26th

## IT PAYS TO BE PERSISTENT

Most of us truly appreciate good books and thank God for so many being widely and readily available! Of course, we ought not to take it for granted that there are such a vast number of volumes easily accessible; this is especially true concerning books on the Christian faith. Numerous authors have given the world the results of their creativity and study; the fruits of their labours have enriched countless lives. We thank God for interpreters of the Bible, such as J.B. Phillips. One of the books he published, *Letters to Young Churches* (a translation of the New Testament Epistles), brought blessing to lots of people, especially young people. Many claimed that certain parts of the epistles were all but unintelligible to them until they read Phillips' book. With all this in mind, it is quite amazing to discover the gigantic struggle he had to get it published! Apparently, Phillips submitted this work to fourteen publishers before his manuscript was accepted. It seems incredible that publishers did not see the potential value of, or need for, such a book. However, by dogged perseverance, Phillips eventually found a publisher, and the book became a great success. It was first published in 1947 and reached the eighteenth impression by 1955, with many others to follow later. For many people, it has brought aid and blessing as it has enabled an informed understanding of the New Testament epistles.

How often, in history, good things have not been initially recognised: authors have submitted books, composers have offered musical scores and artists have presented artworks, only then to face rejection. Sometimes, at a much later date, their works have been taken up, appreciated and honoured or, occasionally, even very highly valued. Quite often, genuine works of art have been saved 'by the skin of their teeth': initially, they have been ignored or neglected, but then someone has perceived their worth. What a tragedy it would have been if Phillips had given up after his manuscript had been rejected a few times, but his persistence won through!

We could say, reverently, that it was just so with the Lord Jesus. Surely, few who listened to the Sermon on the Mount realised they were listening to words of eternal significance, which would be studied for generations to come. They would probably have been astounded to be told that two thousand years later, we would be extolling the worth of these words of Jesus! His teachings have been neglected or even rejected by many, but they still speak clearly of openness to the ways of God. Truth does win through eventually, and we rejoice in the persistent ministry of the Holy Spirit making that truth known. The Spirit reveals the truth as seen in Jesus Christ. Constantly, the Spirit leads us into the truth, so bringing us to real freedom.

Suggested readings: John 8:12-23 and Matthew 22:34-40.

SEPTEMBER 27th

## EVERY CHURCH FELLOWSHIP NEEDS 'HELPERS'

The apostle Paul needed helpers. He was a very able, gifted Christian leader (preacher, teacher, pastor, missionary, counsellor, and apologist), but he knew he required helpers. Scattered through his epistles and the Acts of the Apostles, we get numerous references to men and women who served the Church and co-operated with the apostles in the work of the Kingdom. These references provide a fascinating insight into the variety of people serving God in the Christian fellowship. It is interesting to read Paul's words: 'Now you are the body of Christ and individually members of it. And God has appointed in the church first apostles, second prophets, third teachers, then workers of miracles, then healers, helpers, administrators, speakers in various kinds of tongues' (1 Corinthians 12:27-28). It is quite notable that, in such a significant list, Paul placed the group simply known as 'helpers'.

One of the lovely characters in the New Testament Church was Dorcas: 'Now there was at Joppa a disciple named Tabitha, which means Dorcas or Gazelle. She was full of good works and acts of charity' (Acts 9:36). Those last words are just like a small window through which we can see a loving, faithful and generous Christian. We would like to have known more about her, but this thumbnail sketch of a humble and devout Christian, is very thought-provoking. This one verse could be lifted right out of the New Testament and applied to lots of sincere people today. Ministers and local church leaders (as did Paul two thousand years ago) need other people to help them in the Christian task of outreach, evangelism, fellowship oversight and service. Our Blessed Saviour once spoke of such work: 'Do not let your left hand know what your right hand is doing' (Matthew 6:3). There is a noble army of Christian workers who fulfil that command to the very letter! They faithfully and quietly do good work, often discretely, and so only the heavenly Father knows the exact contribution they make to the worldwide Christian Church. These people are prepared to do lots of humble tasks 'behind the scenes' and rejoice to be 'helpers'. To be a 'helper', of whatever kind, is a significant calling, indeed.

One of the most moving stories in the New Testament is the one recorded in John's gospel where Jesus took a towel and washed the disciples' feet. He then turned and said these challenging words: 'For I have given you an example, that you should do as I have done to you' (John 13:15). There are untold numbers of Christian people who have, quite literally, stooped to serve others and much of their work has been done inconspicuously, but the heavenly Father knows it all. It is always right to be thankful for all those good men and women who are quite content to be 'helpers' in the Kingdom, and whose quiet service is of incalculable worth. For all such workers, women and men, known and unknown, we give thanks to God!

Suggested readings: 1 Corinthians 12:27-31 and 2 Timothy 1:15-18.

SEPTEMBER 28th

## DEATH CAN HAVE A GLORIOUS PROSPECT

There is one sure fact about each and every day: around the country and indeed, the world, babies will be born and many couples will be rejoicing in the sheer miracle of the safe arrival of an infant! It is equally true, that each and every day many people will die, and families will be coping with deep feelings of grief, whatever the circumstances. There is a rhythm to life on this planet: day and night, summer and winter, ebb and flow, life and death. One of the odd things about modern society is that death is seen as a taboo subject. It is even counted morbid to talk about it. However, death is a sure reality for us, as we will all come to the end of our earthly life! For Christians, surely our well-founded faith in God should make a difference!

Dietrich Bonhoeffer was a German pastor and scholar whose writings have attracted much attention. Many who might not agree wholly with his theology, admire his fortitude during his imprisonment, and his courage even when facing death. When the Nazi guards came to take him away to be executed, he uttered these memorable words: 'For you it is an end, for me a beginning'. He saw death – even his own untimely death – as a new beginning. There are many things the scriptures do not tell us about death and the afterlife; in fact, many Christians wish the Bible had said much more about these subjects! Yet, one thing is abundantly clear: for the believer, death is a glorious new beginning, with our hope for eternal life with God.

We might reflect on an elderly Christian who had impressed others by her consistent faith and deep convictions. Towards the end of her life, she had a variety of infirmities; trustingly, she would speak openly of her hope that the Lord would come and call her home. She had a true expectation of the life to come; indeed, so much so, she was like someone who was 'packed ready' for her holidays, just waiting for the transport to arrive! There was a definite, though devout and very reverent 'air of excitement' about it all. She had no fear of death and she readily affirmed the challenging words of scripture: 'O death, where is thy victory? O death, where is thy sting?' (1 Corinthians 15:55). This devout woman, by her strong faith and simple testimony impressed others, especially a young minister, who thereby learned more from her about the Christian hope than from his theological textbooks!

Birth is wonderful; equally so, a timely death – for all its sadness on the part of those grieving – can have a glorious prospect. The apostle Paul wrote of this reality: 'For me to live is Christ, and to die is gain' (Philippians 1:21) He was not morbid about death, but hopeful: he saw death, not as a grievous loss, but as a positive gain. So we can truly rejoice with confidence and serenity in the blessings of this life. We also now look forward with sure hope to the life to come 'with Christ'.

Suggested readings: Philippians 1:19-26 and 1 Corinthians 15:51-58.

SEPTEMBER 29th

## THERE ARE 'MINISTERING ANGELS'

One of the stories in the New Testament which grips the heart is the one of Jesus in the Garden of Gethsemane. Knowing that His hour had come, the Master also knew that, within a very short time, He would be rejected and condemned to death: the cross loomed large. It was to be a time of injustice, rejection, pain and sacrifice. In Luke's account, we are told that the disciples were 'sleeping for sorrow' (Luke 22:45). They were quite out of their depth, so Jesus was wholly on His own: utterly alone in His anguish and sorrow. However, Luke's gospel includes an interesting detail, as Luke tells us of a 'visitation': 'And there appeared to him an angel from heaven, strengthening him' (Luke 22:43). Just at the point of His extreme need as – humanly speaking – He agonised over His vocation to submit to the divine purpose, the Saviour was wonderfully strengthened. Some such surprise visitation is a fact of life for many with eyes to see and ears to hear. Perhaps we have sometimes been facing a serious problem or difficulty, only then to have been marvellously comforted and greatly strengthened. The people of God down many generations and in a wide variety of circumstances, have gladly testified to such divine upholding. Many today would agree that God often works, as it were, through 'ministering angels'.

In the first Book of Kings, we are told of a time when the prophet Elijah won a decisive battle, and this was followed by a period of exhaustion. A message from the king's wife Jezebel (a woman motivated by hate) sent Elijah into a downward spiral. He suffered a frightening spiritual depression so, after going into the wilderness, he made his lament. The story continued: 'He requested for himself that he might die' (1 Kings 19:4 AV). Evidently, he had had enough, and he told God so in no uncertain terms. Then the story went on: 'As he lay and slept under a juniper tree, behold, then an angel touched him, and said unto him "Arise and eat"' (1 Kings 19:5 AV). The narrative records later that the angel came again. Just at the right moment spiritual help and encouragement was providentially granted to him.

God has many 'ministering angels' and some of them are friends or just other people alongside us in everyday life who offer encouragement and support! Of course, in the first instance, there is always the Holy Spirit who prompts and guides us into Christ-like ways: He Who is the Guide, Comforter, Encourager and Strengthener is one with the Father and the Son, God above all. God's people have always experienced the Spirit of God coming to their aid in their hour of need. So, even on difficult days or in baffling or upsetting times, when we ourselves feel unable to cope, we can remember that God has power to bless. God may well use someone else who – guided by the Spirit – becomes a 'ministering angel' to us in our need.

Suggested readings: 1 Kings 19:1-7 and Luke 22:39-53.

SEPTEMBER 30th

A WISE PERSON MAKES TIME FOR THOUGHT

Road accidents occur for many reasons: excess speed, hazardous conditions, alcohol or another substance in the driver's blood, a burst tyre or a mechanical failure. However, sometimes when a person is brought to court to answer for involvement in a traffic accident, the verdict is 'driving without due care and attention'. On a different level, it is sadly the case that so many people live their lives without due care and attention: human foolishness or simply plain selfishness can prevail over common sense and decency at times! As we realise from experience, it is possible to make hasty decisions, form unwise friendships, slip into rather poor habits or even simply utter harsh or inappropriate words, and then live to deeply regret our behaviour.

The failure to stop and consider our choices may bring real trouble. Yet, sometimes, life has a way of restoring the balance by bringing us to a halt and making us 'stop and think'. In one psalm, we have a confession which is quite staggering in its honesty: 'It is good that I was afflicted, that I might learn thy statutes' (Psalm 119:71). We ourselves, like many other people, can testify that this is true of our own experience. Actually, earlier in that psalm, there is a striking testimony: 'I have considered my ways and have turned my steps to your statutes' (Psalm 119:59 NIV). What a wise thing it is to pause in life and to find time to consider our ways. In the wonderful providence of God, it can be decisive in helping us to consider our choices, perhaps change direction, and to live life more honourably before the Lord.

We can reflect on situations that often make men and women 'stop and think': the birth of a little child or the death of one very close to us, a visit to a new place – whether beautiful or ugly – or a close-up encounter with the natural world, or perhaps a recovery from a serious illness or rescue from a dangerous situation. Other such moments might be the experience of falling in love, or simply hearing beautiful sounds or lovely music. God can speak with a thousand different voices. Stanley Jones used to tell the story of a man who was very careless about crossing the road and who would not change. The man used to say to Jones, laughingly: 'If I'm killed, put on my tombstone, "Died looking the wrong way"'. That was obviously a frivolous remark but, having acknowledged that, one might ponder how many people have looked the wrong way and have suffered the consequences for themselves, and perhaps brought pain to others, too. There are so many people of all ages and backgrounds who live without paying 'due care and attention'. We do well to consider the words of the psalmist, and to resolve to live by them each day: 'I have considered my ways and have turned my steps to your statutes'.

Suggested readings: Psalm 119:57-72 and Luke 24:45-53.

# OCTOBER

Who would true valour see,
Let him come hither;
One here will constant be,
Come wind, come weather.
There's no discouragement
Shall make him once relent
His first avowed intent
To be a pilgrim.

Whoso beset him round
With dismal stories,
Do but themselves confound;
His strength the more is,
No lion can him fright;
He'll with a giant fight;
But he will have a right
To be a pilgrim.

Hobgoblin nor foul fiend
Can daunt his spirit:
He knows he at the end
Shall life inherit.
Then fancies fly away,
He'll fear not what men say;
He'll labour night and day
To be a pilgrim.
John Bunyan (1628-1688)

❖ ❖ ❖

God be in my head, and in my understanding;
God be in my eyes, and in my looking;
God be in my mouth, and in my speaking;
God be in my heart, and in my thinking;
God be at mine end, and at my departing.

Sarum Primer, 1558

OCTOBER 1st

## THE RIGHT MIXTURE IS IMPORTANT

Wedding cakes are important! Some clergy might laughingly quip that one of the perks of the Christian ministry is attendance at wedding receptions. Indeed, many beneficial contacts, and even good friends, can be made on these occasions. Those who so attend such functions become connoisseurs of different kinds of cake. Obviously, 'Wedding Cake' can mean many things, ranging from a plain iced cake to an elaborately decorated rich fruitcake of three tiers or more! One particular wedding was a truly happy occasion; the young couple had been courting a number of years and they were entering on marriage with great sincerity. The wedding service was planned with great care and the reception was excellent, with plenty of fun and laughter. However, there was cause for concern when, at the reception, the wedding cake took on the appearance of the 'leaning tower of Pisa'! Guests feared a downfall, but mercifully, it didn't happen. Something had gone badly amiss in the mixture: apparently, according to 'experienced cooks' at the reception, something was wrong with the consistency of the icing, and the tier pillars were disastrously sinking into it!

Mixtures are so important in all walks of life! The chemist or manufacturer, the baker or chef, the painter or sculptor, the composer or poet – just to name a few groups – all know that mixtures are vital. The wise teacher in the Old Testament would agree. Indeed, the third chapter of Ecclesiastes speaks of the 'mixture' of our times in daily life: 'A time to plant and a time to pluck up' (v2), 'a time to weep and a time to laugh' (v4), 'a time to seek and a time to lose' (v6), 'a time to keep silent and a time to speak' (v7). It is a fact of life that quite often people get the wrong balance or mixture in these respects. There can be too much laughing or too much weeping, too much or too little talking, too much or too little toiling, too much uprooting or even, perhaps, too much 'holding on' to something. Relationships, and especially marriages, can go sadly wrong because people can – in effect – get the mixture wrong in their priorities. As individuals, it is wise to consider the 'mixture' of our time.

Sometimes churches can encourage the wrong 'mixture' in life's priorities. A new convert to the faith who had previously spent much time with family, after his conversion, then ends up attending many meetings because of the expectations of the fellowship. In this way, if taken to the extreme, a zealous church fellowship could, unwittingly, undermine the basis of a marriage: the important thing is to get the balance right! Right priorities and a good balance truly count within in our individual lives and in our relationships with others! We thank God that the Spirit will lead us to right choices.

Suggested readings: Ecclesiastes 3:1-15 and Colossians 3:16-23.

## OCTOBER 2nd

## A STEADY CHARACTER BRINGS BLESSINGS

Every Christian minister is asked to give character references and, in most cases, this is a pleasant task. However, in certain instances it can be quite difficult! There are some people who are basically good, but they lack steadiness and there are times when they are rather unreliable. A person, though generally dependable, may sometimes make a foolish mistake or err in judgement. Lacking consistency in this way, it can be difficult to give a satisfactory reference. The vast majority of employers look for reliability. It is certainly a virtue praised in Holy Scripture: 'The faithful will abound with blessings' (Proverbs 28:20). The New English Bible renders it neatly, as those '...of steady character'.

Looking back, we may recall such 'steady characters'. Today, we are increasingly aware of the importance of village life as it used to be in the past. Studies have been made of old customs and crafts and, by the means of recording equipment, these old ways have been documented for the sake of posterity. Significantly, historians have drawn attention to the vital role played by locally-renowned 'village characters'; some of these individuals, even in spite of their very limited education, exercised a powerful influence in the community. These wise and sturdy people were helpers, counsellors, friends and guides to countless numbers, and many of these special men and women of 'steady character' had a firm grounding in the Christian faith. In this regard, the verse from Proverbs, as rendered in the older translation by Moffatt, strikes a familiar chord for lots of people today who have known such dependable individuals: 'Trustworthy men are richly blessed'.

In the Sermon on the Mount, Jesus challenged people to constancy in character. Jesus called people to be the 'salt of the earth' and the 'light of the world', with this challenge: 'Let your light shine before others, so that they may see your good works and give glory to your Father in heaven' (Matthew 5:16). We thank God today for those men and women of 'steady character' who have been such a blessing to others. William Barclay, the New Testament expositor, used to quote this saying: 'One example is better than a thousand arguments'. How true he was! We have all come across living instances of this truth: character speaks volumes.

The wise teacher in the Book of Proverbs asserts that such a steady character 'enjoys many blessings'. These surely include the blessing of being respected and trusted, where honour is duly recognized, as well as the assurance of being used by God, and finding joy in helping others. A 'steady character' living out his or her faith day by day is, in the words of Jesus, like a city on a hilltop or light which is always of benefit to others.

Suggested readings: Proverbs 28:14-20 and Matthew 5:1-16.

OCTOBER 3rd

## OUR GOD KNOWS THE WAY AHEAD

In spite of the often very strong protests made against boxing, it is still a thriving sport. A lot of money is involved and boxers can earn millions of pounds for a special 'title fight'. One of the saddest things in this sport is when a contestant steps into the ring, obviously outclassed, and as a result takes a lot of punishment. Then, after a particularly brutal round, the person's 'seconds' throw in the towel to end the match, meaning defeat or surrender. The expression 'throw in the towel' has entered our English language as a colourful metaphor meaning 'to give up'.

The temptation to 'throw in the towel' comes to us all. The psalmist knew that experience also. He was facing powerful and hostile enemies who were causing great distress, but he also knew that he could turn to God for help. He exclaimed: 'When I am ready to give up, he knows what I should do' (Psalm 142:3 GNB). The psalmist was convinced that the Lord knew the way ahead. There are, indeed, times when believers face uncertainties and have 'had enough', and they simply yearn to 'throw in the towel'. Everyday there are people involved in struggles where there is a big temptation to 'give in'. We might think of a politician fighting for a cause, parents coping with a wayward child, or a couple labouring to keep their marriage intact. There are so many areas where people, both believers and unbelievers, face an exhausting struggle, and they are sorely tempted to 'throw in the towel'. In the sphere of Christian service, the apostle Paul presents a challenge: 'And let us not grow weary in well-doing, for in due season we shall reap, if we do not lose heart' (Galatians 6:9). The resources of God are always available to help us along the way. Even though sometimes we don't know what to do, we can be sure that God knows the way.

At any such point of weariness and exhaustion, it is wise to pause and to think clearly, not only about the consequences of 'giving up', but also about the outcome of merely stumbling on regardless! One notable preacher used to confess how he felt terribly nervous before preaching. He said that before preaching, he would sit in the pulpit and take long, deep breaths until the tension eased. When we feel weary of the struggle and are ready to give in, then perhaps we need space to take some deep breaths. We can pause and reflect on our God Who knows the way. We might well note that after the psalmist made his desperate plea, he offered a final note of confidence to God: 'Thou wilt deal bountifully with me' (Psalm 142:7). Just a few moments of quiet reflection can change our attitude and perspective, and maybe also sometimes, our decisions as well. It is worth pondering always that our loving, heavenly Father knows the way ahead for us, and so we can continue to trust in the Lord that we will be guided and aided on our way.

Suggested readings: Psalm 142:1-7 and Matthew 7:7-12.

## OCTOBER 4th

## GENTLE PERSUASION IS EFFECTIVE

It is quite remarkable how many people are involved, professionally, in some sort of role which necessitates persuasion: lawyers, politicians, business people or sales executives, insurance or estate agents, as well as ministers among others, too! Some who are highly skilled in the art of persuasion could, as it is said, 'sell coals to Newcastle', and they are very clever in their role. This kind of persuasion can often be linked with no small measure of irritation, especially if there is some form of doubt about, or resistance to, what is being advocated. The Holy Scriptures link patience with persuasion, as the ancient proverb puts it: 'Patient persuasion can break down the strongest resistance and can convince rulers' (Proverbs 25:15 GNB).

The parents of a little child were dismayed, indeed, very upset, because he would not talk. Their child understood what was said to him, but his replies to them were only given by pointing at things: he made sounds and gesticulated, rather than engaging in speech. They received plenty of advice from family and friends, and some advocated a much stronger policy, along these lines: 'I'd teach him if he were my child!' The parents resisted these strict methods and kept on their own steady course, showing extreme patience. In the end they won through, and they discovered for themselves that glorious truth given in the Book of Proverbs: 'Patient persuasion can break down the strongest resistance'.

In the story of the Church, there have been people who have spoken with great power; we might think of narrative in the Acts of the Apostles which tells of the apostle Peter preaching on the Day of Pentecost. Peter spoke persuasively with the voice of authority and a tremendous number of his hearers heard the challenge and responded. Later in Acts, we are told the story of Apollos, a bold, effective speaker both fervent and sincere, though in reality his knowledge of the faith was limited. We read this fascinating verse: 'When Priscilla and Aquila heard him, they took him aside and expounded to him the way of God more accurately' (Acts 18:26). To seek to correct someone is a very delicate matter; if Priscilla and Aquila had used an aggressive approach to Apollos, he could have been deeply offended and hurt. However, they were wise and opted for the gentle, patient approach, and they won a signal victory for the Kingdom of God. Very often the Lord uses individuals who practise gentle persuasion; many people will not be swayed by a loud voice and they muster strong resistance to it. People who tend to take a lot of convincing – as any communicator will testify – can only be won over by gentle, patient persuasion with a quiet, winsome approach.

Suggested readings: Proverbs 25:11-22 and Acts 18:24-28.

OCTOBER 5th

## MANY PEOPLE DISPLAY THE 'HELP REQUIRED' SIGN

One positive development over recent decades is that more attention has been given to the needs of those with some kind of disability: shops, businesses, cinemas and theatres, galleries and museums, sports and leisure facilities, public offices and local community venues, as well as places of worship, have been made more accessible. There has been a much greater focus on the problems many people face, while also recognising more keenly their valuable contribution. However, there is still a vast need for more devices, programmes and facilities to allow greater accessibility.

In one Suffolk town quite a few years ago, there was a block of flats with an electronic sign outside which had the bold words, 'HELP REQUIRED' illuminated, if any of the residents who were in need pressed a button in their flat. It meant that anyone passing by would see the sign and, hopefully, take appropriate action to get help. It was a simple idea, but proved a tremendous help to those living within the flats whatever their own circumstances. In one sense, that could be viewed as a parable of life! At certain times, most people need – for some reason – to convey the message 'HELP REQUIRED'. This message can be displayed by a look on the face, a manner of walking, a tone of voice in conversation, or the conspicuous absence of a smile, as well as by other ways which we may not always immediately notice. Much has been written on the theme of 'body language': it is true that, without saying a single word, someone can speak volumes, including the claim that help or comfort is needed.

If a person has a compassionate heart, he or she will be sensitive to read such signs and will detect that help is required. The gospels reveal that Jesus Christ advocated the 'Good Samaritan' type of ministry and lived it Himself. He was always perceptive of, and attentive to, others' needs! In a sermon, Peter portrayed His Master with a lovely explanation: '. . . how God anointed Jesus of Nazareth with the Holy Spirit and with power; how he went about doing good and healing all that were oppressed by the devil, for God was with him' (Acts 10:38). If a person is truly committed to being a disciple of Jesus Christ, he or she will exercise a ministry of helpfulness and will seek to empathise with those in need of assistance.

In Canterbury Cathedral, there are official guides who help multitudes of tourists and visitors; yet there are others who are the 'watchers', ones looking out for the lonely, the isolated, or the despondent people who just drift into the cathedral. These 'watchers' are ready to offer a handshake or a listening ear, or to introduce a person who seems to be in need of help to a priest. There is a sense in which every church needs its faithful 'watchers' who are alert to the signs that there is 'Help Required'. The work of these 'watchers' is vital to the ministry of any church.

Suggested readings: Acts 10:34-43 and Galatians 5:22-23.

OCTOBER 6ᵗʰ

## ENTHUSIASM HAS A PLACE IN THE KINGDOM

Obtaining a place at the performance in the Royal Albert Hall for the 'last night of the proms' is the ambition of lots of people, young and old alike! It is one of the favourite nights of the year for music lovers. In fact, enthusiasm defines the evening! Besides the special music, there is much more: balloons, banners, colourful costumes and headgear, accompanied by much clapping, waving, whistling and hilarity leading to lots of laughter. The enthusiasm is so infectious that the millions watching on television get caught up in the spirit of the evening, too. Enthusiasm can be very catching: people share enthusiasm about sports such as football, rugby, tennis, golf or cricket, or the arts such as music, drama, or literature. Others show enthusiasm for outdoor pursuits such as running, kayaking, cycling, climbing, diving and so on.

Christians, too, who are passionate about their faith, show a genuine enthusiasm for the things of Christ and for living the Christian life. Over the Christian era, there have been men and women who, through following Christ, have displayed in their daily lives a real zeal for the things of the Kingdom. In the everyday world, where people can be passionate in their support of a sports team or an individual player, or some other celebrity group or figure, it should not be frowned upon for a believer to demonstrate zeal for Christ. There should be no surprise that committed Christians seek to exalt Christ as Saviour and Lord of all. The Church now – as always – needs Christians who are wholly faithful, and that includes being sincerely and boldly enthusiastic, though obviously with a due humility and openness.

William Tyndale had a fervent ambition to translate the scriptures into English so that people could read the Bible for themselves – a goal he pursued relentlessly. He had a passionate enthusiasm to do this work, for he believed that the sure way to dispel ignorance and errant faith was through knowledge of scriptural truth. To his informed mind, reformation of both Church and people depended upon it! Equally passionate, was the writer of the Epistle to the Romans, the apostle Paul. After eleven chapters of theological exposition, in chapter 12 he begins the practical application of it with the word, 'Therefore', bringing a wholly new dimension to the epistle. The key to this twelfth chapter is 'enthusiasm' and Dr. Moffatt's striking translation brings this out brilliantly: 'Never let your zeal flag; maintain the spiritual glow; serve the Lord; let your hope be a joy to you; be steadfast in trouble' (Romans 12:11-12 Moffatt). Paul, a faithful servant of Christ, was both, enthusiastic and bold, avowedly unashamed of the gospel. We offer our gratitude to God for all sincere Christians who by their daily life and witness endeavour to make a difference for Christ's sake; we surely also seek such true spiritual fervour and enthusiasm, too.

Suggested readings: Psalm 149:1-5 and Colossians 3:16-23.

OCTOBER 7th

## SOME CHRISTIANS ARE WORTH IMITATING

The apostle Paul is remembered as a person of courage: there was a quality of boldness and fearlessness which impressed both his friends and his enemies. He was bold to proclaim the truth even while facing danger, hardship or hostility, and was courageous to face up to authorities, governors and kings! One aspect of Paul's boldness sometimes goes unrecognised: 'What you have learned and received and heard and seen in me, do; and the God of peace will be with you' (Philippians 4:9). While some might dismiss this directive as arrogance, he had the courage to point to his own life as an example! The New English Bible brings out the sharpness of this challenge in a very apt translation: 'All that you heard me say or do, put into practice'.

If some people today used that expression, they would be heavily criticised, and would no doubt be condemned for having such a proud heart! Anyone who openly invites others to note, and to copy his or her own life would surely attract severe criticism. However, the apostle Paul seemed utterly sincere and does not appear to be drawing attention to himself or seeking praise. We recall that Paul gladly and openly testified to what the grace of God had done for him: 'But by the grace of God I am what I am, and his grace toward me was not in vain' (1 Corinthians 15:10). Paul rejoiced in God's grace: it was divine grace that had forgiven his sin and which had enabled him to live a Christian life and to serve the Kingdom of God, even in spite of hostility and persecution. Divine grace had changed him: he desired that others should have a similar experience of being transformed by that same marvellous – indeed, boundless and amazing – grace, too.

Sometimes, we have been introduced to a father and son, or a mother and daughter, and we've been struck by the remarkable family likeness. The resemblance between children and parents can be astounding! Paul felt himself to be the spiritual father to many people: he had brought them to a saving knowledge of Jesus Christ, and wanted his converts to bear the family likeness so, writing to the Christians at Corinth, he wrote in all humility: 'For I became your father in Christ Jesus through the gospel. I urge you, then, be imitators of me' (1 Corinthians 4:15-16). The apostle actually invited people to imitate him; the boldness of this challenge was based on the confidence that what the Lord had done for him personally, could also certainly be done for others, and so it would redound to the glory of God!

Sadly, the conduct of some Christians does not justify others following their example. Unfortunately, some professing Christians seem petty, critical, smug, censorious, or even selfish. They are not exemplary characters in Christian discipleship! Yet, Paul, with all his faults, filled the word 'Christian' with meaning by his dedicated life and Christ-like example, and so he brought glory to God.

Suggested readings: 1 Corinthians 4:14-21 and Philippians 4:8-13.

OCTOBER 8th

## IT IS HARMFUL TO HAVE AN UNBALANCED VIEW

Jesus must have been hurt by the fact that some people had so little sense of proportion. In this respect, he uttered some strong words which have never been forgotten: 'You blind guides, straining out a gnat and swallowing a camel!' (Matthew 23:23-24). They obviously lacked balance and proportion. On another occasion we are told in the gospels, that on the Sabbath Jesus went into the synagogue and cured a man with a serious disability. It was a marvellous healing and one would have expected everybody to rejoice, but it was not so! The Pharisees in the synagogue were angry that Jesus healed the man on the Sabbath and they couldn't share the gladness. Nor did they seem to realise that in this healing, the power of God was manifested. We read the sequel in Mark's gospel: 'they went out, and immediately held counsel with the Herodians against him, how to destroy him' (Mark 3:6). They had somehow got things out of balance. This meant that the truth of the gospel was being missed, so Jesus became a marked man as plans were made to silence Him.

In 1942, Britain was engaged in a bitter conflict: the British people were in mortal peril and Adolf Hitler, leader of the Nazi regime, stood like a powerful giant – rather like a modern Goliath – poised to pounce and to destroy. At that particular time, a number of bishops were said to be in debate, apparently, discussing what clothing should be worn by the clergy. It seems such a blatant example of stressing the non-essentials. So, in every area of life – home, industry, politics and Church – there can be, as it were, a 'straining out of gnats' and the 'swallowing of camels'. We have probably all faced similar absurdities when issues are blown out of proportion.

One Saturday morning, Mrs Williams went out shopping and, in the hectic rush, lost her purse with a sum of money in it. She returned home really fearing to tell her husband, as he had often chided her for carelessness and she hated his fiery temper. However, as he listened to her story, he remained very calm and composed. Yet, just one week later, she made a silly mistake about the time they planned for the meal to be ready, and he really lost his cool! People sometimes get things quite out of proportion and it can be most harmful to family life and to local church life, too.

In the modern world, most parents are deeply concerned that their children are well-fed and well-educated, but many do not seem to be as interested in their children's spiritual welfare. Surely this is an unbalanced view! Every human being is made up of body, mind and spirit; thus, spiritual, as well as emotional and physical needs, are important. It is very harmful to have an unbalanced view of life; that is true, not just in terms of the things of this world, but also in terms of the spiritual realm, since God has created us for relationship with Him and with one another, too.

Suggested readings: Matthew 23:13-24 and Hebrews 12:1-4.

OCTOBER 9th

## WE MUST LISTEN TO THE OTHER SIDE OF THE STORY

It is true that some people find the Old Bailey criminal courts more exciting than tennis at Wimbledon! Some famous trials at the Old Bailey have a deep fascination for men and women: they listen to the evidence and watch the skills of the lawyers in defending and accusing the defendant. In the course of numerous trials, there are unexpected twists as the witnesses give evidence; sometimes, the surprises are truly dramatic! A defendant appears to be condemned by the weight of the evidence and then a key witness gives clear evidence to prove innocence. So we listen afresh to a verse of scripture: 'The one who first states a case seems right, until the other comes and cross-examines' (Proverbs 18:17). Often, there is another side to the story!

Sometimes, when a marriage breaks down, the evidence seems totally against one partner, and so he or she is shown up as though wholly at fault! Yet, ministers, therapists and marriage guidance counsellors know that, so often, there is another side to the story. Many a person who appears to be thoroughly innocent, and can speak convincingly against the other partner, can actually be implicated to some degree. The other side of the story, probably known to just a few, gives a very different angle on the vexed question of blame. Often in life, there is another side to a story and, sadly, all too frequently, that other side is never told or, at least, the account of the other party is not given any credibility.

The whole issue of 'hearing the other side' applies to thinking about Christian faith, too. There are people who can never find a good word for the Christian faith: they have in their own minds 'the case against God', citing famines, earthquakes and disasters, as well as disease and tragedy, as an argument against a loving heavenly Father. They refer to the problem of evil, and are well versed on the subject, but they tend to overlook the incidence of goodness. Yet, Christians contend that God works through others, such as, firefighters and other emergency responders, rescuers and lifeboat crews, as well as all those who do valiant duty in our health service, in the police, or working within the armed forces. Indeed, the mystery of courage, heroism and self-sacrifice – when the nobility of the human spirit shines like a brilliant light – to believers seems to point to God at work in the world.

There is also a vast array of ordinary people who never hit the headlines but whose lives tell this side of the story. One of those – who later became renowned for her work, startling and challenging the world by her faith, goodness and loving toil – is Mother Teresa. She chose to work in an area of great need, but her own good life presented another side to that situation. People, sadly, can do the most horrible things, but also the most beautiful things. There are always two sides to most stories.

Suggested readings: Psalm 1:1-6 and Acts 3:11-16.

OCTOBER 10th

## GOD SEES TRULY

In Old Testament times, when the prophet Samuel duly went down to Bethlehem, as instructed by the Lord, to look for a king to reign over Israel, he learned a very valuable lesson: God sees truly. The Holy Scriptures are quite specific as to the Lord's command to Samuel: 'Do not look on his appearance or on the height of his stature . . . for the Lord does not see as mortals see; they look on the outward appearance, but the Lord looks on the heart' (1 Samuel 16:7). Seven sons of Jesse were presented to Samuel but none of them was selected. Then David, the other son, who was out in the fields – one not even considered at first – was brought before the prophet, and the inner voice commanded Samuel: 'Rise and anoint him; for this is the one' (1 Samuel 16:12). The complete 'outsider', as it were, was the one chosen by God for high service: the Lord was seeing beyond outward appearances.

How often we judge things by outward appearance and it can prove to be a disastrous decision! Someone purchases a nice-looking car and believes the smart-looking salesperson, but within a few weeks, numerous hidden faults are discovered. A young person marries a wealthy, well-educated and charming partner, but discovers in subsequent days an unacceptable degree of self-centredness. Even a church might call a good preacher to become the new minister, only to find out later, in great dismay, the person is not what they were seeking in a pastor. Of course, such bad choices are made in all kinds of situations in life, and so we ignore – at our peril – some words of the Lord Jesus who gave clear counsel on the subject: 'Do not judge by appearances, but judge with right judgment' (John 7:24). It is so easy to be taken in by outward appearances, and it seems that many – even very sincere – Christians can make mistakes in their assessment of a person; yet God sees truly! God saw the potential in David, though as one not without serious flaws, but even despite those flaws God was able to use him. Of course, if God looked for perfect people, we would all be excluded! What God sees in us is the potential to be used by Him.

When God put it into the heart of Campbell Morgan to be a minister of the gospel, a selection committee turned him down. It was a nasty shock, but even so, he refused just to accept their rejection of his sense of calling, and sought other avenues of service. History now records his effective expository ministry at Westminster Chapel, London. Selection committees can sometimes make mistakes as, sadly, they can be influenced by outward appearance. One of the richest verses in the prophecy of Isaiah reads, 'One who trusts will not panic'; or, in the older translation, the one who believes 'will not be in haste' (Isaiah 28:16). It is good to give a second thought or take a further look, if we would see aright, as God would have us see.

Suggested readings: 1 Samuel 16:4-13 and John 7:16-24.

# OCTOBER 11<sup>th</sup>

## INFLEXIBILITY CAN BE A VIRTUE

A person's flexibility is widely praised as a virtue. We can all appreciate the fact that the employer, employee, business person, politician, leader, statesman or woman who is flexible is able to establish good relationships, and work well in collaboration. However, as we know, flexibility can have its dangers! In Psalm 86 we have these words: 'Turn to me and be gracious to me; give your strength to your servant' (Psalm 86:16). The latter part of that verse makes an interesting study for, in response to divine grace, the strength desired is 'inflexibility'. So we could put it, as it were, as follows: 'Give me the strength of inflexibility'. As strange as it may seem, there is sometimes true virtue in inflexibility!

At one stage in his life, Joseph became very successful: 'The Lord was with Joseph and he became a successful man; and he was in the house of his master the Egyptian' (Genesis 39:2). Joseph found favour with many, including Potiphar, an official under Pharaoh, and Joseph was made overseer of Potiphar's house. At this moment, when Joseph was at the pinnacle of success, there was a blatant attempt by Potiphar's wife to seduce him, as she '. . . cast her eyes upon Joseph and said, "Lie with me"' (Genesis 39:7). We cannot know the force of that particular temptation for him, but Joseph resisted it resolutely. He was absolutely inflexible, and his words of self-examination proved remarkable: 'How then can I do this great wickedness, and sin against God?' (Genesis 39:9).

We remember that there are many different types of strength: physical, mental, emotional and spiritual strength; the latter has many different forms, including strength to endure through adversity, to be patient and to love others, to serve and to obey, as well as the strength to be inflexible when the situation demands it. In the Apostles' Creed, we have words referring to Jesus' ministry: 'suffered under Pontius Pilate'. Pilate is remembered for the fact that he was all too pliable to suit others at a time when inflexibility was required. Luke's gospel shows how Pilate knew that Jesus was not guilty, but also, that he was under pressure to have Him duly crucified; many in the crowd were determined to have their way. Luke's account reveals Pilate as a man who yielded under pressure: 'They were urgent, demanding with loud cries that he should be crucified. And their voices prevailed. So Pilate gave sentence that their demand should be granted' (Luke 23:23-24). Sometimes, in the interests of the Kingdom of God, Christians need the strength to be inflexible, and so to take a stand for righteousness. The apostle Paul wrote 'Finally, be strong in the Lord and in the strength of his might' (Ephesians 6:10). Paradoxically, sometimes, inflexibility is a sign of great strength in the Lord.

Suggested readings: Genesis 39:1-12 and Luke 23:13-24.

OCTOBER 12th

## LIFE'S PINNACLES CAN BE UNSAFE PLACES

In the world of sport there are certain days which are long remembered. On Saturday, 24th September 1988, the Canadian athlete Ben Johnson broke the world record for the men's one hundred metres sprint; Canada, as a nation, was delighted! The world's press had a field day splashing his photograph on their front pages and describing him as 'The fastest man on earth', having run the distance in 9.79 seconds. He received the gold medal on the podium and congratulations came from every quarter. That day, seemingly, Ben Johnson had a secure future, as the money he would earn from participating in advertising would amount to a staggering figure. The final spurt at the end of the race was quite awe-inspiring: fellow athletes and the public could not forget that dramatic acceleration! However, it was not long before a rumour began that he had taken anabolic steroids to enhance his performance. Then, three days after the race, the results of the drugs test revealed that he had cheated by taking steroids, and so he was stripped of his gold medal. One day, he was at the pinnacle of fame and glory, yet three days later, he was in the depths of shame! His family, his friends, and his country were all deeply embarrassed and the downfall was reported on the front pages of the world's newspapers; this man's failure hurt lots of people.

The Holy Scriptures are quite realistic about human frailty and sinfulness and it supplies ample illustrations of our proneness to temptation. Many pages tell the story of David, the young shepherd who became a king. We learn much about his skill, his courage, his perseverance and achievements, but he fell into shame, too. The story of his moral failure is told with great economy of words: David saw a beautiful woman after whom he lusted, so he devised a way that he could commit adultery. All this started off a chain of events which caused pain, injury and death. One day David was at the pinnacle of fame, but then through his folly he fell, and his notoriety caused real pain and so much unhappiness, to himself and to others. From his pinnacle of grandeur, his downfall was striking.

History records many downfalls of the high and mighty, as well as the less well-known figures of the past. Most of us are well aware of the possibility of glorious achievements, but also of dismal – even dramatic – failures. Indeed, we know that in many respects, a pinnacle can be an unsafe place to the unwary or unwise. However, even if we do slip and fall, we know that God's forgiveness is unfailing. There is an assurance from the Lord which brings so much comfort: 'If you, O Lord, kept a record of sins, O Lord, who could stand? But with you there is forgiveness' (Psalm 130:3-4 NIV). We can praise God that His grace is deeper than our sin, broader than our shortcoming: that is our hope and comfort, giving us a blessed assurance, indeed.

Suggested readings: Psalm 130:1-8 and 2 Samuel 11:2-5.

OCTOBER 13th

## CONCERNING THE FORGETFULNESS OF GOD

In Psalm 25, we read the confession of the psalmist who was painfully conscious of his sins and failings: 'For thy name's sake, O Lord, pardon my guilt, for it is great' (Psalm 25:11). An earlier verse sets the context for such trust: 'Remember not the sins of my youth, or my transgressions; according to thy steadfast love remember me, for thy goodness' sake, O Lord' (Psalm 25:7). Here the psalmist is pleading with God in effect: 'Remember not my sins but remember me!' People who have been let down by others often say 'I will forgive but I shall never forget'. The psalmist wants God to forgive and forget, and the affirmation of faith is that God does so! For believers, there is a precious verse in Isaiah: 'I, even I, am he who blots out your transgressions, for my own sake and remembers your sins no more' (Isaiah 43:25 NIV). What a glorious promise based on such wonderful mercy! If we are wholly honest, we remember our own sins, and others also remember them – even those closest as family and friends – but God forgives and forgets. If we sincerely seek His forgiveness, God always accepts us, forgives us and graciously forgets our sins!

In the prophecy of Isaiah, we read how King Hezekiah was very ill and close to death: he prayed to God and was granted, as it were, a special dispensation of an extra fifteen years to live. The words spoken to him were impressive: 'I have heard your prayer, I have seen your tears; behold I will add fifteen years to your life' (Isaiah 38:5). After this remarkable experience of divine mercy, Hezekiah wrote a testimony which included these words: 'Lo, it was for my welfare that I had great bitterness; but thou hast held back my life from the pit of destruction, for thou hast cast all my sins behind thy back' (Isaiah 38:17). We, like Hezekiah, rejoice in divine forgetfulness!

Some people who have erred and have hurt other people often say: 'I have sinned and I just cannot forgive myself'. These indiviudals have the grace in their hearts to forgive others who have wronged them, but they are hard on themselves. There is comfort in the Word of God since, in the New Testament, we have these words of assurance: '. . . for if our heart condemn us, God is greater than our heart, and knoweth all things' (1 John 3:20 AV). God's mercy is greater than ours, God's love is deeper than our sins, God's forgiveness is more wonderful than can be told! We remember with gratitude that the cross of Christ proclaims the possibility and wonder of forgiveness: divine mercy is an actuality for us all to experience! One theologian, deeply versed in the Holy Scripture, used to say that many people would enjoy better mental health if they really accepted the fact that God does amazingly forgive their sins. For all of us, there is a real measure of healing in the truth that God both forgives and forgets.

Suggested readings: Isaiah 38:4-17 and 1 John 3:16-24.

OCTOBER 14th

## LIFE'S BREATHING SPACES ARE VITAL

A clergyman was giving a talk to young people about gifts and made the point that some presents last one day, some last months or years, and a few last a lifetime. In saying this, he produced a large Bible which he had been given to him years before: the Bible was very special because it had extra wide margins for writing in notes. Over the years, he had used the margins to put down comments, references, explanations and ideas. In the early days of printing, the printer filled the pages with a mass of words and the margins were often quite slim or even almost non-existent, so the pages appeared as one block of print and were not so easily readable. Yet, the margins of this particular Bible had increased its value to this minister and therefore, it had proved extraordinarily important to him, as he was able to convey to the youth.

The image of a book with wide margins, in many ways, is a metaphor of life. That is to say, we all need margins, and we must value space! Large cities have parks, as well as other green areas, and these are rightly described as the 'lungs' of the city. London has millions of residents, as well as workers who commute to the city daily. Hence, there are multitudes of buildings, and while green spaces may seem few and far between, amid all the built-up areas, there are parks which serve as the 'breathing spaces'! It is essential to have such wider spaces or margins, as it were. Indeed, life is truly enriched by them. Of course, on the level of our daily lives, some people try to live without margins: their days and nights are so crammed full of engagements and activities that they have little space for other people or pursuits. Adequate margins are actually essential!

As we consider the life of Jesus Christ, we see how he needed such margins for true 'breathing spaces'. Mark's gospel records how one day He said to the disciples: 'Come away by yourselves to a lonely place and rest a while' (Mark 6:31). This brought forth a ready response as Mark records: 'And they went away in the boat to a lonely place by themselves' (Mark 6:32). The Master knew the wisdom of having 'breathing spaces' but, as the narrative shows, the crowds all too soon interrupted His rest. Jesus, Himself, knew the struggle to maintain such margins.

Sometimes, the demands of life are great, and it is difficult to find a space to relax. God has provided spaces in the created order: night and day, Sabbath and the Jubilee year and life is thus enriched. Sabbath and holiday times are not wasted times! With all this in mind, the Christian Church has become aware of the need for conferences, retreats, study times and sabbatical leave to offer such space. We all need 'breathing spaces'. In our lives, vital 'margins' prove to be wholesome, restorative and enriching to all concerned; it is perilous to God's gift of space.

Suggested readings: Psalm 62:1-12 and Mark 6:30-34.

OCTOBER 15th

## OUR GOD IS BEYOND ALL COMPARISON

Over the past century or more, Scotland has produced some remarkable preachers whose influence has been very significant in the land and far beyond. Dr. Alexander Whyte had an outstanding ministry at Free St. George's, Edinburgh. His noted ministry is now a part of the sacred record of what the Holy Spirit has wrought through faithful servants in that great city. He was a fine individual as preacher, scholar, lecturer, pastor and author as well as a 'friend of sinners'. The apostle Paul once prayed: 'Unto Him be glory in the church' (Ephesians 3:21). History affirms that Dr. Whyte certainly sought to do just that! There were particular occasions when his preaching reached such sublime heights that it had an awesome quality and a tremendous impact for good on his hearers. Words found in the Book of Genesis aptly describe the effect that Whyte's ministry evidently had: 'How awesome is this place! This is none other than the house of God, and this is the gate of heaven' (Genesis 28:17). To those attending, the times of dynamic preaching were quite unforgettable; for hundreds of men and women, the preaching proved a turning-point, when they made their commitment to Jesus Christ and rejoiced in Him as their Lord and Saviour. There were three special biblical texts which Dr. Whyte returned to again and again: each time he preached from them, he gave fresh insight and inspiration. The three texts were: 'The Lord, the Lord God, merciful and gracious', 'Who is a God like unto Thee?' and 'Lord teach us how to pray'.

Some testified that Dr. Whyte's greatest preaching came when he expounded the verse, 'Who is a God like unto thee?' We know, of course, that God is beyond description. Our God is above our highest thoughts, beyond our furthest vision and deeper than our most profound experience: His grace and love, His purposes of mercy, are all beyond comparison. So Isaiah the prophet uttered these stark and challenging words: 'To whom then will you liken God, or what likeness compare with him?' (Isaiah 40:18). In another place, the Lord also spoke through Isaiah: 'My thoughts are not your thoughts, neither are your ways my ways, says the Lord. For as the heavens are higher than the earth, so are my ways higher than your ways and my thoughts than your thoughts' (Isaiah 55:8-9). God is beyond all compare.

No human mind can ever calculate the greatness of God: nothing can ever measure it and no one can ever compute it, as it is beyond all earthly estimation! Best of all, God's love is deeper than our sin; His mercy is greater than our mistakes and His purposes are broader than our utmost and loftiest expectations. It is a privilege to ponder each new day the greatness and the faithfulness of our living God!

Suggested readings: Genesis 28:10-17 and Isaiah 55:8-9.

OCTOBER 16th

## JESUS HAD A WINSOMENESS OF SPEECH

In every age, there are certain speakers who can hold the attention of the general public: they may be far above their hearers intellectually, but somehow they keep the common touch. There are leaders, cabinet ministers, commentators, trade union leaders, government officials and members of the clergy who have a winsomeness of speech which is both attractive and compelling. Jesus of Nazareth was also One so powerful in His manner of speech. He had an ability to communicate effectively to ordinary people. Mark's gospel puts it evocatively: 'The common people heard him gladly' (Mark 12:37 AV). His speech struck a chord deep within ordinary people.

In each of the gospels, it's fascinating to see how many times it is recorded that Jesus was speaking to a local crowd or even a great multitude. Luke gives an indication of the great size of the crowds around Jesus as He taught: 'As thousands of people crowded together, so that they were stepping on each other . . .' (Luke 12:1 GNB). We might ask why so many listened so attentively to Jesus. It is clear that they appreciated the simplicity of His words, the sincerity of His person, and the authority of His voice. Yet, most important over everything else, was His loving concern seen in His everyday life: His speech and actions were one.

When Dick Sheppard was the minister of St Martin-in-the-Fields, London, he suffered from terrible bouts of asthma. It was said that he used the words 'Give us this day our daily bread' and said for himself, 'Give us this day our daily breath'. However, in spite of all his difficulties with health, people from all walks of life, in all conditions and from every kind of background listened to him. They did so because they recognised in him those four basic things: simplicity, sincerity, authority and a genuine loving concern, and so he exercised a remarkable ministry. Those who feel God's call to teach and preach do well to remember these cardinal virtues in seeking to be those through whom God's Word would be made known in their own day.

Jesus spoke to the crowds – often using stories – and they remembered His words. Think of three famous parables: the Prodigal Son, the Good Samaritan, and the Sower, which are widely known and used in everyday – even parliamentary – speech from time to time. Jesus once said: 'Heaven and earth will pass away, but my words will not pass away' (Luke 21:33). How true those words were! The Master was, indeed, right. His teaching was of eternal significance and of lasting worth; little wonder the winsomeness of His words has captivated millions of hearts over the centuries. We give thanks for Jesus' timeless teachings which spoke plainly of the love of God and, even now, continue to show us more about God's grace and mercy.

Suggested readings: Mark 12:35-44 and Luke 21:28-38.

OCTOBER 17th

## GOD OFTEN USES THE MINORITY

Unfortunately, people can sometimes become obsessed with numbers! There is so much in modern life that moulds our thinking to accept that numerical strength is of prime importance, and such an attitude can even permeate the Church. So, even in a fellowship, there can be much stress on the size of the congregation and the quantity of the offering! However, we remember that there is a glorious strand of truth running through the whole of scripture which testifies that God can use the many or the few, as well as larger or smaller means; indeed, often God uses the minority group. In the first Book of Samuel we read about Jonathan. He was a good character; his loyalty as a friend, his strength of purpose, his fine courage and loving heart are well recorded in the Bible. Less emphasis has been placed on his wisdom, but he certainly possessed it. In one place, we read how he and his armour-bearer were in a tricky and fearful situation. Jonathan spoke reassuring words: 'It may be that the Lord will work for us; for nothing can hinder the Lord from saving by many or by few' (1 Samuel 14:6).

As we look back on history with the hindsight of faith, we can see how God has often used the tiny minority to achieve His purposes, whether a small group or a family, a married couple or simply an individual. Dr. Moffatt's translation of the above verse makes the position crystal clear: 'The Eternal never has any difficulty about delivering his people by means of many or by means of few'. God can work through a tiny minority as seen so often in the Old Testament. We think of this truth illustrated in the lives of Abraham and Sarah, Tamar, Moses, Gideon, Deborah, Rahab, Ruth, Samuel, Elijah, and so on. The same could be said of many in the New Testament including Elizabeth, Mary, and John the Baptist; of course, there have been countless more in the history of the Church ever since the earliest days.

While millions of people have acclaimed Jesus Christ as Lord, confessing Him to be 'Prophet, Priest, and King', as Saviour of all, the truth of the incarnation is that God intervened in a particular way to use One Who was unique – Jesus of Nazareth – Who came among us as His Son. He was born to a lowly mother and grew up among the poor. His life, death, resurrection and ascension surely give ultimate expression to the way God takes what is small, and often considered weak and unimportant in the world, to do His work. According to Luke, when Jesus ascended, He challenged His disciples to be witnesses (Acts 1:8). At that time, the group of disciples made up a minority, and the task given to them seemed impossible; yet today, we know that Christianity has spread all over the world! We thank the Lord that He often uses the few, as well as the many, to His sovereign glory.

Suggested readings: 1 Samuel 14:1-12 and Hebrews 11:8-12.

OCTOBER 18th

## A PAINFUL EXPERIENCE CAN BE A MINISTRY

One of the marks of the ministry of Jesus of Nazareth is the profound way in which He used parables. His wonderful skill at telling simple stories, using homely subjects and making them shed light on spiritual truths, is unsurpassed. In Luke's gospel chapter 15, we have the Parable of the Prodigal Son, a story which over the centuries, has been used powerfully by the Holy Spirit. We reflect on all the people – thousands upon thousands – who have been brought to faith, or challenged to renewed faith, by the retelling of this story by Christian ministers and teachers!

The parable can be quickly retold: the younger of two sons grew restless and left home, taking his inheritance which he very quickly spent on worldly pleasures far away. Then, after times became difficult, with no money and no friends, and in desperation – looking after pigs, in that culture seen as unclean beasts – he realised he would be better off at home as a mere servant of his father. At this critical stage of his life, the lowest point of his experience, he made the wise decision to return home to his father. His long-suffering father was on the lookout for him and gave him a warm, loving and generous welcome back. The broken relationship is restored and, as such, tells of the everlasting mercy of the heavenly Father who longs for the return of all who have erred and strayed far from Him.

One of the lessons of this parable is that when he reached rock bottom, the prodigal son came to his senses; he returned to his father and received love and forgiveness. A verse in Proverbs links up splendidly with this fascinating story: 'Sometimes it takes a painful experience to make us change our ways' (Proverbs 20:30). This is an ancient truth from centuries ago, but it is still just as relevant in our modern world today. There are so many different ways in which men and women learn life's important lessons; sometimes, the deepest lessons in life can only be fully learned personally, through a challenging – even painful – experience.

In any church there will be people who began attending services, or made a wholly new commitment to Christ, after a difficult experience. Some came for forgiveness after making a significant mistake, or for comfort after a sad bereavement, or for renewed hope after their world had crashed about them, or seeking peace after being rocked by adversity. The truth is that when a person reaches 'rock bottom', that moment may be the very time when they find God granting a new experience of His love and power. The Bible speaks of 'grace to help in time of need', and myriads of people have proved that true in their own experience! It is a reality of life: by God's mercy even a most painful experience can have a positive effect (or 'ministry to the soul') as it is used by the Spirit of the Lord to draw us closer to God.

Suggested readings: Luke 15:11-32 and Hebrews 4:14-16.

OCTOBER 19th

## WE NEED EYES TO SEE – REALLY SEE

Years ago, Pauline Neville wrote a book called *My Father's House* that was very well received by readers. It is a beautiful book telling of her childhood in a Scottish Manse. It pays a fine tribute to her father with whom she had a close and loving relationship. He was a preacher, scholar and a dedicated worker in the service of the Kingdom of God. Yet, he had such a caring way with his two children: he allowed them to ask all sorts of questions about the Christian faith and he patiently gave answers in a way that, perhaps, others might not always do. She testified that he taught her 'the little areas of perfection in life', such as rainwater slowly dropping from a leaf or the glistening of morning frost. He helped her to observe, appreciatively, the natural world around her in terms of really seeing, and giving thanks to God for such beauty.

We thank God for all those men and women who have 'seeing eyes' and, as we walk and talk with them, they open our eyes to see beauty, too. When we think of the ministry of Jesus, we know that He had 'seeing eyes'. He saw truth in ordinary things! He taught truth from a woman making bread, a farmer sowing seed, a shepherd seeking a lost sheep, good and bad fruit trees, an unfinished tower, birds and flowers, and many other things of everyday life. The Blessed Master had 'seeing eyes' and He greatly desired that men and women should also really see. So, one day He said to the disciples who were conducting themselves rather unwisely, 'Do you not yet perceive or understand? Are your hearts hardened? Having eyes do you not see, and having ears do you not hear? And do you not remember?' (Mark 8:17-18).

One of the tragedies of modern life is that sometimes people get caught up in a mad rush of activities, and they have little time 'to stand and stare' or to drink in the beauty of this wonderful planet. So often, sadly, people look, but do not see! Even good Christian people can get so very deeply involved in various activities that they have no time to enjoy 'the little areas of perfection in life'. One verse in the Psalter helps us to see our life in perspective clearly: 'When I look at your heavens, the work of your fingers, the moon and the stars that you have established; what are human beings that you are mindful of them, mortals that you care for them?' (Psalm 8:3-4). Then, this most profound psalm comes to a lovely climax of final affirmation: 'O Lord, our Sovereign, how majestic is your name in all the earth' (Psalm 8:9). The scriptures teach us that sun, moon and stars, rivers and seas, mountains and valleys, trees and flowers all, in their own special way, reflect something of God's resplendent glory. While we are conscious of the needs of those with visual impairment, we can give thanks for the blessing of sight (along with our other senses, too) allowing us to rejoice in the wonders of creation, and to observe the Lord's handiwork.

Suggested readings: Psalm 8:1-9 and Philippians 4:8-13.

OCTOBER 20th

## COMMUNICATION IS VITALLY IMPORTANT

We all know how crucial close communication is in our modern world. This is especially true in the realm of travel, and in particular, with the mode of flight. In our ordinary lives, we are well aware that any aircraft – but especially one with many crew members and passengers – needs good communication to be able to travel safely. This is most apparent in the final approach to landing since, should there be a system failure or sudden radio blackout – leading to a breakdown in communication between the pilot and the air traffic controllers – it can be terribly dangerous. In flight, as in so many other modes of transportation or mass transit, it is absolutely essential that there should be good communication between pilots, navigators, drivers or operators and all who manage the control of the systems. That is a parable of life: good communication is so vitally important in all walks of life.

In 1988, there was a ghastly disaster on an oil rig in the North Sea. There was a terrible explosion and an uncontrollable fire: some escaped, but sadly, many did not. This particular disaster brought distress and indescribable sorrow to numerous homes. Subsequently, it was revealed that there had been a breakdown in communication between two sets of workers and that this led to a serious mistake being made. This fire cost many lives, bringing much grief and heartache, as well as causing a massive financial loss. Communication failure brought about untold harm.

Of course, we know of other communication failures. We all know that some marriages falter because there is a failure to communicate properly: excessive work, a passion for something else, or other avoidable obstructions can cause a 'conversation blackout'. Yet, true communication is obviously more than just conversation or exchange of information. A lack of sharing wreaks havoc in other areas: we think of parents and children not communicating, members of families losing touch, or business partners drifting apart; such issues can even occur in church life. Communication, at its best, involves a depth of relationship and understanding.

All relationships can be damaged by lack of communication, even our relationship with God. We are often reminded in scripture of the need to make time for God in daily life and in the regular routine of worship. In the Epistle to the Romans, the apostle Paul presents a challenge: 'Never let your zeal flag, maintain the spiritual glow, serve the Lord' (Romans 12:11 Moffatt). While we may think of being zealous in the faith in terms of evangelistic activities, it is also true that our zeal for God is revealed in our desire to spend time with God in prayer. Paul says clearly: 'As therefore you received Christ Jesus the Lord, so live in him, rooted and built up in him' (Colossians 2:6). Above all else, communication with God is vitally important!

Suggested readings: Romans 12:9-18 and Colossians 2:1-8.

OCTOBER 21st

## GOD IS FAITHFUL THROUGH ALL LIFE'S CHANGES

Changes, whether expected or unanticipated, certainly come our way! Sometimes, they come with breathtaking swiftness; at other times, they come very slowly, indeed. Swift change can be a wonderful joy, as when an athlete wins, perhaps unexpectedly, an Olympic gold medal. Or, it can be an awful upset, such as when a person is called into the manager's office and made redundant. All kinds of surprises come along, sometimes very pleasant, at other times quite devastating: a substantial legacy is received from a distant relative or a person loses mobility in an accident. Such sudden changes – happy or sad – occur all around us every day.

A woman was interviewed on television about a difficult decision she had made: a nerve-shattering decision. One evening, she and her husband sat in their car and he told her of his involvement in serious crime, leaving her numb with shock. Those few moments of intimate talk were devastating and ruined her happiness! In the following days, she was torn between two conflicting loyalties: her loyalty to her husband and her loyalty as a citizen. His crime was not only a danger to individuals, but also a threat to the nation. She wrestled with this complex problem and, finally, went to the police: it was a devastating decision and the sequel was a long prison sentence for the man she loved. Few people could enter into the terrible trauma of her emotions; her life was dramatically and drastically changed.

The psalmist wrote: 'My heart breaks when I remember the past' (Psalm 42:4 GNB). It is a poignant verse which speaks of recalling the time of being gloriously free to go up to the house of God to worship. The psalm testifies wistfully to glad days of gathering in friendship: 'My heart breaks when I remember the past, when I went with the crowds to the house of God and led them as they walked along, a happy crowd, singing and shouting praise to God' (Psalm 42:4 GNB). The psalmist was looking back to a happy past – not simply looking through rose-tinted spectacles – and speaking of the reality of pleasant experiences before something changed life for the worse. Yet, despite that blow, after that personal word of lament, we read of the psalmist's resolution: 'I will put my hope in God and once again I will praise him, my saviour and my God' (Psalm 42:5 GNB).

Changes will, indeed, come to us in life, some good, some dramatic, some sad, some traumatic, but our sure faith is that God remains. The apostle Paul knew disappointments and much suffering in life, but he gladly testified to the Christians in Rome: 'God's love has been poured into our hearts through the Holy Spirit which has been given to us' (Romans 5:5). Without a doubt, changes for good or ill will come upon us, but God's love in Christ is the constant factor, and so we can be thankful.

Suggested readings: Psalm 42:1-11 and Romans 5:1-5.

OCTOBER 22nd

## GOD USES THE HUMAN VOICE

As we read the Bible, it is important not to underestimate the key ministry of John the Baptist. The fourth gospel tells how a group once came to ask John 'Who are you?' They persisted in firing more questions and, finally, John replied to them quoting a verse from the prophecy of Isaiah: 'I am the voice of one calling in the desert' (John 1:23 NIV). His was a powerful voice, uttering a remarkable challenge to all the people of the land in his day, just as the ancient prophecy had foretold!

The voice is a remarkable instrument which has a wide range and potential: a single voice can have such a resonance. When we think of the human body, we are, in the old language of Psalm 139, 'fearfully and wonderfully made'! We are amazed at the complexity of the eyes, ears and nose, the marvels of the brain, heart and the various organs, not least the capacity to speak! Those who have assessed the contribution that Winston Churchill made to British national life during the Second World War, often speak of the power of his voice. In the depths of the war, when the situation was both difficult and dangerous, his distinctive voice uplifted and emboldened depressed and fearful people. One of his stirring speeches could raise the morale of millions of people giving them new hope and courage.

A study of Holy Scripture reveals that God has always used the human body surrendered to His service: eyes and ears, hands and feet, and the faculties we associate with mind and heart, have all been used in the service of the Kingdom of God. However, most particularly the voice has been used both in speech and song! We think of Miriam, Aaron and Moses, Hannah, Joshua, Samuel, Elijah and then other prophets, including John the Baptist, as well as the apostles, all using their voices for God. The women, who were the first witnesses to the empty tomb, verbally conveyed the message, 'He is risen'! All through the Christian era, other voices, both of men and women, have been dynamic in declaring the truth of Christ.

In the modern age, the power of the spoken voice was demonstrated when Dr. Martin Luther King Jr. delivered his famous speech 'I have a dream . . .' His voice had awesome power and authority: millions have heard recordings of that speech and have found it deeply moving and profoundly significant. Of course, even as we recall special voices in history, we also remember that ordinary voices can be used to comfort or to persuade, to inspire hope or to stimulate faith. In the Book of Proverbs, significantly, there are many passages which mention human speech: 'The lips of the righteous nourish many' (Proverbs 10:21 NIV). One sincere voice can help in so many ways, indeed, offered to God, the voice of a person – whether in speech or in song – can be an effective instrument used to God's glory.

Suggested readings: Proverbs 15:23-33 and John 1:19-29.

OCTOBER 23rd

## CHRISTIANS SHOULD WATCH THEIR PURSUITS

While we may not always acknowledge it, we are sometimes tempted to live in a spirit of covetousness. It happens in a variety of ways: occasionally, we may have an inordinate and unworthy desire to have someone's house, car, garden, or their job or possibly even their partner, besides other things, too. People also crave a position of power and the Bible gives a blatant example: two brothers (James and John) came to Jesus with a special request: 'Grant us to sit, one at your right hand and one at your left, in your glory' (Mark 10:37). There is quite a shock in this story: first, that these two brothers had such barefaced covetousness, and then, also, that they had so neglected the plain teaching of their Master. It seemed that their attitude was far from His gracious spirit and way. The story continues: 'And when the ten heard it, they began to be indignant at James and John' (Mark 10:41). Dr. Moffatt's translation puts it very clearly: 'They burst into anger'. It seemed as if this selfish request had lit the touch-paper to set off a reaction and so, in the end, all the disciples revealed their frailty in their loyalty to Jesus' teaching. It seems that none of them were blameless.

The behaviour of the disciples in this story, could be likened to a large forest fire that has been set by careless picnickers unwisely lighting a small fire out in the countryside. In fact, in the New Testament the image of a fire is used as a stark reminder: 'So the tongue is a little member and boasts of great things. How great a forest is set ablaze by a small fire!' (James 3:5). So these two disciples, James and John, by their brazen selfishness – actually, plain covetousness – sparked off a blaze of anger amongst the disciples. It can only have hurt Jesus.

In his letter to the Romans, the apostle Paul gives some valuable advice about attitudes within the church fellowship: 'Let us then pursue what makes for peace and for mutual upbuilding' (Romans 14:19). That word 'pursue', used by the apostle, suggests the idea of a lion stalking its prey. Its whole body and instinct is geared to making that pursuit successful. Some people ruthlessly pursue their career, their promotion, their ambition or their cause with lion-like enthusiasm, hungry for fame, wealth or power. Indeed, their goal is to achieve what they have always coveted. Paul urges the Christians to be zealous in pursuing the things which make for peace: they should earnestly strive to build up other believers in their faith. As a lion pursues its prey, so the Christian should pursue true peace. A fine passage in the New Testament, Philippians chapter 2, has deep theological insights and perceptions, and ends with a very practical verse: 'Let each of you look not to your own interests, but to the interests of others' (Philippians 2:4). What a revolution might come about if we always took note of our pursuits and, like a lion pursuing prey, focused intently on the needs of others instead of seeking, merely, to please ourselves.

Suggested readings: Mark 10:32-45 and Romans 14:13-19.

## OCTOBER 24th

## GRACE HAS APPEARED

Every year multitudes of people travel to Cornwall for their holidays and return with vivid photos and descriptions of its rugged beauty. The dawn on the Cornish coast is something very special. It is, as if with first light, there is the appearance of luminescent colour, splendour, and majesty; the sheer glory of sunrise and sunset are beyond description. In many ways, we might compare this beauty to the coming of Jesus Christ, the Saviour of the world. He came revealing the grace of God like the sunrise, so the scriptures include this verse: '. . . the kindness and generosity of God our Savior dawned upon the world' (Titus 3:4).

There is no way to adequately describe the significance of the coming of Jesus Christ into this world; Jesus Christ was the Son of God, the Word made flesh, the divine light, the good shepherd, the true fulfiller of ancient prophecy, the ultimate messenger of grace. We read in John's gospel: 'And the Word became flesh and dwelt among us, full of grace and truth; we have beheld his glory, glory as of the only Son from the Father' (John 1:14). The apostle Paul said simply: 'For the grace of God has dawned upon the world with healing for all mankind' (Titus 2:11 NEB). In effect, we might say that there had been a terrible darkness – a great forsaking of the ways of righteousness – but, in due time, God's grace appeared, a new day had indeed dawned, bringing healing (or really, 'salvation') for all humankind.

Jesus' coming was like a glorious dawn revealing God's grace, and we might say that we see God's grace in so many different 'colours'. We see grace when Jesus reached out to heal the sick, or the possessed, when he welcomed people whom others rejected, when He shared a meal with those regarded as 'sinners', and when He exercised patience towards His disciples who were so slow to understand. Supremely, this grace was manifested when, on the cross, He prayed the remarkable prayer: 'Father forgive them; for they know not what they do' (Luke 23:34).

Artists, poets and photographers have sought to capture a glorious sunrise in Cornwall, but they have never been completely successful. In the same way, people have sought to describe the life of Jesus Christ revealing God's grace, but their very best efforts have always been wholly inadequate. So much has been written and spoken about the incarnation, as well as the ministry of Christ, but no mere words can really do justice to such truth, or express the full richness and depth of this gospel. It is a glorious mystery now made known, but still loftier than all our best thoughts! Yet, we pray that something of this dawning grace may be seen in our lives.

Suggested readings: John 1:1-14 and Titus 2:11-15.

OCTOBER 25th

## SPIRITUAL TRAFFIC LIGHTS ARE VERY IMPORTANT

Drivers, and their passengers, know that traffic lights can be irritating! On the very days when we are running short of time to meet a deadline or to get somewhere in a hurry, they all seem to be red! Obviously, that's just a perception, but we all know that's just how it is, and we accept that traffic lights have saved many lives and serve a very useful purpose in public safety. Of course, sometimes people take unnecessary risks: people jump ahead to try to save a few seconds! There are times when it is absolutely necessary for us to stop in order to give other people a chance. That not only applies to road junctions but, indeed, to life in general. This seems especially true when it comes to our communication with one another.

In the New Testament, there is a very challenging verse on this theme: 'You must understand this, my beloved; let every one be quick to listen, slow to speak, slow to anger; for your anger does not produce God's righteousness' (James 1:19). Someone has comically pointed out that God gave us two ears but just one mouth; that is a good reminder since it is possible to speak too much and too often, and occasionally for too long, even carelessly. There is sound advice in the Book of Proverbs: 'A gossip reveals secrets, therefore do not associate with a babbler' (Proverbs 20:19). In the rendering of another Bible version, it has been translated: 'A gossip betrays a confidence; so avoid a man who talks too much' (NIV).

Reflecting on the interaction of Moses and the Israelites, the psalmist wrote: 'They made him so bitter that he spoke without stopping to think' (Psalm 106:33 GNB). Even Moses, the servant of the Lord, who was a significant prophet and leader of God's people, spoke without first thinking. We might say that he was speaking hastily, almost like driving straight through the traffic lights! There is a time to speak boldly and a time to speak cautiously; yet, there is also a time when we need to stop and 'weigh our words' before uttering a single syllable.

John Bunyan, in *Pilgrim's Progress*, has a character named Mr. Talkative, someone with whom we are surely familiar. Most of us can remember times when we have 'driven recklessly' straight through such red traffic lights, as it were, unwisely 'speaking without thinking'. Our conscience reminds us of unnecessary words, careless or hurtful comments, superficial judgements, or hasty remarks and we, no doubt, all have our regrets. In the Book of Proverbs, there is a sober truth stated: 'When words are many, transgression is not lacking, but the prudent are restrained in speech' (Proverbs 10:19). We all know how easily speaking too soon, or too much, can be harmful. Traffic lights are important in our travels through life, and especially so, in a spiritual sense, in the course of our conversation!

Suggested readings: Proverbs 20:6-19 and James 1:19-25.

OCTOBER 26th

## GOD'S LOYALTY LASTS FOR EVER

The scripture says, 'A friend loves at all times' (Proverbs 17:17), and for all such wonderful friendships we thank God. We are grateful to God for those people who are wholly consistent and who have proved themselves 'friends for all seasons'. These are people in whom we can place confidence, whether our road is easy or difficult. Yet, the plain fact of life is that loyalty can be strained to breaking point. Under certain difficult situations, the most trusted people can sadly prove to be disloyal. Today, we rejoice in our affirmation that God's loyalty and faithfulness endure forever. We can stake our confidence on the scriptural truth that God is never disloyal and His love never turns us away.

In Psalm 117, we read these lovely words: 'Praise the Eternal, all ye nations, laud him, all ye races; for his love to us is vast, his loyalty will ever last' (Psalm 117:1-2 Moffatt). While we rejoice in this affirmation, we know that even God has been accused of disloyalty! We think of the very sensitive prophet Jeremiah, who suffered because of his faithful ministry, and cried out in despair: 'O Lord, thou hast deceived me and I was deceived; thou art stronger than I, and thou hast prevailed' (Jeremiah 20:7). These are quite shocking words for a prophet of the Lord to utter, but we face the fact that lots of God's people in dire sadness, illness or other serious difficulty have felt that God has been disloyal to them. Even Jesus, when on the cross, experienced the sense of being abandoned for our sake as He cried out to His Father: 'My God, my God, why hast thou forsaken me?' (Matthew 27:46). No scholar or disciple of Christ has ever truly plumbed the depths of those words, but as we read the gospel stories, we realise that after the dereliction of the cross, there was the victory of resurrection. On Easter Day, the crucified One, Jesus of Nazareth, was gloriously raised from the dead, and God's ultimate loyalty and love were fully revealed.

God's loyalty is immovable, far more than even the solid mountains. As the psalmist wrote: 'His love to us is vast, his loyalty will ever last'. Similar testimonies are also found: 'Thy faithfulness reacheth unto the clouds' (Psalms 36:5 AV), 'His mercies never come to an end; they are new every morning; great is thy faithfulness' (Lamentations 3:22-23). While we know well our potential – as human beings – for betrayal and disloyalty, we may give thanks that the steadfast love of God knows no bounds. Whatever we have done, or failed to do, God is faithful and true.

Suggested readings: Isaiah 25:1-9 and Psalm 36:5-12.

OCTOBER 27th

## OUR GOD DOES UNDERTAKE

When we think of William and Catherine Booth, the founders of the Salvation Army, we remember their great faith, lofty ambitions, tremendous drive and energy, clear vision and warm hearts. However, in spite of all their good work, we know that the Booths experienced difficulties which tested their faith. William Booth knew the loss of Catherine in 1890 and then, in 1903, their beloved daughter Emma was killed in a railway accident: it was a terrible tragedy because she, too, was much involved in the Salvationist work in America. In a letter written at the time to his son, Bramwell, General Booth expressed his faith: 'God will undertake for us'. William Booth's faith was sorely tested; yet, through all the tears, he realised that he must go on trusting in God. Words of the psalmist come to mind: 'Trust in him at all times, O people; pour out your heart before him; God is a refuge for us' (Psalm 62:8).

In the Old Testament, there are many stories about those who continued to place their trust in God in the midst of difficulty. David, as a young boy about to face Goliath, expressed his faith; 'The Lord who delivered me from the paw of the lion and from the paw of the bear, will deliver me from the hand of this Philistine' (1 Samuel 17:37). He believed, on the basis of past experience, that he could rely upon God, even though the odds seemed rather stacked against him surviving the battle! In the Book of Isaiah, we read how Hezekiah was facing a major crisis, and he prayed: 'O Lord, I am oppressed; undertake for me' (Isaiah 38:14 AV). We might ponder for a few moments all the people down the centuries oppressed by guilt, sorrow, illness, or tragedy, who have simply prayed, 'Lord . . . undertake for me'.

In our own day, many people can testify from the heart that, in their hour of need, God did undertake for them and they were wonderfully helped! This important fact helps us understand the significance of Paul's words: 'When I am weak, then I am strong' (2 Corinthians 12:10). Put plainly, when we are at the end of our own resources, we are at the beginning of God's! God does, indeed, undertake for us: 'So we can say with confidence, "The Lord is my helper; I will not be afraid. What can anyone do to me?"' (Hebrews 13:6). That is the assurance of our faith as we seek daily to be followers of the Lord Jesus. We may face an uncertain future, but always we may know that our God will undertake for us. Even in those moments when we, like the apostle Paul, may feel weak, we know that God will never fail us.

Suggested readings: 1 Samuel 17:31-37 and Isaiah 38:1-16.

OCTOBER 28th

## IN OUR DESPAIR, THERE IS YET HOPE

Sometimes, television news bulletins picture scenes which are highly controversial: they seem to be an intrusion into private grief and suffering. When the Pan American aircraft flying to the USA in 1988 exploded in mid-air over Scotland (as the result of a terrorist bomb), there was a total loss of life. The television cameras focused on the place where friends and relatives were told the tragic news that Flight PA103 had crashed: in front of the cameras, one woman, hearing this terrible news, dropped to the floor and gave vent to her grief. It was a terrible scene to witness and may have evoked deep feelings of pain as other grief was remembered by those watching the broadcast; the Lockerbie media coverage caused much dismay and criticism.

The feeling of loss is graphically depicted in some Bible stories. In the Old Testament, there is a terrible scene of despair when Job feels that his prayer has not been answered, his friends have let him down, his inner resources have disappeared and even God seems to be against him. Job cries despondently: 'If my troubles and griefs were weighed on scales, they would weigh more than the sands of the sea, so my wild words should not surprise you' (Job 6:1-3 GNB). Reading of Job's trouble, many people can identify with this sense of complete despair – as deep as the ocean itself. Yet, as scripture teaches, with God's help, it is possible come through such anguish to find a new perspective and to discover hope afresh.

One of the psalms cherished down the centuries by countless people contains this marvellous verse: 'Why are you cast down, O my soul, and why are you disquieted within me? Hope in God; for I shall again praise him, my help and my God' (Psalm 42:5). Admittedly, at times, it is easier to speak of hope than to feel hopeful. However, there are moments when, in an encounter or a dawning awareness, we are reminded that despair does not need to have the final say. One evening there was a remarkable sunset in Bedford: the evening sky was dotted with lots of dark clouds, but each one was lined with red and gold. The darkness of the clouds added significance to the glorious edging and it seemed that the poet's words were revealed: 'Every cloud has a silver lining'. It was a reminder that while it sometimes seems that the clouds of despair are all-pervasive, the Bible testifies that – in the darkest moments of life – there is still hope to be known in God Who is never far away.

The darkest day in history was when the Saviour was rejected and unjustly treated, crucified upon a cross. However, those heavy, dark clouds of seeming defeat and hopelessness were edged with gold at the dawn of Easter: God acted to bring about victory over death and so we rejoice in that triumph and the hope it affords in His Son, our Lord Jesus Christ. Amid the despair, hope gloriously won through.

Suggested readings: Psalm 107:23-32 and 2 Corinthians 1:8-11.

OCTOBER 29th

## SECRET DISCIPLESHIP SHOULD BE CHALLENGED

We might ponder how many people really believed in Jesus Christ during His earthly ministry. Actually, that is an exceedingly difficult question to answer with any degree of certainty! There are verses which give vital clues that there was a wider acceptance than might have first appeared to be the case. John's gospel indicates the situation: 'Nevertheless, many even of the authorities believed in him. But because of the Pharisees they did not confess it, for fear that they would be put out of the synagogue: for they loved human glory more than the glory that comes from God' (John 12:42-43). We could name this particular brand of belief as 'faith with reservations'; they believed, but fear prevented an open confession of faith. The impact of those words 'but for fear . . .' is certainly relevant in modern society, too.

President Roosevelt once said: 'There is nothing to fear but fear itself'. That is a fine and quotable saying, but fear can be a terrible reality. We can easily think of five reasons why people are sometimes frightened to confess their faith in Jesus Christ: some fear a partner's reaction, some fear the scorn of family, friends or colleagues at work, some fear their employer's response, some fear that they will not be able to 'keep it up', and some fear what it may cost them. The Bible gives us a fascinating insight into the character of Nicodemus. He was a ruler of the Jews and John's gospel records: 'This man came to Jesus by night and said to him, "Rabbi, we know that you are a teacher"' (John 3:2). He came by night (under the cover of darkness) and, undoubtedly, it was because of fear: he did not want others to observe his visit to Jesus. Of course, it was better to come by night rather than not at all!

Today, we may recall many stories of those who have had to overcome fear in order to take a stand for Christ. There is the true story of a married man who had a strong desire to confess Christ openly in a service of Believers' Baptism (which is the Christian rite of baptizing confessing believers by total immersion at a public worship service). He feared his wife's reaction and it was a perfectly genuine concern on his part. Even so, he publicly confessed his faith, was duly baptized and, as a result, his wife stubbornly refused to speak to him. She showed her anger for a number of days, but he remained resolute and true to Christ.

So much in life involves the conquest of fear: the warrior, the mountaineer, the explorer, the astronaut, the diver, the pioneer, the reformer and the prophet all need courage to overcome natural fear. We think of the noble army of martyrs who confessed Christ in the full knowledge that their confession could result in rejection, suffering, and death. Surely, timid, or even secret, discipleship needs to be challenged! While we may face fear in our discipleship, we know God will give us courage.

Suggested readings: John 3:1-16 and John 12:42-50.

OCTOBER 30th

## ALL DO FOOLISH THINGS

Many people all over the world love the story of King David as it is found in the Holy Scriptures: the humble shepherd who became a famous king! David was not a perfect man and perhaps that explains why he's so popular: he was very human and he knew it. Consider this confession: 'But now, O Lord, I pray thee, take away the iniquity of thy servant; for I have done very foolishly' (2 Samuel 24:10). These and other verses, reveal how David was so often quite conscious of his own weakness and sinfulness, as well as his occasional foolishness, too! We can all identify with him.

In Bedford there is a large roundabout which takes motorists on a slight detour: it is amazing how many drivers have been observed breaking the rules to make a dangerous turning right rather than go all round the roundabout. In trying to save a few seconds, they recklessly risk their own lives and put others in serious danger, too. Actually, although most of us would condemn such foolish behaviour, if we are honest, we know that we are guilty of some folly in our own lives, too! We can remember foolish plans or decisions, foolish talk, and sometimes, foolish friendships. Naivety or downright folly is an age-old shortcoming and people of every generation and culture have – to some extent – shared in it. So it is not surprising that in the Psalter there are a number of honest confessions, and one stands out in particular: 'O God, thou knowest my folly; the wrongs I have done are not hidden from thee' (Psalm 69:5). It is undeniable that, sometimes, we can hide our foolishness from our own family and friends, but we can never conceal it from God. However, God is patient and so we may draw near with our sins, our guilt, our foolishness and our utter unworthiness, knowing that God is always willing to show mercy and to grant forgiveness.

In the Old Testament, we have the honest confession of Saul: 'I have done wrong . . . I have played the fool and have erred exceedingly' (1 Samuel 26:21). Those words have a very authentic ring about them but – to his shame – Saul's foolishness continued to the end. In our world, we know that there are lots of people deeply saddened by the fact that their poor behaviour has estranged them from family and friends, but they are comforted by God's acceptance of them. God's forgiveness is not simply a fine theological doctrine: it is indeed a renewing and life-giving reality which can be surely known and experienced daily in our walk with the Lord. Of course, it takes God's power to overcome our foolishness; we cannot do it in our own strength. The wisest thing for a person to do is to always turn to the Lord.

Suggested readings: 1 Samuel 26:17-25 and Psalm 69:1-6.

OCTOBER 31st

## THE CHRISTIAN NEEDS A DAILY WALK WITH GOD

In our modern world, it is quite amazing how many people consult their horoscope. The media caters for this desire, and so we have all manner of newspapers, magazines, and other media sources giving their particular predictions and, strangely, even in our sophisticated society and quite rational context, still, people consult the stars to determine their choices day by day. Many are anxious to know about the future and think that such supposed means of information will help them find good fortune. Concern for the future, of course, is not new. Near the end of the Book of Daniel, the prophet asks this question: 'O my Lord, what shall be the end of these things?' (Daniel 12:8). The reply to this question comes fully in the last verse of that same chapter: 'Go your way, and rest . . .' (Daniel 12:13 AV). God calls men and women to have faith and to express it by their daily walk in fellowship with Him. Believers may, quite naturally, want to 'know the end from the beginning', but God desires all who confess faith, simply to place trust in His goodness and loving care.

We recall the dramatic call to Abram: 'The Lord had said to Abram, "Leave your country, your people and your father's household and go to the land I will show you"' (Genesis 12:1 NIV). Then, came the heart-moving words: 'So Abram left, as the Lord had told him' (Genesis 12:4). It was obedience: God called, and Abraham and his wife, Sarah (as they became known) both went forward, confident that God would work out His purposes. This kind of unquestioning obedience day by day is revealed in the story of Gladys Aylward. She felt God had called her to work in China, but people with responsibility did not agree with her. On a human level, there was so much to say against her working in China, but – duly convicted she had to do so – she went anyway. History now simply records that, at a time of crisis, she was wonderfully used by God to help the Chinese people. Her story is quite remarkable: she felt God's call and obeyed, daily walking by her faith in God.

So, on this particular day, when the Church recalls the 'Saints and Martyrs of the Reformation' era, we remember that they certainly didn't 'know the end from the beginning', and had to walk by faith. Luke records how Jesus Himself was informed that He was in a dangerous situation, and then replied: 'Nevertheless, I must walk today and tomorrow and the day following' (Luke 13:33 AV). Jesus was committed to the daily walk with God His Father above, content to leave the outcome in the Father's hands. The apostle Paul put it this way: 'For we walk by faith, not by sight' (2 Corinthians 5:7). That is our Christian pilgrimage: God does not reveal all His plans in advance, but calls people to serve, daily trusting in the Lord's faithfulness.

Suggested readings: Daniel 12:4-8 and Hebrews 11:8-16.

# NOVEMBER

Blessed assurance, Jesus is mine!
O what a foretaste of glory divine!
Heir of salvation, purchase of God;
Born of His Spirit, washed in His blood.

Refrain:
*This is my story, this is my song,*
*Praising my Saviour all the day long;*
*This is my story, this is my song,*
*Praising my Saviour all the day long.*

Perfect submission, perfect delight,
Visions of rapture burst on my sight;
Angels descending, bring from above
Echoes of mercy, whispers of love.

Perfect submission, all is at rest,
I in my Saviour am happy and blest;
Watching and waiting, looking above,
Filled with His goodness, lost in His love.

Fanny Crosby (1820-1915)

Lord, make us, we beseech thee, like-minded with all saints whether on earth or in heaven; that we may worship thee as they worship, trust as they trust, rejoice in thee as they rejoice, love thee as they love; for the sake of our Saviour Jesus Christ.

Christina Rossetti (1830-1894)

# NOVEMBER 1st

## GOD'S SPIRIT CAN BRING ORDER OUT OF CHAOS

One of the mysteries of the Spirit of God is proclaimed in the opening verses of the Bible: 'In the beginning God created the heavens and the earth. The earth was without form and void, and darkness was upon the face of the deep; and the Spirit of God was moving over the face of the waters' (Genesis 1:1-2). At the beginning, by God's mighty act, order was brought out of chaos. From Genesis to Revelation, the Holy Scriptures remind us of the gracious work of God's Spirit. The Spirit of God has redeemed situations which often seemed terribly muddled, erratic or chaotic, and we affirm that God's Spirit still does so, bringing order and renewal.

One such occasion was when Saul of Tarsus was converted on the road to Damascus; it was a miraculous triumph of the Spirit of God. As with some other extraordinary instances in the Biblical narratives, it took a little time for those observing to understand how God was at work. Knowing that Saul had persecuted Christians, when Ananias was instructed by the Lord to visit the new convert, he protested: 'Lord I have heard from many about this man, how much evil he has done to thy saints at Jerusalem' (Acts 9:13). Even after Saul (who became known as Paul) began to proclaim the gospel, many people found it hard to believe that this could be true. In fact, when they heard Paul proclaiming Jesus, they said: 'Is not this the man who made havoc in Jerusalem among those who invoked His name? And has he not come here for the purpose of bringing them bound before the chief priests?' (Acts 9:21). They were astounded by the surprising work of the Spirit.

Before his conversion, Saul of Tarsus, had wrought havoc among the followers of Jesus, but now he was engaged in Christian service. The Spirit of God had, as it were, brought order out of chaos and Paul became the strident apostle and effective servant of God in proclaiming the gospel. Through the Spirit's work, the persecutor became a preacher, the destroyer become a builder, all brought about by a radical change of heart and mind. Paul became an advocate for building up the Church: 'You are, I know, eager for gifts of the Spirit; then aspire above all to excel in those which build up the church' (1 Corinthians 14:12 NEB). God's Spirit within him, shaped and transformed him, enabling him to use his gifts for Christ.

Today is known in the Christian Church as 'All Saints' Day': all those devoted people who have served God faithfully knew, as we now know, that the invisible power of the Holy Spirit is beyond our comprehension in bringing order out of seeming chaos. In biblical thought, the saints are not just historical figures, but men and women of all sorts and conditions, in both the past and the present, by whose lives we see God's Spirit at work in the world. We thank God for the Spirit of truth and grace, and surely offer ourselves again today to the Spirit's renewing power.

Suggested readings: Acts 9:10-22 and 1 Corinthians 12:1-13.

NOVEMBER 2nd

## THERE IS A DIVINE COMPANION

When Dr. Alexander Whyte was the minister at Free St. George's, Edinburgh, he exercised a remarkable pastoral ministry. Hundreds of people flocked to hear his powerful expository preaching, but he was truly valued for his remarkable gifts as a good pastor. By letter, by visitation, by personal help, he showed himself to be a loving pastor and gracious friend. So, when people were plunged into a personal crisis through accident, trouble, illness or loss, he could be relied upon to comfort and to encourage. He no doubt believed, and took to heart, the sound advice found in the Book of Proverbs: 'A word in season how good it is' (Proverbs 15:23) and also 'The tongue of the wise brings healing' (Proverbs 12:18).

One terrible day, the message came through to Dr. Whyte that his son, Robert, had been tragically killed. This particular son was just twenty-three years of age and possessed remarkable gifts of intellect and personality. The news brought Dr. Whyte and his wife inexpressible sorrow, with a deep grief. Yet, his congregation noticed that he faced this bereavement with courage and fortitude. For years he had been profoundly conscious of the nearness of God, and the Lord's presence was a living reality for him. Therefore, following the tragedy, when he returned to the pulpit, he preached on the words: 'Lo, I am with you alway' (Matthew 28:20 AV). This was the faith he believed, proclaimed and lived out in true witness. His sense of God's presence daily was a powerful witness.

In John's Gospel we are told that the disciples were in the grip of fear following the dreadful events of the crucifixion and burial of Jesus, and then something happened: 'On the evening of that day, the first day of the week, the doors being shut where the disciples were, for fear of the Jews, Jesus came and stood among them and said to them "Peace be with you"' (John 20:19). The words have a haunting beauty as they remind us that the risen Lord came to His disciples bringing peace and, as Dr. Whyte testified in the midst of his own grief, the Lord still comes as the One Who stays by our side in every situation we face.

Of course, we never know what a day will bring. In a sense, each year is like three hundred and sixty-five unopened envelopes. With each new day opening before us, we don't know what it may bring in terms of joy or sorrow. Indeed, the ancient proverb is correct: 'Do not boast about tomorrow, for you do not know what a day may bring forth' (Proverbs 27:1). It's true that there are days of gain and loss, of sickness and health, of joy and sorrow, as well as ones of hope and despair; yet, Christ has promised to be with us day by day. That is, indeed, a 'blessed assurance'.

Suggested readings: Matthew 28:16-20 and John 20:18-22.

## NOVEMBER 3rd

## SOME PROBLEMS ARE SOLVED BY SPIRITUAL MEANS

A young man was having a whole series of difficulties in his professional life; put plainly, a few of his colleagues belonged, as it were, to the 'awkward squad'. He was anxious to find a fresh position in a new area, so he confided in a trusted friend and the reply he received was significant: 'We change our jobs and change our problems, but we never escape the necessity of facing problems'. Wise words, for surely, we all face difficulties. Some problems are a little bit like toothache nagging away, taking their toll day after day. For example, the issues of a marriage under severe strain may not be resolved immediately, but eventually, over time a resolution may be found.

In many different contexts, the solution to a quandary which seemed impossible to solve, suddenly becomes clear; almost like 'a flash of lightning', the answer is found. There is the story of a scholar who faced a complex mathematical problem which seemed quite insoluble; he pondered this particular conundrum for many months. One day, as he waited for a bus, the solution suddenly came to him! This story reminds us that the mind has different levels of consciousness and, sometimes, the subconscious appears to be working overtime as we go about our daily lives. Such is our human make up, that this may even occur during a good night's sleep. What a blessing it is to discover the solution to a thorny problem!

Often when wrestling with difficult issues, we need to find a place to be quiet in order to gain perspective. In Psalm 73, a person of faith is troubled and claims: 'I tried to think this problem through but it was too difficult for me until I went into your Temple' (Psalm 73:16-17 GNB). It was being in the house of the Lord that brought calmness of spirit, and a fresh perspective on life. Since that confession, made centuries ago, many people have found that through quiet reflection in a special place, or gathering for worship in God's house, they have discovered new angles on, or answers to, life's difficulties. We should not be surprised. After all, Jesus taught his followers: 'The Holy Spirit, whom the Father will send in my name, he will teach you all things, and bring to your remembrance all that I have said to you' (John 14:26).

Surely this is true in all of life – though especially in times of trial – that the Spirit opens our minds to new insight and gives clarity, no matter how seemingly intractable the problems that we may face. Countless Christians can testify that, in an hour of great perplexity, a passage of scripture or a single verse 'bubbled up from the deep levels of the mind', and proved to be significant in helping them to face a difficult problem! This is surely the work of God's Spirit. As we place our trust in God, we know divine aid to help us overcome all obstacles, and to help us find solutions to our problems.

Suggested readings: Psalm 73:1-17 and John 14:23-26.

## NOVEMBER 4th

## JESUS STILL GIVES THE GRACIOUS INVITATION

One precious word in the Bible which has, as it were, been polished smooth for us by constant use down many generations of people, is this verse from Matthew's gospel: 'Come unto me, all ye that labour and are heavy laden, and I will give you rest. Take my yoke upon you, and learn of me, for I am meek and lowly in heart: and ye shall find rest unto your souls' (Matthew 11:28-29). This is a unique passage in Matthew's record which reminds us of the gracious invitation of Jesus found at the heart of so many of the other gospel stories. In essence, these stories picture Jesus with open arms of welcome and blessing to young and old alike. They unite to say Jesus looked at the people, knew their needs and, without reservation, drew them to Himself.

A verse in John's gospel confirms Jesus' knowledge of the people who came to Him: 'He knew all people and needed no one to testify about anyone; for he himself knew what was in everyone' (John 2:25). So, as Jesus looked at a crowd of listeners, He discerned their needs: He knew their fear and weariness, their sorrows and burdens, their anxieties and perplexities, and especially the heavy loads they had to carry. For many of that era, one burden it seems was a standard of religious practice which demanded more than they could fulfill. The multitude of rules and regulations made everyday piety seem like a massive burden to shoulder. Jesus perceived their burden and had harsh words for the religious leaders: 'They tie up heavy burdens, hard to bear, and lay them on the shoulders of others; but they themselves are unwilling to lift a finger to move them' (Matthew 23:4).

We can picture Jesus looking with compassion on all the people and saying: 'Come unto me . . . and I will give you rest'. Whatever the burden that people faced, whether it was linked to religious practice or merely a sense of failure, trouble or rejection in life, the gospel stories record that Jesus opened his arms to extend a welcome. His offer of 'rest' signified an invitation to receive peace as a gift from God, a peace which was deeper and richer than anything they had ever known.

Over the centuries, many have responded to this invitation to come to Christ: those of every race and culture, of every background and age. Jesus always greets us with open arms. This is pictured in a lovely way at the end of Luke's gospel when the Lord was preparing to send the apostles out with His gracious invitation, and He blessed them: 'Then he led them out as far as Bethany and lifting up hands he blessed them' (Luke 24:50). As we ponder these pictures of the Lord's gracious invitation, we are reminded that the Lord still sees the needs of people and invites them to know the peace which only He can give. He is a welcoming, gracious Saviour.

Suggested readings: Matthew 11:25-30 and Luke 24:44-53.

## NOVEMBER 5th

## FAITH CAN BE SORELY TESTED

Sometimes, it may seem that God has let us down, or failed us, or that God's faithfulness is open to question. In Psalm 73, we have the words of a person who was simply appalled by the prosperity of the wicked. The psalmist seems to feel sorry for himself because, in spite of all his spiritual endeavours, he had suffered and life had been difficult for him. He explains his earlier disquiet on this subject: 'Yet had I let myself talk in this fashion, I should have betrayed the family of God. So I set myself to think this out but I found it too hard for me' (Psalm 73:15-16). His complaining about God's ways could have been discouraging or disheartening to others!

God does not always appear to act fairly. When a minister made a pastoral visit to a family on the fringes of a local church after they had suffered a tragic bereavement, he faced stark questions about God. One of the family looked straight into his face with the challenge: 'But where is God?' We have to be honest and say that, in similar circumstances, firm believers have posed that same question. There are pains so deep, injustices so vile, circumstances so evil, that one may begin to doubt the power, love and faithfulness of God. Many believers suppress their feelings, though others more openly confess their doubts or even find it helpful to admit that their faith is tested.

Jeremiah was a faithful prophet but his message was not popular with the people: great hostility was aroused by parts of his prophetic utterances. In the narrative we read: 'Then Pashur beat Jeremiah the prophet, and put him in the stocks that were in the Upper Benjamin Gate of the house of the Lord' (Jeremiah 20:2). Later these startling and shocking words were uttered by the prophet: 'O Lord, thou hast deceived me and I was deceived' (Jeremiah 20:7). One spiritual teacher used to say that the first rule of prayer is honesty: Jeremiah was certainly honest in his prayers. Sometimes, life simply doesn't seem fair, and we cry to the Lord.

When the psalmist felt overwhelmed with difficulty, he claimed that he found solace in worship: 'So I set myself to think this out but I found it too hard for me, until I went into God's sacred courts; there I saw clearly what their end would be' (Psalm 73:16-17 NEB). Despite his qualms over the ways of God, in the sanctuary, this worshipper found perspective. Countless people can echo that testimony. Only God knows how many come to the sanctuary tossed by perplexity and doubt, but in the context of worship, they find the 'peace of God which passes all understanding' (Philippians 4:7). In the presence of God, we can be our truest selves and plead from the heart to the Eternal One, Who knows us through and through. While our faith may be tested at times, we can be sure that God will, indeed, always heed our cry.

Suggested readings: Psalm 73:1-17 and Jeremiah 20:7-9.

337

NOVEMBER 6th

## THERE ARE DIVINE SURPRISES

Sometimes, when a question is asked it is loaded with prejudice! In John's gospel we read how Philip told Nathaniel about the ministry of Jesus: 'We have found him of whom Moses, in the law and also the prophets wrote, Jesus of Nazareth' (John 1:45). In his reply, Nathaniel revealed his perspective: 'Nathaniel said to him, "Can anything good come out of Nazareth?"' (John 1:46). The answer to that is in the affirmative: through the wonderful providence of God, out of that ordinary place, came Jesus Christ, the Saviour of the world. God often uses a humble village or town to produce a revolutionary or challenging figure. When Susannah Wesley gave birth to her fifteenth child in the rectory at Epworth, Lincolnshire, no one would have anticipated that the child, named John, would be used to begin a mighty revival of faith. However, that child of Samuel and Susannah was greatly used by the Holy Spirit.

That extraordinary event was a divine surprise, as has happened many times in the history of the faithful. Over and over, God has used a humble mother living in an ordinary place to bring forth a person, who despite her or his lowly birth, became someone of utmost significance. On another level, but in the same vein, when some people are faced with an unpromising situation, they query, in effect, 'Can anything good come out of this?' So often the answer is undoubtedly in the affirmative! God can use a disappointment, a sorrow, a difficult situation, even an illness or accident, to bring forth something good, positive and beneficial. Out of humble Nazareth came Jesus Christ, and out of many inauspicious situations, there has come blessing in the form of confidence and courage, new beginnings and fresh hope. God is neither limited nor constrained by our 'poor reach of mind', to quote the well-known hymn writer. God can bring good things out of the most unusual circumstances or ordinary situations, and the gospel records reveal this very clearly!

When the Son of God was mocked and scourged, nailed to a cross and crucified, it destroyed the confidence of the disciples. They were terribly distressed: the very foundations of the world seemed to be trembling, as if the question was being posed, 'Can any good come out of this?' Yet, God worked out His sovereign purposes in spite of such injustice. In his first epistle, Peter offers these remarkable words: 'For Christ also died for sins once for all, the righteous for the unrighteous, that he might bring us to God' (1 Peter 3:18). Who would have ever thought that the place called Calvary (the place of unspeakable cruelty and shame) would become the very place where people are reconciled to God? Using the most unlikely people and the most unpromising places, God brings forth choice blessings, and so we stand in awe of God's amazing, indeed, surprising grace.

Suggested readings: Judges 6:1-16 and John 1:45-51.

NOVEMBER 7th

## THE VICTORY OVER EVIL IS ASSURED

The Holy Scriptures leave us in no doubt that the spiritual life is a battle. In a sense, right at the heart of things there would appear to be a constant struggle between good and evil. So the directors within the film industry have produced scores of films featuring 'goodies' and 'baddies', so to speak. Such is real life, to a large degree! We all know that there is within the human heart an everlasting struggle, just as the apostle Paul put it: 'When I want to do right, evil lies close at hand' (Romans 7:21). This inner struggle gives a clue to the incidence of bigger conflicts, particularly those between various communities and nations.

In the modern era, Adolf Hitler rose to power with a death-dealing philosophy towards other races and groups, which led directly to the appalling extermination of millions of Jews, as well as others. A wicked, powerful man had to be confronted: history records that it was a bitter struggle involving so many, and costing so much sacrifice, but it was a conflict which had to be won. Of course, the battle between right and wrong has been fought in many different places and in all generations. In his letter to the Ephesians, the apostle Paul gives theological content to the thought that life is a battle: 'For we are not contending against flesh and blood, but against the principalities, against the powers, against the world rulers of this present darkness, against the spiritual hosts of wickedness in the heavenly places' (Ephesians 6:12). Sometimes, the battle is very fierce and, frankly, it looks as if evil will win the day. However, prophets and seers, psalmists and apostles, always truly believed that the victory over evil is assured, and that God will ultimately triumph. Paul knew from personal experience how strong forces of evil assail the Christian, so he exhorted the believers: 'Put on the whole armour of God' (Ephesians 6:10). In the broad sweep of scripture, there is a confidence that the last word is with God: in the end, the victory over evil will be complete.

In our pilgrimage of faith, we can look back and see God's marvellous work, and so look forward in hope. We may ponder what God did at Easter: when Jesus Christ was crucified, it looked as if the power of evil had triumphed. The sight of Him on the cross seemed to indicate defeat. Yet, then came Easter Day: the empty tomb, the risen Saviour, and the glorious victory! We can be sure the Lord will not allow His purposes to be ultimately thwarted, since God always has the final word with us. We rejoice that God is surely sovereign over all.

Suggested readings: Ephesians 6:10-20 and Revelation 5:9-14.

## .JRNING BACK IS A BIG TEMPTATION

Human nature reveals a variety of faults and it is fascinating to consider the way we react to them in others! Some people's failings annoy or irritate us, other faults amuse us, and yet still others shake our confidence. One such human frailty – which is highlighted in Psalm 78 – is the fault of all too easily giving up or turning back: 'The children of Ephraim, being armed, and carrying bows, turned back in the day of battle' (Psalm 78:9 AV). It appears that – for no good reason – the people faltered, they failed and they turned back, and so, in modern jargon, they let the side down.

This seems to a widespread foible. For instance, in one of our English towns, there was a very large estate which presented a challenge to Christians to do pioneer work. A young minister courageously accepted the call to bring a Christian presence into this needy area; there was no church building, so he set about the task of enlisting help. He duly went around the locality contacting carpenters, bricklayers, electricians, plumbers and labourers. There was real enthusiasm as the foundations of the building were laid and the walls began to rise. A new church was springing up before the people's eyes! The believers in the area rejoiced in this success and, it seemed evident that, even as Luke recorded of the early church: 'The hand of the Lord was with them' (Acts 11:21). Then, a curious thing began to happen: people began to make excuses and some failed to turn up for assignments, the number of helpers dwindled, and the work began to slow down! A small band of workers bravely and stubbornly toiled on, but many others faltered and lost interest in the work. Like the people of God of old, they turned back 'in the day of battle', so to speak. Sadly, this attitude may be seen in other areas of life, too. People sometimes turn back on promises made, withdraw from life's responsibilities, and fail to keep commitments solemnly pledged. It takes courage to maintain a steady and consistent witness.

In the life of faith, people are sometimes tempted to turn back. When faced with difficulties, it is so easy, simply to forget our pledge to the Lord. Yet, we think today of the words of Jesus: 'No one who puts a hand to the plough and looks back is fit for the kingdom of God' (Luke 9:62). On this day in the Church calendar, we remember the 'Saints and Martyrs' of England who showed a great courage and a sure fortitude which was truly praiseworthy; they refused to turn back even in the scorching heat of battle! Such people in the history of our land have, by their steadfastness and endurance, truly honoured God and lifted up on high the name of Jesus Christ our Saviour. We thank God that so many have set an example of faithful endurance, and have trusted in God to guide and strengthen them on the way.

Suggested readings: Psalm 73:1-10 and Hebrews 10:19-25.

# NOVEMBER 9th

## MINDS CAN BE POISONED AGAINST THE FAITH

Sometimes much attention is given to the study of the missionary travels of the apostle Paul without appreciating the essential message he conveyed! It is good to look at the actual events that took place in Paul's missionary work and to study the reaction to Paul's message. When Paul and Barnabas came to Iconium, they adopted a well-tried method, going first to the synagogue to give the initial proclamation of the gospel: 'There they spoke so effectively that a great number of certain Jews and Gentiles believed' (Acts 14:1 NIV). One reality of Christian mission is that so often, after a moment of triumph and advance, there comes a determined opposition. So it was with Paul and Barnabas that, after the first flush of success, a small group of people in the synagogue stirred up trouble: 'But the unbelieving Jews stirred up the Gentiles and poisoned their minds against the brethren' (Acts 14:2). With this kind of assault, the apostles faced a stiff opposition to their work: the minds of many had, indeed, been 'poisoned', as it were.

One of the most terrible weapons of war has been poisonous gas: the story of the First World War includes an infamous chapter where this hideous weapon was used. Thousands of men suffered, and many continued to do so years after the war ended. The pain and misery inflicted are beyond all human estimation. On another plane, in the spiritual realm, one of the deadliest weapons is to seek to poison people's minds against the Christian faith and against those who proclaim it. There are some people in our day who appear to take delight in poisoning others against the faith: some people who – from a variety of motives – seek use every opportunity to speak against Christians and the faith. Sadly, there are stories of young people discovering the Christian faith, wanting to come to church, and facing their parents' disapproval. Sometimes, this has triggered off a process of trying to change the minds of the newly converted: there can be a determined effort to unsettle them.

There was one occasion, when a school teacher spoke in class very critically against Jews which, of course, was an abuse of his position of authority. A young student stood up and objected, saying, 'My best friend is a Jew: Jesus Christ'. Apparently this brought a stunned silence to the class! Prejudice is blind: prejudice against Jew, Gentile, or even the Saviour Himself, is like a 'spiritual poison.' It is a sad reality that people can be turned against the Christian faith by words and attitudes, and sadly, also, by the bad example of some professing Christians. We thank God today for all those who stand up against religious – and other – prejudice of this kind; and we also recall the fortitude of steadfast believers who defend their faith gladly and effectively, by living it out day by day with boldness and courage.

Suggested readings: Acts 14:1-7 and Titus 1:9-16.

NOVEMBER 10th

## WE HAVE TO LIVE WITH OUR MISTAKES

One of the Ten Commandments in the Old Testament is especially important: 'Honour your father and your mother, that your days may be long in the land which the Lord your God gives you' (Exodus 20:12). This particular command has been obeyed by multitudes of people and it has brought great blessing. The apostle Paul takes up this theme in his epistle to the Ephesians: 'Children, obey your parents in the Lord, for this is right' (Ephesians 6:1). Christians have pondered this command, and the implication of it, for relationships. Questions arise: for parents, there might be hesitations about the wisdom of certain activities of their children, and equally, some children do not agree with the ethical or moral choices of their parents! When parents and children see things differently, there is often tension in the home.

Many sons and daughters have married contrary to their parents' wishes, and yet, the marriage has been a wonderful partnership. However, that is not often the case, as in the story of Doreen who became infatuated with a man that her parents disliked intensely. They talked with her, reasoned with her, and explained things to her, yet, she was completely blind to all his evident faults and she married him in haste. The subsequent years sadly brought heartbreak and unhappiness. However, Doreen had to live with her regrettable, poor decision, and later she lamented: 'If only I had listened to my parents'.

Scripture reminds us of people who made mistakes in life: Lot's wife, David, Jonah, Peter, Ananias and Sapphira, as well as others, like Demas. In our world, there are numerous people who have to live with the consequences of their poor choices which might include: wrong investment of money, foolish relationships, missed opportunities to study or to change direction, and broken promises. Guilt can be a heavy burden as Doreen discovered: she carried the burden of her mistake for many years, but she also came to know for herself the cry of the psalmist: 'Have mercy on me, O God, according to thy steadfast love; according to thy abundant mercy blot out my transgressions. Wash me thoroughly from my iniquity, and cleanse me from my sin' (Psalm 51:1-2). While Doreen sorely felt the pain of knowing that certain things in her life could never be unscrambled, she also came to realise that by God's grace, she was able to go on in life trusting in God's mercy to forgive and to renew.

As we all recognise, mistakes are a reality for us each. Yet, thankfully, God's forgiveness towards us is a sure reality, too. These words from the Old Testament have been a great comfort: 'The Lord our God is merciful and forgiving, even though we have rebelled against him' (Daniel 9:9 NIV). We give thanks for God's mercy and love. While we cannot erase our mistakes, God can give us a knew way forward.

Suggested readings: Psalm 51:1-12 and Ephesians 6:1-10.

NOVEMBER 11th

## JESUS CHRIST IS LIFE'S STRONG ANCHOR

The annual Festival of Remembrance held at the Royal Albert Hall in London, each November is an important event in the British calendar. Millions of people watch it on television and there are always representatives from the Royal Family to support this event in person. In November 1988, one of the musical items presented by the Royal Navy was most significant. The Royal Navy military band stood in the shape of an anchor and played music: a group of people forming, as it were, an anchor, which seemed to be a remarkable portrayal of life as we know it!

There are many situations when our family, or close friends or even our church fellowship, can be like an 'anchor' for us. How often when a believer is overtaken by some serious setback or tiresome difficulty, the Christian fellowship seems to form itself into an 'anchor', as it were, exercising a steadying influence! Very often this kindly support has occurred at extremely difficult times, and brought a sense of security to those who seemed quite vulnerable. Of course, those who provide support in this way, are being used by God and, by their actions, they point us to Christ, Who is our hope and stay. As the writer of the Epistle to the Hebrews affirmed: 'We have this as a sure and steadfast anchor of the soul, a hope that enters into the inner shrine, behind the curtain, where Jesus has gone as a forerunner on our behalf, having become a high priest for ever' (Hebrews 6:19-20). This verse has brought assurance to many, and is significant to the Boys' Brigade movement, since the badge on the uniform consists of an anchor which has these words from the above text inscribed upon it: 'Sure & Steadfast'.

We can never calculate the good which has been achieved through the work of the Boys' Brigade in all parts of the world. There are countless people, including ones in various professions, as well as many in other jobs, who can testify that their B.B. Company provided support and related the message of an 'anchor' to them in the testing days of adolescence. Furthermore, through its ministry, a large number of the members growing up in the ranks, found Christian faith and placed their trust in Jesus Christ as their personal Saviour.

The reference in the sixth chapter of Hebrews is to Christian hope as an anchor but, in a real sense, in that image, we can see an allusion to Christ Himself, in Whom is our hope. So many have found that, in the storms of life, Jesus Christ has been the 'anchor' for the soul. Most of us can point to dear friends or loved ones who, in Christ's name, have been a steadying force for us, in such a way, too. Christians can truthfully testify that the Saviour of the world is their best, most trusted, friend: the sure and steadfast 'anchor', in their lives. Generations of believers have placed their trust in Christ and known God's marvellous assurance and blessing.

Suggested readings: Psalm 42:1-11 and Hebrews 6:19-20.

## NOVEMBER 12th

## REFUSAL TO LISTEN CAN BE DANGEROUS

Lots of people who live in Britain dislike the month of November! It brings with it strong reminders that summer is ended and the chilly, stormy, winter months are ahead: it usually brings numerous cold and grey days, and sometimes there is fog. Sadly, the coming of foggy mornings and evenings increases the number of bad road accidents. On the motorways, one accident can easily involve a dozen or more vehicles, as others racing along crash into the rear of those that have stopped. Again and again, police and motoring organisations have appealed to drivers to take extra care in foggy conditions, but some just will not heed the warnings. Occasionally, drivers speed along with reckless abandon and, as a consequence, there are injuries and even deaths, which perhaps, might otherwise have been avoided.

When we ponder the Old Testament, we see that so often God's people behaved foolishly, refusing to listen to God's commands. In the Psalter, we read these poignant words: 'O that my people would listen to me, that Israel would walk in my ways' (Psalm 81:13). So many of the problems which arose for the people of God were the direct result of their refusal to listen to God. One of the great affirmations of faith is found in the Book of Nehemiah: it tells of God's power, mercy, love and goodness. In chapter nine, right at the centre of this testimony of faith, there is a true confession: 'But they, our forefathers, became arrogant and stiff-necked, and did not obey your commands. They refused to listen and failed to remember the miracles you performed among them (Nehemiah 9:16-17 NIV). This story has been repeated over and over in subsequent centuries, and serves as a reminder that it is a wanton folly to refuse to listen. to God's commands. Of course, people of all ages and times have been guilty of refusing to listen carefully to God.

The topic of listening often comes up in family life. When the first child comes along, a couple rejoice and their joy is shared by so many friends and family members. Yet, while the joy of parenthood can be truly wonderful and uplifting, there can be real pain, too. Parents can recall moments when their son or daughter showed a stubborn resistance, and determinedly refused to listen. We may all identify with the father in the parable Jesus told of the 'prodigal son', when the son was determined to go his own way and simply not listen. Likewise, we may admit that such obduracy is an attitude we sometimes know in ourselves, as well as in others. Yet, the consequences of refusing to listen can be avoided if we heed the broad sweep of the teaching of the Bible. When we listen carefully to the scriptures, and heed the advice and warnings, we discover that in God's Word, there is guidance and help for every situation in life.

Suggested readings: Nehemiah 9:7-19 and Psalm 81:10-14.

NOVEMBER 13th

## THERE ARE PLENTIFUL RESOURCES IN GOD

Riverside walks in Bedford give much pleasure to locals, and visitors from elsewhere, alike. The walk along the river embankment is so pleasant: the trees, the gardens, the lawns, the swans, geese and ducks – as well as the craft on the water – all combine to provide plenty to observe with great interest. Just by the Suspension Bridge, which crosses the river at a strategic point, there is a magnificent horse-chestnut tree. Its roots are at a plentiful water source and they are embedded deep down where there is a good supply of moisture and so – to the delight of the children passing by – it bears much fruit in the form of conkers galore each autumn!

This splendid tree encapsulates the truth, portrayed in various Scripture passages, which speak of the plentiful resources found in knowing God. We recall one verse which puts this truth very simply: 'My flesh and my heart may fail, but God is the strength of my heart and my portion for ever' (Psalm 73:26). Similarly, in the Book of Jeremiah, there is a word picture which is exceedingly beautiful as it describes people who have discovered good spiritual resources: 'Blessed are those who trust in the Lord, whose trust is the Lord. They shall be like a tree planted by water, that sends out its roots by the stream. It shall not fear when heat comes, and its leaves shall stay green; in the year of drought it is not anxious, and it does not cease to bear fruit' (Jeremiah 17:7-8). Likewise, the psalmist shares Jeremiah's vision of the people who draw their strength from God: 'They are like trees planted by streams of water, which yields their fruit in its season, and their leaves do not wither' (Psalm 1:3). Such people of faith have deep and wonderful resources in God. The apostle Paul puts all this splendidly in a letter to his friends: 'My God will supply every need of yours according to his riches in glory in Christ Jesus' (Philippians 4:19). Many have proved that these witnesses – prophet, psalmist and apostle – were right in testifying that, in God, there are adequate resources for all to be able to grow and to flourish in the spiritual life.

Charles Simeon is remembered as a faithful minister who was the vicar of Holy Trinity, Cambridge, for fifty-four years. He was a staunch evangelical and had an immense influence with undergraduates. However, his ministry was not without opposition. Yet, Simeon's spiritual roots were firmly placed in the resources of the God in Whom he trusted. So, in season and out of season, he preached the Christian gospel with authority and power, and his ministry bore much fruit. He could say with the psalmist: 'God is the strength of my heart'. That is, indeed, surely the grateful confession of all those who have come to a truly personal experience of the Lord. We, too, can daily draw strength and nourishment from the living God.

Suggested readings: Psalm 1:1-6 and Jeremiah 17:5-8.

## NOVEMBER 14th

## JESUS CHRIST BRINGS RENEWED CONFIDENCE

Loss of confidence can be a shattering experience! A young doctor who was very highly motivated to help people once made a big mistake. It all happened at a weekend when he faced enormous pressure at work: long hours and lack of sleep meant less than complete efficiency, and a serious error of judgement occurred. Others who knew this physician had every confidence in him as one who was very sincere and conscientious. However, the mistake haunted the doctor for a long time, and finding the confidence to practise as a physician took him a great deal of time.

There are lots of situations where confidence can be shaken: a woman discovers that her husband has lied about a relationship, or vice versa, a father learns that a trusted child has been mixing with bad company, an employer finds out that an employee has been stealing material from the workplace. Of course, sometimes, people can, and do, lose confidence in God! Believers might point to a time when – in their view – prayer has not been answered: a blessing has not been granted, a struggle has not been won, or things have turned out rather differently than expected. The Bible is very honest about people who have been badly shaken and lost their confidence in God. When the enemy besieged, then invaded and finally ransacked Jerusalem, and many of God's people were transported to Babylon, it seemed like the end of the world. One can imagine the questions which arose: 'Where is God?', 'Is God faithful?', 'Does God have power as we have been taught?'. Many of the people found their faith in the Lord badly damaged or nearly wrecked when Jerusalem fell. Still today, there are lots of situations in life, some of which come swiftly and unexpectedly, where believers find their confidence takes a serious knock.

In this context, one New Testament verse refers to confidence in the Lord: 'Through him you have confidence in God, who raised him from the dead and gave him glory, so that your faith and hope are in God' (1 Peter 1:21). The life, ministry, death and resurrection of Jesus Christ mean many different things, but Peter points out that they meant a new confidence in God. Here the wording could not be more specific: 'Through him you have confidence in God'. When people witnessed the crucifixion of Jesus, it must have shaken their confidence, and the disciples must have asked, 'Where is God?' On the third day, God manifested His power and Jesus was raised from the dead; so began a new era of confidence! The Acts of the Apostles records the boldness and courage of those first Christians. The words of the psalmist of old can be filled with an even deeper, richer meaning now: 'I will call to mind the deeds of the Lord' (Psalm 77:11). We recall that our once crucified, now risen, Lord Jesus Christ ever present with us, gives every believer much confidence!

Suggested readings: Psalm 77:5-15 and 1 Peter 1:13-23.

NOVEMBER 15th

## GOD NEEDS CHRISTIAN AUTHORS

A book can be a wonderful present for both children and adults! Lots of people enjoy receiving the gift of a good book, and it is amazing what a large selection of books is available. Books can prove to be very influential in a person's life. Some of God's most celebrated servants were first influenced by the reading of a fine book which had a profound effect. In Psalm 102, there is an interesting verse on this very theme: 'Write down for the coming generation what the Lord has done, so that people not yet born will praise him' (Psalm 102:18 GNB). We thank God for all Christian authors: the men and women who spend time and thought writing books for our edification and for the upbuilding of the Church. Countless people all over the world recall the impact of Archbishop William Temple as a very sincere and devout clergyman, who worked so tirelessly for the Christian cause. He preached, lectured, conducted missions, presided over meetings, and led great congregations in worship. However, we also thank God that he took the time to write his seminal work, *Readings in St John*, a volume which even today still brings much insight and blessing.

We thank the Lord for those used of God to write the books of the New Testament, but also for the long line of authors who have written good Christian books to the glory of God. Books such as Mother Julian's *Revelations of Divine Love*, John Bunyan's *Pilgrim's Progress*, Martin Luther's *Commentary on Romans*, or John Wesley's *Journal* have been a blessing to generations of believers. The wonderful truth is that, long after the tongue of a faithful gospel expositor is silent, that person's witness can still be heard in the words of a book! In the gospels, we hear the Master commending humble, personal prayer: 'But when you pray, go into your room and shut the door and pray to your Father who is in secret; and your Father who sees in secret will reward you' (Matthew 6:6). There are people who spend many quiet hours, often alone, prayerfully writing a book for the Christian public: they research, meditate, write, redraft, and write again. While this is often an unseen labour, the heavenly Father knows. God hears solitary prayers, and in the same way God knows secluded authors, and surely will, in His due time, reward them evidently.

At the outset of his much-loved gospel, Luke explains the reason for his writing: 'It seemed good to me also, having followed all things closely for some time past, to write an orderly account for you, most excellent Theophilus, that you may know the truth' (Luke 1:3). Luke's gospel has been treasured through the Christian centuries and the Holy Spirit has gloriously used it to inform, challenge and inspire believers beyond all measure. We thank God for the Bible and for other Christian literature that continues to teach and inspire us!

Suggested readings: Psalm 102:12-22 and Luke 1:1-4.

## NOVEMBER 16th

## OUR GOD GIVES THE FINISHING TOUCH

Every year thousands of people visit the Cotswolds as tourists, many from abroad! This area has plenty of attractions: ancient churches, stately homes, renowned parks, beautiful gardens, quaint old-world towns, glorious countryside, thriving markets and lovely orchards. Lots of people enjoy touring the area because of the fascinating opportunity to explore the various antique shops: there is certainly an abundance of them! There are numerous tourists who love looking for antique items, some looking for furniture such as tables, chairs, writing desks, cabinets and bookcases. How often these pieces of furniture have a special quality, which show that they have received, what we might call, 'the finishing touch'! This touch makes all the difference in the world. So we observe that skilled craftsmen and women, as well as writers, poets, painters, sculptors, composers, gardeners and decorators often share a passion for the 'finishing touch'.

During his amazing ministry, the apostle Paul both spoke and wrote some magnificent truths about God. Every Sunday, a multitude of preachers and teachers take Paul's words, as well as the gospels too, as a basis for giving sermons and addresses, to interpret Christian faith! We might ponder one of the loveliest thoughts Paul ever expressed: 'And I am sure that he who began a good work in you will bring it to completion at the day of Jesus Christ' (Philippians 1:6). One biblical interpreter, Dr. Handley Moule, splendidly rendered the last part of that verse: '. . . will evermore put his finishing touches to it'. We are thankful to God who is so gracious and creative in the art of adding the 'finishing touch'! Dr. Andrew Bonar exercised a remarkable ministry: he was 'first and last' a preacher of the gospel of the Lord Jesus Christ. He was a good man, known by his friends and flock alike, as one who possessed rich qualities of devotion and dedication. His diary is a wonderful book to read. In it, he makes honest reference to what he perceived to be his slow growth in grace: he rebukes himself for lack of prayer and for various 'spiritual weaknesses', as he always yearned for the finishing touch! He wanted to be wholly dedicated to the Lord and to the Kingdom of God, and ever sought the Spirit's sure work in his life.

Sometimes, we point an accusing finger at ourselves because, as we look within, we may despair. Yet, as the popular quote says: 'Be patient – God hasn't finished with me yet!' This is a humorous quip, but there is a lot of truth in those words. The Bible reminds us that we are God's handiwork. God fashions us like a master craftsman with great skill. God continues to work patiently within us to make something beautiful! The Lord is, as it were, a 'great finisher', and this is the ground of our hope and confidence, even as we seek to remain open to God's Spirit.

Suggested readings: Psalm 19:1-14 and Philippians 1:1-11.

NOVEMBER 17th

## THERE ARE TIMES WHEN HELPERS NEED HELP

It is interesting to note the slogans which are painted on vans and lorries: sometimes, they can stimulate spiritual thoughts. For example, a van used to be driven around East Anglia with three words painted on its side: HELP! HELP! HELP! It caused many smiles, and was obviously some kind of service van used to assist others. However, one evening, it raised a bigger smile than usual because it was broken down itself: it was not giving help, but actually needed it! The words displayed on its side, HELP! HELP! HELP!, took on a new meaning, and that highlights a reality of life.

There are thousands upon thousands of people in the helping professions including medical, social, emergency, rescue and other workers, as well as ministers. While they are dedicated to offering help, they themselves occasionally need assistance, too. These people answer numerous calls for help and willingly give of their skill and care, but they are also vulnerable to weariness and fatigue. Nurses and carers can become exhausted, doctors and therapists can face burn-out, emergency and other support workers can succumb to stress and, equally, ministers too, can become, in the words of the apostle Paul, 'weary in well-doing' (Galatians 6:9). There are times when professional helpers need help themselves.

One of the outstanding chapters in the Old Testament is Isaiah 40: it speaks of the power and the gentleness of God. It also speaks, as it were, of God's never-failing care: 'Have you not known? Have you not heard? The Lord is the everlasting God, the Creator of the ends of the earth. He does not faint or grow weary, his understanding is unsearchable' (Isaiah 40:28). The prophet is confident of God's power and faithfulness, and offers some beautiful words of comfort and promise: 'He gives power to the faint, and strengthens the powerless' (Isaiah 40:29).

When Charles Haddon Spurgeon exercised his remarkable ministry in London, he lived a very full life as preacher, lecturer, author, philanthropist and more besides! At one time, when thousands were depending on his ministry, illness struck: it was so obvious that the great pressures of his ministry had eroded his strength, and that experience clearly illustrated the vulnerability of God's servants. Spurgeon was a human vessel whom God used, but he always remained subject to weariness and exhaustion. We are thankful that our God – as the psalmist put it – never slumbers nor sleeps, never tires nor grows weary: our assurance is that God's love is inexhaustible. It reminds us of a prayer of another of God's servants in the past: 'Lord, I'm at the end of my strength – I now receive yours'. That is surely often a prayer for us, too! All we need to do is to call upon the Lord in faith.

Suggested readings: Isaiah 40:25-31 and Psalm 86:11-17.

NOVEMBER 18th

## INGRATITUDE CAN BE A ROOT OF REBELLION

One of the slightly more acceptable forms of pride is that which parents have in their children's achievements. There are numerous occasions in family life which call for celebration: passing exams, gaining a qualification, receiving a university degree, passing the driving test, achieving a promotion, being selected for a team and winning a medal, and so forth! Parents can 'live again' to a certain extent in the accomplishments of their children. Most people think this form of pride in the success of one's daughters or sons is legitimate, but obviously, it must not be overdone! Every day, families celebrate for various reasons, but sadly, there are many parents who have little cause for celebration. There are sons and daughters who get into the wrong company and develop attitudes hostile to their parents. In the Bible, we read how David's son, Absalom, organised a conspiracy against his own father: 'And the conspiracy grew strong, and the people with Absalom kept increasing' (2 Samuel 15:12). David's heart-rending cry at Absalom's death, echoes down the centuries: 'O my son Absalom my son, my son, my son Absalom! Would I had died instead of you, O Absalom, my son, my son!' (2 Samuel 18:33). We sense here, a parent's anguish.

Children can bring so much happiness, but they can bring terrible pain, too. One person in despair said to a friend, 'If I had known, I would never have had any children!' If we are among those who rejoice in a happy family life, and we have children who are kind and thoughtful, we ought not only to give thanks to God, but also to pray for those parents who are suffering unimaginable pain at the disappointment caused by their children. Even better, we might go out of our way to befriend and support them!

As we consider family relationships, we think, too, of our own relationship with our heavenly Father. Just as we might recognise how a child's rebellion is often due to ingratitude – his or her blindness in not seeing the generosity and love of human parents – so also it may be true on a spiritual level. Our rebellion against the heavenly Father is often due to a failure to accept, with thanksgiving, what God has done for us. There is a passage in Isaiah which is worthy of some careful thought: 'Hear, O heavens, and listen, O earth; for the Lord has spoken: I reared children and brought them up, but they have rebelled against me' (Isaiah 1:2). People do rebel against God; the books of the prophets, and so many biblical narratives, remind us that people reject God and turn away from His grace. The basis of that rebellion is often a profound selfishness and ingratitude. So it is important that we ponder day by day the multitude of blessings bestowed upon us, and give thanks to God.

Suggested readings: 2 Samuel 15:1-12 and Isaiah 1:1-4.

NOVEMBER 19th

## PASTORS AND LEADERS NEED THE BREATH OF LIFE

The apostle Paul loved to preach the gospel and rejoiced when people responded to the message of faith. However, the New Testament makes it abundantly clear that Paul was a pastor, as well as an evangelist, and his pastoral heart longed that converts should mature and make progress in the Christian life. Sometimes, he feared that they might find the way too hard and turn back from Christ. One of the passages which illustrates Paul's concern is in 1 Thessalonians chapter three. It is a good example of the apostle's pastoral care and oversight. He wrote to those who were threatened, voicing his concern 'that somehow the tempter had tempted you and that our labour would be in vain' (1 Thessalonians 3:5). He sent Timothy to visit and encourage them. Timothy soon realised that there was faith, love and loyalty in the fellowship, and so, he returned to Paul with the good news. The apostle was so happy to receive the news that, writing to the Thessalonians, he spoke warmly of their faith: 'It is the breath of life to us that you stand firm in the Lord' (1 Thessalonians 3:8 NEB).

What gives a pastor joy? There are a number of things: an increase membership in the congregation, an enrichment of the fellowship, members maturing and using their gifts, sufficient financial resources in the church, the joy of receiving or nurturing new converts, as well as the satisfaction of seeing believers 'go on with the Lord', in spite of the cost of the Christian way. It is gratifying to witness the growth of faith, love and loyalty, and it is, indeed, the 'breath of life' that pastors and other Christian workers need. It certainly brings them renewed confidence and boldness. There are special delights that thrill a pastor, and one of them is to see people obeying the command which Peter urged upon believers: 'But grow in the grace and knowledge of our Lord and Saviour Jesus Christ' (2 Peter 3:18). Obviously, Peter and Paul had the same desire for all the believers to whom they were ministering.

The joy of pastors and leaders may be likened to the joy of parents watching their children grow and mature. Christian parents rejoice over many things, among them, their children developing wise relationships, or gaining meaningful employment. However, one of the deepest joys is when their children 'stand firm' in the faith and reveal, in their own character, Christian disciplines and virtues. Using this parenting image, John, in his third epistle, speaks pastorally to his congregation: 'No greater joy can I have than this, to hear that my children follow the truth' (3 John 1:4). Rather like the joy of observing lovely scenery and breathing the fresh air, for the pastor or Christian leader, to see people progress into a rich faith and deep maturity in Christ is, as it were, a spiritual breath of 'fresh air'. Surely, that 'fresh air' of divine blessing invigorates and enthuses not only Christian leaders, but us all.

Suggested readings: 1 Thessalonians 3:1-13 and 3 John 1:1-4.

NOVEMBER 20th

## PEOPLE MAKE MANY EXCUSES

It was a lovely summer's day and the minister had been out in the parish seeking to encourage people to attend public worship on Sundays. He called at one house and was told: 'I'm sorry that I don't come to church, but there are too many people'. In the normal course of ministry, members of the clergy might hear many different excuses to give reasons for non-attendance: 'too wet', 'too hot', 'too cold', 'too busy', 'too tired', 'too far'. Yet, this was a wholly new excuse: 'too many'!

In Luke 14, Jesus of Nazareth told the story of a person who arranged a great supper and sent his servants out with the invitations: 'And they all with one consent began to make excuses' (Luke 14:18 AV). One had purchased a piece of land, one had bought some oxen and the other had got married, and they all made excuses. We all know that, so often, the excuses given are not real reasons! Some people are experts at making excuses. In fact, they can think of a good excuse in a split second. Some are so skilful at it, that we can easily be deceived, but not God; for God knows our hearts, and so sees the reality of the situation. In Paul's letter to the Galatians we get a stark warning: 'Do not be deceived; God is not mocked, for you reap whatever you sow' (Galatians 6:7). There are certain poor decisions, covered at the time by 'excuses', which are destined by their nature, to bring forth a bitter harvest in due course. Poor excuses are not just lame, but can also prove to be quite destructive.

In the Holy Scriptures, we read of a number of people who made excuses. Moses was called to leadership and he said to the Lord: 'I am slow of speech and of a slow tongue' (Exodus 4:10 AV). God called Gideon to save Israel from the hand of the Midianites and his reply was 'My family is poor in Manasseh, and I am the least in my father's house' (Judges 6:15 AV). Centuries later, God called Jeremiah to exercise the ministry of a prophet, and the sensitive youth replied: 'I cannot speak, for I am a child' (Jeremiah 1:6 AV). In all these cases, there was more than a grain of truth in the excuses, yet, under God's sovereignty, they reluctantly took on the task assigned.

There are some excuses which are spiritually perilous: the excuse not to accept full personal responsibility for failings, not to accept Christ's offer of life abundant in personal renewal, or not to be active in the service of the Kingdom of God. One could make a rather long list! The apostle Paul had something to say about those who, perhaps, would have offered many excuses for rejecting God: 'Ever since the creation of the world his invisible nature, namely, his eternal power and deity, has been clearly perceived in the things that have been made. So they are without excuse' (Romans 1:20). We are urged by scripture to be fully open to the Lord, and so find our true selves, in God alone. Surely, there is no need to look for an excuse!

Suggested readings: Exodus 4:10-18 and Luke 14:16-24.

NOVEMBER 21st

## THERE ARE EVEN BENEFITS FROM AFFLICTION

Sometimes, a verse of scripture 'hits you between the eyes', as it were; it is so startling and powerful that it's like a blow striking us! We might think of one particular verse: 'Before I was afflicted I went astray; but now I keep thy word' (Psalm 119:67). Then, a few verses later, we read an even more remarkable verse: 'It is good for me that I was afflicted that I might learn thy statues' (Psalm 119:71). The psalmist had no doubt about the benefits of affliction! In the face of such stark verses, an important question is posed: 'Was the psalmist actually right and can people really learn valuable lessons in a time of affliction or 'humbling' (as it is put in a modern rendering)? The answer is a clear affirmative. In looking back, plenty of people of faith will readily acknowledge that this was their experience.

In Suffolk, there was a very ambitious man who worked seven days a week; he was a workaholic! He had no time for the Church, nor for the Christian faith. He literally 'lived to work', until he was laid low with a serious illness and was forced to lie on his back and think. One day, a Christian worker visited him and the man simply said: 'For the first time in my life I've been looking up'. He meant that in a 'double sense': physically, because of his bodily position, and yet, metaphorically, it applied – as he realised – to the spiritual realm, too. We can put alongside this quite telling story another verse from the Bible, with reference to King Manasseh of Judah: 'In his suffering he became humble, turned to the Lord his God, and begged for help' (2 Chronicles 33:12 GNB).

If we were to ask why people begin coming to church there is a wide variety of reasons. Times of distress, difficulty, bereavement or personal loss are the moments when a person's heart is sometimes softened towards spiritual things. Charles H. Spurgeon, the minister of the Metropolitan Tabernacle, London, used to say that lots of ships come into port on the north wind! He testified that, during his ministry, he knew plenty of people who had found their 'spiritual harbour' when, as it were, the bleak north wind was blowing in their experience. One of the deep mysteries of life is that there are definitely 'benefits' from affliction. The mystery deepens when, arguably, at the very time that people might, perhaps, have more reason to turn against God, instead, they turn to the Lord. In the Old Testament, on one occasion when the people were facing trouble, this prayer was offered: 'For we are powerless against this great multitude that is coming against us. We do not know what to do, but our eyes are upon thee' (2 Chronicles 20:12). For those who face a very difficult or testing situation – and who really do not know what to do – the Lord's counsel is: 'Look up'. God is ready to help, if only we will call upon Him.

Suggested readings: Psalm 119:65-72 and James 1:1-12.

## NOVEMBER 22nd

## JESUS CHRIST LOVES EVEN JUST THE ONE

Mark's gospel is cherished by many people. It has a style which is quite compelling: it is short, compact, vivid and lifelike, and has a simple freshness which is immensely attractive. Lots of people have come to their first understanding of Jesus Christ as they have read this gospel. The words 'straightway' and 'immediately' are frequently used, so this lovely gospel has been likened to a series of 'snapshots', and one of the loveliest of these, is the story of Bartimaeus, found in Mark 10:46-52. Bartimaeus was a person who had no sight at all until he met Jesus. In reading the story, we discover that Bartimaeus spent his days begging by the roadside. One day, when he heard that Jesus of Nazareth was passing by, he realised this was his chance find help: 'He began to cry out and say, "Jesus, Son of David, have mercy on me!"'(Mark 10:47). At this point, the crowd became very impatient with Bartimaeus and told him to be quiet, but this did not deter him, as Mark recorded it: 'But he cried out all the more, "Son of David, have mercy on me!"' (Mark 10:48). Then we read the marvellous words: 'And Jesus stood still' (Mark 10:49 AV). Jesus Christ stopped as He went on His way, and He had time for just one needy person, a beautiful scene, indeed.

In pondering these few words, 'And Jesus stood still', we catch a glimpse of the glory of the gospel of the Saviour's redeeming love. Jesus heard the man's cry above the din and confusion of the crowd. His ears were attuned to hear the plea of one person. The good news is for families, for communities, for nations and for the whole world, and surely, it is for individuals, too. Throughout history, at times, the individual has been discounted, and or at least it seems that a person becomes little more than a number among many others. Yet, we are reminded in this story, and in other places in scripture, that the Lord is attentive to the needs of 'even just one' who calls upon Him.

The New Testament abounds with stories of Jesus relating to individuals, and for some, we know their names: Matthew, Nicodemus, Zacchaeus, Jairus, Mary Magdalene. Yet, there were many whose names were not recorded including the Samaritan woman, the woman accused of adultery, the one, though not welcomed by the others guests, anointed Jesus in Simon's house, and others whom Jesus healed. God loves the world, but loves each of us as individuals, too. The apostle Paul, giving voice to his personal faith and commitment said of Christ, poignantly: 'The Son of God, who loved me and gave himself for me' (Galatians 2:20). As the apostle Paul knew that he was loved by God, so we, too, may each know that divine love for ourselves, even as individuals before the Lord.

Suggested readings: Mark 10:46-52 and John 3:1-16.

NOVEMBER 23rd

## TRUE LIVING INVOLVES MAKING RIGHT JUDGEMENTS

A young mother was in a newspaper shop selecting wrapping paper for her son's birthday present. A queue began to form, and people were patiently waiting for their turn to be served. One elderly woman piped up saying: 'Don't worry about the wrapping paper, love – he won't even notice it'! Actually, it was a good ruse to pressure the young mother to make up her mind, but it wasn't really quite so true! Many have had the experience of taking great pleasure in selecting a lovely toy for their child's present, then wrapping it up in really colourful paper, anticipating their child's delight; only then to watch with loving eyes as the present is unwrapped, opened and put to one side, as the child plays with the colourful paper! It causes amazement, and perhaps a little disappointment, but also serves as a parable of life. How easily we can be taken up with lesser things and miss the more important ones!

In every walk of life there are people who emphasise the trimmings and neglect the things at the centre. There are brides and bridegrooms who pay endless attention to the details of their wedding, but give scant heed to the promises they are going to make to each other. There are students who give much energy to the social life of their university, and carelessly neglect their studies. There are countless people who make detailed arrangements for the approach of Christmas but, when it arrives, miss out on what really matters. In a similar way, there are churches which stress the importance of maintaining buildings and fund-raising, and yet, almost forget that the primary task is to proclaim Christ! How often the plain truth is that people 'play with the wrapping paper', as it were, failing to be alert, observant and diligent to the primary, deeper, matters of life – a failing we've probably all known.

It is easy to get priorities mixed up. William Temple, the beloved Archbishop of Canterbury (1942 to 1944), often used to say that life is like a shop window where the price tickets have been rearranged, so that cheap things are given an expensive label and precious things are given an inexpensive price tag. Jesus Christ knew all about this human tendency and, in Matthew chapter 23, we read of His challenge to the religious leaders of His day. This particular chapter is very significant, but does not make easy reading. Bluntly the Lord speaks of how even avowedly religious people can get their priorities wrong! In speaking of their scruples about 'keeping the religious law', Jesus commented sharply: 'But you have neglected the more important matters of the law – justice, mercy and faithfulness' (Matthew 23:23 NIV). Before the hectic rush of the Christmas season gets into full swing next month, it is important that we focus on what really matters, a truth which is, of course, applicable throughout the whole year, if we would live wisely and well!

Suggested readings: Matthew 23:1-24 and 1 Corinthians 15:1-3.

NOVEMBER 24th

## WORDS HAVE A MIGHTY POWER, BUT ACTIONS SPEAK LOUDER

Words can be razor sharp and can pierce like a sword, a truth found in Proverbs: 'Rash words are like sword thrusts' (Proverbs 12:18). In addition to all the physical suffering that Jesus experienced on the cross, in Matthew chapter 27, special attention is paid to the verbal abuse hurled at the Saviour: 'If you are the Son of God, come down from the cross' (v40), 'He saved others; he cannot save himself' (v42), 'Let him come down now from the cross, and we will believe in him' (v42), 'He trusts in God; let God deliver him now' (v43). These hurtful words must have cut very deeply into the Saviour's heart. Yet, His love for humankind was so real and enduring that, indeed, as many have commented, 'it was not the nails which held Him there, but rather His love'. The apostle Paul put it this way: 'The saying is sure and worthy of full acceptance, that Christ Jesus came into the world to save sinners' (1 Timothy 1:15). The meaning of the cross remains a deep mystery. However, we know that on the cross, Jesus accomplished His saving work, by revealing God's love in self-giving.

Jesus Christ once taught: 'No one has greater love than this, to lay down one's life for one's friends' (John 15:13). Truly, the sacrifice of self for the sake of love is the greatest gift one can give. History abounds with illustrations of men and women who gave themselves for others: we can think of courageous firefighters who have entered a blazing building to rescue people but, in so doing, have literally laid down their lives. Similarly, brave lifeboat crews have launched out in terrible conditions to rescue people from danger at sea. Some of these courageous rescuers have lost their own lives. Brave actions generally speak louder than just fine words.

Often those who give to community life, do so at great cost. In many different jobs, people make sacrifices for the sake of others. The story is told about a tunnel through the Alps which was opened in 1965. It was costly to construct: it cost time, money, effort and, sadly, human lives. In the case of this Alpine tunnel, those who, accidentally and tragically died, did so in their endeavour that others might have a way through. Similarly, Christians affirm that the Lord's sacrifice of love on the cross was absolutely unique: its nature and its significance are for all eternity. However, as we read in the letter to the Hebrews, in His sacrifice of love, Jesus opened 'the new and living way' for us (Hebrews 10:20). So we give thanks for God's love made know supremely in Jesus Christ. He is indeed the truth, having opened that new and living way: His loving words were borne out in what He did on the cross for us, and for all.

Suggested readings: Matthew 27:38-50 and 1 Peter 3:13-18.

NOVEMBER 25th

## CONCERNING GOD'S MIGHTY POWER

Every day people stroll along urban or rural riverbanks, and the riverside at Bedford is no exception: 'the silvery Ouse' has a fascination of its own, whatever the season. Almost hidden, on the walled bank of a quiet backwater by the river, there is a small plaque which testifies to an historic site: John Bunyan was baptized near this spot. How many of his day and age imagined all that would follow from it? John Bunyan is known worldwide as the seventeenth-century tinker who preached the gospel and who wrote the famous book *Pilgrim's Progress*. Thinking of his life, the words in the first epistle of Peter seem fitting: 'Humble yourselves therefore under the mighty hand of God, that in due time he may exalt you' (1 Peter 5:6). While Bunyan must have grown weary as his faith was challenged, he was confident that God's power was greater than his weakness. Indeed, in his life, he affirmed the truth of the apostle Paul's words: 'Now unto him that is able to do exceeding abundantly above all that we ask or think, according to the power that worketh in us...' (Ephesians 3:20 AV).

God's power is a sure element of our faith; to the eye of the believer it is demonstrated in nature, and vividly displayed in the lives of men and women, as in some lovely Bible stories. The Lord took Rahab (a dubious innkeeper), Hannah (a humble childless woman), David (a plain shepherd boy), Jeremiah (a sensitive young man), Peter (an ordinary, uneducated fisherman), Saul of Tarsus (an educated religious zealot), and used them mightily in His service. We also remember that, in God's profound and unsearchable wisdom, He took a humble young maiden, Mary, and selected her to carry in her body the Son of God, the Saviour of the world. The deep mystery of God's selection of people gives hope and joy; even today, we can give thanks that God still works through people. Did the mother of John Bunyan or the mothers of other well-known Christians envisage what their daughters and sons might accomplish? Almost certainly not; yet, we can give thanks to God!

As we ponder the glorious power of God, we have to leave aside ordinary measures of calculation: the might of our God cannot be known by human reckoning, for it is 'exceeding abundant'. This truth brings a new dimension to our thinking, as well as to our attitudes! On the threshold of very important changes in our lives, we might find inspiration in prayerfully reading Ephesians 3:20. A reminder of God's power – 'above all that we ask or think' – brings strength and encouragement. In Britain, this time of year brings shorter, cooler days, and the occasional icy or foggy morning! Yet, however dreary or daunting the day, we do well to remember, above all, that God's power is both great and unfathomable.

Suggested readings: Psalm 8:1-9 and Ephesians 3:8-21.

NOVEMBER 26th

## SMALL THINGS CAN BE VERY IMPORTANT

How important a small thing can be! Some time ago, a man was driving a new powerful car: he was delighted that during his long journey home, it had well demonstrated its power. Just a light touch on the accelerator and he could overtake other cars quickly and safely. However, when he was almost home, suddenly, the car stopped: there was no power in the engine at all! While he was trying to discover the source of the trouble, his small son (who looked at things from a different level!) said: 'Look Dad, there's a tiny wire dangling'. The boy was absolutely right! The little wire was speedily reconnected as required, and it brought the power back to the engine. The small wire, though seemingly inconsequential, had an important part to play.

So often, small things are very important. There is an old saying 'out of the acorn grows the mighty oak', and that is true to life. One brief conversation or one small act of kindness, can make all the difference in a person's life. In so many places, the Bible reminds us that small things can be tremendously significant. In itself, Psalm 98 is very small – just nine verses – but what an ocean of comfort is to be found there, as we are reminded of God's grandeur and love.

While it is human nature to associate important events with the spectacular, strangely, God often chooses to work in quiet, seemingly insignificant ways. When Mary held the infant Jesus in her arms and when, later on in childhood, the people of Nazareth looked at Him, how many of those humble folk could ever have imagined the importance of this little boy? Jesus would grow up to be recognised as One unique in history. As Saviour, His Kingdom would never fail, His reign would be eternal, and His glory would never cease nor fade. Furthermore, untold millions of every race, colour and tongue would call Him 'Lord'. While at the time, hardly recognised by others, this humble birth at Bethlehem would prove to be an event which would change the world! It is true to say, especially as we think of the story of the birth of Jesus, but also in our lives, too: small things can be important.

When James Irwin was travelling in a spacecraft towards the moon, he looked back and saw planet Earth. It was an awe-inspiring sight: there it was, hanging in space like a small ball – a tiny disc of bright light in the blackness of space. How small the Earth seemed! As the spacecraft sped further away from this 'terrestrial ball', he was aware that all he held dear was left on that seemingly small sphere. Yet, Irwin was struck by the significance of the world, and not just to him and his colleagues. He had a new awareness of God's love for the world. In fact, that divine love was so great that once, in history, the Son of God came among us as a real individual, abiding with us, living our life to reveal the very character of God. For such love, we offer our heartfelt thanks.

Suggested readings: Psalm 98:1-9 and Matthew 13:31-32.

NOVEMBER 27th

## OUR HEAVENLY FATHER IS GENEROUS

Parenthood brings so many joys and so much blessing! While being a parent brings responsibility and sometimes heartache, for many people, it also brings an abundance of pleasure and joy: the joy of seeing children develop, the joy of sharing their various successes, the joy of seeing them launched on a career or discovering a meaningful vocation, and the joy of seeing them develop wholesome relationships. Above all, for parents there is the joy which they experience in giving to their children and to succeeding generations, too.

Jesus had some remarkable words about giving which remind us that God's generosity far exceeds our own. He taught: 'If you then, who are evil, know how to give good gifts to your children, how much more will your Father who is in heaven give good things to those who ask him?' (Matthew 7:11). The significant words in this passage are 'how much more'. Here, Jesus was making a comparison between God's ways and our ways. In other words, Jesus was pointing out God's generosity as compared to our own by saying, if we love our children and find joy in giving, how much more does the heavenly Father love us and want to give to us.

As we well know, there are parents who do not give generously or put their children's needs first. Moreover, even the best parents occasionally get things wrong, make mistakes, and may make unwise or poor choices. However, the point that is being made in this teaching is that even our best acts of love and care will fall far short of the love that God has for us and for all. God loves even those who seem to us to be unlovely. God's generosity and care really is beyond compare. The Bible teaches that we can be certain that our heavenly Father knows best and can, indeed, be fully trusted. God does not make mistakes, nor does He have any unloving attitudes: the heavenly Father is consistent and generous in every way.

Of course, as we look to the Lord for particular blessings, we acknowledge that our Father above can grant or withhold, and this is always done from the deep divine yearning for what is best for each of us. The Lord bestows good gifts on His children. God's generosity and love for all people is reflected in a thought-provoking verse in the New Testament in which Jesus teaches that we, too, should be generous in our love and forgiveness. Jesus' urges us to love those we might consider unlovable or even ones who show enmity toward us. The command was to do this: 'So that you may be children of your Father in heaven; for he makes his sun rise on the evil and on the good, and sends rain on the righteous and on the unrighteous' (Matthew 5:45). That verse causes us to ponder the Lord's abounding goodness for all and to consider how we might in gratitude reflect that same generosity to others.

Suggested readings: Psalm 63:1-8 and Matthew 7:7-12.

NOVEMBER 28th

## CALCULATIONS ARE TREMENDOUSLY IMPORTANT

Italy has, like other nations, sadly experienced a number of natural disasters in its long history. However, in 1985, a terrible disaster – sadly, of human making – occurred there. A massive dam burst and a wall of water 120 feet high cascaded down the mountainside and engulfed a community in a sea of mud; there was total devastation in the area. It was said that the engineers and builders had made a series of mistakes through costly miscalculations in its construction. How often a miscalculation can precipitate a crisis or even a tragedy. We all know that calculations are tremendously important in every aspect of life. For example, the success of a space mission depends upon a whole series of extraordinarily complicated calculations. The lives of the astronauts or cosmonauts depend upon these being wholly correct! Even a small error in undertaking these calculations can have catastrophic consequences, as the history of space travel has shown.

Calculations are vital in so many respects, including our everyday routines and the things we so take for granted: we depend on the accurate work of engineers, pilots, surgeons, physicians, architects, scientists, as well as all those who provide for our daily needs. This attention to detail is relevant in the spiritual life, too. As we seek to follow in the way of Christ, we inevitably must make choices, and there is a deep sense in which choosing a lifestyle is a form of calculation! We think of Moses' choice as it is described in the New Testament: 'By faith Moses, when he was grown up, refused to be called the son of Pharaoh's daughter, choosing rather to share ill-treatment with the people of God than to enjoy the fleeting pleasures of sin' (Hebrews 11:25). Over the centuries, much has been spoken and written about Moses, but these few words give insight into his spirituality and judgement. He made an exemplary decision on the basis of faith.

To dismiss the teachings of Christ is always a serious miscalculation. In this respect, there is a verse in the Epistle to the Hebrews which issues a challenge: 'How shall we escape if we neglect such a great salvation?' (Hebrews 2:3). Numerous people who have held positions of great responsibility have been deeply aware of their accountability to God. Of course, accountability to God is expected of us all. Everyone must give an account of their stewardship before the Lord and, indeed, the apostle Paul put it this way: 'We shall all stand before the judgement seat of God' (Romans 14:10). The most serious miscalculation is to forget, or to reject, the living God as we go about our lives. However, as is God's power, so is His love, and thus, we thank God that – like His power – His mercy is inestimable! As we make our decisions, God longs for us to know His presence and to discover His peace.

Suggested readings: Romans 14:5-12 and Hebrews 11:22-28.

## NOVEMBER 29th

## PERSISTENCE IS A SPIRITUAL VIRTUE

In Luke's gospel, we have a rather humorous story which Jesus told as one of His parables. It is of a man who had an unexpected visitor at the untimely hour of midnight, and he had next to no provisions to set before this visitor! So the householder goes to a friend's house and knocks on the door asking for help, but the friend is most reluctant to assist: 'Do not bother me; the door is now shut, and my children are with me in bed; I cannot get up and give you anything' (Luke 11:7). 'Some friend . . .' we might be tempted to comment. We all know that, once children are disturbed at night, they can really play up and refuse to settle back down, so the excuse seems an honest one! Jesus then continues the parable telling how this reluctant neighbour might not get up on the basis of friendship, but he will do so because of the sheer persistence of the man. Unceasing knocking did the trick in the end, and finally, the neighbour got up to share his supply of bread with the one relentlessly asking for provisions late at night. Persistence can bring results: so we are urged by this parable to persevere in prayer, knowing that God heeds our cry.

Perseverance is key in many experiences of life. The person tragically blinded in an accident feels that he will never learn Braille, but he presses on and eventually succeeds. The medical researcher works with a sure and steady persistence to try to find a cure for a disease. So, likewise, the mountaineer, the detective, the explorer, the pioneer, and many others, who just 'keep on keeping on', all testify that persistence wins through in the end. The basic requirement of missionaries is persistence: so often they can work many months – even years – without seeing much spiritual harvest. They need both courage and a willingness to persevere, realising also that their work needs to be supported by faithful, constant prayer. We can ponder the apostle Paul's heartfelt request to his Christian friends: 'Continue steadfastly in prayer, being watchful in it with thanksgiving; and pray for us also, that God may open to us a door for the word, to declare the mystery of Christ' (Colossians 4:2-3).

Oswald Chambers loved one special verse in Luke, and for many years, it dominated his thinking about God: 'If you then, who are evil, know how to give good gifts to your children, how much more will the heavenly Father give the Holy Spirit to those who ask him?' (Luke 11:13). Those words 'how much more' are important. We must get a right perspective: prayer is not seeking to overcome what we might think to be God's reluctance. However, we are to continually and persistently turn to God in prayer. Indeed, persistence in prayer has been a spiritual virtue in the daily devotion of countless believers.

Suggested readings: Luke 11:1-13 and 1 Thessalonians 5:12-22.

NOVEMBER 30th

## JESUS CHRIST IS A PERFECT SAVIOUR

Many British people have enjoyed the occasions when there was a Royal Wedding! It is the best excuse to 'down tools' and have a happy day of celebration: thousands of people line the streets of London and the whole affair is a magnificent party! When Prince Charles married Lady Diana Spencer, they selected St Paul's Cathedral for their wedding and this decision brought joy and pleasure to countless people: it set the scene for a fine Royal Wedding. That service itself seemed to have just the right music and hymns, the beautiful words and prayers, plus the glorious ceremonial and the pageantry, along with the service. A vast global television audience heard the couple say their vows to one another. However, there was a mistake in the repetition of them! This couple in the limelight, shared the fate of numerous couples before them in making mistakes: the bridegroom fluffed his lines a bit, and the bride mixed her words. In a strange way, these simple mistakes seemed to make the appeal of the royal couple even more endearing to those watching or listening avidly around the globe. Being human, mistakes are common to us all!

There is an old saying 'no one is perfect'. How true that is, as we all know well that Monarchs and Governors, Presidents and Prime Ministers, Statesmen and women, judges and juries, Members of Parliament – even bankers – make mistakes. Indeed, all members of the human race are liable to err, but are also prone to failings in life. The Bible puts it plainly: 'All have sinned and fall short of the glory of God' (Romans 3:23). As we reflect on this sober fact, we know there is one glorious exception: namely, the Lord Jesus Christ. We have a perfect Saviour, who was sinless, as Pilate in his assessment reported: 'I find no fault in him' (John 19:4). Jesus Christ, the Saviour of the world, never makes a mistake, never breaks a promise, never fails in mercy; as such, He is different, indeed, unique. He is the One who was the 'only-begotten of the Father'. Many, in humility and sincerity, both great and lowly, have worshipped Him, our glorious Lord. He alone was without sin, and is worthy of our adoration and our whole-hearted devotion.

Today is St Andrew's Day, when the Church gives thanks to God for this true follower of the Lord Jesus. One of the truths about Andrew was his passion and skill in introducing people to Jesus. John's gospel reveals this with beautiful simplicity, as the story is narrated thus: 'He first found his brother Simon, and said to him, "We have found the Messiah". He brought him to Jesus' (John 1:41-42). Andrew knew in his heart that Jesus had a special ministry and was a unique Saviour, and so at every opportunity, he gladly brought others to find in Jesus, the true Lord all (John 12:22).

Suggested readings: Romans 3:9-23 and John 1:35-42.

# DECEMBER

Love came down at Christmas,
Love all lovely, Love divine;
Love was born at Christmas,
Star and angels gave the sign.

Worship we the Godhead,
Love incarnate, Love divine,
Worship we our Jesus:
But wherewith for sacred sign?

Love shall be our token,
Love be yours and love be mine,
Love to God and all men,
Love for plea and gift and sign.

Christina Rossetti (1830-1894)

God, who makest us glad with the yearly remembrance of the birth of thy only Son
Jesus Christ: grant that as we joyfully receive him as our Redeemer, so we may with
sure confidence behold him, when he shall come to be our Judge, who liveth and
reigneth with thee and the Holy Ghost, now and ever.

Prayer Book, 1549

# DECEMBER 1st

## JESUS CHRIST WANTS FAITHFUL PEOPLE

The works of the Italian painter, architect and sculptor, Michelangelo, have thrilled countless people, bringing him worldwide acclaim. His most famous work is seen on the ceiling of the Sistine Chapel at the Vatican in Rome. One of his finest skills was to sculpt marble into marvellous works of art. At one point in his career, he carved out of marble a beautiful tribute to Mary, the mother of Jesus. In the statue, Mary is forlornly holding Jesus in her arms and looking upon His torn body with a mother's love and tenderness. Michelangelo called this sculpture 'PIETA' (*Pietà* is a Latin word meaning piety, pity, faithfulness to natural ties). As this work depicted, Mary trusted God even when she did not fully understand the Lord's ways and purposes; she trusted His wisdom, love and faithfulness, and she persevered in that devotion even through the darkest of hours.

There are Christians the world over who, of course, acknowledge that Mary was an outstanding person of virtue, but do not necessarily subscribe to the particular doctrines of Marian devotion which are held by some Christian traditions. However, all believers perceive that Mary was 'a chosen vessel' for the gracious fulfilment of God's purposes. Her supreme virtues were faithfulness and obedience. Jesus once said: 'He that is faithful in a very little is faithful also in much' (Luke 16:10). It is quite easy to believe that Mary, the mother of Jesus, was faithful in things great and small; that was her shining virtue which stands as an example to all.

The apostle Paul, writing to the church at Corinth (a body of believers in a city notorious for idolatry and immorality), maintained that faithfulness and trustworthiness were the qualities clearly needed in the work of the Kingdom. He wrote: 'Moreover it is required of stewards that they be found trustworthy' (1 Corinthians 4:2 AV). He also commented on one whom he considered faithful: 'I sent you Timothy, who is my beloved and faithful child in the Lord' (1 Corinthians 4:17). Peter expressed a similar sentiment when he wrote: 'By Silvanus, a faithful brother, as I regard him, I have written briefly to you' (1 Peter 5:12).

As we look over the long period of Church history, we recognise the service of those who were faithful to Jesus Christ and who sought to bring honour and glory to His name. They deserve the words found in Matthew's gospel: 'Well done, good and faithful servant' (Matthew 25:23). It is clear that all the scriptures – although the many and varied parts were written at different periods of time – unite to commend faithfulness as a worthy response of believers to the Lord. It is a quality that Christ can use to His glory, as history has proved over and over. Faithfulness is a virtue to which, with the aid of the Spirit, we would surely all aspire in our daily lives.

Suggested readings: Matthew 25:19-28 and Romans 12:1-21.

## DECEMBER 2nd

## OUR GLORIOUS GOD IS MERCIFUL

There are some parts of the Bible which are like a truly 'spiritual tonic'! As they are read and meditated upon, they invigorate the soul of the believer, so bringing life and hope. Such a passage is Psalm 103 in which the psalmist speaks of the mercy of God. 'The Lord is merciful and gracious, slow to anger and abounding in steadfast love' (Psalm 103:8). One hymn writer, H. W. Faber, puts it beautifully: 'There's a wideness in God's mercy, like the wideness of the sea . . .' Other hymn writers, composers, poets, and authors have also taken the thought of the sea (or the ocean) reflecting the endless breadth of God's boundless love.

A Christian was celebrating her eightieth birthday and her pastor called to congratulate her and to say a prayer of thanksgiving. It was a very happy and interesting pastoral visit: the elderly lady had a warm sense of humour, as well as a deep devotional spirit. At one point, the conversation took an unusual turn, as the woman passed a comment: 'I'm eighty years old today, but I've never seen the sea!' Just a few weeks later, she died, passing peacefully into the presence of her Lord. She had lived in the British Isles all her eighty years, but died without having ever visited the seaside.

This story prompts thought of those who live many years, even to a very ripe old age, who never glimpse the 'wideness of the sea', as it were, in terms of God's love and mercy. It seems that many seem unaware of the 'ocean' of God's love and the abundance of divine mercy. Perhaps they have lived a long life, but don't seem cognisant of the need for God's forgiveness. It seems to us, to be rather sad that an eighty-year-old could die without ever having viewed the sea. However, it is infinitely sadder, that anyone should live the whole of his or her earthly life without experiencing for themselves the rich mercy and love of God, and not discovering for themselves in a personal way, that the ' heart of the Eternal is most wonderfully kind.'

As the psalmist reminds us: 'For as the heaven is higher than the earth, so great is his mercy toward them that fear him' (Psalm 103:11). The Hebrew word for mercy used in this verse is *chesedh*, and it is often translated 'loving-kindness' but can mean, 'help in time of need'. It has been rendered: 'God's active intervention to help'. So, when we may feel oppressed by the multitude of our mistakes and failings, we do well deliberately to recall the words in the opening verse of Psalm 51: 'The multitude of thy tender mercies' (Psalm 51:1). We know that God does intervene for us bringing sure help and showing great mercy. We can be thankful, at all times and in all places, that God's mercy is inexhaustible, 'vast like the ocean'. Divine grace is truly boundless, amazing and all-sufficient, whatever our need or circumstance!

Suggested readings: Psalm 103:1-18 and John 21:11-17.

## DECEMBER 3rd

## HUMAN FAILING IS SURPRISING

Major airports all over the world are alert to the cunning of people involved in the illicit drugs trade. The lengths to which drug smugglers go are quite amazing! One Colombian man, on a flight from Bogata to Madrid, was seen carrying a Nativity scene. At the Madrid airport, he handed it over to another person, and a sharp-eyed official had his suspicions aroused. On closer inspection, it was discovered that the figures of Mary, Joseph, the Shepherds and Baby Jesus were all made of cocaine! The drug dealers were obviously motivated by greed, and went to great lengths to further their illegal activity. One might say that this activity reveals the depths to which human depravity can sometimes sink in rebellion against God.

In the Book of Jeremiah, there is a verse about human sinfulness: 'The heart is deceitful above all things, and desperately corrupt; who can understand it?' (Jeremiah 17:9). The words, 'desperately corrupt' might seem an exaggeration, but it is actually a fair description. The proceedings in the courts of this land endorse the plain fact that there is 'corruption', to some extent, endemic in the hearts of people, though perhaps only a minority end up facing legal proceedings. There is, as it were, a deep-seated sickness which variously affects us all, but sorely blights so many lives. The New English Bible renders the verse thus: 'The heart is deceitful of all things, desperately sick; who can fathom it?' Many people who appear to be quite reasonable in nature with pleasing personalities and important responsibilities, may yet have 'heart' trouble: a sickness of spirit, which permits them to do the most hurtful things to other people. For example, a woman living alone in London once went, with a joyful heart, to the Christmas morning service. She enjoyed seeing her friends and singing the carols. Sadly, when she returned home, she discovered her house had been burgled: her Christmas celebration had been completely wrecked. It seems inconceivable that a criminal could do such a thing, but it bears out Jeremiah's words.

At this early stage of the forthcoming Christmas season, we pause to remember the heart of the gospel: 'Christ Jesus came into the world to save sinners' (1 Timothy 1:15). We acknowledge, of course, that we all come into that category: we have all erred and strayed from God's ways. However, there are people today suffering from a deep spiritual malaise. There was a time when the apostle Paul – who became a proclaimer of Christ – had this sort of 'spiritual sickness', which led him to persecute Christians. Yet, after Christ came into his life, he bore testimony: 'The grace of our Lord overflowed for me' (1 Timothy 1:14). When Paul met the risen Lord, his heart was renewed and his life was transformed. We, too, may know God's grace: divine mercy can change and renew even the most troubled soul.

Suggested readings: Jeremiah 17:5-10 and 1 Timothy 1:12-17.

DECEMBER 4th

## GOD'S BOOK IS THE BEST BOOK

Certain ancient university cities, alongside London itself, have huge bookshops with a massive stock and a worldwide reputation. Generations of students and academics, along with other keen readers, have purchased books for study and reference, as well as for pleasure. In any such bookshop, within the theology section, there is a salutary reminder of the many numerous learned books written about our Christian faith, quite beyond the more popular ones. As one stands and looks at the masses of books in any such place, the mind is given a severe jolt! Indeed, such a sight is a timely reminder that there is so much more to learn about any subject, and that includes our faith. However, Christians all around the world believe that the most significant volume which stands paramount above all others, is the Bible, a volume which itself is actually a wonderful collection of many varied books.

In a quiet moment, we might reflect on all the wonderful things the Bible has inspired: lovely poetry, inspirational hymns, cherished prayers, beautiful music, memorable quotations, famous paintings and other works of art. It has inspired some to give themselves in dedicated care of others, it has evoked a spirit of loving service, and it has summoned men and women to both fortitude and devotion. The Bible's contribution to the well-being of humankind is beyond all reckoning. Every Bible Society in the world lists exciting testimonies of what the Holy Scriptures have done in the lives of people once they were able to read the words in their own language or dialect, and so discover the truth of God's Word for themselves.

One Christmas season, a bookshop in St Neots in England had a very special sale of books, and numerous people found it useful in purchasing suitable presents, but there were some curious titles, including a book entitled: *This book will change your life*. Actually, that seems to be a most appropriate title for the Bible! The Word of God has challenged people and, under the powerful ministry of the Holy Spirit, it has changed people, too. In the Epistle to the Hebrews there is a splendid verse which illustrates this key point: 'For the word of God is living and active, sharper than any two-edged sword, piercing to the division of soul and spirit, of joints and marrow, and discerning the thoughts and intentions of the heart' (Hebrews 4:12).

Dr Martyn Lloyd-Jones was renowned for his love of scripture; he even gave up a career in medicine to be a proclaimer of the Word. The Bible has been likened to many things: a lamp, a sword, a guide, spiritual food or drink, but interestingly, also as medicine for the soul. There is good reason for asserting the Bible as the most important book, and the best one, too, because it is life-changing!

Suggested readings: Psalm 119:97-105 and Hebrews 4:11-16.

## DECEMBER 5th

## THE HEART KNOWS WHERE TO TURN

Much space is given in the Old Testament to the record of the journeying of God's people through the wilderness towards the Promised Land. It was a journey with many difficulties, so much so, that the story tells of the trouble the people faced: 'And they journeyed from mount Hor by the way of the Red Sea, to compass the land of Edom: and the soul of the people was much discouraged because of the way' (Numbers 21:4 AV). The Good News Bible gives further insight into this episode by translating this verse: 'But on the way, the people lost their patience'. The record also reveals that when they lost their patience, they spoke harshly against God and Moses.

How often people want to blame others, their leaders or even God, when the going gets rather tough! In this story, it is revealed that the people's impatience brought them into further difficulties, so they queried what should they do next. As the people face further adversity, the story continues with a remarkable verse: 'And the people came to Moses, and said, we have sinned, for we have spoken against the Lord and against you; pray to the Lord, that he take away the serpents from us' (Numbers 21:7). The man they had heavily criticised was the very man, to whom they then in desperation turned, pleading: 'Pray to the Lord'. Furthermore, the gracious God, Whom they had spoken against, was the very God from Whom they wanted help and deliverance. Ironically, given the situation of their waywardness, the recalcitrant people of God knew exactly where to turn when in trouble!

It is a remarkable fact that often, the human heart has an innate capacity to know where to turn when the road is difficult, as it were. In a strange but real way, the people of God were paying Moses a great compliment. They knew that, in spite of their bitter criticism of him, Moses was generous enough to forgive them and continue to serve. When we ponder Jesus' Parable of the Prodigal Son, we perceive that the rebellious son knew where to turn! In the hour of his great need when, as it were, he had hit rock bottom, he said: 'I will arise and go to my father, and will say to him, "Father, I have sinned against heaven and before you; I am no longer worthy to be called your son; treat me as one of your hired servants"' (Luke 15:18-19). As he returned to his father, he anticipated the largeness of his father's heart. Yet, even then, he wholly underestimated the breadth and depth of his father's love and mercy.

However difficult the situations that we may face, we may be assured that the Spirit of God continues to prompt and to draw us, and also always points us to God. As we make our journey through life, we remember that it is always the right time to turn to God. God is the One upon Whom we may rely, not only during tough times, but also during all the good days, too!

Suggested readings: Numbers 21:1-7 and Luke 15:11-20.

DECEMBER 6th

## OUR GOD IS SOVEREIGN

In the second book of Samuel there is a thought-provoking story of how David 'sat before the Lord' (2 Samuel 7:17). It was a time of deep reflection and confession of faith, and one verse stands out: 'Therefore thou art great, O Lord God; for there is none like thee, and there is no God beside thee, according to all that we have heard with our ears' (2 Samuel 7:22). Running throughout scripture we have stories of people rejoicing in the Lord's love, power and creativity, as well as God's awesome majesty, and His divine sovereignty. This doctrine of God's sovereignty both inspires and comforts.

We think of the disciples Peter, John and the other men and women who were followers of Jesus, and the comfort they gained from knowing God's sovereignty. After the crucifixion of Jesus and the events of Easter Day, Jerusalem was a dangerous place for His disciples: misplaced zeal, bigotry and spiritual blindness posed a threat to them. Yet, a few weeks after the resurrection of Jesus Christ, Peter and John boldly witnessed there, and they 'didn't pull any punches', as it were! The authorities were extremely agitated and they sought to stop the spread of the new proclamation. They had Peter and John arrested and, at a hearing of the Council, then threatened them and '. . . charged them not to speak or teach at all in the name of Jesus' (Acts 4:18). So the two apostles returned and shared this situation with their Christian friends. Their united response to these threats was to turn to God in prayer. Luke recorded: 'And when they heard it, they lifted their voices together to God and said, "Sovereign Lord, who didst make the heaven and the earth and the sea and everything in them"' (Acts 4:24). They turned their problem over to their sovereign God, continuing in prayer with a specific request: 'And now, Lord, look upon their threats, and grant to thy servants, to speak thy word with all boldness' (Acts 4:29). They found both comfort and courage in God's sovereignty, and this is how women and men down successive generations have faced their difficulties before the Lord.

Livy, a famous historian (born 59 BC), once claimed: 'In difficult situations when hope seems feeble, the boldest plans are safest'. This Roman historian was wise enough to commend boldness and, rightly placed, it is a most honourable human attribute. However, the boldness of the first Christians, as shown in Luke's glimpse of them at prayer under dire threat of harsh persecution, was based on their belief that God is sovereign. John Calvin, the sixteenth-century Reformer in Geneva, stressed this particular doctrine, and it shaped both his teaching and his attitude towards life. If we simply place our trust daily in God, we too, can pray with the psalmist: 'But my eyes are fixed on you, O Sovereign Lord' (Psalm 141:8 NIV).

Suggested readings: 2 Samuel 7:18-29 and Acts 4:23-31.

DECEMBER 7th

## THE PROVIDENCE OF GOD IS A SOLID FACT

How often in life men and women cast their vote for short-term policies! Numerous people make decisions thinking about the immediate future rather than distant horizons. Yet, this short-term perspective is not God's way. We confess that God in His wisdom, always takes the long-term view, as it were, preparing men and women to be in the right place at the right time. So in Psalm 105, we read of a time when even though famine was approaching, God had plans for His people: 'He sent a man before them, Joseph sold as a slave' (Psalm 105:17 NIV). Looking back with the eye of faith, one could say that Joseph was 'prepared' by God to handle a particular situation and, with hindsight, Joseph recognised God's hand at work in his life. While his brothers had sold him into slavery, years later and after a long separation, Joseph met his brothers, and he said to them: 'God sent me before you to preserve for you a remnant on earth, and to keep alive for you many survivors. So it was not you who sent me here, but God' (Genesis 45:7-8). Scripture teaches that our God sees a long way ahead, as it were, and we may therefore trust that His timing is always perfect.

This particular day, many Christians will remember with gratitude the life of the fourth century Church leader, Ambrose, Bishop of Milan. At that time, an emperor was guilty of a massacre at Thessalonica; Ambrose, with much courage and fortitude, and at great personal risk, rebuked him. His attitude was a potent influence on the relationship between state and Church for generations. Ambrose declared with profound courage that the emperor was within the Church and not over it! He was a man who took the long-term view. It would have been easy to take a short-term view, and so avoid risking the displeasure of a powerful figure. As it happens, history simply records that the rebuked emperor did, indeed, accept ecclesiastical discipline.

Sometimes, life does look fragmented like an incomplete jigsaw puzzle, but God holds all the pieces in His hands. We suffer setbacks, experience big disappointments, and doors of opportunity seem to close. Yet, God is still at work. We find hope in affirming that God has a gracious plan. Even while facing persecution, John the Divine, proclaimed his faith that even the death of Christ can be seen to have an eternal dimension. He saw this Christian assurance in terms of 'the Lamb slain from the foundation of the world' (Revelation 13:8 AV). With John, Christians affirm that Christ was born, He lived and ministered, He was crucified and raised to resurrection life, He was taken up into glory, and He will surely come again. The scriptures remind us that God takes the long-term view. In our lives and in the life of the world, we know God's purposes are being worked out. So we pray together in sure hope: 'Thy Kingdom come, thy will be done on earth as it is in heaven'.

Suggested readings: Psalm 105:8-24 and Acts 2:22-24.

# DECEMBER 8th

## OUR SALVATION IS THE REAL CAUSE FOR REJOICING

Today, as with each day of the year, lots of people in many different places will assuredly be rejoicing for one reason or another! The reasons might vary considerably from an examination passed, a new job secured, a marriage celebrated, a quarrel healed, a prayer answered or some victory won. While in some places, there will be grief, undoubtedly, in other homes there will be great joy, as well as relief. In his very warm letter to the Philippians, the apostle Paul encourages those Christians to be joyful: 'Rejoice in the Lord always; again I will say, Rejoice' (Philippians 4:4).

While Christians are called to rejoice, the Bible also warns against a triumphalist attitude. In the gospel story, we are told how Jesus sent out seventy disciples on a special mission: it was a very successful enterprise. In fact, it was more successful than their wildest dreams, so we read: 'The seventy returned with joy, saying, "Lord even the demons are subject to us in your name"' (Luke 10:17). What a report to give their Master! He listened, and then introduced a surprising note: 'Nevertheless do not rejoice in this, that the spirits are subject to you; but rejoice that your names are written in heaven' (Luke 10:20). Jesus was simply pointing to the fact that what they felt they had accomplished was actually God's work through them!

Sometimes we may forget that the greatest cause for rejoicing is at God's work in our lives and in the life of the world. Over the recent decades in particular, many people have written books which stress that our salvation is a wonderful free gift of God. The apostle Paul put it this way 'For by grace you have been saved through faith, and this is not your own doing, it is the gift of God – not because of works, lest any man should boast' (Ephesians 2:8). Plainly, divine grace is the ground of our salvation and this is the real cause for our rejoicing. Our names are not written in God's book, as it were, because of any human achievements; salvation is the sheer gift of God who has received us, forgiven us and given new hope.

Occasionally, hearing some Christians talking, one might get the impression that they think that God is in their debt! Yet, as a verse in Luke's gospel reminds us: 'When you have done all that is commanded you, say, "We are unworthy servants; we have only done what was our duty"' (Luke 17:10). Everyone who has served the Lord faithfully knows that the real cause for rejoicing is our experience of God's grace. Our part is simply to be trusting and obedient in response to the glorious love of the Lord. God has reached out to us in Christ, and our part is to follow faithfully, knowing His presence, and relying upon His Spirit. We do, indeed, rejoice at so great a salvation, which we – and all others – can come to know in Christ Jesus: we have such cause to be glad in the Lord.

Suggested readings: Luke 10:17-24 and Philippians 4:1-7.

## DECEMBER 9th

## IT IS A GOOD THING TO BE FRIENDLY WITH YOURSELF

It may sound a strange question but it is one worth asking: 'Are you a good friend to yourself?' It is quite astonishing how many people have a hostile attitude towards themselves! We might think of some of the things we hear people say: 'I despise myself', 'I'm so ashamed of myself', 'I'm cross with myself', and some even say 'I hate myself'. In many respects, there is a surprisingly large proportion of the population who are less than friendly with their own person. Strange, but true! Every minister of the gospel, who has had long experience in pastoral work, can testify to the destructive attitudes some people have towards themselves, which then also affect others. The problem is in knowing a sense of true self-worth before the Lord.

The Holy Scriptures have a word for this: 'He who grows wise is a friend to himself' (Proverbs 19:8 Moffatt). So the best way to befriend oneself is to become wiser! For example, lots of things have been written about Zacchaeus (the tax-collector who climbed a tree to see Jesus), and his character does provide an interesting study. There are some Bible students who believe that Zacchaeus was a person who despised himself. Zacchaeus' profession attracted criticism and hostility, and perhaps, to a degree, he even shared these negative views of himself. Yet, Jesus Christ set him free from such self-hatred and self-despising. Zacchaeus learned spiritual wisdom from the Saviour and rejoiced in the Saviour's kindness and love. We believe that, because of the gracious and healing ministry of Jesus, this tax-collector, in a sense, became a friend to himself. Then, having accepted divine mercy, he was wholly reconciled to God and to others.

The folly of hostility towards one's self is very evident in some people's lives: individuals who take unnecessary risks, overlook the spiritual life or neglect their own person. Self-hatred takes many different forms but is very dangerous and damaging to the personality, and it can have a wide impact, too. Someone who was really unkind to himself was Martin Luther: there was a period in his life when, deeply conscious of spiritual failure, he literally engaged in self-punishment. However, when a new understanding of the Holy Scriptures came to him, he rejoiced in God's love and mercy. Luther then had no doubt that Jesus was the Saviour of the world. With God's help, Luther befriended himself and undertook his great work for the Lord.

Many people around the world today do not know the love and forgiveness of God. In fact, there are many whose self-loathing has blighted their own lives and the lives of others. Yet, healing is possible; let us pray that one day, everyone will come to know that they are 'accepted in the Beloved' (Ephesians 1:6). The love and acceptance God offers is a vital part of the gospel, and we rejoice to share in it.

Suggested readings: Proverbs 19:1-11 and Luke 19:1-10.

## DECEMBER 10ᵗʰ

## GOD IS WITH US IN LIFE'S CHANGES

Changes certainly do come upon us! Sometimes they come with unexpected swiftness; at other times, they come painfully slowly. We can think of the rapid, sudden changes: a young athlete wins an Olympic Gold Medal unexpectedly, a person is seriously injured in a road accident, a young couple receive property left to them in an older relative's will. Such changes (both happy and sad) occur every day in someone's home, somewhere. Sometimes, the swiftness of the change comes as a tremendous shock! Not all changes can be foreseen, and not all changes are good.

As we go on our life's journey, and face up to change, we often come to a fork in the road, as it were. We have to make a decision which may prove to be monumental for our future whether in our career or in our relationships. Sometimes, we have a choice thrust upon us, over which we have little or no control. At other times, we can take more responsibility for our destiny, but as the psalmist cried to God, so we should always pray, 'my times are in your hands' (Psalm 31:15). Often, in looking back later on, we can say of our lives, as the psalmist said of God's people: 'He led them on safely' (Psalm 78:53).

Of course, we might look back wistfully over certain poor choices and with the psalmist cry: 'My heart breaks when I remember the past' (Psalm 42:4 GNB). At this point, the psalmist, while facing trouble was looking back on a happy past and lamenting an unwelcome change. He was not looking through rose-tinted spectacles, but rather was remembering the reality of his happiness before a big change struck his life. He recalled glad days of warm friendship and said: 'My heart breaks when I remember the past, when I went with the crowds to the house of God and led them as they walked along, a happy crowd, singing and shouting praise to God' (Psalm 42:4 GNB). Then a resolution is declared: 'Hope in God; for I shall again praise him, my help and my God' (Psalm 42:5). Changes may indeed come, but God remains forever constant. God can be trusted and that is the source of new hope and confidence. Reflecting Psalm 34, the hymn writer, Nahum Tate (1652-1715), wrote:

> 'Through all the changing scenes of life,
> In trouble and in joy.
> The praises of my God shall still
> My heart and tongue employ'.

As the psalmist knew well, God is ever faithful, with us throughout all life's changes to bless and to renew us, according to His great mercy, so we are thankful.

Suggested readings: Psalm 42:1-11 and Romans 5:1-5.

## DECEMBER 11th

## FORGIVENESS BRINGS FRUIT

Jesus told the parable of an unfruitful fig tree which was given another chance. For three years, the vineyard owner had been disappointed because it failed to bear fruit, so orders were given to cut it down. His servant, the gardener, made an interesting suggestion to his master: 'Leave it alone for one more year, and I'll dig round it and fertilise it. If it bears fruit next year, fine! If not, then cut it down' (Luke 13:9). One more year, one further reprieve, one last chance. Within this little story there is a philosophy of life which shows graciousness to another: a little extra patience, a hint of further waiting, a shade more persistence in order to show compassion, or maybe a quiet willingness to give someone the benefit of the doubt.

If we consider people we know well, we are bound to find a variety of responses to failure. There are those who have been let down who then say: 'I'll never trust him (or her) again. Never'. No second chance there! Such people exercise a sort of 'excommunication', as it were: no forgiveness, no further trust, no time allowed for amendment. However, this attitude is certainly challenged by the words of the Lord's Prayer: 'Forgive us the wrong we have done, as we have forgiven those who have wronged us' (Matthew 6:12 NEB).

The Bible is full of stories of people who made grievous mistakes: Moses lost his temper, Aaron was led astray into idolatry, David committed adultery, Peter denied knowing Jesus three times, and John Mark turned back when the going got tough. Yet, all these – and many other nameless men and women – found forgiveness and were given another opportunity. We can probably each think of times when we were temped to lose our patience with someone out of sheer exasperation, whether a partner or sibling, or grown-up son or daughter, or friend or colleague. The challenge to us is whether we might, for the Lord's sake, give such an offending person 'one more year', meaning another chance for the good of all. When God forgives someone, and we too forgive, it is like a door to blessing being flung open for us all.

History records a remarkable reconciliation: there was once real trouble in the Wesley home at Epworth, so husband and wife separated. After some weeks, the relationship was restored, and in due time, their son John was born. He then would go on share the gospel of God's forgiveness far and wide. Whatever, mistakes we make or troubles we face with others, God calls us, also, to be forgiving and to offer people another chance. Indeed, as we, too, forgive one another, we may discover the truth that the apostle Paul shared with the Christians in Corinth: 'As the abounding grace of God is shared by more and more, the greater may be the chorus of thanksgiving that rises to the glory of God' (2 Corinthians 4:15).

Suggested readings: Luke 13:1-9 and 2 Corinthians 5:11-21.

DECEMBER 12th

## DESTINY COMES IN SMALL CONTAINERS

The morning of Monday, 12th December 1988, will be long remembered. This was the day when there was a major train disaster at Clapham Junction, London. Thirty-three people were killed, many were seriously injured and a large number deeply shocked. The routine 6:20am Bournemouth to (London) Waterloo service is the regular train for hundreds of commuters, but that morning, sadly things went tragically wrong. Sometimes, truth is stranger than fiction! Although one woman usually took the train and sat towards the front – ready for a speedy exit at Waterloo station – that morning, she missed the train. Remarkably, a strange thing had happened: the battery in her alarm clock had faltered and the alarm went off twenty minutes late. Despite rushing around to catch the train, she missed it: an amazing escape for her. If she had caught the train, and sat in her usual seat, she would probably have been on the casualty list. So often life is like that, 'on trivial matters, big things turn'!

There is a quaint, though very true, old adage: 'Large doors can swing on small hinges'. That is, indeed, a valid description of daily life! How often, along the journey of life, a seemingly small occurrence turns out to be crucial to our path in a career or a relationship! In the Old Testament, there is the story of Saul who was sent by his father to find some lost animals. Three days' searching brought about no result. However, coincidentally (so it seemed to observers), Saul met the prophet Samuel who gave him generous hospitality. Moreover, there and then, Samuel felt constrained by the Lord to bestow upon Saul a position of leadership in the nation. Quite a leap from lost donkeys to promised leadership! That sounds ridiculous, but it is true, and so began the tale of the monarchy in ancient Israel (I Samuel 9 -10).

Though we know the whole life of this planet depends upon the sun's light and warmth, a small object held over one's eye can blot it out. In the same way, small events can hold within them the seeds of destiny: a visit, a letter, a phone call, a conversation, a glance at a book or leaflet, or an encounter with an issue through the media. All these small things can be used by God to prompt, guide and direct us. The nativity story found in Luke's gospel, seems a relatively short one, but what power it has been for good! It tells the story of the birth of a little baby in Bethlehem. No one, in their wildest dreams, could have imagined all the good that was going to come into the world through the birth of that tiny baby. However, as we too, may affirm, God often works in quite small, even inauspicious or unexpected ways. That knowledge surely inspires us to continue trusting in God day by day.

Suggested readings: 1 Samuel 9:1-10:1 and Hebrews 13:20-21.

DECEMBER 13th

## PLANNING BRINGS VICTORIES

One of the very important lessons we can learn from history is that an energetic minority can end up influencing the majority. We know such small groups (even against overwhelming odds) have won big victories! By skillful planning and enthusiastic endeavour, the seemingly impossible can happen. For example, a few years ago, people who were supportive of 'green' politics (interested in matters such as pollution, conservation and the environment), were considered to be a minority group. Yet, the numbers of this political persuasion have now increased dramatically, and their voices are being heard throughout the world. Pollution, waste, exploitation, environmental threats and the 'greenhouse effect' are today increasingly worldwide concerns. This is primarily due to the fact that a resolute, active and determined minority planned very carefully and alerted the majority to these critical issues.

Scripture affirms that people who have patiently made long-term plans and who have been both energetic and persistent, have won many great victories. As a verse in the Book of Proverbs notes: 'Victory is the fruit of long planning' (Proverbs 11:14 NEB). This remarkable verse can be illustrated time after time from history. The people who have patiently made long-term plans, and who have been both energetic and persistent, have won many great victories. This is true in the political world and the social sphere, but also in spiritual matters, too. Sometimes, men and women make quick plans and expect immediate results, and are disappointed. Even Christian workers can get caught up in feverish activity, expecting victory by sheer effort, but without much planning. Yet, the Holy Scripture reveals that our God is – in our poor human expression – 'a long-term planner', and so often has used a small minority to fulfil His purposes.

The people of old, who were in many respects viewed as a powerless minority, maintained a deep yearning for God to act. They continued to hope for a new day and a long-awaited deliverer. What seemed impossible, actually, in the fulness of time – through God's mysterious and inscrutable ways – came about when God sent Jesus to be the Saviour of the world. The first group of disciples, who were called by Jesus, were also a small group who seemed to have no power. The first Christians were a tiny minority and, humanly speaking, they didn't stand a chance of influencing the world! Yet, following Jesus' command to, 'Go into all the world and preach the good news to all creation' (Mark 16:15 NIV), they had a world-changing impact. While it may have seemed an impossible task God had, as it were, the 'long-term plan. Truly, victory is the fruit of planning. It is always God's work, undertaken at God's prior initiative, of course, and yet, we all have our necessary part to play.

Suggested readings: Proverbs 11:11-19 and Mark 16:9-20.

DECEMBER 14th

## THE LORD HAS A WONDERFUL STOREHOUSE

The wide pavement was full of large trolleys laden with goods: it was difficult for pedestrians to find their way through. The local shopkeeper was restocking for the final Christmas rush! Earlier shoppers had depleted his storehouse, and so he was making a determined effort to restock from the warehouse: groceries, toiletries, drinks, household goods and a wide variety of Christmas gifts. Storehouses are important places and filled with needful supplies. To see such a storehouse of goods, is to be reminded of the abundance of good things which we enjoy in life.

In the Bible, we are often reminded of what we might call the Lord's 'storehouse'. Numerous verses in scripture indicate that God gives plentifully without reservation. In God's own storehouse, as it were, there are many blessings which are freely available. The Lord has boundless love, grace, forgiveness and power, generously offered to all humankind. One of the rich verses of Holy Scripture is found in the opening chapter of John's gospel: 'Out of his full store we have all received grace upon grace' (John 1:16 NEB). The Lord gives abundant grace, and yet more grace. As we read in the gospels, the Lord Jesus gave and gave and, as the risen One, has not ceased to give. Knowing such generosity, we are called to be generous.

In the Old Testament, we read how the people gave generously to the building of the temple at Jerusalem and uttered sincere words in prayer: 'O thou Eternal, our God, all these stores which we have prepared to build thee a temple for thy sacred majesty, come from thine own hand and are all thine own' (1 Chronicles 29:16 Moffatt). Humbly, we remember that even the gifts we offer to God were first received from above! God generously gives from His vast storehouse and as we delight in His great abundant gifts, so we are to give generously to others.

In Luke's gospel, we read the parable of a farmer who had an abundant harvest and this created a problem: 'And he thought to himself, "What shall I do, for I have nowhere to store my crops?" And he said, "I will do this: I will pull down my barns, and build larger ones; and there I will store all my grain and my goods"' (Luke 12:17). The farmer in the story already had a vast storehouse, but had not considered gratitude to God, nor sharing any of his overflowing harvest with others. He was a rich man, a very successful farmer, but it appears that he was motivated by greed and selfishness, as he was not 'rich toward God' (Luke 12:21).

As we remember all that God has given to us from His vast storehouse, we acknowledge, in the words of the hymn writer, that 'all good things around us . . . sent from heaven above', are God's gift to us. Having experienced God's generosity, we, in turn, are to share with others with a glad and generous heart.

Suggested readings: 1 Chronicles 29:10-20 and Luke 12:15-21.

## DECEMBER 15th

## LIFE CONTAINS HIDDEN TREASURE

Picture a group of friends chatting together about childhood memories and, very specially, recalling the Christmases spent with their families. One of them speaks of the old tradition of hiding sixpenny pieces in the Christmas pudding. Once it was then served, when someone found a concealed coin, there was a whoop of delight! One of the great 'mysteries' of the family was that all the children received a slice of pudding with 'hidden treasure', but mother and father were always unfortunate! This old custom brings to mind how a devoted daughter once described her father. She said that he was 'a man rich as a Christmas pudding stuffed with sixpenny bits'! She was, of course, not referring to wealth, but thinking of the generosity of his character.

There are people who reveal their goodness in a surprising number of ways: the more we get to know them, the more a certain 'treasure' within is revealed. Seeing this goodness in others points us to God's Spirit in their lives. In Matthew's gospel, we read: 'The good person brings good things out of a good treasure' (Matthew 12:35). There are lots of people who might appear quite ordinary but, as we experience their company and friendship, they reveal previously unknown treasures of goodness. To use the graphic language of the appreciative daughter, they are truly 'like a Christmas pudding stuffed with sixpenny bits'. In the Acts of the Apostles, we read of a remarkable person called 'Barnabas, (which means, 'son of encouragement'), a Levite, a native of Cyprus, who sold a field which belonged to him, and brought the money and laid it at the apostles' feet' (Acts 4:36-37). 'Son of encouragement' was a wonderful, but very apt name. He showed a rich goodness. The first Christians discovered that 'every slice' of his friendship, and service contained, as it were, a treasure within it. As Luke describes him, he was seen as good, inspired by the Holy Spirit.

Every church needs to have at least one real encourager, a 'Barnabas' character, whether male or female! Often such kindly people are found within a church fellowship, and their qualities of generosity, loving care and encouragement, which, at first seem 'hidden', are perhaps only discovered over time. In a wonderful way, the fact that these treasures seem concealed, serves as a reminder that Jesus taught His disciples: 'Do not let your left hand know what your right hand is doing' (Matthew 6:3). Jesus meant, of course that whatever we do for others, it should be done without fanfare or drawing attention to ourselves. As we humbly and quietly follow in the footsteps of Jesus, we remember that He went around – in the words of the apostle Peter –'doing good' (Acts 10:38). As we seek to do likewise, day by day, we will glorify God.

Suggested readings: Acts 5:32-37 and Matthew 12:33-37.

DECEMBER 16th

## SOME PROMISES ARE PRICELESS

It was during the Christmas season some time ago, and the town centre shops were busy stocking their windows to attract potential customers. One jewellery shop stood out as it simply blazed with light, and there was a magnificent selection of very costly jewellery: rings and bracelets, watches and brooches. One window featured a small pair of golden scales, and placed on one side of the scales was an exquisite engagement ring priced £525 (then a huge sum). The ring on the scales was a graphic illustration which prompted thought of life and relationships. Surely, there is a spiritual truth in that scene, as well, which might be expressed in this way: it may be possible to weigh the gold and the diamonds, but you cannot weigh the promise. We may think of people who have been married for many years, indeed, over several decades, and their engagement rings and their wedding rings possess a value – not just sentimental value – far beyond the jeweller's price tag. The real value for them is a reminder of the promises which were made. While the ring, itself, may have a monetary value, the promise behind it escapes actual valuation.

Thinking of the value of promises, we recall that this season of Advent is all about God's promise, as we look to the coming of Christ. Christian believers rejoice in the wonderful promises found in scripture. The Lord's promises have brought inspiration, comfort, strength and blessing to generations of people. Three glorious ones are these: 'As I was with Moses, so I will be with you; I will not fail you or forsake you' (Joshua 1:5), 'Anyone who comes to me I will never drive away' (John 6:37), 'And my God will supply every need of yours according to his riches in glory in Christ Jesus' (Philippians 4:19). No one can ever calculate what the promises of God have meant to the Lord's people down the centuries. They have been like a light in a dark place, and they stand out brightly as beacons of hope and encouragement!

One particular verse in the New Testament, makes an extraordinary promise. Extolling God's wondrous grace, the writer claims that we are granted 'exceeding great and precious promises: that by these ye might be partakers of the divine nature' (2 Peter 1:4 AV). Here, we are reminded of God's inexpressible gift in Christ. This gift will never be fully described, and is priceless and beyond any human measure. We know of God's love for us, and for all, as we behold the cross as God's pledge of love toward us. Here the promise of God's love is fully revealed: a priceless gift, which is beyond all comparison, and above our loftiest conception. Untold myriads of people, have claimed the promises of God made known in Jesus Christ and have discovered the fulfillment of all that God has promised in the hope, joy and peace which only Christ can bring. As we look to the Christmas celebration, we remember that in Christ we have the guarantee of all of God's promises.

Suggested readings: Joshua 1:1-9 and 2 Peter 1:1-11.

## DECEMBER 17th

## UNHOLY THINGS CAN HAPPEN AT HOLY TIMES

In December there are lots of Nativity plays presented in schools and churches, and the children just love the drama! They enjoy being involved and dressing up as angels, Magi, shepherds, innkeepers, Mary and Joseph (or even as the donkey, sheep, oxen or Herod himself). Of course, there is pride of place for the person acting as Mary. These simple enactments of the Christmas story bring much pleasure to parents, relatives and friends. The Christmas message is proclaimed by this activity, but there can be complications! In 1988, a Nativity play was staged at a school in Bury St Edmunds, and in the course of the presentation, there was a disturbance as two shepherds began to argue and push each other. To the utter dismay of the audience, there was a nasty squabble: they both wanted to be the nearest one to Mary. So angels, innkeepers and Magi rushed to separate them. How 'out of place' that seemed, but also how true to life! Unworthy things can ruin special times and places.

In Mark's gospel we're told how Jesus and the disciples were going up to Jerusalem. It was a turning-point: '. . . and taking the twelve again, he began to tell them what was to happen to him' (Mark 10:32). Jesus spoke of mocking, spitting, scourging, and death. It appears that two of the disciples were thinking in terms of privilege, and they came to Jesus with their own special request: 'Grant us to sit, one at your right hand and one at your left in your glory' (Mark 10:37). This stirred up the indignation of the others as Mark records their reaction: 'And when the ten heard it, they began to be indignant at James and John' (Mark 10:41). So the disciples argued with one another. Their conduct was not exactly true to Christ's way!

The Bible has many stories of people who, at the most inconvenient times and places, spoke out of turn or acted foolishly. We know it in our lives, too. At one wedding in East Anglia, the bride and bridegroom openly quarrelled at their wedding reception, much to the dismay of their relatives and friends. People do, of course, squabble unnecessarily, sometimes even at the most awkward, embarrassing or inconvenient times. Regrettably, we know that numerous families have quarrelled at the time of a loved one's death, when there's been a disagreement about the funeral arrangements or the deceased's will. Even at Christmas – the season of goodwill – couples, and indeed, whole families can have a serious quarrel; sadly, unholy things can happen at the holiest of times. Yet, we can thank God that even though we may prove unfaithful so often and act foolishly in such failings, God never ceases to be faithful toward us. God is an ever-present help in time of trouble. He stands ready to guide, to heal, to reconcile and to bless; our part is to be always open to God's grace.

Suggested readings: Mark 10:32-45 and Colossians 4:29-32.

DECEMBER 18th

## THE LORD STANDS BY HIS PEOPLE

Paul was having a tough time. Acts 22 and 23 reveal how difficult things were and also how bravely the apostle faced up to the situation. He spoke to a crowd and they listened for a while and then they said: 'Away with such a fellow from the earth! For he ought not to live' (Acts 22:22). The following verses tell how he narrowly escaped the dreaded 'examination by scourging'. The next day, Paul was brought before the authorities and he gave a very forceful speech. As the story goes, there was a division of opinion and a big disturbance erupted: 'The dispute became so violent that the commander was afraid Paul would be torn to pieces by them. He ordered the troops to go down and take him away from them by force and bring him into the barracks' (Acts 23:10 NIV). Paul's enemies were determined, but by divine grace, Paul came through a nasty experience. However, Paul still had fears, anxieties and much foreboding, but as we read in Acts, help was near: 'The following night, the Lord stood by him and said, "Take courage, for you have testified about me at Jerusalem, so must you bear witness also at Rome"' (Acts 23:11). We might ponder those wonderful words of comfort: 'the Lord stood by him'.

Over the Christian era, lots of God's champions have been in difficult situations after a bold act of witness. Yet, in their time of adversity, such believers have been very aware of the divine presence supporting them. Likewise, ordinary men and women in the ups and downs of life have also experienced the Lord standing near, as it were. Indeed, they knew the presence of the Lord amid difficulty, and we may, too.

One middle-aged woman received the devastating news that her husband had committed suicide, bringing her a terrible shock and deep grief. It seemed that he had everything to live for with a nice home, a loving wife and family, as well as a good job. She was terribly shaken by this awful tragedy, and wondered: How could she cope? To whom could she turn? There were problems which seemed impossible to solve on her own. A friend gave her an illustrated Bible text on a card: 'God is our refuge and strength, a very present help in trouble' (Psalm 46:1). She, like so many before her, found these words a wonderful source of comfort in her sorrow. While the assurance brought by the verses did not, of course, remove the pain and anguish of loss, she found strength to get through very tough times. The affirmation of scripture is that God is never far away from the brokenhearted, and always hears our cry to Him when we are in despair or anxiety. As God's servants of old testified, the Lord is always near, not only when we turn to Him for help in crisis moments, but also in the ordinary days, too. Indeed, God is with us throughout our lives.

Suggested readings: Acts 23:1-12 and 2 Timothy 4:7-18.

## DECEMBER 19th

## THE ETERNAL GOD DOES INTERVENE IN HUMAN AFFAIRS

Some older ministers of the gospel have gladly acknowledged down the years that Dr. Moffatt's translation of the Holy Scriptures has been of enormous value to them. Many sermons have been inspired by his insight into the vital truth of certain verses. For example, Moffatt's translation of Psalm 138:8 is, 'The Eternal intervenes on my behalf: Eternal One, thy kindness never fails, thou wilt not drop the work thou hast begun'. The divine intervention is a matter of our faith, but according to the scriptural record, it is also a fact of history: a situation arises, then God steps in. There are countless Christians who can bear testimony to God's marvellous intervention in their lives. They speak of encounters which plainly manifested the faithfulness of God to them. God's intervention is a glorious aspect of our faith in Christ as we endeavour to be His disciples today. Of course, it is so easy at times, to look at our own situation without the perspective of faith and resign ourselves to say: 'This and that will inevitably happen'. However, we can be assured that God can and does intervene – in His time – to bring about good even through great difficulty.

In Daniel chapter 6, we see how Daniel was elevated to a position of power and authority. A group of powerful men were jealous and hatched a plot against him. They were determined to undermine this godly, honourable man and to get him in disfavour with King Darius. They succeeded in this treachery. In his loyalty to God, Daniel was found to have transgressed royal commandment, and so was put in a den of lions; it seemed there was no escape for Daniel. Yet, as the story is told, God intervened, and the next morning Daniel was found alive. 'Then Daniel said to the king "O King, live for ever! My God sent his angel and shut the lions' mouths and they have not hurt me"' (Daniel 6:21-22). It is a dramatic story of deliverance which is loved by people of all ages. Likewise, there are plenty of Christians in the modern world who can truthfully bear witness to God 'stepping in' on their behalf.

At this season of the year, we think of God's most significant time of 'stepping in' when Christ came into our world, born of Mary. It was a divine interruption, indeed, an intervention! His coming shaped history and so, we speak in terms of dates being BC and AD. His coming was as light coming into darkness, or love breaking into 'lovelessness' or even like water refreshing a thirsty land. The apostle Paul puts it theologically: 'But when the time had fully come, God sent forth his Son, born of a woman, born under the law, to redeem those who were under the law so that we might receive adoption as children' (Galatians 4:4-5). At the right moment, as the apostle proclaimed, in Jesus, God intervened, and the world has been transformed by His coming.

Suggested readings: Daniel 6:1-23 and Acts 2:22-24.

DECEMBER 20th

## KINDNESS IS A STRONG VIRTUE

In the Genesis story, Joseph suffered at the hands of his brothers: their jealousy led them to devise an evil plot against him. However, in the providence of God, Joseph survived and prospered way beyond his wildest dreams! Many years passed, and then in a position of authority, he had a perfect opportunity to take his revenge. Finding themselves in submission to him, his brothers had reason to fear: 'It may be that Joseph will hate us and pay us back for all the evil which we did him' (Genesis 50:15). Yet, Joseph, enriched by life's experiences, had grown much wiser, and we read his response to them: 'So do not fear; I will provide for you and your little ones'. Then we read: 'Thus he reassured them and comforted them' (Genesis 50:21). The New International Version translates the last part: '. . . and spoke kindly to them'.

If all the kindness shown by successive generations of humanity were written down, there would be a vast library of books! We can ponder the rich ministry of kindness: kindness has comforted the sorrowing, and it has overcome hatred or distrust by breaking down barriers. Kindness has naturally been shown within families and between friends but, most remarkably, has been shown quite often by strangers. Thus, kindness has won numerous victories over mistrust, suspicion and fear. Kindness is often thought of as a 'weak' virtue, but how far that is from the truth! The kindness which Joseph showed towards his estranged brothers, was something which demanded real strength of character and purpose.

Especially, at this time of year, we think of the kindness of God in revealing Jesus Christ to the world. As the epistle of Paul to Titus says: 'But when the kindness and love of God our saviour appeared, he saved us, not because of righteous things we had done, but because of his mercy' (Titus 3:4 NIV). While we remember God's kindness to us, we also reflect on the words of scripture: 'Be kind to one another, tenderhearted, forgiving one another, as God in Christ forgave you' (Ephesians 4:32). We could name many examples of those who have shown kindness and, in so doing, have reflected God's love. In the early twentieth century we know of Edith Cavell, the nurse who was executed for tending to the injured on both sides of the conflict in the First World War. We have all known friends who have extended kindness to us, and in their love and compassion, we sense something of the kindness which is at the heart of God. For many people, the kindness of others, has been a key element in coming to understand more of the Christian faith. Indeed, kindness is a strong virtue: expressed not as 'weak' tolerance, but as 'strong' compassion.

Suggested readings: Genesis 50:14-21 and Titus 3:1-7.

# DECEMBER 21st

## JESUS CHRIST REVEALED THE CHARACTER OF GOD

How indebted we are to men and women who spend time studying the Holy Scriptures and who then share their insights! Dr. William Barclay was a well-known New Testament scholar of a generation or so ago: he was noted as a preacher, lecturer, translator of scripture, and the author of many books. It is interesting to reflect on his testimony concerning the single most important Bible text for him. After so many years of study, he selected this verse: 'And the Word became flesh and dwelt among us, full of grace and truth; we have beheld his glory, glory as of the only Son from the Father' (John 1:14). This is the message at the heart of our faith. Jesus Christ came to us as the messenger from God, but was – indeed is – the message. He came to bring the gospel, but was Himself the gospel. Jesus Christ is the living demonstration of the divine attributes of grace and truth: in Himself, He reveals the character of God.

Down the centuries believers and unbelievers alike have posed a searching question: 'What is God like?' The answer is clearly found in the life and ministry of Jesus Christ, Son of God, the Saviour of the world. The writer to the Hebrews uses daring language to state this: 'Long ago God spoke to our ancestors in many and various ways by the prophets, but in these last days he has spoken to us by a Son, whom he appointed heir of all things, through whom also he created the worlds. He is the reflection of God's glory and the exact imprint of the God's very being' (Hebrews 1:1-3). We do well to mark and ponder the striking phraseology: 'He is the reflection of God's glory'. In Jesus Christ, God is truly seen.

Norwich Cathedral has a most beautiful ceiling and visitors from all over the world come to see it but, of course, looking straight up can be very difficult. So the cathedral, like many other ancient places of worship open to visitors, has a large – almost horizontal – mirror fixed to a moveable table in the aisle, so a person can manoeuvre it and look down into the mirror to observe the splendid ceiling above. This mirror obviously gives an exact representation of the ceiling for people to see, but at an easier angle. Just so, in the life of Jesus Christ, the love, patience, mercy and grace of God are faithfully mirrored to perfection. While people may wonder what God is like, we confess that God has chosen to reveal Himself supremely in the person and work of Jesus Christ. The early nineteenth-century hymn writer, Josiah Conder, was inspired by the cherished verse in John's gospel when he wrote of 'The heart of God revealed' in his hymn 'Thou art the everlasting Word. . .' This is our faith that, though God has been made known in many ways, the Father is beheld most clearly in His only-begotten Son, who dwelt amongst us 'full of grace and truth'.

Suggested readings: John 1:1-14 and Hebrews 1:1-4.

## DECEMBER 22nd

## GOD'S PROMISES ARE DIFFERENT

There was much excitement in the home – Eric was coming home for Christmas! He was a young man with great artistic ability, and had discovered that his best option was to work abroad. He was a poor letter writer and phone calls home were rather infrequent, but he was coming home for a short Christmas holiday. This was going to be some Christmas! Eric's mother had decided that nothing less than the best would do! Rejoicing in the prospect of this great reunion, loved ones were preparing a loving and warm welcome. Three days before Christmas, Eric rang home with a message: 'I'll not be coming now'. These few words brought pain, heartache and deep distress. This broken promise really hurt all those who had been so excited about the reunion: whatever his reason, his promise proved unreliable.

In the Upper Room, Jesus had a conversation with His disciples and He spoke of the impending desertion He faced, but Peter answered abruptly: 'Though they all fall away because of you, I will never fall away' (Matthew 26:33). Then, as if to doubly underline his loyalty, he said to the Blessed Master: 'Even if I must die with you, I will not deny you' (Matthew 26:35). Peter surely meant it; yet, it is a sad fact of history that, under the pressure of circumstances, Peter did deny Jesus, and thereby broke his solemn promise. It is easy in pleasant circumstances to make promises, but much harder in tough times to keep them, and we all know that broken promises cause much pain and deep hurt. People do break promises, but God never does so!

In the Second World War, the East End of London took a terrible hammering, facing days and nights of relentless bombing. Sometimes, it is very difficult to imagine how those Londoners coped with the terror and havoc, as well as the many hardships. One London minister testified that a popular hymn in those traumatic days was the Sankey hymn, 'I'm standing on the promises of God'. His congregation used to sing this lovely hymn with deep feeling and faith. At the time when the very foundations of life seemed to be in terrible danger, those brave men and women in that congregation were affirming the faithfulness of God.

For all those suffering from trouble, bewilderment and hurt today, there is a sure word, which speaks into their situation however desperate: 'I will strengthen you, I will help you, I will uphold you with my victorious right hand' (Isaiah 41:10). As we ponder that text, we note the repetition of the glorious 'I will' in it! The blessed hope of Christian men and women is that God will never break His promises: that itself is a sure foundation. Like Peter of old, as well as the others, too, we falter and fail at times, and we may end up breaking our promises, but our glorious God is utterly dependable. In view of that, we can be thankful and confident each day.

Suggested readings: Isaiah 41:8-13 and Romans 4:20-25.

## DECEMBER 23rd

## MOST PEOPLE HAVE THEIR LOW DAYS

One evening, a neighbour said to a young married woman, 'Your little boy has been crying a lot today!' In a flash, the young mother replied with a glint in her eye: 'Yes, he's going cheap today!' The vast majority of parents know exactly what that mother meant and have experienced it themselves. With or without a crying young child to deal with, we all have those days when we feel low in spirit and everything seems to go wrong. One of the strange things is that it can easily happen just before Christmas. Sometimes, by December 23rd, people feel exhausted, and after the build-up to Christmas Day itself, they are almost too tired for a celebration of the festive season.

Revd. John Hunter was a powerful preacher and a zealous worker and, at one period during his ministry at King's Weigh House, London, he reached a point of deep weariness. He had spent much energy coping with the demands and responsibilities of ministering to his congregation; he badly needed a break so a holiday was arranged on the continent. On the day he was to leave for his holiday he received two letters: one letter was from his church secretary resigning from office, and the other was from his oldest friend in London withdrawing from service because of a failure of faith. He was shocked and dismayed. Then to crown everything, he mislaid the bank notes which were to pay for his holiday! It was a Monday morning he was never to forget; he felt a deep weariness of spirit, for it was a very low day, indeed. Most of us have had similar experiences of multiple troubles.

Men and women in the Bible are shown as people who knew both high days and low days: they knew times of blessing, but also of testing and loss. Psalm 55 is an important example, as we hear the anguish of the psalmist: 'Give ear to my prayer, O God; and hide not thyself from my supplication! Attend to me, and answer me; I am overcome by my trouble' (Psalm 55:1-2). A little later on in the psalm, the psalmist expressed a sentiment which has echoed in many hearts: 'And I say, "O that I had wings like a dove! I would fly away and be at rest"' (Psalm 55:6). He needed God's help so very badly, and cried out to the Lord with a longing for divine blessing.

We might ponder the testimony of the apostle Paul in the New Testament: he tells of an experience which is known only from his reference to it as 'the thorn in the flesh'. Whatever that meant, he sought relief from it, and he bore witness that he received this amazing answer from the Lord: 'My grace is sufficient for you, for my power is made perfect in weakness' (2 Corinthians 12:9). If anyone feels a sense of deep weariness, it is never because the grace of God has changed. God grace is ever available to all those who turn to the Lord in faith. 'My grace is sufficient for you': that has been a help to generations of believers and still remains a reality for us today.

Suggested readings: Psalm 55:1-8 and 2 Corinthians 12:7-10.

## DECEMBER 24th

## SOME MINUTES ARE ETERNALLY WORTHWHILE

He had left home for good, as – this time – the quarrel was really serious and, in spite of his love for his two children, he felt the situation was unbearable. He packed his bags, went out of the door, and left. It was the most painful decision of his life and, of course, it was a terrible shock to his wife. Days passed, then weeks: there was no going back, no forgiveness, no reconciliation, but only a deepening sense of hurt. The grey and wet weather didn't help either. Or did it? On Christmas Eve, there was a knock on his door and there stood a local clergyman. It was absolutely pouring with rain, so the visitor was allowed in. (Even a rebellious heart has finer feelings!) The conversation was difficult: it was stilted, awkward, then rather heated. The minister quietly said, 'Will you go back on Christmas morning, just for a few minutes, for the sake of the children?' This question was persistently asked, until finally, the husband gave a reluctant: 'Yes'. Next day, Christmas morning, the husband went back; he stayed longer than just a few minutes, too. There was a new start: reconciliation followed and the marriage was healed. Those few minutes of conversation on Christmas Eve, were beyond any price for a Christmas gift: they were to prove eternally worthwhile.

If a book were commissioned with a title such as, 'The Five Minutes Which Changed My Life', the general public could supply plenty of material for it to be written. We all know various illustrations from history: John Bunyan overheard the conversation of a few Christian women which stirred holy desires, John Wesley was in a room hearing a book being read and his heart was 'strangely warmed'. In the twentieth century, we know of Albert Schweitzer who spent just a few moments reading a leaflet which led him to service for others. Hugh Redwood, a Fleet Street journalist (later a Christian author), heard a religious broadcast and he was challenged.

Sometimes, of course, it is something wonderful like a birth which brings such redirection. Other times, it is a tragedy which strikes and makes one face up to change after a very nasty jolt. For the vast majority of people, life has plenty of ordinary stretches, including many rather boring days! Yet, there are little periods of time, just moments, minutes or perhaps an hour, which can shape a destiny. We remember that a few minutes spent being in touch with someone, whether by writing a letter, making a phone call, paying a visit, or simply by stopping to chat and show friendship, or even by sharing one's faith, could prove to be eternally worthwhile. The ministry of 'five minutes' can be undertaken anytime, anywhere; the time so seemingly insignificant to us, can prove of immense significance to others!

Suggested readings: Matthew 8:1-4 and Ephesians 5:6-20.

# DECEMBER 25th

## THAT BEHIND CHRISTMAS IS GOD'S GENEROSITY

Every Christmas season large crowds of people take the opportunity to pay a visit to Canterbury Cathedral. It is a very special place of worship: rich in craftsmanship and music, as well as in history and tradition. This fine building, with its great heritage, along with its beauty and charm, stirs the hearts of many. Somehow, at the great festival of Christmas, this ancient place of worship has a particular attraction. For instance, at the cathedral, there is a doorway which has a carving of Jesus Christ and behind the carving, there is a large image of a hand, signifying a divine hand giving Jesus to the people. This hand represents the generosity of the heavenly Father; it is a powerful illustration, in stone, of the eternal truth at the heart of Christmas.

On Christmas Day, we rejoice in the birth of Jesus to Mary, but behind it all is the Father's hand. John's gospel puts it magnificently: 'For God so loved the world, that he gave his only begotten Son, that whosoever believeth in him should not perish, but have everlasting life' (John 3:16 AV). So, on this joyful day, people all over the world, think again about the Christmas story: Mary, Joseph, angels, shepherds, Magi, the star, and the little baby destined to be the Saviour of the world. Yet, in all our celebrations, we remember the unseen hand, which made it all possible. We rejoice today in our heavenly Father's generosity, for the birth of Jesus was an integral part of God's gracious plan and purpose for the world. It was all motivated and initiated by divine love, a wonderful, indescribable power at work.

The apostle Paul described the coming of Jesus in this majestic way: 'But when the time had fully come, God sent forth his Son, born of a woman' (Galatians 4:4). The hours of God's purposes were always unfolding, as it were. Yet, this was a special time, a moment when the unseen hand would give a marvellous gift from the Father's heart of love. The gift of God, as we celebrate on Christmas Day, has brought redemption to all humankind, and brings enrichment to impoverished souls, ones whose lives are lived seemingly, out of communion with God. We recall the splendid words of the apostle Paul: 'Blessed be the God and Father of our Lord Jesus Christ, who has blessed us in Christ with every spiritual blessing' (Ephesians 1:3).

The truth enshrined in the doorway at Canterbury Cathedral reminds us that we must praise the heavenly Father for this gift above and beyond all words. Paul urged such gratitude: 'Thanks be unto God for his unspeakable gift' (2 Corinthians 9:15 AV). Today, as we share in the giving and receiving of gifts, we offer thanks to God and we reflect on God's generosity toward us every day of our lives. In this way, we are mindful of our great need and God's generosity to us day by day.

Suggested readings: Luke 2:1-20 and Galatians 4:1-7.

DECEMBER 26th

## GOOD CAN TRIUMPH OVER EVIL

During the Second World War, a considerable number of churches in England were severely damaged by enemy action. One of the saddest days of the war, in this respect, was when Coventry Cathedral was destroyed. People were stunned because weapons of hate ruined the lovely ancient cathedral. However, when the awful tragedy struck, the clergy there, and elsewhere, discovered that Christian people were very resilient and proved that the worst events can often call out the best in people. Another fine example of human enterprise was the response of parishioners of St George's Church, Bristol. Enemy action made a hole in the roof of their church and they fitted it with a 'Star of Bethlehem'! The gaping hole in the roof spoke of human hatred and violence: the bomb had done its deadly work. However, the special star, which filled and covered the hole, spoke of the work of the 'Prince of Peace'. Out of the bad, came something exceedingly good, and this was a sign of divine grace.

There is a very powerful verse in the New Testament which has been an anchor in the lives of many believers: 'We know that in everything God works for good with those who love him, who are called according to his purpose' (Romans 8:28). Very many believers have found this verse a tremendous comfort and a rich blessing, too, but of course, the verse has also been seriously misunderstood and thus misapplied. Yet, God can, by His sovereign power, bring good things out of the most unlikely circumstances. Indeed, as scripture affirms, there have been many times when a gulf caused by bitterness has been replaced by a star of hope, as it were. For example, Jacob's son, Joseph, was betrayed by his brothers, but God transformed the whole situation so that, as a man of authority, he was then used to bless many lives, including theirs. David sinned grievously, but he was inspired by God to write the words of Psalm 51, which have been a blessing to women and men. Paul was put in prison for the sake of the gospel but, whilst there, wrote letters which have blessed millions down twenty centuries. Out of so many bad situations, God has brought faith, hope and love.

The Christmas story in Luke's gospel, points out a key detail worth pondering: 'There was no room for them in the inn' (Luke 2:7 AV). Those few words in the narrative of Jesus' birth, may be used by the Holy Spirit to prompt us to consider if we have 'made room' for the Lord in our own lives. On this Boxing Day, as we continue our celebration of the incarnation of our Lord, born to lowly Mary, with faithful Joseph's care, we remember, too, the death, resurrection and ascension of our Lord. The question is: 'Have we made room for Him in our lives'? It's truly the ongoing challenge of Christmas.

Suggested readings: Genesis 45:1-9 and Acts 2:22-36.

# DECEMBER 27th

## THE LIFE OF JESUS CHRIST MOVED THE WORLD

At the height of the Second World War, Horace Shipp published a book with a very intriguing title: *Lives That Moved The World*. It is a record of the achievements of such people as Thomas Barnardo, Father Damien, Elizabeth Fry, William Carey and Lord Shaftesbury, with other women and men, too. It was a slender book published on 'economy paper', but it proved both interesting and valuable. It was not only a fine title for a book, but thought-provoking, too. It is especially inspiring at this time of the year, as we remember the birth of Jesus and recall that he came to show us the love of God and in so doing, to 'move the world'. The gospel of John says it best: 'And the Word became flesh and dwelt among us, full of grace and truth; we have beheld his glory, glory as of the only Son from the Father' (John 1:14). His coming among us as the 'only-begotten' of the Father truly shaped human history, and through His life, death and resurrection, He transformed and changed the whole world. As the apostle Paul put it, 'In him all the fullness of God was pleased to dwell' (Colossians 1:19).

Let us think of five truths concerning His life and ministry: (1) through Him we have the Bible, the Old Testament anticipating His Coming and the New Testament declaring it, (2) through Him there is a Christian faith which is loved and honoured by millions on this planet, (3) through Him gifted individuals have been inspired to write, paint, sculpt or compose, as well as build noble edifices to His glory, (4) through Him men and women have entered into a new and profound understanding of God, (5) through Him untold numbers have felt called to live beautiful lives of service for other people. The life of Jesus Christ shifted the centre of gravity, indeed, 'moved the world', and still continues to influence countless people. Surely, the coming of Jesus Christ changed the course of history.

As we think of the Christmas story in Luke's gospel, we recognise that no one at that time in Bethlehem – in rural Judea, a rather ordinary, obscure corner of the then known world – could possibly have known the earthshaking significance of the birth of Jesus! In Luke's narrative, we are told of the message of the angels to the shepherds: 'Be not afraid; for behold I bring you good news of a great joy which will come to all the people; for to you is born this day in the city of David, a Saviour, who is Christ the Lord' (Luke 2:11-12). Looking back over the years, we might say that the birth of Jesus Christ was the most significant turning point in history. His birth, redemptive life and death, then His glorious resurrection and ascension 'moved the world'. This was indeed, 'good news' bring great 'joy to the world'!

Suggested readings: John 1:1-18 and Colossians 1:15-20.

DECEMBER 28th

## GOD GIVES SPECIAL DAYS

At this late stage of the year, we always have an opportunity to look back over the past months. For a considerable number of people, the year will have been a strange mixture of good and bad things, no doubt including some surprises, too! While many days of the year now closing have been ordinary, most of us will all have known an extraordinary occurrence when something wonderful happened. In Luke's gospel, we are told of a man who was paralysed, but who met Jesus since he had four good friends determined to get him to the Master. This was not an easy task because of the crowds; yet, as Luke describes it, they found a way to let him down through the roof. Jesus healed the man and he got up and walked. The people's reaction was recorded: 'They were all completely amazed! Full of fear, they praised God saying, "What marvellous things we have seen today"'(Luke 6:26 GNB). They had witnessed an extraordinary miracle and it turned out for them to be no ordinary day at all. It was a special day, a God-given glorious moment.

Most of us can testify that, at certain points, life has brought a wonderful day, and we have come to the evening saying, 'What marvellous things we've seen today'. We might ponder a few situations: parents experience the birth of a child, a child comes successfully through critical life-saving surgery, a person has a fantastic sightseeing trip on holiday, a family sees a loved-one recover consciousness after being in a coma, a wildlife photographer catches a unique shot of an animal, bird or fish rarely spotted, or a scientist makes a once-in-a-lifetime discovery! As this year draws to its end, we thank God for all the ordinary days, as well as the most unforgettable, truly wonderful days. For each and every day we are grateful to God.

On this Earth and in 'the heavens' above, there are marvellous things to behold, just as the psalmist declared, as he expressed joy and delight in Psalm 8. The last verse reads: 'O Lord, our Sovereign, how majestic is your name in all the earth!' (Psalm 8:9). In the centre of this lovely psalm, there are verses which tell of the psalmist's wonder: 'When I look at your heavens, the work of your fingers, the moon and the stars that you have established; what are human beings that you are mindful of them, mortals that you care for them?' (Psalm 8:3-4). Dr. William Sangster was a much-loved minister of the gospel: his powerful preaching drew lots of people to faith in Jesus Christ, and the value of his godly life and ministry reached far and wide. He used to tell his people that they must never lose their sense of wonder: the ordinary day, can be a wonderful day, if only we have the eyes to see! God, in His mercy, blesses us all with very special days. Yet, there can be joy in the ordinary day, too, and so we offer gratitude for every new day and each new year.

Suggested readings: Psalm 8:1-9 and Luke 5:16-26.

## DECEMBER 29th

## ONE OF THE BEST PRAYERS IS 'LORD, INCREASE OUR FAITH'

One of the hardest things in the Christian life is to obey the teaching of Jesus Christ on the subject of forgiveness. The plain fact is that His teaching on this particular subject is so deep and profound, and some people find it both ridiculous and unrealistic! In Luke 17, the Blessed Master speaks about showing forgiveness to another: 'If the same person sins against you seven times a day, and turns back to you seven times, and says "I repent", you must forgive' (Luke 17:4). We note that very clear wording, 'must forgive'. We also know that forgiveness is costly! No wonder the disciples, after listening to this teaching, cried to the Lord: 'Increase our faith' (Luke 17:5). Even those people who have been Christians for decades readily admit that there is still room for a deeper, richer and stronger faith. We can probably all think of a number of areas where our faith needs to be broadened or strengthened. For instance, we can grow in our trust in the promises and purposes of God, and deepen our confidence in the power of prayer. Indeed, throughout life, this may be the prayer of us all: 'Lord, increase our faith'.

One of the most moving experiences for a Christian is to stand in the ruins of the old Coventry Cathedral, which was bombed in the Second World War, and to see the altar which bears a rugged cross made of two charred beams. Over the altar are two words: 'Father forgive'. Few people can stand there and reflect without emotions welling up within, or even shedding a tear. It is a powerful and overwhelming reminder of the wretchedness of sin, but also of the loving forgiveness of God. The Christians in Coventry were deeply shocked and pained by the destruction of their beautiful cathedral. Yet, the church leaders in that city courageously and boldly directed the thoughts of the people to the subject of forgiveness.

Forgiveness is very demanding, but it is at the heart of the Saviour's teaching. On the Cross of Calvary, Jesus suffered much, but He prayed, 'Father forgive them for they know not what they do' (Luke 23:34). As his persecutors were stoning Stephen, the first Christian martyr, to death, he knelt down and prayed likewise: 'Lord, do not hold this sin against them' (Acts 6:60). So, as this old year ends, we meditate on the theme of forgiveness: our own need to be forgiven, and our duty to show forgiveness to others. Forgiveness is not easy, but we can be thankful to the Lord that the Spirit of God never fails to come to our aid to help us to discern truth, to bear faithful witness, to pray aright and to serve well in God's sight! So we pray one of the best prayers: 'Increase our faith' and we also ask, 'even as we have been forgiven, so help us to forgive'.

Suggested readings: Luke 17:1-10 and Ephesians 4:25-32.

# DECEMBER 30th

## WE HAVE NO IDEA WHAT TOMORROW WILL BRING

As this old year draws swiftly to its close, we are reminded that life has a great mystery about it in facing each day, indeed, each hour. We don't know what might happen next, or what a day might bring. We all know the difference just one day might make: there are lots of people of all ages who can testify that, within the space of twenty-four hours, life has been turned upside-down. A person climbing the career ladder is summoned to the manager and given notice of redundancy, a family living on the edge of poverty receives a solicitor's letter informing them they have been left a substantial legacy, a young person who has been promised a place on a course fails to get the required standard in the school examinations. On a humorous note, the true story is told of a young woman who attended a wedding reception, and met a friend of the bridegroom, and they fell instantly in love. Actually, she tripped over and literally fell into the arms of the one who later became her husband. So their romance began with a near accident, and blossomed through courtship, thereafter!

In the Book of Proverbs there is a verse which reminds us of the uncertainty of life: 'Do not boast about tomorrow, for you do not know what a day may bring forth' (Proverbs 27:1). Plenty of people would say 'Amen' to that as they have experienced unexpected joys and sorrows, with one single day making a whole world of difference. It is possible that the events of the day can radically change one's attitude to spiritual matters, too. Many people have started the day as an unbeliever, or uncommitted to the Christian way, and ended the day having experienced God's nearness which brought them to saving faith in the Lord of life, joy, peace and hope. The story of Zacchaeus is well known, as is the fact that the tax collectors in that era were both disliked and despised. One day, Zacchaeus met Jesus and that encounter brought a radical change in his life and attitude. In the space of one day, his life underwent a revolution. This story has been retold countless times, and through it, people have come to know the boundless, transforming grace of the Lord.

There is an apt verse in James which speaks of being mindful of time: 'A word with you, you who say, "Today or tomorrow we will go off to such and such a town, and spend a year there trading and making money". Yet you have no idea what tomorrow will bring' (James 4:13 NEB). We each have no idea what is in store for us tomorrow, for good or ill. The hymn writer, speaking of such times in life, gives us reassuring and comforting words: 'It can bring with it nothing, but He will bear us through'. As we face the future, we know Who holds the future in His hands, and in Whom we can trust to the uttermost. Thanks be to God for the confidence and assurance this hope grants us!

Suggested readings: Luke 19:1-12 and James 4:8-17.

## DECEMBER 31st

## THE LIVING GOD FORGIVES SIN

Psalm 51 could be seen as one of the shorter psalms; it has just 19 verses but its value is out of all proportion to its size. It speaks of sin and God's forgiveness so this psalm is very relevant on the last day of the old year. The psalmist is very realistic in the assessment of life: 'Wash me thoroughly from my iniquity and cleanse me from my sin! For I know my transgression and my sin is ever before me' (Psalm 51:2-3). Those last words '. . . my sin is ever before me', speak volumes. From somewhere in the past, this person recalled grievous sin or, indeed, a pattern of sin against the Lord: this failing could not be forgotten or erased, as it was like a deep stain.

On one memorable occasion, Dr. Leslie Weatherhead (minister of the City Temple, London) preached a powerful sermon on sin and forgiveness. He gave a simple but telling illustration: he spoke of a boy playing with a ball and breaking a window of his home. His father chides the boy, but forgives him, yet the fact of the broken window remained. An ancient theologian, Origen, talking about sin, once memorably noted: '. . . the scars remain'. Countless people can echo the words of the psalmist, 'My sin is ever before me'. There was the unhappy case of a man who became infatuated by a young woman at work and, for what he later accepted were 'three mad months', he left wife, children and home. Finally, he came to his senses and – begging the forgiveness of his wife and family – pardon was duly granted. Yet, while forgiveness brought a new beginning, the man found it difficult to forgive himself. The memory of the pain he had caused, remained like a scar.

One morning a person went for a long walk by the sea: the tide was out and the seashore had many jagged rocks which jutted out of the sand, looking rather like rotten teeth. Later, returning back along the shore, the tide was in and all the ugly rocks were completely covered: the perspective was transformed! This scene came as a reminder of past failures: the jagged rocks now hidden were like old sins erased and mistakes covered. In the same way, the grace of God comes in like a full tide and covers the ugliness. As the hymn writer, Charles Wesley wrote: 'Plenteous grace with Thee is found, grace to cover all my sin'. As the apostle Paul wrote: '. . . though I formerly blasphemed and persecuted and insulted him; but I received mercy because I had acted ignorantly in unbelief, and the grace of our Lord overflowed for me with the faith and love that are in Christ Jesus' (1 Timothy 1:13-14). As the year draws to a close, we can ponder the abundant, overflowing, rich mercy of the Lord! We have every opportunity today to reflect on the past that is over, and to prepare our hearts to face the challenges of the dawning year. The calendar changes, but God's love is unchanging! So we give humble and hearty thanks to God!

Suggested readings: Psalm 51:1-19 and Acts 13:38-39.

# FOR FURTHER REFLECTION

Teach us, good Lord,
to serve thee as thou deservest;
to give and not to count the cost;
to fight and not to heed the wounds;
to toil, and not to seek for rest;
to labour, and to ask for no reward,
save that of knowing that we do thy will;
through Jesus Christ our Lord.

        St Ignatius Loyola (1491-1556)

Included in this section are three further meditations for Good Friday, Easter and Whitsun. In addition, among Norman's papers, were several hymns that he had written. While he had not planned to include them in the devotional volume which he and Jessie were preparing, it seems appropriate to publish them in this collection.

All the hymns below keep the original wording, and they have not been amended to take into account inclusive language. Written in an older style, reflective of that era, it was thought best to allow the original verses to stand. The tunes noted are ones selected by Norman, and quite possibly Jessie, too. Some of the hymns were written, as Norman noted, for particular occasions and these annotations have been included here to show the context for the hymns.

## GOOD FRIDAY

## YOU CANNOT BLINDFOLD JESUS CHRIST

One of the most moving passages in the whole world of literature is Luke's account of the arrest, trial and crucifixion of Jesus. He tells the story with simplicity and sincerity: Luke chapters 22 and 23 make a fascinating study of the ways of sinful humanity and the Saviour's response. We recall the way the authorities treated Jesus: they denied Him justice, then scourged Him, clothed Him with a purple robe, while mocking and mistreating Him, even placing a crown of thorns on His head. They jeered Him, spat upon Him and struck Him, and those guarding Him at the foot of the cross even cast lots for His garment. Luke records a key detail about Jesus' tormentors: '. . . they also blindfolded him and asked him, 'Prophesy! Who is it that struck you?' (Luke 22:63). We can well ponder the fact that there is a real sense in which it is actually impossible to blindfold Jesus Christ.

Earlier in His ministry, a man named Nicodemus had come by night to talk with Jesus saying: 'Rabbi, we know that you are a teacher come from God; for no one can do the signs that you do, unless God is with him' (John 3:2). However, Jesus knew the heart of Nicodemus: he could not 'pull the wool' over the Saviour's eyes, and lest there be any doubt about it, Jesus replied: '. . . no one can see the kingdom of God without being born from above' (John 3:3). Jesus knew that the heart of Nicodemus needed renewal. Although he was a mature Pharisee, a truly religious man and even a ruler of the Jews, Jesus realised that he still did not comprehend the new life of the Kingdom. So He challenged Nicodemus, yet again, with the same stark counsel: 'You must be born from above' (John 3:7). Of course, that expression also had overtones of being 'born again'. Truly, Jesus could see into this man's heart.

In the Old Testament there is a verse: 'The Lord does see not as mortals see; they look on the outward appearance, but the Lord looks on the heart' (1 Samuel 16:7). When we shall stand at the last before God, our Judge and our Hope, the One who judges us is the all-seeing Lord of everyone. God knows our virtues and our faults. The Lord sees our secret failings, the dryness of our heart and our inner rebelliousness; God also knows our longing for peace, our hunger and thirst for spiritual things and our hope for reconciliation. One cannot blindfold Jesus, Who knows all about us, but, nevertheless, Whose heart overflows with love and compassion. As scripture reminds us: 'For Christ also died for sins once and for all, the righteous for the unrighteous, that he might bring us to God' (1 Peter 3:18). Even from the cross, He prayed: 'Father, forgive them; for they know not what they do' (Luke 23:34). The cross reveals for all time that there is One Whose love will never let us go, offering forgiveness to all those who turn to Him in faith and repentance.

Suggested readings: Luke 22:63-71 and 1 Peter 3:21-25.

## EASTER SUNDAY

## EASTER TELLS OF GLORIOUS MERCY

The gospel narrative is direct in its clarity. Jesus endured such rejection, betrayal and denial by those closest to Him. He endured the terrible death of crucifixion, seemingly abandoned by God, after He had been forsaken by His disciples. How did Peter feel? He had wept bitterly after the cockerel crowed, following his denial of his Master and once he had caught the eye of the One who had prophesied his downfall. He had let Jesus down in that he had broken a promise, played the coward, fled in terror and failed to live to the high standard of loyalty he had boasted about. We might try to imagine Peter's sense of guilt and remorse: once he had been 'riding high' as a foremost disciple of Jesus, but after the crucifixion of his Master he was in the depths of despair. However, on Easter Day, there was a dramatic turn of events: the miracle of the resurrection surprised Jesus' followers, both the men and the women. The impossible had happened as Jesus had said it would: the tomb was empty, the Saviour had been raised, and the Risen Lord appeared to them.

In Mark's account we are told of a special message: 'Ye seek Jesus of Nazareth, which was crucified: he is risen; he is not here: behold the place where they laid him. But go your way, tell his disciples and Peter that he goeth before you into Galilee: there shall ye see him, as he said unto you' (Mark 16:6-7 AV). We note the profound significance of those two words, 'and Peter'. Within those two words we perceive mercy, hope, forgiveness and love. The man who had failed and had desperately experienced the abyss of guilt and remorse, the one who had stained his discipleship, was the very one specially selected to receive the glorious message of Jesus Christ's resurrection and continuing friendship! The lovely words, 'Go your way, tell his disciples and Peter', give new hope to all those people who have made mistakes and feel terribly guilty or even deeply disturbed. The Lord receives people again, with a glad welcome and a gracious forgiveness.

There is a special sense in which God's love and mercy are directed towards those who know they have failed in the past, and Peter knew it, as did Saul who became the apostle Paul. He knew himself to be the unworthy recipient of divine love. In 1 Timothy chapter 1, he calls himself 'the chief of sinners', 'a blasphemer', and 'a persecutor'. Then, he adds: 'But I received mercy for this reason, that in me, as the foremost, Jesus Christ might display his perfect patience for an example to those who were to believe in him for eternal life' (1 Timothy 1:16).

Easter means new beginnings. It tells of God's mercy: there is hope and forgiveness. This day and, indeed, every day, we find assurance in the Easter message of joy and peace in believing, even though we, like Peter, have known failure.

Suggested readings: Mark 16:1-7 and 1 Timothy 1:12-17.

# WHITSUNDAY

## THE HOLY SPIRIT IS MARVELLOUSLY POWERFUL

For decades, people relied on encyclopaedias as a great source of knowledge. Young and old, teachers and preachers, and people of all backgrounds found them tremendously helpful. Yet, even such storehouses of knowledge proved somewhat inadequate! One older set of encyclopaedias, curiously, showed a strange imbalance: it gave over thirty pages of information about the Pope and yet, less than three pages about the Holy Spirit of God. Whatever our tradition of faith or conviction, from a Christian perspective, that discrepancy seems strange. For Christians everywhere, the work of the Holy Spirit is extremely important!

We recall the much-loved passage in the Acts of the Apostles: 'When the day of Pentecost had come, they were all together in one place. And suddenly a sound came from heaven like the rush of a mighty wind, and it filled all the house where they were sitting' (Acts 2:1-2). We all know that the powerful and mysterious ministry of the Holy Spirit made the ongoing story, narrated in Acts, possible: the Spirit came in power and so the Church was formed and inspired, the gospel was preached and lives were transformed as obstacles were overcome and the Kingdom extended. More than one scholar has suggested that the 'Acts of the Apostles' ought to be called the 'Acts of the Holy Spirit'. This book and the New Testament epistles make it abundantly clear that the Holy Spirit is marvellously powerful.

In the Christian Church people believe in the Holy Spirit of God as divine Comforter, Interpreter, Guide, Counsellor, Helper and much more! On Whitsunday, we think about the mighty power of the Holy Spirit. The Spirit is the One Who has power to change hearts and minds, attitudes and lives. Church history endorses the wonderful fact that people can experience a radical transformation by the dynamism of the Spirit. The Bible shows how Saul the persecutor became Paul the preacher, how John Mark (one early missionary who somehow let others down) became the writer of a gospel, how Peter the fisherman became a trusted, leading apostle. The New Testament speaks of the Spirit of God at work always transforming us.

So, in the Christian era, there have been dramatic instances of people being convicted, convinced and renewed, by the Spirit of God. High winds are nothing new, but in the winter of 1989/1990, Britain experienced the awesome power of the wind as over a matter of weeks, there were severe gales. For some, this provided a timely reminder of the mighty 'Wind of the Spirit' forcefully at work, unseen, but mysteriously encountered. That early, small group of disciples, experiencing anew the Holy Spirit on the Day of Pentecost, came to accomplish so much in the spread of the gospel. It was all because the Holy Spirit of God is marvellously powerful!

Suggested readings: Acts 2:1-16 and Acts 11:21-26.

## HYMN 1

Father we come to Thee, bringing our praises,
Thanking Thee now for Thy wonderful Son,
We love this House of Prayer for it reminds us
Of our great Saviour and all He has done,

*Chorus: Praise to Thy Holy name, Father we render!*
*Now as we supplicate, hear us again.*

Father we come to Thee, pleading for mercy,
Sure Thou art ready this blessing to give;
Stirred with the memory of Thy great goodness,
Simply we ask, of Thee, 'Father forgive'.

Father we come to thee, praying for others,
Those who are faithless and love not Thy word;
Now as we intercede, let Thy Good Spirit,
Speak to them plainly and let Him be heard!

Father we come to Thee, thinking of Jesus,
Filling our minds with His beautiful Truth,
Inspiring many hearts, comforting others,
Bringing a challenge to age and to youth.

Father I come to Thee, looking at Calv'ry
Where Thy dear Son gave His life-blood for me,
Help me to think again of its great message,
Telling the sinful 'Today you are free'.

(NLH 18th February 1963)

Note: This hymn is written to express in each verse a different reason for worship.

Tune: Rescue the Perishing  11.10                    W.H. Doane (1832-1915)

## HYMN 2

Give me, O God, a greater love
Which flows from Calvary's tree;
A love inspired by Jesus Christ
Who gave His all for me.

Give me, O God, a greater faith
Which dares to trust Thy word;
A faith which soars with eagle's wings
And knows that Christ is Lord.

Give me, O God, a greater care
For those who walk in sin;
A care which prays and works and strives
To bring the stranger in.

Give me, O God, a greater strength
To face the world of doubt;
A strength which speaks the word of truth
And spells the gospel out.

Give me, O God, a vision true
Of Thy great Love and Power;
A sight of Thee which nerves the heart
To face this present hour.

Give me, O God, Thy very Self
And keep Thy promised word.
Let Thy Good Spirit dwell within –
So let my heart be stirred!

(NLH      29th October 1967)

Text: THE PRAYER OF JABEZ: 'Oh that thou wouldest bless me indeed and enlarge my coast' (1 Chronicles 4:10).

Tune: St Stephen  CM                                      William Jones (1726-1800)

## HYMN 3

We praise Thee Lord for Thy great gift,
Of Thy forgiving Love;
It helped us first our hearts to lift
To seek those things above.

We praise Thee Lord for Thy dear Son;
His Life! His Cross! His Word!
We now confess that He has won,
His call to follow, heard.

We praise Thee Lord for Thy strong Hands,
Which helped us on our way,
Keeping us true to Higher Plans,
Unto this present day.

We praise Thee Lord for blessed times,
Spent in this House of Prayer;
The memory of which refines,
Our present thought and care.

Help us, O Lord, to ponder still,
The path that has been trod,
Never let us forget the thrill,
Of serving such a God.

(NLH          10th July 1962)

(Written for the last service of their ministry at Breachwood Green held on Sunday, 26th August 1962).

Text: 'The memory of Thy great goodness' (Psalm 145:7).
Tune: Martyrdom  CM                                    H. Wilson (1766-1824)

## HYMN 4

I hear the rustle of the breeze
And think of Christ's own word;
The Spirit moves in human hearts
He comes and men are stirred!

Within my heart, I feel a need
To have my faith made strong;
Read Thou my heart and hear my prayer
Help me to conquer wrong.

Be still, my heart, and wait again
To feel the Spirit's power;
He comes to bring vitality
In this refreshing hour.

I love to read God's Holy Book
And see the Lord of grace;
He loves the old, He loves the young
To each He gives a place.

I see the Lord in many ways
This earth tells forth His love!
The mighty mountains speak of Him
And lift my thoughts above.

Give me, O Lord, a noble aim
To help men see the right –
Give me a heart that truly seeks
To serve the Lord of Light.

Within this world of noise and strife
Temptation has its power.
Help me, O God, to look to Thee
Each day – and every hour.

(NLH        October 1968)

Text: 'I will lift up mine eyes unto the hills. From whence cometh my help? My help cometh
from the Lord' (Psalm 121:1-2).
Tune: St Fulbert  CM                                          H. J. Gauntlett (1805-76)

## Hymn 5

I am ready Lord to learn,
Teach me what to shun and spurn!
To Thy highway, now I turn;
But Lord, in thy strength.

I am ready Lord to serve,
Give me faith and give me nerve,
Never from Thy highway swerve;
But Lord, in Thy strength.

I am ready Lord to press,
Forward! Onward! – and possess!
Godly things my happiness;
But Lord, in Thy strength.

I am ready Lord to fight,
For the things so good and right;
Spread the Kingdom of Thy Light!
But Lord, in Thy strength.

I am ready Lord to pray,
By the new and living way,
Help me walk there every day;
But Lord, in Thy strength.

I am ready Lord to seek,
Give the words that I should speak!
Helping others who are weak;
But Lord, in Thy strength.

(NLH      29th January 1968)

Text: 'I am ready . . .' (2 Corinthians 12:14).
Tune: Capetown  777 5                                    (Adpt.) F. Filitz (1804-76)

Hymn 6

Teach us, Good Lord, to view,
This world through Christian eyes;
The hills, the woods, the sea, the land
All these – Thy enterprise!

Teach us, Good Lord, to meet,
Thy Presence every day,
Each season tells of goodness royal,
Thy Love along the way!

Teach us, Good Lord, to see
Thy power in harvest time!
The summer fruit and ripened corn;
Tell men of might sublime.

Teach us, Good Lord, to look
At love in graceful flowers;
Their colour speaks of higher things –
The God with mighty powers!

Teach us, Good Lord, to voice
Our praise with hearts sincere.
If God so loved this sinful world –
Why should I ever fear?

Teach us, Good Lord, to know
That every single day;
Brings gracious gifts from God's good hand
And shows His Loving way.

Teach us, Good Lord, to sow
A thousand precious seeds;
Thy word is true! Thy word is right!
It meets men in their needs.

(NLH          22nd June 1968)
(Offered in thanksgiving to God 'for a prayer that was answered').

Text: 'He will teach us of His ways' (Isaiah 2:3).
Tune: Sandys  SM          English traditional carol from W. Sandys', *Christmas Carols*, 1853.

Printed in Great Britain
by Amazon